H. P. Lovecraft

# Letters to Alfred Galpin

*Alfred Galpin*

# H. P. Lovecraft

# letters to
# ALFRED GALPIN

Edited by S. T. Joshi and David E. Schultz

Hippocampus Press

New York

Published by Hippocampus Press
P.O. Box 641, New York, NY 10156.
http://www.hippocampuspress.com

Cover design and Hippocampus Press logo by Anastasia Damianakos.
Cover production by Barbara Briggs Silbert.

First Edition
3  5  7  9  8  6  4  2

ISBN 0-9673215-9-X

# Contents

# Introduction

It is unfortunate that the long and complex relationship of H. P. Lovecraft (1890–1937) and Alfred Galpin (1901–1983)—spanning nearly two decades and covering the entire period of Lovecraft's mature creative career—is exhibited only fragmentarily in their surviving correspondence; for around 1930 Galpin, apparently ashamed of some of his youthful enthusiasms, destroyed many of Lovecraft's letters up to that time.[1] In any case, it is evident that Lovecraft valued this relationship highly, attributing to Galpin the development of his philosophical outlook at a critical period in his maturation. Lovecraft remained cordial to Galpin to the end of his life, although it is clear that by the 1930s Galpin had outgrown the role of "adopted grandson" and had matured into but one of Lovecraft's many congenial colleagues with whom he enjoyed exchanging points of view.

Because of the fragmentary nature of the correspondence, it is not certain when the two first became acquainted. In his autobiographical notes Galpin variously dates their first epistolary contact to 1916 or 1917;[2] but elsewhere he states that the earliest extant letter (26 January 1918) was perhaps the second he received. Lovecraft clarifies the matter somewhat in a letter to Anne Tillery Renshaw dated 24 August 1918, where he states: "Galpin first dawned above my horizon a year ago . . ."[3] Lovecraft had been elected president of the United Amateur Press Association (UAPA) in September, and he sought a promising high-school student to be fourth vice-president (at the time the third and fourth vice-presidents were not elected but were appointed by the president) to lead efforts at recruiting young people to join the United. Galpin had entered high school in 1915 and had quickly become a fixture in the Appleton (Wisconsin) High School Press Club, headed by Lovecraft's colleague Maurice W. Moe. It was not Moe, however, who brought Galpin to Lovecraft's attention, but Joseph Harriman, a recent graduate of Appleton High School.

The two quickly engaged in copious correspondence—one far more intellectually substantive than many others in Lovecraft's early career. From the first, Lovecraft was impressed, even awed, by Galpin's precocity. As early as 1918 he wrote: "It is hard for me to realise that eleven years separate me from

---

1. Biographical information on Galpin is chiefly derived from his own writings, including his memoir of Lovecraft ("Memories of a Friendship," 1959) and several unpublished documents at JHL (titled "HPL" [1971], "Native's Return" [1975?], "Old Friends and New Horizons" [1976], and "A. G. (II)" [1979]).
2. The original ms. of "Memories of a Friendship" (at JHL) bears the title "1916–1937: Memories of a Friendship."
3. *SL* 1.71.

Galpin, for his thoughts fit in so well with my own. I am convinced that he has a mighty future. He is passing me already in the intellectual race, and in a few years will have left me behind completely."[4] Three years later he supplied a definitive account of Galpin's influence upon him:

> It is odd that an old man should be so much influenced by a kid so vastly his junior, but it remains a fact that no other one human creature has moulded my thought and opinions as extensively as has that Alfredus child. The secret is this: that he is intellectually *exactly like me* save in degree. In degree he is immensely my superior—he is what I should like to be but have not brains enough to be. Our minds are cast in precisely the same mould, save that his is finer. He alone can grasp the direction of my thoughts and amplify them. And so we go down the dark ways of knowledge; the poor plodding old man, and ahead of him the alert little link-boy holding the light and pointing out the path. . . .[5]

Taking into account the wry exaggeration and excessive modesty characteristic of Lovecraft at this time, this assessment is very likely true, though it is difficult to document. For example, Galpin probably introduced Lovecraft to the great iconoclastic German philosopher Friedrich Nietzsche, well before he published his perspicacious essay, "Nietzsche as a Practical Prophet," in 1921. Galpin admitted that his father raised him an atheist, but he never subscribed to what he mischaracterizes as Lovecraft's "dogmatic monism"; and in a startling shift, he converted to Roman Catholicism a year after Lovecraft's death. But their early anticlericalism—and no doubt both of them used the pious Maurice W. Moe as a foil in this regard—helped to establish an intellectual bond. Galpin's skepticism regarding the vagaries of modern poetry (see his essays "Some Tendencies of Modern Poetry" and "Form in Modern Poetry," as well as the parody "Two Loves," published in Lovecraft's *Conservative*) may have assisted Lovecraft in honing his own arguments against the Imagists and Modernists.

In many ways, Galpin reminded Lovecraft of his own boyhood. His delight in Galpin's various schoolboy crushes—manifested in numerous poems, such as "Damon and Delia, a Pastoral" (*Tryout*, August 1918) and "Damon—a Monody" (*United Amateur*, May 1919)—became mortifying to Galpin in later years. The evidence points to one Margaret Abraham (who, oddly enough, shared Galpin's birthday, 8 November) as his chief *inamorata,* and the whole business led to Lovecraft's send-up of Elizabethan tragedy, *Alfredo* (September 1918). Galpin paid homage to Lovecraft in his own literary works, including the story "Marsh-Mad" (1918)—which led the diffident Lovecraft to postpone writing his story "The Tree" for three years because he felt that Galpin had anticipated his use of the "living tree" idea—and the poem "Selenaio-

---

4. *SL* 1.72.
5. HPL to Rheinhart Kleiner, 23 April 1921 (*SL* 1.128).

Phantasma," an affectionate tribute to Lovecraft's "Nemesis" (1917). Galpin does not seem to have had any overwhelming enthusiasm for weird literature, but he doubtless appreciated Lovecraft's early macabre tales—more so than the later, longer, more complex works that did not meet his favor and that led to a gradual cooling off of their friendship.

In the early years of their association—roughly the period 1917–24— amateur affairs were largely on their agenda. After his fourth vice-presidency in 1917–18, Galpin served as first vice-president in 1918–19; Rheinhart Kleiner was president during this term, and Lovecraft had resumed his chairmanship of the Department of Public Criticism, a position he had held in 1915–17. The next term (1919–20) Galpin himself was chairman of the Department, retaining that office until 1922. Anomalously, Galpin simultaneously held the presidency of the UAPA in 1920–21. Lovecraft, for his part, was Official Editor for 1920–22 and 1924–25. It could well be said that Lovecraft and Galpin were among the stars of the UAPA for the entire period. Galpin's literary contributions were not as extensive as Lovecraft's, and he produced only one number of his own publication, the *Philosopher* (December 1920)—a choice issue for its several contributions by Galpin and the first appearance of Lovecraft's story "Polaris" and his poem "The House."

Galpin states that much of his correspondence with Lovecraft during the period 1918–22 was embodied in the so-called Gallomo, the round-robin correspondence cycle including Galpin, Moe, and Lovecraft. Only seven Gallomo letters are now extant of perhaps dozens that were written; but they are among the most illuminating of Lovecraft's letters of the period. In what seem less like letters than rambling stream-of-consciousness essays or autobiographical vignettes, Lovecraft expounds at length upon his bizarre dreams (including the one that led directly to the writing of "The Statement of Randolph Carter"), provides a wondrously illuminating account of the genesis of his early fiction, pontificates on the world political scene (in particular the establishment of the League of Nations and the Anglo-Irish conflict of the early 1920s), and relates at length his gradual emergence from the hermitry of 598 Angell Street (especially following the death of his mother on 24 May 1921), as he ventures to Boston and elsewhere to socialize with amateur writers. Galpin himself was at this time undergoing changes in his scholastic life: he had graduated from Appleton High School in 1919 and entered Lawrence College in Appleton; two years later he transferred to the University of Wisconsin, from which he graduated in 1923.

In the summer of 1922 occurred the first and, as it proved, the last meeting of the two associates. Galpin, having struck up a friendship with Samuel Loveman, decided to spend the summer in Cleveland, and persuaded Lovecraft to join him. Lovecraft did so, taking the long train ride from Providence on 29 July and arriving in Cleveland the next day. He stayed more than two weeks, leaving on 15 August. It was a critical trip in many ways: not only did Lovecraft meet Galpin and Loveman (the latter of whom he had first met in New York only a few months earlier), but he also met George Kirk, Hart Crane, and Crane's numerous cronies, and also began writing to Clark Ashton Smith after Galpin and Kirk had lent him some of Smith's early volumes of poetry. All these men (except Crane, whom Lovecraft met sporadically up to 1930) became close and lifelong associates of Lovecraft. Naturally, the visit is not recorded in their surviving Lovecraft correspondence to Galpin, but echoes of it can be found in letters to others.

In 1923 Galpin became a fellow in Romance Languages at the University of Chicago. On 23 June 1924 he married a Frenchwoman, Lillian M. Roche (whom he called "Lee"), a junior at the University of Chicago. In June 1925 Galpin left for France, ostensibly to study French; but by this time he was becoming enraptured by music, and he devoted much of his time to its study. Lee objected to this change in Galpin's intellectual horizons and decided to return to Appleton; it was on her way home that she stopped off in New York, briefly meeting Lovecraft and his wife and later complaining that the room in which she was lodged for a night—an apartment in the boarding house at 169 Clinton Street where Lovecraft and his wife Sonia dwelt—was infested with bedbugs.

By this time the two men's friendship had cooled somewhat. Lovecraft, in 1927, expressed a certain bewilderment at the change in Galpin's interests when he noted, "The boy for whom I predicted the quickest success—a veritable infant marvel whose cerebral gymnastics left me beaten and amazed—has dropped literature altogether and is desperately studying *music* in an effort to become a composer . . ."[6] When Galpin returned from France in 1926, he became an instructor in French and Italian at Northwestern University; but he remained devoted to music, notably piano and composition. In 1930 he obtained his M.A. in music at Northwestern, then spent a year (1931–32) in Paris; but this time when he returned, in the midst of the Depression, he found no position available to him at Northwestern, so he went on to Appleton and took a job at Lawrence College.

Galpin reports that the letters from 1932 onward probably survive in their entirety. It was at this time that Galpin, although having destroyed many Lovecraft letters a few years earlier, decided to reestablish contact. He found Lovecraft a changed man, and one gains the impression that Lovecraft found Galpin changed also—and perhaps not entirely for the better. The philosophical discussions of 1933–34 seem to reveal an impatience on Lovecraft's part at Galpin's growing mysticism and emotionalism, a far cry from the steely intellectual sharpness that Galpin had exhibited a decade earlier. As with many other correspondents, Lovecraft expatiated upon the economic and political situation in the nation and the world, but there is little here that we do not find in other letters of the period. Galpin continued to display intellectual vagaries, produc-

---

6. HPL to Zealia Brown Reed (Bishop), 28 August 1927 (*SL* 2.161).

ing in 1936 a detective novel—first entitled *Death in D Minor* and later *Murder in Montparnasse*—as a means of gaining income while continuing to pursue his musical studies. Although August Derleth—then already a published author of mysteries—reviewed the manuscript and suggested several changes that Galpin evidently made, it was submitted to only one publisher and then shelved when it was rejected. The manuscript does not appear to survive.

Galpin was working on several musical compositions when he learned of Lovecraft's death in March 1937. Accordingly, he titled one of these pieces "Lament for H. P. L." Set in the unusual key of B major, it is a haunting and touching rhapsody. In 1977 Galpin, by then having moved to Italy and married an Italian woman, played the composition during the course of an international conference on Lovecraft. It is, certainly, one of the most distinctive tributes to Lovecraft's passing that any of his colleagues ever paid.

The Lovecraft-Galpin relationship is unique not only for its intellectual substance but also for the literary works that it spawned. Aside from the "Damon" poems, "Nathicana" (a poem on which the two associates apparently collaborated), and *Alfredo*, we must cite Lovecraft's "Old Bugs" (1919), a whimsy written to warn Galpin not to indulge too strongly in liquor prior to the onset of Prohibition. For Galpin's part, we have "Marsh-Mad," "Selenaio-Phantasma," and one installment of "The Vivisector," a column published under the house-name Zoilus in the *Wolverine*. (The other four installments were all written by Lovecraft, as correspondence between Lovecraft and Horace L. Lawson, editor of the *Wolverine*, makes clear.[7]) Galpin's Zoilus column discusses Lovecraft's "Facts concerning the Late Arthur Jermyn and His Family" at length, and is one of the more insightful early assessments of Lovecraft. About a year later Galpin became embroiled in the heated controversy between Lovecraft and amateur writer Michael Oscar White over the merits of Samuel Loveman's poetry, contributing a pungent article, "A Critic of Poetry," to the *Oracle* (August 1923). Galpin's devotion to Clark Ashton Smith's work impelled a substantial review of *Ebony and Crystal* (1922) and *Sandalwood* (1925), published in the *United Amateur* (July 1925) under the title "Echoes from Beyond Space."

Alfred Galpin may not have achieved the fame Lovecraft once predicted for him, but he remains one of the most astute and perceptive of Lovecraft's colleagues, and his writings—particularly his memoirs of his association with Lovecraft—attest to his perspicacity and creative fertility. His accomplishments as writer, philosopher, teacher, and musician are far from insignificant, and he would deserve remembrance even if he had done nothing else than to inspire the engaging letters contained in this volume.

—S. T. JOSHI
DAVID E. SCHULTZ

7. "I enclose Galpin's review of *The Wolverine*, written at your request." Horace L. Lawson to HPL, 19 September 1921 (ms., JHL).

## A Note on the Texts

The texts of the letters in this volume are derived from manuscripts at the John Hay Library of Brown University, with the exception of the seven letters to the Gallomo and two of the three letters to Alfred Galpin and Frank Belknap Long, Jr., which exist only in the form of transcripts of Lovecraft's letters prepared by Arkham House for use in publishing *Selected Letters*. Apparent transcriptional errors in the latter have been silently corrected.

The works by Galpin volume derive chiefly from the amateur publications in which they first appeared; the manuscripts of unpublished items are found in the John Hay Library.

Abbreviations used in the introduction and notes are as follows:

ALS autograph letter, signed
AHT Arkham House transcripts
*AT* *The Ancient Track: Complete Poetical Works* (San Francisco: Night Shade Books, 2001)
JHL John Hay Library, Brown University (Providence, RI)
*LL* S. T. Joshi, *Lovecraft's Library: A Catalogue*, rev. ed. (New York: Hippocampus Press, 2002)
*MW* *Miscellaneous Writings* (Sauk City, WI: Arkham House, 1995)
NAPA National Amateur Press Association
SHSW State Historical Society of Wisconsin (Madison, WI)
*SL* *Selected Letters* (Sauk City, WI: Arkham House, 1965–76; 5 vols.)
TLS typed letter, signed
UAPA United Amateur Press Association

The editors and publisher are grateful to Robert C. Harrall, of Lovecraft Properties LLC, for permission to publish the letters by Lovecraft contained in this book, and to the John Hay Library for granting permission to publish autograph letters by Lovecraft and unpublished works by Galpin. They also wish to thank Mike Horvat, Jean Rainwater of the John Hay Library, Patrick Harrigan, and Brian Showers for their assistance in locating information in rare publications.

# Letters to Alfred Galpin

[1] [ALS]

598 Angell St.,
Providence, R.I.,
Jany 26, 1918

Dear Hasting:— [1]

This is just a note to display to you the latest feat of my slow-moving wit, regarding the name of the book you recommended to me: *Etidorpha*.[2]

This name, obviously Hellenic, puzzled me; since I assumed it to be a compound of ἔτι. Then I saw light, and perceived that the initial □ might as easily be an ητα as an επσιλου□ —thus: ΗΤΙΔΟΡΦΑ. Now what is this, unless it be *Aphrodite* (Ἀφροδίτε) *written backwards?* Thus you see, my dear Niplag, that I have made a discovery! At least, it appears to be a discovery; though I cannot for the life of me conceive why a reversed Aphrodite should have anything to do with metaphysics and the philosophy of the ultimate. I should like to see this curious Ἡτιδορφα. Of course, I *may* be all at sea about this name—*but* if it be a coincidence, 'tis one of the most singular coincidences I ever encountered. I spent full half an hour looking up an hypothetical word δορφα in Liddell & Scotts Greek Lexicon,[3] to match the supposed ἔτι, before the analogy dawned upon me!

Trusting you are not completely prostrated by that massive letter of a few days ago, I remain

Most humbly & respectfully yours,
L. P. Drawoh

*Notes*

1. In his autobiographical notes, Galpin explains that his pseudonym Consul Hasting is derived from the etymology of *Alfred* (*Elf-Red* = wise in counsel; hence *Consul*), and a play on his surname (*gallopin'* = hasty).
2. John Uri Lloyd (1849–1936), *Etidorhpa; or, The End of Earth* (Cincinnati: John Uri Lloyd, 1895). The novel, dealing with a journey to the hollow center of the earth, may have influenced *The Dream-Quest of Unknown Kadath* (1926–27). There is a modern reprint (Pocket Books, 1978).
3. Henry George Liddell and Robert Scott, *A Greek-English Lexicon* (1843; LL 533). Still the standard Greek-English lexicon.

[2] [TLS/ALS]

Nowhere, May 27, [1918] 10 p.m.

O thou of microscopic years but telescopic mind:

My reason for replying before waiting for an inspiration is this: Through a singular combination of circumstances I have disposed of *all* the accumulated correspondence which has so long vexed me, including even the dreaded letters to possible laureate judges, so that tonight there await me only your much appreciated treatise and a brief and unimportant note from a mediocre recruit named Thalheimer.[1] Tomorrow I may be "swamped" with a burden of portentious [*sic*] mail, hence find it best to write whilst I have the leisure, even though my thoughts are likely to prove the very reverse of scintillant. I wonder if I am wise in doing this? I note that in my last communication, fatigue led me to perpetrate a puerility which attracted your immediate notice—i.e., the silly comparison of instinct and *knowledge*. I am glad that you cannot know the deadly fatigue and lethargy which accompany a state of health such as that under which I have been staggering for ten years and more. At times the very effort of sitting up is insupportable, and the least added exertion brings on a sort of dull tiredness which soon shews itself in the lagging brilliancy and occasional incoherence of my literary and epistolary productions. I fear you will find me disappointing as a fellow-philosopher— if, indeed, my current contributions to the world's fund of mediocrity have not already removed any illusions you may have entertained in this direction.

Buckling down to business, I see the fatuity of my statement regarding *knowledge*, but strangely enough, do not withdraw my original contention! I concede an error of expression, but do not yet see the error in deduction. (how dense!!!) My amended statement is this: instinct is born in the young animal *in full working order*—all the major instincts are at once capable of expression, and require absolutely no *instruction* for development. The young animal or human (pardon the distinction—I do not make it scientifically) would develop the same instincts if utterly isolated and without external impressions. Young lions do not have to be taught their fierceness, nor human beings their greedy treacherousness. The qualities are innate and unconnected with the genuine intellectual faculty. Turning to reason, we see that it is only a *capacity*—not an automatically working function—which may or may not be developed according to environment. You refer to the *instinctive* use of very simple reasoning processes—the addition of 2 and 3 to obtain 5, as you express it. Now I believe that this is not *inborn*, but that it is the result of elementary observation. Only the *capacity* is inborn. On the other hand, the cry of a child for food *is* instinctive and inborn, as is its automatic flinching if approached by a seemingly menacing object, or its fear of the dark—or any of those things which develop without so much as a glance at surroundings or hint of instruction. Let me elaborate: I maintain, rightly or not, I leave it for you to judge—that a human being born without the five senses and utterly isolated from intercourse with the world, would *never* develop the slightest trace of manifested rationality, even though endowed with a mind of high grade and perfect soundness. That same man, if trained by particular methods, might become a genius. BUT—the *instinctive* processes of that man would develop exactly the same in either case! Do you perceive my trend? Reason requires something to work with—instinct does not. My error lay in calling *reason itself* acquired. I meant to say, and should have, had I been less fatigued, that the *manifestations* of reason are acquired, whilst those of instinct are innate. The distinction which I draw satisfies me of the essential difference of the two attributes, though I should be the last to assert dogmatically that reason is not a product of evolution from instinct. As to the matter of *aphorisms,* or seemingly innate displays of the reason, I will not try to be too precise in arguing with so great an opponent as yourself. So little is known of the true inwardness of psychology, that I would hesitate to deny the existence of some borderland betwixt reason and instinct. But I will say that in my opinion, even the simplest reasonings are the result of observation and experience—conscious or subconscious. Instinct is otherwise.

N.B.—Do not mistake me—beasts have an appreciable share of reason, and many of their seemingly instinctive acts are doubtless compounded of instinct and reason, just as many of man's seemingly rational acts have in reality a liberal share of instinct in them. If I have revealed any new fallacies and absurdities this time, pray do not hesitate to let me know about them. I am very humble at heart, despite my forbidding and dogmatical exterior.

Concerning the correct personnel of the staff of an average 8-page city daily, I cannot even guess, for dailies hereabouts are inclined to run over that size to a considerable extent. The *Evening Bulletin* has never published less than 18 pages within my recollection, whilst it frequently runs up to 48. 30 is the average number. The late *Evening News* was not a paper—it was a joke.[2] And I am not much interested in its successor, since the request of its editor for me to make my articles "so simple that a child might understand them" caused me to withdraw from the field. He did not use "child" in the sense which the word conveys at 779 Kimball St. He meant the grade of mentality prevailing in the ranks of the Democratic party—of which the reconstructed *News* is an organ and exponent. But as to the *Crescent* [3]—it is easy to see that the paper is sadly undermanned—reminding one of the late *News.* I never thought I could take much interest in Sporting Editors—but circumstances alter cases! If you wish to develop a sporting vocabulary, read Thomas Moore's comic piece, "Tom Crib's Memorial to Congress", published about an hundred years ago, with very learned notes, and beginning:

> "Most Holy and High, and Legitimate *squad,*
> First *swells* of the world, since *Boney's* in *quod,*
> Who have everything now, as Bill Gibbons would say,
> Like the bull in the china-shop, all your own way—
> Whatsoever employs your magnificent *nobs,*
> Whether *diddling* your subjects, and *gutting* their *fobs,*"—etc[4]

And now for the puzzle—*Dreams*—which may be destined to reveal to you in all its hideous reality my unutterably and infinitely Boeotian density and slug-gishness of wit. Possibly the safest way to reply and not reveal the clumsiness of my guessing, is to be as enigmatical as you, and ask you to *guess* what my guess is!! I will oil the way with a compliment or two—the language and atmosphere of your piece are really quite captivating and haunting; nor is it in a spirit of un-intelligent and obvious comment that one may compare the style to that of Mr. Poe. I shall send this to Cook, minus the N.B.'s, for though he was forced to return your "Two Loves",[5] he asked me for a piece of your *prose* if I had any-thing of the sort on hand. (Note my playing for time—I am trying to distract your attention whilst I neglect to try for solution of the mystery!) But what is the use? You can penetrate all shams and pretences, so I might as well face the ordeal: I fancy you are—er—er—thinking of theories advanced in the Kleico-molo[6]—er—er—which I disputed to some extent, yet which I admired for their boldness of conception and so forth—(I hope I am indefinite enough to be able to make this sound like the right solution after I learn the truth from you. The gentle art of non-committal ambiguousness is a great asset to a would-be philosopher.) But again, wot's de use? I think you are hinting at your dream theory—that all entity is but an agitation in the ether, and that it is coexistent and identical with the pitiful unrest known as human consciousness. Now you know all. I stand revealed. Have pity!

Once more the fair—and otherwise. I appreciate your position, which is the average one, and am glad you are not to be classified as a "fusser"—a term not so new or local as you think, since it existed in full glory in my day, many, many, years ago. As to the Massachusetts monstrosity—you have my sympathy—a sympathy of comprehension rather than experience, since so far as I know, no feminine freak ever took the trouble to note or recognise my colossal and transcendent intellect. "It" must be an interesting caricature. Why not use It to excite the jealousy of your Hibernian Chloë, thereby awak-ing the interest of the latter? Such is the approved method of fiction. Or pos-sibly Its utter ridiculousness precludes the course! [ALS begins here:] I paused a moment for a somewhat humorous poetical note—& find the hour too late to admit of Remingtonian clattering.[7] Pardon the relapse. The following may apply to your heart entanglements:

A PASTORAL TRAGEDY
of Appleton, Wisconsin
By
Kleinhart Reiner, Esq.[8]

Young Strephon for his Chloë sigh'd
In accents warm but vain;
Th' Hibernian nymph his suit deny'd,
Nor melted at his pain.

But one day from an Eastern scene
     Fair (?) Hecatissa came;
She eye'd the swain with fav'ring mien,
     And felt the Paphian flame.

No answ'ring flame the youth display'd;
     He scorn'd her doubtful charms,
And still implor'd th' Hibernian maid
     To seek his outstretch'd arms.

Thus Strephon, both unlov'd and lov'd,
     Both pleading and refusing,
Plann'd, that to passion might be mov'd
     The maiden of his choosing.

With seeming scorn he ceas'd his sighs,
     And careless turn'd away;
Then courted with dissembling eyes
     The maid from Boston Bay.

The willing fair (?) his wooing heard;
     With bliss his suit receiv'd;
Bright Chloë, list'ning, notes each word,
     With jealous longing griev'd.

At length the nymph for Strephon frets,
     And mourns the lonely lack;
In tears her frigid course regrets,
     And yearns to win him back.

One kindly glance the fair one sends,
     And Strephon's at her side;
In grief poor Hecatissa bends—
     Forsaken ere a bride!

And on that joyous nuptial morn
     When Strephon wed the fair,
A hooded figure, wan, forlorn,
     Stole thro' the dewy air.

Down to the dam the sad one went,
     Pray'd Heaven to forgive her,
Then leap'd with desperate intent
     Into the swift Fox River!

P.S. The river-god her face espy'd,
     And felt a sudden pain—
Declin'd to claim her as his bride,
     And cast her back again!

Your adaptability, to which you refer, is a very enviable characteristic; and one which I share to the extent of relaxing gravity & perpetrating things like that on the other side of this sheet. However, my own adaptability is very limited, and I lack interest in a vast number of things that others are deeply concerned about. As I said before—*games* form one of the provinces in which I am unable to take much interest. The reason for this is undoubtedly my feeble store of energy. I am only about half alive—a large part of my strength is consumed in sitting up or walking. My nervous system is a shattered wreck, and I am absolutely bored & listless save when I come upon something which peculiarly interests me. However—so many things *do* interest me, & interest me intensely, in science, history, philosophy, & literature; that I have never actually desired to die, or entertained any suicidal designs, as might be expected of one with so little kinship to the ordinary features of life.

Regarding your absorption of ideas in class—I always found that a *written* fact remained in my memory far better than a *spoken* one. I could, with the same amount of mental energy, obtain twice as much from a book as from a lecture. On the same principle, I am a much better writer than conversationalist. (Heavens! what a confession to make after the written trash I have revealed to the public!!)

As to *concentration*—I am a bit baffled as to the proper method of cultivating that gift, since my own "single track mind" (I borrow a phrase from a statesman of whom I am none too fond) is always so *stupidly* concentrated on whatever I am doing. I think lack of excess mental vitality is an aid to concentration—that is why I, and the statesman alluded to, are such d—n fools. Pardon, please!! My innate concentration is so complete that I cannot be diverted from a subject by any amount of digression on the part of those with whom I may be conversing. I am the direct antithesis of the person who says—"Yes, I wrote that last Friday; you know, the day we went down town and met John Smith who had just bought such a pretty cottage in Riverside, where the Joneses live—you know, the Joneses that are related to the Browns who used to live in Auburn—and by the way, isn't it too bad how the fare has been raised to 7¢ on the car line to Auburn; oh, I think these war prices are *terrible*—what a terrible war it is, anyhow! I wonder how this new German offensive will be met—and—dear me! What *was* I talking about?"

But *your* lack of concentration is *not* of this familiar type. Yours is obviously based on a mental vigour which calls for more exercise than the external aspects of one ordinary topic afford. You perceive obscure analogies—the *overtones* of your subject, as it were—and in an effort at following all the parallel lines of thought, find a lack of concentration on the dominant phase. In my abysmal ignorance of the subtleties of psychology, I can suggest nothing but a conscious comparison of relative values—a recognition of the ascendancy of some *one* phase of the subject before you—a phase to & from which the lesser phases must of necessity lead. Do not think of *concentration* in a concrete way.

Simply think of the *main topic*—the *thing itself*. Probably this so-called "advice" is valueless & unintelligent. At least give me credit for suspecting its emptiness!

As to "Sherlock Holmes"—I used to be infatuated with him! I read every Sherlock Holmes story published,[9] and even organised a *detective agency* when I was thirteen, arrogating to myself the proud pseudonym of S.H. This P.D.A.*—whose members ranged between nine & fourteen in years, was a most wonderful thing—how many murders & robberies we unravelled! Our headquarters were in a deserted house just out of the thickly settled area, and we there enacted, and "solved", many a gruesome tragedy. I still remember my labours in producing artificial "bloodstains on the floor!!!" But in conformity with our settled policy of utter candour, I must admit to you that the entire venture was more dramatic than psychological in objects & essence; and that our "deductions" were generally pretty well provided for in advance.

As for deducing your habits & biography from the letters I have received—pray assign me an easier task! You & Sherlock are beyond me! But if you have any more discoveries about me to tell, let me hear them! Your conclusions about my typing are practically correct. I use forefingers only, & employ a Remington machine—though *not* #11. [Query—is this machine, or is it not, a visible writer?] As to your mode of deduction—did I *tell* you about my typing methods—as I may have mentioned to many—or did you judge from the *kind* of mistakes I am prone to make—or from the evident pressure I give the keys—or from the fact that I prefer to write by hand? About my *speed*—here is something to think over. I began this note at 10 p.m. When the household retired, I changed to handwriting—ergo, the two pages typed represent what I can do in the time between ten & the retiring time of the average household. But on the other hand, this was not copying but original argumentative composition. Obviously, I may have ceased work from time to time to frame a reply to some point, or think up a new line of defence.

About current detective stories—I have read only a few, which I happened to stumble upon in the ordinary course of human events. Most of them seem to me too artificial to be interesting. I read two or three of the Craig Kennedy[10] tales several years ago, but deemed them too *mechanical* to be really absorbing. It all comes from Poe, *via* Doyle. M. Dupin[11] is the prototype of Holmes, & Holmes is the prototype of every other detective of fiction, if we except Nick Carter and Old Sleuth,[12] dear to the small boys of other generations, and studied almost invariably without knowledge or consent of the reader's parents! There is, though, another sort of mystery story, in which the detective plays rather a minor part. This is the type of which "The Moonstone"[13] & the first tales of Anna Katherine Green[14] are the earliest examples. A few months ago I happened upon a new atrocity of this sort—"Faulkner's Folly"—by Carolyn Wells.[15] I knew the outcome before I

---

*Providence Detective Agency

had read the thing a quarter through—and sure enough—I was right! But as you remark—it was not by genuine deduction based on the circumstances that I solved the murder mystery—it was merely by a familiarity with the conventions & technique of this sort of novel. So far as real evidence went, there were two persons more likely to be guilty than the real culprit—but I knew that owing to their *positions* in the narrative, they simply *could not*. If you have read this effort, I will speak of it more in detail.

Your analysis of the Sherlock Holmes technique is very acute, & coincides with my own views on it. (egotism) However—did you notice how, a few years ago, Mr. Doyle excited considerable newspaper attention by actually solving a simple case by methods akin to those with which he invested his hero? He succeeded in establishing the innocence of a man unjustly accused of the very singular crime of injuring live-stock on a farm by stabbing. I wish I could recall more of the case.[16]

About the word *"peruse"*—possibly I do employ it to excess, but Mr Addison was ever my model of style in prose. Owing to my devotion to many very un-Addisonian subjects, I have strayed far from the classic diction of the Spectator in many ways; but the original impress is ineradicable—at least, I *hope* it is. Addison hath never been surpassed in grace, and the most pleasing of American essayists, Mr. Washington Irving, obtains much of his charm & urbanity by a close adherence to the manner of the older and greater writer.

Your procedure in *apparently* curtailing the length of your St. Nicholas poems, is very ingenious—quite worthy of a master mind. "Nemesis"[17] metre readily lends itself to such condensation. I sincerely hope you win a prize. Concerning the *American Magazine* contest, I shall try to investigate the matter, though I have not been out lately & have not seen the magazine for uncounted aeons. I could compete with serene consciousness of injuring no chance of yours. My own entry could not begin to equal yours in merit, for I am little in touch with the present interests of people. I do not write for the public, but only for my own satisfaction. I wish you could win first prize and I second, if second there be.* But probably I shall never get around to accomplishing the labour.

I hope you can find a way to win renown in the Sankt Nikolai League before old age shall debar you. Seventeen! What a weight of years for a tiny tot only 73 inches in height to sustain! You are well headed toward that celestial infinity which we love so well. My own altitude is 70.5 inches in ordinary shoes, hence we can both claim kinship with the lofty. Another old gentleman, Mr. Hoag,[18] claims an even 72 inches—we of the United[19] are not at all inclined to be lowly!

Concerning Alfred the Lesser[20]—I will not forbear to pay homage to his undoubted art and excellence. He had a remarkable command of smooth

---

*I see there is a second—and seven more—according to your later allusion.

melody & imagery, and never fell below a high standard.* I respect him. But as a matter of personal preference, I select older & more vigorous bards. I never seem to turn of my own accord to A. T.—or to recall bits of his composition—as I do with my favourite Georgians & pre-Georgians. I hardly think Tennyson, or even Milton, can be compared to Shakespeare in excellence. I am slightly unappreciative of Shakespeare, but I can easily see that he is the leader of all. No other writer possessed so universal a genius, & so broad an understanding of mankind. All this notwithstanding a multiplicity of defects, including some positively puerile errors & anachronisms.

In my ultimate definition of poetry, I presume I am not so far as you and M[r.] Poe. As you will see in a forthcoming article of mine,[21] I subscribe to a great extent to the dicta of the Baltimore Bard. Beauty is certainly the prime object; Truth is to be considered only when coincident with Beauty—which is not so often as the late J. Keats believed. I am aware that my favourite Georgians lacked much in the true spirit of poesy—but I do admire their *verse*, as *verse*. I have often felt that I possess but a slight grasp of the poetic principle, & but a fragmentary appreciation of genuine poetry. (See previous *Kleicomolos*) You will shudder with outraged poeticism when you read my latest effusion—a 48-line XVIII[th] century pastoral in octosyllabic couplets!!!!![22]

Your poetical contrasts are illuminating—I appreciate their force—but I realised all this before. I entertained no notion of Mr. Pope's literalness or Grecian simplicity in his Iliad. Dr. Bentley, indeed, told M[r] Pope, 'that it is not Homer'.[23]

Your *retentiveness* is to be envied. Mine varies with my state of health—I am very dull when prostrated with a headache, or struggling with a less obvious tangle of refractory nerves—not that I am ever so *very* far from dulness!! (I have enough constitutional stupidity to keep on liking the Georgian atmosphere despite all evidence against it!) I sincerely trust you may receive your expected 100% in the Commercial Law examination—it will certainly constitute a varied testimonial of your genius.

The general reception of your "Two Loves" is most gratifying to me, both as an endorsement of my own opinion and otherwise. I cannot suggest just the professional magazine for it, but Mo's suggestion will undoubtedly be satisfactory. In amateurdom, I think you had best send it to the new recruit—James J. Moloney, 430 Main St., Athol, Mass. He will, I am sure, be delighted to print it in his coming paper—which according to all accounts will be a somewhat ambitious venture.[24] The Association must not be denied the privilege of seeing it, after having endured the original. Did I tell you that Miss Gidlow is President of the rival "United" Amateur Press Association which split off from ours in 1912? It is a puerile thing, with very easy literary

---

*Someone has said T. is too artistic—that he is the slave of his style, & that sometimes he KEEPS ON WRITING after INSPIRATION has gone.

standards. Some idea of its calibre may be gained by noting the opinion of the majority of its members regarding the weird & wondrous work of the Mills-Gidlow duet. They call it "*very highbrow*"!! At least, this is what Cook informs me, & his acquaintance with this circle is fairly representative.[25]

About your sonnet—pray do not think *I* consider it poor. In analysing it, I merely suggested why *you* might deem it below your usual standard. The experimental nature of its construction would never have impressed me, had you not revealed the secret voluntarily. It is, as I have remarked, an excellent production, with the one slight technical exception previously noted. I am sure Moloney will appreciate it. My own recent ode is akin in purpose & construction. It is a pure experiment, which I am never likely to repeat. Up to date I have written *one* sonnet and *one* ode—no more.[26] Couplets & quatrains are my specialty, with blank verse in rare homœopathic doses.

As to Klei—you will see a most touching eulogy of his recent poem "Ruth", by our friend Mo in the May Dept. of Public Criticism. Mo compares my "Astrophobos" to "Ruth", much to the disadvantage of the former.[27] This incident has impelled me to perpetrate a gentle parody on "Ruth"—which here behold:

GRAYCE

(With Unstinted Apologies to the Author of "Ruth")

by Kleinhart Reiner, Esq.

In the dim shade of the unrustled grove,
    Amidst the silence of approaching night,
I saw thee standing, as thro' boughs above
    Filter'd the pencils of the dying light.

Grayce! I had thought thou wert by far too proud,
    Too weary of the world and all its pain,
To pause so wistfully, with fair head bow'd,
    Forgetting all thy coldness and disdain.

But in that instant all my doubts and fears
    Were swept away, as on the evening breeze,
When I beheld thee, not indeed in tears,
    But rack'd and shaken with a mighty *sneeze!*

N.B. If you have not read "Ruth", you can find it in the February *Brooklynite*.[28]

Klei edits *The Brooklynite* now, & if he can surmount the difficulties of his task—the thankless task of recording social gossip—he will produce a paper worth a more careful reading than most *Brooklynites*. He has owed me a letter for ages—in fact, he has not yet acknowledged the *Kleicomolo* I sent him a month ago. I am still debating with myself whether or not to send

Ἠτιδορφα around the circle. Would it, or would it not, be beyond Kleico.? I wonder! Co likes imaginative flights—but Lloyd brings in just a trifle too much science and pseudo-science for the absolutely wild & woolly reader. And as for Klei—I fear there is not enough soft Cyprian romalince for him!

I am trying to issue a July *Conservative,* as I think I told you before. I expect to produce some 8 pages, with your "Selenaio-Phantasma" as one of the leading contributions.[29] My Klei parody may be included, though this is amongst the items to be dropped if any space congestion occurs. I have already sent the MS. to Cook for printing, but on account of his pressure of work, hardly expect to be able to publish it for a month or two. I have usurped a vast deal of the space for myself, though there will be in all five other contributors.

I note your reference to the beauteous Miltonico-Shakespearian fellow-prodigy at A.H.S., & trust that you may succeed in arousing within her soul any possible 'dormant genius of authorship'! However—you prejudice me against her when you relate her naive estimate of my precious heroic measure! One thing, though, shews good sense—her apparent aversion to the much overrated peasant warbler R. Burns. This fellow fatigues me, though he succeeded in gaining the qualified approval of as great a poet as W. Cowper.

I have not yet purchased *Sankt Nikolai,* nor taken any steps toward League recruiting—in fact, I have not been out at all since last addressing you. After the Presidency is off my hands, I may be able to assist you a bit in the recruiting department; in fact, I will accept appointment as your subordinate on the committee. I could handle a very limited number of cases. You will make the best 1st Vice-President since the term of Chester L. Sharp—1913–1914—the year I joined. I never corresponded with him, but find glowing testimony of his ability on the official records. As you know—the Hon. Don Eduardo Daas "roped me in"—an utter stranger.[30] He had seen some of my metrical heroic wails in the back of a mediocre magazine.[31]

Note the *envelope* in which this missive will reach you—unless it bursts or pines away & dies. It is home-made, an excellent example of Theobaldian craftsmanship. Wherefore, sayest thou? I reply! I am all out of envelopes, & not wishing to encroach on my mother's rather different supply, have utilised my matchless constructive skill in supplying my needs. This is an age of conservation, & I fancy I have made good use of waste paper.

Have I been too boresome? Pray let me hear from you when you have recovered.

> Yr. ob[t] humble Serv[t]
> L. Theobald Jun[r.]

*Notes*

1. Joseph Thalheimer, Stanford University, Stanford, California.

2. HPL wrote monthly astronomy columns for the Providence *Evening News* from January 1914 to May 1918.

3. Presumably the *Appleton Crescent*, the major daily newspaper in Appleton.

4. Thomas Moore (1779–1852), *Tom Crib's Memorial to Congress* (1819), ll. 1–6.

5. The poem, as by Consul Hasting, appeared in the *Conservative* (July 1918). W. Paul Cook (1881–1948) was publisher of the *Monadnock Monthly*, the *Vagrant*, and other amateur journals and books. In 1927 he issued the *Recluse*, containing HPL's "Supernatural Horror in Literature."

6. HPL refers the correspondence group the Kleicomolo, consisting of Rheinhart Kleiner, Ira A. Cole, Maurice W. Moe, and HPL. In "Memories of a Friendship," Galpin mentions "a monstrosity called the Kleicomagallo," which ultimately became the Gallomo, consisted of Galpin, HPL, and Moe (see letter 6). Letter 13 makes mention (twice) of a Gremolo—presumably consisting of Sonia Greene, Moe, and HPL—but nothing is known of this cycle, and no letters from it are extant.

7. I.e., typing. HPL had a 1904 Remington typewriter.

8. A spoonerism of the name of HPL's friend Rheinhart Kleiner (1882–1949), who wrote many light love lyrics.

9. Later HPL confessed that he had read only the first three Sherlock Holmes collections (*The Adventures of Sherlock Holmes* [1892], *The Memoirs of Sherlock Holmes* [1894], and *The Return of Sherlock Holmes* [1905]), three novels (*A Study in Scarlet* [1888], *The Sign of the Four* [1890], and *The Hound of the Baskervilles* [1902]), and "an odd (& rather mediocre) pair or series of tales appearing about '08" (HPL to A. W. Derleth, 26 March 1927; ms., SHSW).

10. Arthur B[enjamin] Reeve (1880–1936) created Craig Kennedy, scientific detective. His work appeared in *Hearst's Magazine, Cosmopolitan,* and *Nash's Pall Mall Magazine.* The tales were gathered in many collections, beginning with *The Silent Bullet: Adventures of Craig Kennedy, Scientific Detective* (1912). Reeve also wrote several novels featuring Kennedy.

11. Poe's detective, C. Auguste Dupin, featured in "The Murders in the Rue Morgue," "The Mystery of Marie Roget," and "The Purloined Letter."

12. Nick Carter was created by John R. Coryell (1848–1924). Old Sleuth was the dime novel detective created by Harlan Halsey (1839?–1898).

13. Wilkie Collins (1869–1942), *The Moonstone* (1868).

14. Anna Katharine Green (1846–1935), the first American mystery writer to remain consistently on the bestseller lists.

15. Carolyn Wells (1870–1942), *Faulkner's Folly* (New York: George H. Doran Co., 1917).

16. Written up by Doyle in "The Case of Mr. George Edalji," serialized in the *Daily Telegraph* in 1907, and published in book form as *The Story of Mr. George Edalji* (1907).

17. HPL alludes to his poem "Nemesis," the meter of which is derived from Swinburne's *Hertha.* Galpin's "Selenaio-Phantasma" uses the same form.

18. Jonathan E. Hoag (1831–1927), a poet from Greenwich, NY.

19. I.e., the United Amateur Press Association.

20. I.e., Alfred, Lord Tennyson.

21. "The Despised Pastoral" (*Conservative*, July 1918).

22. "The Spirit of Summer" (*Conservative*, July 1918).

23. Richard Bentley (1662–1742) was the leading classical scholar of his time. He made a celebrated comment upon the publication of Pope's translation of the *Iliad* (1715–20): ". . . it is a pretty poem, Mr. Pope; but you must not call it Homer" (quoted in G. Birkbeck Hill's notes to Samuel Johnson's essay on Pope in *Lives of the English Poets* [Oxford: Clarendon Press, 1905], 3:213).

24. Moloney edited *The Voice from the Mountains*, whose issue for July 1918 contained an essay by Galpin, "Man and the Supernatural," as well as a poem, "Sonnet to Poetry." The latter presumably is the item discussed in the next paragraph.

25. For this split in the UAPA, see HPL's "A Matter of Uniteds" (*Bacon's Essays*, Summer 1927). HPL addresses the amateur paper, *Les Mouches Fantastiques*, ed. Elsa Gidlow and Roswell George Mills, in the essay "*Les Mouches Fantastiques*" (*Conservative*, July 1918).

26. The sonnet is "Sonnet on Myself," *Tryout* (July 1918); the ode is "Ode for July Fourth, 1917," *United Amateur* (July 1917).

27. "'Astrophobos,' by Ward Phillips, is another recipe poem; although his recipe is so much more intricate that it is not to be recommended for the Freshman. The critic would denominate a poem composed according to this recipe, a ulalumish poem, as it has so many earmarks of Poe. True to type, it is ulaluminated with gorgeous reds and crimsons, vistas of stupendous distances, coined phrases, unusual words, and general touches of either mysticism or purposeless obscurity. Such a poem is a feast for epicures who delight in intellectual caviar, but it is not half so satisfying to average poetic taste as Mr. Kleiner's 'Ruth.'" "Department of Public Criticism," *United Amateur* 17, No. 5 (May 1918): 95.

28. *Brooklynite* 9, No. 2 (February 1918): 5. HPL's "Grace" was published as part of the article "Ward Phillips Replies" (*Conservative*, July 1918).

29. Galpin's poem "Selenaio-Phantasma," "Dedicated to the Author of 'Nemesis,'" a pastiche of HPL's "Nemesis," was published in the *Conservative* (July 1918). A manuscript entitled "Luna-Phantasma" survives among HPL's papers at JHL.

30. Edward F. Daas was Official Editor of the UAPA in 1913–14 when he recruited HPL into amateur journalism.

31. I.e., the *Argosy*. See *H. P. Lovecraft in the* Argosy: *Collected Correspondence from the Munsey Magazines*, ed. S. T. Joshi (West Warwick, RI: Necronomicon Press, 1994).

[3] [TLS]

598 Angell St., Providence, R.I.,
August 21, 1918.

Theobaldus Tertius, Esq.,
Esteem'd Godson:—

I am overwhelmed! How can I possibly convey a suitable idea of the pleasure and gratitude I experienced, and am still experiencing, as a result of your communications of 18th inst.? I will begin with the verses, which are, if grossly flattering, excellent indeed; and which must represent a great aesthetic sacrifice on your part, considering the medium in which they are cast.[1] I am so used to the heroick atmosphere that your delightful tribute does not sound at all like doggerel to me. I think it most graceful. Should you desire Private Criticism, I will say that (1) In line 5 the word "questioners" might be shortened to "doubters" to get rid of a syllable, (2) The word you have as "e'er" should be "ere", (the two are different), (3) "I-*de*-als" has 3 syllables, and cannot rhyme with "feels". I have substituted

> The Gods themselves thy high ideals guide;
> They only know the passions that preside.

(4) The word "omnipresent" contains no "c". I felt like sending the lines somewhere for publication, but on second thought decided that I could not, good as they are, since to do so would savour of egotism. They are too complimentary to me! Therefore for once in my life I am going to let something of yours languish in unpublished obscurity! But I will have revenge—and last night celebrated my birthday by scribbling a reply which I shall copy on the machine for your perusal. Theobald II can scarcely equal Theobald III, but the enclosed is the best I can do.

And now about the book—!!!² Words fail me in describing my pleasure at receiving this exquisite volume, whose appearance is as delightful as its contents—and that is saying much. I fancy it covers a great deal of ground with which we are familiar, and shall probably have a few words to say about it in my next epistle. I may have perused this among other Emersoniana in the dim past, but I recall it not, and shall read it with all the zest of first acquaintance. I generally neglected the more recent philosophers in favour of the ancients, and have never quite understood the habit of so many of my acquaintances in proclaiming their undivided allegiance to the Sage of Concord. Your timely gift has reawakened my interest in him, and it is not unlikely that I shall in the near future give him a good share of my attention. I am like a great many others, who neglect the riches near at hand whilst searching in far fields. Whilst I have been roving through antient Hellas in the company of Democritus,³ I have slighted my fellow-New-Englander! You are helping me broaden my education! Again I will attempt to suggest all the abounding thanks which I cannot visibly frame, both for the delectable poem and the appropriate and artistic book. Your thoughtfulness is most highly appreciated!

I am hopelessly engulfed in your "hyperbolic oleaginity"! Pray do not slander yourself so! Your intellect is no more imitative than any other—you are seeking the truth, and therefore examining all men's thought and selecting what appeals to you. That is the only way to form ideas—and your genius for assimilation is all that is needed to stamp you as a remarkable thinker. The curiosity which leads you to consider philosophical questions, supported by your discriminating method of selecting and analysing opinions, is an ample testimonial of your genius. Others hear the same things you hear—but never stop to think about them—or if they do think they become confused and give it up. You have a plenitude of years in which to work out an original eclectic system of thought—and you certainly will work one out! As a disillusioning proof of my lack of super-intellect, I refer you to the Sonneberg article. Illness, withdrawing me from active duties, has relieved my mind of an infinite amount of concentration on details and left it free to wander at will through the realms of the abstract and unpractical. It is not likely that I expend any more actual brain activity in considering infinite space, than the average business man expends in attending to the innumerable trying details and responsibilities of his office work. It is merely a matter of direction—and so prone to fatigue am I, that I occasionally feel that my mind must be very mediocre. Mr. Pope, for one, triumphed over greater bodily illnesses than mine—yet I get nowhere.[4] So you see that I have enough self-derogatory material to match the modest remarks you make at the head of your epistle. It is rather fortunate we ran across each other, since we are both dwellers in a rather singular region of thought, with few near at hand to share our views. My family are as delightful and kind as any family could be—my mother is a positive marvel of consideration—but none the less I am not thought any particular credit socially—I am awkward and unpleasing—much more so than you, I am certain. Comparing us, I find you most like me of anyone I know—yet with real impartiality I must concede the brighter mentality to you. Your rate of assimilation really surpasses mine by far. To trace, for instance, my philosophical views. I began to study astronomy late in 1902—age 12. My interest came through two sources—discovery of an old book of my grandmother's in the attic,[5] and a previous interest in physical geography. Within a year I was thinking of virtually nothing but astronomy, yet my keenest interest did not lie outside the solar system. I think I really ignored the abysses of space in my interest in the habitability of the various planets of the solar system. My observations (for I purchased a telescope early in 1903) were confined mostly to the moon and the planet Venus. You will ask, why the latter, since its markings are doubtful even in the largest instruments? I answer—this very MYSTERY was what attracted me. In boyish egotism I fancied I might light upon something with my poor little 2¼-inch telescope which had eluded the users of the 40-inch Yerkes telescope!! And to tell the truth, I think the moon interested me more than anything else—the very nearest object. I used to sit night after night absorbing the minutest details of the lunar surface, till today I can tell you of every peak and crater as though they were the topographical features of my own neighbourhood. I was highly angry at Nature for withholding from my gaze the other side of our satellite! It was not till 1904 that I dabbled much in philosophy, and even then I used to smile at extravagant speculation. I had always been an agnostic because I saw no proof of Deity, but I was not by any means a cosmic sage. My real philosophical interest began when I was just your age—1906. I then set about writing a book—a complete treatise on astronomy[6]—and in doing so I resolved to use all the best material at hand. I would not write till I had made myself absolute master of my subject. Wherefore I commenced a campaign of intensive reading, devouring everything I could find on astronomy. This perforce turned my attention to the structure of the universe, and to problems in cosmogony, and literally obtruded upon my attention the matters of infinity and eternity which have since interested me so keenly. Before 1907 I was deep in speculation, and have not been able to get out yet! When I look back, I can see that I always held the idea of the earth's insignificance—but it was in a passive way before 1906. I knew it, but it made no impression on my thought. I was a great reformer then—(in my own mind), and had high ideas about uplifting the masses. I came across a superficially bright Swedish boy[7] in the Public Library—he worked in the "stack" where the books are kept—and invited him to the house to broaden his mentality (I was fifteen and he was about the same, though he was smaller and seemed younger.) I thought I had uncovered a mute inglorious Milton[8] (he professed a great interest in my work), and despite maternal protest entertained him frequently in my library. I believed in equality then, and reproved him when he called my mother "Ma'am"—I said that a future scientist should not talk like a servant! But ere long he uncovered qualities which did not appeal to me, and I was forced to abandon him to his plebeian fate. I think the experience educated me more than it educated him—I have been more of a cynic since that time! He left the library (by request) and I never saw him more. Pardon the autobiographical reminiscences, but I seem to be in a retrospective mood—perhaps as a result of my birthday, which is a natural time of recapitulation.

Mention of your heroic couplets, written in a lady's album, reminds me of some correspondence I had with Klei last fall. At the 1917 convention of the National he was called upon to perpetrate some album verse, and he retained a copy to send me. I thought it excellent, but believed I could equal it—hence dashed off five specimens in this vein for Klei's approval. I will copy them here if I can find them, and will leave it to your judgment whether or not I succeed in the field of poetical gallantry. First Klei's effusion:

FOR THE ALBUM OF
MISTRESS MARJORIE OUTWATER[9]—JULY, 1917

> Sweet girl, be always good and kind,
> And you in each glad hour shall find
> Some fragrance ere the time is flown;
> Some beauty rising to your own.
> Give love, and hearts will ever bow
> Before your tender spell, as now;
> So you in other lives may shine—
> But not more brightly than in mine!

RHEINHART KLEINER

Now behold the products of the Master Mind—sheer abstractions, written coldly and without the inspiration of the fair:

### TO THE INCOMPARABLE CLORINDA

You ask for verse—yet who cou'd justly write
When dazzled by your beauty's radiant light?
What line so smooth, but 'twould seem harsh and weak
Beside the velvet softness of your cheek?
My ill-scrawl'd words can win no greater praise
Than having drawn the glory of your gaze;
And much I fear, 'twill seem too rash in me
To rise from mere Olympian themes to thee!

(Very confidential P.S.)

With this, Clorinda, must thou rest content:
'Twou'd be no better, *even if 'twere meant!*

KLEINHART REINER

### TO SACCHARISSA, FAIREST OF HER SEX

When Nature fix'd the lamps of space
    To gild the plain and light the blue,
She made thee orbs of diff'ring grace—
    The silver Moon, the Sun, and You.

The lesser two she plac'd aloft
    As Guardians of the Night and Day;
But You she left, whose magick soft
    Rules *both* with sweet resistless sway!

EDVARDUS SOFTLEIUS[10]

### TO RHODOCLIA—PEERLESS AMONG MAIDENS

Were the blue of the sea and the blue of the skies
Half as sweet and as pure as the blue of your eyes;
Were the scent of the fields, and the flow'r-laden air
Half as potent and rich as your dear { golden / nut-brown / raven / silver / crimson } hair
Then the world were an Heaven, and mine were the bliss
To write verses forever as freely as this!

A. SAPHEAD

Note the adaptability of the above gem to all varieties of maidens. True, the [*sic*] is no alternative for *blue* eyes—but in poesy all eyes are blue.

### TO BELINDA, FAVOURITE OF THE GRACES

Nymph, whose glance demure and kind
    Turns the darkest hour to joy;
In whose witching face are join'd
    Venus and the Paphian Boy;
Take this tribute, tho' my hand
    Ne'er cou'd pen a tribute meet.
Labour done at thy command,
    Howe'er fruitless, still is sweet!

### TO HELIODORA—SISTER OF CYTHERAEA

When Paris made his fateful choice
    According to his duty,
To Venus with unfalt'ring voice
    He gave the prize of beauty;
Her godlike sisters, hard to please,
Grew piqued, and turn'd his enemies.

Now were that prize bestow'd today
    Poor Paris needs must tremble;
For greater ills wou'd haunt his way,
    Cou'd he not well dissemble:
For *ev'ry* god his foe wou'd be,
Since Beauty's prize belongs to *Thee!*

ANACREON MICROCEPHALOS.[11]

You may use any or all of these specimens if occasion arises—I have given them to no one else but Klei, and his field of conquest is widely remote from yours—Brooklyn and Appleton are well separated! They ought to melt even the beautiful perverse Delia! You young gallants are a sad lot!

Ascending—or descending—to seriousness, I am flattered that you should think my idle comment on "Progress" worthy of publication in *The Open Court*.[12] I did not write it with an eye to the publick, and fear the rhetorick is somewhat lacking in elegance. Also—one or two plainly personal and epistolary comments may have crept in between the lines. But I will trust to your good sense to prepare a revised version should you find the magazine still flourishing and willing to print comment on so obsolete an article. Ye Gods! For 'Eaving's sake abstain from sending my "mission in life" letter to Mistress Durr.[13] I recall saying in it that I thought she was minding other people's business! I have given her a 22-page broadside, calculated to demolish any pragmatical notions which may still becloud her mentality, but have not gone into personal excuses for idleness beyond saying that my constitution does not permit of systematic endeavour, else (of course) I should be doing something the same as any other rational human being. What does she think I am—a corner loafer! She might know better—for if I were, the "work or fight" law would have "got" me long ago, and I should be toiling in some munition factory or shovelling sewers at some cantonment. I am not particularly anxious to discuss my affairs with relative strangers—my letter was for you, not for her. I wished to demonstrate to *you* why I am such an apparent parasite on society. And just to prove how anxious I am to labour—if the *Crescent* wants a New-England correspondent, and is willing to take a thorough anti-Hun, I speak fer de job!

I trust you are satisfied with your critical assignment—to which I will add one trifle—Glause's new venture, *The Pathfinder.*[14] Follow your own methods, and nothing essential will be changed—though I should like the privilege of going over the copy for details before publication. One thing—guard against the so-called "split infinitive", the use of which sometimes appears in your work. THE "TO" OF AN INFINITIVE MUST NEVER BE SEPARATED FROM THE MAIN VERB-FORM BY ANOTHER WORD. It is incorrect to say TO SLOWLY GLIDE. You must say either SLOWLY TO GLIDE or TO GLIDE SLOWLY. At all events keep TO GLIDE as an unbroken unit. This is one of the tests of mature scholarship, as Kleiner told me some time ago. In amateurdom and elsewhere there are many fearful offenders in this little nicety—but it pays to be on the side of perfection. Details count in the long run. I have to correct vast numbers of split infinitives in the U.A. Both Miss McG[15] and Cook are confirmed infinitive-splitters, though I have lectured both on the subject. As to the improved style of criticism which you suggest—by all means give it a trial. The main argument for detailed revision in print is that most of the faults corrected are universal faults of crude writers, and that correction is therefore of general benefit. The public see just what sort of errors need mending, and learn what verses to copy and what not to copy. This idea is not mine—Father Mo was doing the same thing before I ever heard of amateurdom—for proof, see your file of back U.A.'s. But I am no enemy to rational innovation, and bid you go as far as you like. I have much respect for your taste, despite the few years in which you have had an opportunity to exercise it. I may even alter mine own critical style if your idea meets with general approval. Write Klei and Father Mo about it—they will be interested. One thing about my criticism—it is liable at times to become hackneyed and unoriginal. I have been at the task so long, that I fall into ruts and mannerisms, repeating myself unconsciously. The United deserves a better critic, and I am expecting you to become the Young Sam Johnson of the Association in a few years.

I can see how the *Flatbush* may have failed to impress your sense of humour. Different persons react differently to Hasemann. Cook, for instance, feels only *disgust* when reading the F.A.P.[16] I feel amusement and pity—whilst another, such as you, may with equal naturalness feel nothing but boredom. To members of my amateur generation, Hasemann is something like a Ford car. If you hear his name, you think you must laugh.

As to Klei's silence—I will enclose a card from him which came today. As you see, he is with us in thought, e'en tho' the cares of commerce keep him occupied to the exclusion of all else. I think you are wise to exercise a certain amount of Vice-Presidential concentration on your home town. A local club, if active, is a vast incentive to general enthusiasm. See if you can interest former press club members, whose names you can glean from old *United Amateurs*. There were some very passable poets among them, I believe. The only two veterans that "stuck" are Schilling and Miss Merkel;[17] the rest have evaporated into infinity. I am corresponding lately with a lady friend of yours—or your mother's—the would-be poetess Mrs. Agnes Richmond Arnold, who thinks you are a very bright child indeed. She seems to be a nice old lady, though she uses simplified spelling. She is very much interested in the Association, and if you can secure her aid you may be able to capture some adult recruits. Also—for Heaven's sake teach her how to use metre. She wants to be a poet very much, but must master many a technical rule first. I have amended one of her effusions and have offered to do more, for I have a very keen sympathy for the old folks who develop their ambitions too late in life to improve them. I judge Mrs. Arnold (though not from any real evidence) to be about 70—and if Mr. Hoag can succeed (with aid) at 87, there ought to be hope for her. I think she would appreciate your help, and in return might help your recruiting, as I said before. By the way—in her latest note, Mrs. Arnold says she hopes you have not "imbibed any of your father's Ingersollism."[18] I told her that while like all deep thinkers you could not be orthodox, you were not at all an anti-clerical, and had a keen respect for the church. She admires your mother's staunch Presbyterianism! Turning to the younger generation, I trust you can capture the Shakespeario-Miltonick person for the United, though if she lived to high-school age without indulging in original composition I doubt if she is a really natural-born author. Most writers began about as soon as their hands were strong enough to hold a pencil. My poetical career started at the age of seven. (Pardon implication that I am a typical great author!) I shall endeavour to write the fair nymph, whom I hope you will choose as your new divinity in place of the cruel Delia. The French are patriots and worthy folk, whilst the Irish are slackerish and seditious. If I write, I shall allude to the 1st Vice-President in a way calculated to heighten her interest in that young gentleman! I am much interested in your allusion to "the town's most prominent poet", and hope you can "land" him for the Association. Any poet more prominent than Alfredus Aurelius Galpinus Secundus must be prominent indeed! If you will send me the names of all your prospects, I will supply them with *Conservatives* and application blanks, and possibly form letters. The latter I shall carbon in lots of six. Special recruits like Miss Shakespeare or the poet, I shall seek to write individually, though I cannot promise speed. I wonder who will finance the new application blanks? There is no constitutional provision for them, and it is usually left to the Secretary, though for the past two years private individuals—Campbell[19] and Miss McGeoch—have philanthropically come to the rescue. I would aid this time if I could, but my financial situation is not bright just now. You might suggest as diplomatically as possible to the Secretary that she could well use a bit of her *Crescent* salary in having some nice new blanks printed, with her name on them.

I am still struggling with the typing of *Hesperia*.[20] It is execrably boresome work, and I shall be lucky if I can finish it alive. I shall await with interest your opinion of my dime novel—the conclusion of the "Mystery of Murdon Grange".[21] A vast amount of the magazine is critical—confined to British amateur journals. Since but few American amateurs have seen these journals, I am thinking of omitting this section in the American edition—for the sake of paper conservation. (To say nothing of my readers' patience.) British amateurdom is relatively undeveloped, and confined to a not aristocratic section of the population. The only thoroughly cultured British amateur is Rev. W. F. Pelton, (Wilfrid Kemble), and he says he has not time to bother with his less erudite fellows. I induced him to revise a little of Sub-Lieut. M'Keag's verse, but he found the task uncongenial. But I must break off abruptly, else I shall never finish.

Sincerely, gratefully, and godparentally yours,
Ludovicus Theobaldus Secundus

*Notes*

1. The poem must have been a tribute to HPL; it does not appear to survive.
2. Evidently a de luxe edition of Emerson's *Culture* (cf. *SL* 1.73); perhaps the edition published by Barse & Hopkins (New York, 1910).
3. Greek philosopher (c. 460–370 B.C.E.), one of the founders of Atomism.
4. Pope suffered from curvature of the spine (he was only four and a half feet tall) and also from some tubercular condition.
5. Elijah Hinsdale Burritt (1794–1838), *The Geography of the Heavens, and Classbook of Astronomy: Accompanied by a Celestial Atlas*, A New Edition, Revised and Illustrated by Hiram Mattison (New York: F. J. Huntington, 1853; *LL* 139).
6. Presumably *A Brief Course in Astronomy* (1906), which HPL notes as having reached 150 pp. (*SL* 5.140–41). It does not survive.

7. Arthur Fredlund, who was briefly made editor of HPL's juvenile periodical the *Scientific Gazette* in 1905–06.

8. Thomas Gray (1716–1771), *Elegy Written in a Country Churchyard* (1751): "Some mute inglorious Milton here may rest . . ." (l. 59).

9. Marjorie Outwater (Roxbury, MA) was a member of the NAPA.

10. A Latinization of HPL's pseudonym "Edward Softly."

11 "Anacreon" refers to the Greek poet (6th century B.C.E.) known for his drinking songs. "Microcephalos" is HPL's coinage meaning "small-head."

12. The *Open Court* (1887–1936) was a magazine published by the Open Court Publishing Company, devoted to the critical study of religion, science, and philosophy.

13. Mary Faye Durr, who would be elected President of the UAPA for 1919–20.

14. The *Pathfinder*, ed. Edwin H. Glause of Cleveland, reviewed by Galpin in "Department of Public Criticism," *United Amateur* 18, No. 2 (November 1918): 29–30.

15. Verna McGeoch, Official Editor of the UAPA (1917–19).

16. *Flatbush Amateur Press*, ed. John H. Hasemann, Jr., of Flatbush, NY. At least six issues were produced from January 1918 to April 1920.

17. George S. Schilling of Madison and Gertrude L. Merkel of Appleton, WI.

18. Robert G. Ingersoll (1833–1899), renowned agnostic lecturer and writer.

19. Paul J. Campbell, former President of the UAPA (1916–17).

20. "'Hesperia' is a manuscript magazine which I circulate in Great Britain" (*SL* 1.136, 4 June 1921). See also *SL* 1.68 (27 June 1918): "My 'Hesperia' will be critical & educational in object, though I am 'sugar-coating' the first number by 'printing' a conclusion of the serial 'The Mystery of Murdon Grange'." No issue of *Hesperia* has been discovered.

21. "The Mystery of Murdon Grange" seems to have been a round-robin serial appearing in *Spindrift*, an amateur journal edited by Ernest Lionel McKeag (1896–1976) of Newcastle-upon-Tyne, England, who later wrote boys' fiction. One segment—published in *Spindrift* 5, No. 1 (Christmas 1917): 26–27, and signed "B. Winskill"—has been located, but no other segments have come to light. HPL, however, discusses several segments in his "Department of Criticsim" columns of January, March, and May 1918.


[4] [ALS]

598 Angell St.,
Providence, R.I.,
Aug. 29, 1848. [i.e., 1918]

Edgar A. Poe, Esq.,
Appleton, Wis.:——

My Dear Mᵣ Poe:——

      I beg to acknowledge receipt of your favour of 25ᵗʰ inst., enclosing the story "Marsh-Mad",[1] written under the pseudonym of "Alfred Galpin, Jr." I deem the tale fully up to your usual standard, though in some respects surpassed by your former story "The Fall of the House of Usher". The ascription of sentient life to something not usually considered conscious reminds me of "Usher", but in detail your newer story is markedly original and splendidly developed. Atmosphere & vocabulary are alike remarkable, & I anticipate no trouble in placing this masterpiece in a prominent magazine.

Your development of the "living tree" idea will probably cause me to change a plot of my own, long conceived but never elaborated into literary form, which also involves such a thing. For your edification I will outline this plot:

Two close friends, either artists or authors, live near each other, and maintain their early intimacy & cordiality despite strong rivalry for fame. Finally the *more successful* man sickens and dies of a *mysterious malady*, causing the devoted friend to mourn long and unconsolably. The dead man is buried in a neighbouring meadow which he loved in life, and from his grave springs a tiny green shoot which grows into a tree. As long years pass, the other man works toward a celebrity almost equal to that of him who died. Finally he completes a masterpiece which, when shewn to the world, will bring him a fame *greater* than that of his departed friend. The tree had grown very rapidly—much more rapidly than is the wont of such a tree—and on the 25th anniversary of the buried man's death, it is of great size. On that night the surviving man, about to gain supreme laurels and earthly triumph, goes to his friend's grave and looks long at the grassy mound. And his lips twist strangely, even considering his great grief. There was no wind that night, but the next morning (just as the long-bereaved friend was to have enjoyed his new fame) the tree was found uprooted—as if the roots had voluntarily relinquished their hold upon the ground—and beneath the massive trunk lay the body of the faithful mourner—crushed to death, & with an expression of the most unutterable fear upon his countenance.[2]

---

Such is the plot I was *going* to develop—but *now* it seems weak & futile indeed! You have (in the language of the masses) "beaten me to it", & exhausted the possibilities of living trees. Likewise—my plot is pathetically ordinary & prosaic beside yours. I congratulate you!! You are master in the regions of the dimly terrible and ineffably hideous. I need not be so anxious for you to see "Dagon" & "The Tomb".[3] They will appear tame to you, for you have outdone my best. Last night whilst vainly trying to sleep, some wildly sinister verses crept through my brain so insistently that I arose & set them down. After 2½ lines my inspiration gave out, but I think I shall some day concoct a suitable plot & conclusion to go with this promising (?) prelude. The following is what I wrote:

'Twas at a nameless hour of night
When fancies in delirious flight
About the silent sleeper reel,
And thro' his mindless visions steal;
When flesh upon its earthly bed
Sprawls corpse-like and untenanted—
Vacant of soul, which freely flies
Thro' worlds unknown to waking eyes.
The hornèd moon above the spire

This sounds
like something
I have heard
before. I shall
investigate in
order to avoid
subconscious
plagiarism. Does
it sound familiar
to you?

With ghastly grace was crawling high'r,
And in the pallid struggling beams
Grinn'd memories of ancient dreams.
Aloft in heav'n each starry sign
Flicker'd fantastic and malign,
Whilst voices in the gaping deep
Whisper'd to me, I must not sleep.
(This scene, one night in chill November,
I shall thro' many a year remember.)
Beneath that selfsame moon I spied
A bleak and barren countryside,
Where spectral shadows darkly crept
Across the moor————————4

P.S. I have just looked up in Poe where I *thought* I had read something like this, & find it is not so! Perhaps this is fairly original after all! But Mo, even if he would not call it "rubber-stamp" work, would dub it a "recipe poem"—so what's the use??

Perhaps, after reading this d——— foolishness, you will advise me not to complete it. Nor do I blame you for such advice!

As to our exchange of heroics—allow me to correct something in my own answer—line 22. For *become*, read *becom'st*. Archaism must be consistent. If you keep the verses, I wish you would make the change on the copy. If not, you are at least informed of the error, and aware that I am as alert in spying out mine own faults as those of other poets & poetasters. Goodenough's tribute, according to latest evidence, seems to have been absolutely serious.[5] He acknowledged my counter-tribute in a very kind note.[6] He is 47 years of age, & in October will celebrate the 30th anniversary of the publication of his first poem. His *serious* tribute sounded more comical than your semi-serious one—hence it is not remarkable that Miss McGeoch should fail to grasp the spirit at the bottom of your graceful lines. I agree that they are (considering the unworthy subject) scarce suitable for publication in the official organ. I am glad Miss McG speaks so well of me. It would be easy to say a great deal more in reciprocity, for I have seldom encountered her equal in kindly breadth of opinion, exalted ideals, high sense of duty, dependable efficiency, conscientious responsibility, & general nobility of character. This sounds like Theobaldian oleaginousness, but since nearly every other amateur can give a similar verdict, you may see that it has much foundation in fact. She is certainly one of the pillars of amateur journalism. You surprise me when you state that even other favourable references to me have reached you. I have always had a sort of sensation of unpopularity—knowing how odd and utterly boresome I am. I fear most of my correspondents would be sadly disappointed on meeting me—I hope Klei did not find me so uninteresting that he will lose his zest for further correspondence![7] In his case, I think I am safe, for his letters *since* calling me are just as cordial as those which he wrote *before*.

I am glad Father Mo found Miss D's epistle so interesting. She has a sort of pert, laconic humour or smartness, of which she is evidently fairly proud, & which she is not at all reluctant to employ. Anent the new and Gallic charmer—Mlle. Shakespeare—I am glad your *affaire du cœur* is progressing so well. Surely she is a much more worthy helpmate than the scornful Delia—whose attitude can be ascribed only to inherent cruelty of temperament & absence of good sense. In the evening of life, after youth & beauty are fled, you would find Delia a monstrous dull companion; since lacking intellectual interests, she would have naught in common with her transcendently gifted spouse. On the other hand, you will find Mlle. Shakespeare—or Mme. Shakespeare-Galpin—eternally congenial & delightful in literary discussion, so that down to your very graves you may be blessed with the most perfect mutual understanding and harmonious fellowship. Long live Lycë the fair—Down with Delia! Incidentally—I made it a point the other day to write your Lycë a full recruiting letter. Assuming that you had roughly outlined the United to her, I used the "second letter" text, which aims to set forth the especial advantages of amateurdom very vividly. In my Galpinian interpolations, I took care to avoid any appearance of fulsomeness, but merely stated casually that Mr. Galpin is indeed a very remarkable young man, who despite his few years has come to be one of the leading workers in our cause, *& who has a great future before him.* Note this last item. By predicting a great future, I imply, of course, that anyone who *shares* that future will be fortunate indeed! I gave her to understand that her new gallant is esteemed & respected by all his elders—which ought to count in your favour. I did not lay my praise on thickly—but worked scientifically & psychologically! If she replies & thereby gives me a chance for more scientific pro-Galpinism, I will have her proposing to you in a month or two! All hail to Theobald the Matchmaker!! And by the way—in excavating old papers to send her as samples, I came across one I am not sure I sent you—*The Providence Amateur*—relic of my philanthropic club experiment of 1914–16. If you have not a copy, let me know; for I have two extra. I also sent a letter to Secy. Kelly[8] as you suggested, seeking to arouse her interest in outside amateur journals. My plan was to describe at some length, & a trifle humorously, each of the papers which are now receiving contributions; urging her to submit stories already written if she had nothing new or was especially busy. Accompanying my letter I despatched a set of Chase's *Amateur*

*Journalist?* as a possible stimulus of interest. [Have I sent you a set—5 numbers? If not, I will] If all this does not make an amateur out of Misthress O'Kelly, you had best secure a more potent persuader than I. My guess as to M^rs. Arnold's age was based on her exceedingly tremulous & uncertain handwriting. Few persons as young as 55 have such an outwardly senile chirography. She has just offered to pay me professional rates for verse revision, but I shall not accept remuneration for anything designed for the *amateur* press. However—if she has any large amount of work to be prepared for outside publication, I shall be pleased to handle it as I handle Rev. David V. Bush's.[10] It will not be such hard work, since Mrs. A. could not possibly perpetrate such utter & unqualified asininity as Rev. D.V.B.

Concerning philosophy—it flatters me to learn that so much of your present system came from a perusal of mine own humble attempts & speculations. You place me in a position of grave responsibility—the pious & the orthodox will revile me as a pernicious corrupter of youth!! And yet—since it was MO who first shewed you my lucubrations, I cannot so deeply blame myself. Some day, when you have left me far behind & formulated a new system of your own, I may return the compliment by borrowing ideas from you!

The science of chemistry, in which I am glad to find you interested, first captivated me in the Year of Our Lord 1898—in a rather peculiar way. With the insatiable curiosity of early childhood, I used to spend hours poring over the pictures in the back of Webster's Unabridged Dictionary—absorbing a miscellaneous variety of ideas. After familiarising myself with antiquities, mediaeval dress & armour, birds, animals, reptiles, fishes, flags of all nations, heraldry, &c. &c., I lit upon the section devoted to "Philosophical & Scientific Instruments", & was veritably hypnotised with it. Chemical apparatus especially attracted me, & I resolved (before knowing a thing about the science!) to have a laboratory. Being a "spoiled child" I had but to ask, & it was mine. I was given a cellar room of good size, & provided by my elder aunt (who had studied chemistry at boarding school) with some simple apparatus & a copy of "The Young Chemist"—a beginner's manual by Prof. John Howard Appleton of Brown—a personal acquaintance.[11] "The Young Chemist" was just the book for me—devoted to easy & instructive experiments—and I was soon deep in its pages. The laboratory "work"—or play— seemed delightful, and despite a few mishaps, explosions, & broken instruments, I got along splendidly. Soon I acquired other books, & began (March 4, 1899) to issue a chemical magazine called *The Scientific Gazette*, which I maintained for eight years. This was, I suppose, my entry to amateur journalism! By 1901 or thereabouts I had a fair knowledge of the principles of chemistry & the details of the inorganic part—about the equivalent of a highschool course, & not including analysis of any kind. Then my fickle fancy turned away to the intensive study of geography, geology, anthropology, &

above all *astronomy,* after which came a revival of classicism, latinity, &c. Not until 1906 did chemistry come into my life again. In that year I encountered *physics* in high-school, which reawaked my dormant laboratory instincts, & led me back to the study of matter, its constitution and properties. I increased my chemical library by fully 20 volumes—to say naught of the physics text books I bought—& obtained a plenitude of new instruments. I was now in a smaller house, with a smaller laboratory, but the new room was ample for the purpose. In 1907 I took chemistry in high-school, but since I knew all the course before, had more fun than instruction in the class room. I left high school certified in physics & chemistry, & intended to specialise in those subjects at college; but just then my nervous system went to pieces, & I was forced to relinquish all thought of activity. Yet at home I continued my chemical studies, dabbling in a correspondence course which helped me in matters of *analysis & organic chemistry,* hitherto neglected by me. But in the mean time literature had been on the increase once more, & I found my interest centreing more & more in old-fashioned scribbling. By 1912 I had practically ceased to be active in chemistry, & have since partially dismantled my laboratory, owing to my mother's nervousness at having deadly poisons, corrosive acids, and potential explosives about the place. One tangible memorial of my hobby remains—a bulky manuscript entitled "A Brief Course in Inorganic Chemistry", by H. P. Lovecraft. 1910.[12] There is also a physical memorial—the third finger of my right hand—whose palm side is permanently scarred by a mighty phosphorus burn sustained in 1907. At the time, the loss of the finger seemed likely, but the skill of my uncle—a physician[13]—saved it. It is still a bit stiff, & aches in cold weather—as no doubt it always will. During the bandage & splint days I had to pick out my verses & articles with my left forefinger only on the typewriter. I am not at all regretful of the time I spent in chemical pursuits, for I have time & again found use for the information I imbibed. I should not feel competent to make philosophical conjectures, were I without at least a moderate knowledge of the laws & properties of matter & energy.

About the constitution of *common sand*—I should say it is mainly $SiO_2$ with perhaps a few intermixed silicates—i.e. salts of silicic acid. Probably—in fact positively—its exact constitution varies according to the geological nature of the locality. It is safe to say that the leading constituent is silicon dioxide. I should be interested to hear the details of the A.H.S. controversy which exposed the ignorance of the instructor. What book do you use? In Hope Street we had Hessler & Smith's,[14] but I disliked the latter half, owing to the unscientific order in which it discusses the metals. It is out of harmony with the periodic system. I like Remsen's text-book much better.[15] My earliest favourite—he whose name is even as your native town—is not so successful with non-elementary treatises, hence though I own all his works, I have found little inspiration in any save "The Young Chemist". I have some archaic text-books which my grandfather used in his youth, but they are quite obsolete. Chemistry has changed vastly in the past sixty or seventy years. At one time I was especially interested in the more minutely theoretical aspects of chemistry—atoms—ions—electrons—&c., but find all this has changed immensely since my day. Some articles which your father recommended to me showed how radically the science has progressed since I ceased greatest activity. One phase of chemistry in which I dabbled was spectrum-analysis, & I still have my spectroscope—a rather low-priced diffraction instrument costing $15.00. I have also a still cheaper *pocket* spectroscope,[16] which was the delight of my fellow students at H.S.H.S. It is unbelievably tiny—will go into a vest pocket without making much of a bulge—yet gives a neat, bright little spectrum, with clear Frauenhofer lines when directed at sunlight. Many are the times I have passed it around at school. Radio-activity interested me enough to cause me to obtain a spinthariscope—containing, of course, a minute quantity of radio-active matter. Speaking of science in general—I have an excellent *microscope*, which I have used for various purposes. I must again ask pardon for an autobiographical lapse. My boyhood, on account of my slightly better health & consequently more active life, is crowded with events as compared with my older years; hence its memories are still of utmost vividness. All these things seem as but yesterday—in fact, it would not be at all hard for me to forget the last decade altogether, & imagine myself not much older than you!

I am sorry that modesty caused you to refrain from telling your early experiences in "uplifting the public", for I am sure they must be interesting. My last attempt was in 1914–16, when I laboured with a "literary" club of Micks who dwelt in the dingy "North End" of the city. The brightest of them was an odd bigoted fellow named Dunn,[17] two years older than I. He hated England & was a violent pro-German—& I was foolish enough to waste time trying to convert him—as if an Irishman could reason!! Even after I gave up the club as hopeless, I continued corresponding with this fellow, for he was well-meaning & quite intelligent in his way. But in 1917 came events which caused me to drop him. He took the war very badly, & wrote treasonable letters by the score. When the draft came, he refused to register, & was arrested by government agents. In July he was drafted, but refused to respond to the summons—hence was court-martialled & sentenced to 20 years in the Atlanta Federal Prison—where he still languishes, I presume.[18] I am done with Dunn!

Your repertorial work has assuredly been most exacting of late—yet it must be interesting in its way. To a recluse it seems very picturesque. I wish I lived in Appleton & could help you on some of the hard assignments—though I should probably be more of a hindrance than a help.

August 30.

Since adjourning yesterday the following self-explanatory post-card has come to hand:

8/27/18

My dear Lo:

I have received a post-card from my local board advising me to "be ready to go between Sept. 3d & Sept 6th." I expect the final notification this wk. This will mean a change of plans in regard to the U.A.P.A.

Sincerely,

R. Kleiner

In other words, Klei hath been drafted at last, and the burden of the Presidency is likely to fall at once upon Consul Hasting, Esq. It is possible that if Klei is placed in some clerkship on this side of the sea, [he goes only for limited service as a clerk] he may be able to finish his term without nominally resigning—but in any case you will be the real leader, & will most probably be elevated to supreme office. I hope you may not find your new duties oppressive—count on me to give you all the assistance & coöperation in my power. Your promotion will automatically make M^rs. Jordan 1st V.P., leaving another 2nd V.P. to be appointed. (At least, this is what I think the Constitution says, though I have not a copy before me) But first let us see just how nearly total Klei's cessation of activity will have to be.

I have been re-reading "Marsh-Mad"—& the more I analyse it the better I like it! I shall make every effort to get this in the official organ—failing which I shall send it to Cook with positive instructions *not* to give it to Moloney but to use it himself. That is far too good to waste on any but a first-rate paper! Try it on the *Black Cat*[19] professionally. I have been thinking about how to modify my own living-tree plot, & I think I see a way to convey the central idea without resorting to ligneous consciousness. It will make the narrative somewhat more complex & elaborate, but that will [be] all the better.

August 31

Still another interval! Before I forget to mention it, let me express my appreciation of Emerson's "Culture", which is assuredly full of sensible precepts & acute observations. Measured by the Emersonian standard, I am certainly lacking in even culture, for many phases of life in its fuller sense have been, & are likely to continue, sealed pages to me. To be actually cultured, one must needs possess a multiplicity of exquisite tastes and social graces, and a range of mild interests, far beyond the sphere of a feeble & sequestered egotist. I have far too much impatience of disposition to become absorbed in many of the minor aspects of perfect beauty which are theoretically essential to absolute culture. I am not so sensitive to beauty that I require every nicety of perfection in stationery, bookbinding, and furnishing, as is the case with some persons I know. Many pictures on my wall, for example, are lacking in artistic perfection, yet are retained for various reasons, and do not outrage my aesthetic sense every time I contemplate them. In art also I show a lack of breadth and profundity. I used to think I was a devotee of classic art—but when I analysed my predilection I found it was not so much intrinsic & intelligent, as because classic art reminded me of the classic Graeco-Roman age which I so much admired as a whole. Still—I think I possess a distinct preference for the ideals & technique of the ancients. In modern art—painting—I am as one-sided as in most things. I have no appreciation of portraiture, but am captivated by landscapes—mostly quiet rural scenes in England. In this connexion—I have a curious fondness for *one particular type* of scene—a rustic panorama with much verdure & possibly a quiet river in the foreground, and in the background many low hills, with a steepled hamlet resting in their midst. In my own disastrous attempts at pictorial art, I have tried to reproduce innumerable modifications of this favourite subject. I am more acutely sensitive to *architecture* than to any other form of visual art—in fact, certain architectural combinations have the power of pleasing & repelling me very powerfully. I have never yet been able to understand how human beings *can live* in absolutely ugly localities. Just as you might surmise, I love 18th century architecture above all else for residences and gardens—though for other types of buildings Gothic & Graeco-Roman forms appeal to me. I do not care over much for the Italian Renaissance types now so prevalent in local public edifices. As a rule, I have the ancient classical preference for form as opposed to colour. I appreciate *contour* much more than harmonious blending of tints in a decorative scheme. This I take to be an Aryan, western trait. It is Asia & the East that are completely devoted to chromatic beauty. I dislike gaudy hues of every kind except occasionally *in nature*, as, for instance

> The bursting blossoms that bedeck the scene,
> And gaily pie the smooth enamell'd green.

Detached flowers charm me singularly little, & I find it nearly impossible to go into ecstasies over a bouquet. I demand the *natural environment.*

My Poe tastes make me fond of wild scenery and nocturnal landscapes, and I have a great liking for the weird creations of Doré.

But it is in *music* that my crude, uncultured, gothic, barbaric, unappreciative nature makes itself most manifest. Frankness impels me to confess that in this field I have the most execrable & altogether abominable & deficient taste conceivable. The musical classics not only fail to attract me, but actually repel me. An infantile fondness for simple tunes led my mother to start me on violin lessons when I was seven years old, and through the insistence of a teacher who said I had musical genius, the farce was kept up for two years. I played the exercises because I had to—but abhorred all the classics that came before me, and for *pleasure* would go back to whistling those utterly light & frothy tunes which I really enjoyed. In 1899 violin practice made me so nervous that it was stopped by doctor's orders—and thus closeth one branch of L. Theobald's culture. To this day I have not improved, & though I revel in absolutely frivolous light opera & musical comedy airs, I cannot bear serious Music with a capital M. However, I am not so narrow that I do not understand its aesthetic value, & I never laugh at it in the manner of Lord North[20] and other celebrated anti-musical personages. So fond am I of *light* and catchy music, that I tried to write a comic opera when about ten years old! But pardon the relapse of autobiographical mania. My egotism is appalling in its thoroughness & persistency. In this case, though, I shall use my sad one-sidedness to point a moral. Let me urge you, in your own aesthetic development, to slight no phase of culture, however uninteresting it may seem to your young mind; lest you become subject to eccentricities & prejudices such as mine. I have sadly few points of contact with the majority of minds, and my mother deems me a rural barbarian indeed. Let thine own culture be more even. Probably you do not need this advice, since you seem to shew remarkable catholicity of interests; yet an old man ever feels it incumbent upon himself to advise his juniors.

I have been reading a great deal of Emerson's work since writing you last, & find him something of a Platonist. He is too humanocentric to furnish a model for such an infinity-roamer as I, yet his ideas are all of remarkable soundness & appeal. He is less annoyingly human than most writers; his poems in particular being almost esoteric. He deals with ψυχή unalloyed, yet never seems to reach out beyond the sphere of the familiar. He seems to forget that there may be such a thing as *mind* utterly unlike anything we know—whose only trait in common with human mind is the one eternal entity of *pure reason*. All in all, I think I can see how he became, as he did, the centre of a sort of cult in New-England. His qualities united profound insight with acute common sense. He was typical of the best thought of his era & locality. Comparing Emerson with Poe, my choice falls to the latter. The Baltimorean had the more genuine Pierian spark, and both in boldness of thought & beauty of art was the superior. Emerson is an excellent guide to practical living, but as a creative artist Edgar A. outruns him. Emerson's conception of poesy was as an exalted expression of philosophical truth—which is not correct. Poe hated the metaphysical bards, & vowed beauty to be the poet's goal. Both men were intellectual giants, & will forever add to the lustre of literature & the pride of their native land.

Speaking of Poe—I hope you received the letter I wrote you discussing his "Eureka".[21] In your last, I noticed no specific reference to it; & knowing the uncertain state of the mails, I take this occasion to enquire. It contained also the latest copy of *Les Mouches*.[22]

But I must conclude at last, since I have a fearsome amount of typing to do. I trust you will send me your critical report when it is complete.

I enclose a bit of Latinistic nonsense for your amusement. It need not be returned.

With customary expressions of esteem, and the hope that I may ere long be favoured with an epistle from your direction, I beg y^e honour, my dear Sir, to subscribe myself as

Yr. most humble, most obedient Servt.

Alexander Pope

## Notes

1. Published in Galpin's amateur journal, *The Philosopher* (December 1920).

2. This is HPL's "The Tree" (1921).

3. HPL wrote both stories in the summer of 1917, after an eight-year hiatus in fiction writing.

4. An early version of HPL's "The Eidolon" (*Tryout*, October 1918).

5. "Lovecraft—an Appreciation" (*Tryout* 4, No. 8 [August 1918]: 1–2; rpt. in Goodenough's "Further Recollections of Amateur Journalism," *Vagrant* [Spring 1927]: 101–2). HPL was taken aback by Goodenough's somewhat grotesque compliment: ". . . I make no doubt / Laurels from thy very temples sprout."

6. "To Arthur Goodenough, Esq." (*Tryout*, September 1918).

7. Kleiner visited HPL in Providence in 1917 and 1918.

8. Muriel P. Kelly, Secretary of the UAPA.

9. Cf. HPL, "Report of First Vice-President" (*United Amateur*, November 1915): "A less spectacular but nevertheless considerable work is the gradual free distribution of files of *The Amateur Journalist*, Mr. James H. Chase's extremely valuable but now discontinued magazine, among the newer members of high grade. The complete file consists of five numbers, and will be sent on application to any person who has not already received it. The undersigned has at his disposal, through the generosity of Mr. Chase, the entire remaining stock of the magazine, approximately one hundred complete sets."

10. David Van Bush (1882–1959), "psychological lecturer," founder of *Mind Power Plus*, and longtime revision client of HPL. HPL proposed Van Bush's reinstatement in the UAPA in 1922 (he had joined originally in 1916).

11. John Howard Appleton (1844–1930), *The Young Chemist* (1876; *LL* 36).

12. Non-extant.

13. Dr. Franklin Chase Clark (1847–1915).

14. John C. Hessler (1869–1944) and Albert L. Smith (1866–?), *Essentials of Chemistry* (Boston: B. H. Sanborn, 1902).

15. Ira Remsen (1846–1927), *The Elements of Chemistry* (New York: Henry Holt & Co., 1887).

16. The spectroscope is a key instrument employed in "The Colour out of Space."

17. John T[homas] Dunn (1889–1983) was Irish-American living in North Providence who came in touch with HPL in late 1914 in the Providence Amateur Press Club and corresponded with him for the period 1915–17. He assisted HPL in editing two issues of the *Providence Amateur* (June 1915, February 1916). HPL's

letters to Dunn were published as "H. P. Lovecraft: Letters to Joh. T. Dunn," ed. S. T. Joshi, David E. Schultz, and John H. Stanley, *Books at Brown* 38–39 (1991–92): 157–223.

18. Dunn was released shortly after the war and later became a Catholic priest.

19. An early magazine (1895–1922) devoted to horror and suspense.

20. Frederick North, Earl of Guilford (1732–1792), prime minister of England during the American Revolution.

21. *Eureka: A Prose Poem* (1848), a philosophical study of the mystical and material unity of the universe.

22. See letter 2, n. 25.


[5] [ALS]

ROMAE.

A.D. XIV. KAL. NOV. [1918][1]
M. RINARTIO CLINA.
A. GALPINIO. SECVNDO. COSS.[2]

L. METADIVS. CAELO. A. GALPINIO. SECVNDO. S.D.
SI. TV. VALES. BENE. EST. EGO. QVOQVO. VALEO.[3]

Let me open this document with a spirited defence of your colleague in the consulship, M. Rinartius Clina, who to you a pain administereth. It is not through negligence but through misfortune that our leader is so silent. His mother is gravely ill with Spanish influenza, & though he has assistance in the daytime, he has to act as her nurse throughout the night. He is utterly exhausted, & to cap the climax is now fighting a cold which may prove to be the same affliction from which his patient is suffering. This influenza is nothing light, & I certainly hope Appleton may escape. I fancy you will agree that under the circumstances we must admire Klei's fortitude & filial devotion, rather than criticise his unavoidable inactivity! Klei offers once more to resign, but I really think we should not accept his resignation. Care after care seems to beset him, & he deserves all the encouragement & displays of confidence which we can give him. Once he is "out of the woods", I am sure he can conduct a tolerably efficient administration. He now asks me to instruct the following officers in their duties—a task he would cheerfully discharge if able:

> 1st Vice-President
> Secretary
> Laureate Recorder.

Beginning with the 1st V.P., I find it hard to lay down any set programme; mainly because Vice-Presidents have hitherto been very independent (when not inactive) folk—working on their own initiative & according to their own ideas. When I was V.P.[4] my work was overshadowed by the 2nd V.P. department, then under the direction of that incredibly energetic recruiter Mrs. Renshaw; & I did little save follow up the multitudinous prospectives she unearthed. But in general, I fancy the following things should be done.

(a) Form your committee by securing definite acceptances from as many persons as you can. Tell them their duties—to write all persons whose names you may send for such a purpose—and make up some suitable form letters for their use. If the men I suggested on my postal card will not serve, try others. Try young Nixon of Florida, whose letter I enclose. Get Ingold to join & act if you can.[5] New members sometimes make the best recruiters, being enthusiastic & impressed with the novelty of amateurdom. If you cannot secure the full quota of seven, less will do. I never knew all the members of a committee to be faithful workers, anyway!

(b) Unearth as many prospectives as you can, & ask your subordinates to do the same. For young boys, an element we desire very strongly, cull the names of prize-winners from the B.K.B. department of *Browning's Magazine*.[6] For mature persons, look up the names of authors in *religious* (!) papers—who are never paid for their work, & are therefore potential amateurs. Also—scan the "readers' column" in various magazines; where the public express opinions & sometimes give bits of verse. Ask Mrs. Jordan to send you lists of *Boston Post* prize-winners. High-school & college publications ought to furnish many names, which you & the 4th V.P. can apportion betwixt yourselves. Rely not at all on the 3d. V.P., but write her anyway—see if you can accomplish the impossible by awaking her.[7] A new voice might arouse her dormant sense of responsibility. Prepare your lists of "prospects" for distribution amongst committee members, giving in addition to each name a brief description of the person in question, as judged from what you have read. Whenever you receive a reply, pass it around amongst your committee, so that each member can send "follow-up" matter. Tell your members to send their replies around in the same way. It is much easier to write a person whose letter you have seen. Finally—go ahead with the *St. Nicholas* idea you outlined a few months ago.

---

If there is nothing new or enlightening in these simple bits of advice, blame my stupidity & incompetency rather than question my intent or willingness to help. I desire to assist as much as I can, & will be glad to answer to the best of my limited ability any question you may ask. As to the critical question, my resignation has met with considerable disapproval, and Klei refuses to accept it; implying that I am deserting the United in time of need. In view of this, & in view of his own inability to be active just now, I have left the matter in his hands & am hanging on a while. But I shall make you do more work—July *Brooklynite, Pathfinder,* & all the *Silver Clarions* which come your way, & anything else I can think of to burden you with. There is no hurry, though. Influenza is holding up the work at Athol, & there may be an amalgamation of Sept$^r$ & Nov$^r$ numbers of the U.A. I hope Cook's family is better, & that Moloney lived through his attack after all. His life was despaired of at the time of Cook's last note.

As to Secretary's instructions—I will ask you to see that this official does the following things:

(a) Send Kleiner a large batch of blank certificates for Presidential signature.

(b) Record each application received; send the applicants their certificates, properly filled out, with suitable words of welcome; and send all credentials to one or both of the MS. Bureaux—preferably the *Eastern,* unless she can endure dealing with that utterly impossible Haughton creature.[8]

(c) Once in two months make out a report of all new members, reinstatements, & renewals, sending it in duplicate to Official Editor & President—or better still in *triplicate* to O.E., PRES., & 1st V.P. In this list should be included all changes of address.

(d) Once in two months send all money received to the Treasurer, specifying whether from new members, or for reinstatements or renewals. It is best to itemise it—thus:

From John Smith, membership fee -------------------------- 0.50
"     Robert Jones,    "       " ---------------------------- 0.50
"     James Brown, reinstatement --------------------------- 1.00
"     Joseph Addison, renewal ----------------------------- 1.00
Total ------------------------------------------------------------ 3.00

(e) Notify by postal card EVERY member whose dues lapse—telling him his membership has expired & urging him to renew. Acknowledge all voluntary renewals & re-instatements.

Let me furthermore ask you to initiate your 4$^{th}$ V.P. in any manner you deem wise. This official is legally your subordinate, & is of course to work as the 1st V.P.'s department sees fit. Of course, as you say, Mistress חשוב[9] will not need such explicit guidance as a less bright & competent person might require; but her department is under yours according to the constitution, & the two must necessarily coöperate closely. No one knows yet, just how the 4$^{th}$ V.P. dept. ought to work out its details of administration. It was devised by the nebulous Miss Lehr, who was expected to supervise the development of her idea, but failed as usual to do so. As the only living ex-4$^{th}$ V.P., you ought to know more about the thing than anyone else. Miss A. is indeed a bright infant—she quoted Cicero & has decided opinions on many questions. Had I not encountered the young consul A. Galpinius Secundus first, I should consider her rather a prodigy—a species in which your town seems unusually rich. I have notified Klei of Miss Merkel's selection for the Reception Comm. Chairmanship, & presume he will endorse it as usual. It is very generous of Appleton to finance the blanks. I will help out if necessary, since so much of my peerless prose adorns their reverse side.

Daas complains of not hearing from you. He tells me *I* am Chairman of the Directors, & wants me to take the first steps in unearthing the true inwardness of the old official organ debt—conflicting statements concerning which emanate from Campbell & Cheney.[10] I expect to see him in December when he visits New England—& Cook also expects to see him. At present he is busy organising a local club in Washington, D.C., assisted by Mrs. Renshaw.[11] I hope it will be more literary than his Milwaukee *vereins.* Probably it will be, since Mrs. R. is a genuine litterateuse, & likely to be prominent in anything she is concerned with.

Turning to your epistle, I am impressed by your super-active life—which reminds me of our colleague Mo & his incessant whirl of duties. The *Crescent* near-scoop is very interesting. Our papers took no such trouble last Saturday, being content to issue the "big news" in the Sunday editions. But perchance the⊄and [drawing of a post] have no Sunday editions. Let me congratulate you on your success as a newsboy—I hope you shouted "Extry!" "Extree!" in approved style.

I have witnessed "Hearts of the World",[12] & agree with the approbation which your recommendation implies. It is certainly effective in the highest degree, histrionically, mechanically, & artistically in general. As presented in Providence, an appropriate orchestral accompaniment enhanced its vividness & appeal. If it is less striking than "The Birth of a Nation",[13] it is because of a necessary lack of quaintness, (which, however, Griffith does his best to supply) a certain remoteness of locale which contrasts with the immediate scene of the older picture, and a lack of traditionary background such as is afforded by Civil War problems, which have been discussed & portrayed for half a century by every fireside. Then too—the excellence & magnitude form less of a *surprise.* The "Birth" prepared us for something great, and we are *satisfied* rather than taken off our feet. Continuing in the dramatick line, but ascending the scale several degrees, I find "Hamlet" a most absorbing character, even as you do. It is hard for me to give an original estimate or opinion, since other commentators' opinions are so abundant; but I find in Hamlet a rare, delicate, & nearly poetical mind, filled with the highest ideals and pervaded by the delusion (common to all gentle & retired characters unless their temperament be scientific & predominantly rational—which is seldom the case with poets) that all humanity approximates such a standard as he conceives. All at once, however, man's inherent baseness becomes apparent to him under the most soul-trying circumstances; exhibiting itself not in the remote world, but in the person of his mother & his uncle, in such a manner as to convince him most suddenly & most vitally that there is no good in humanity. Well may he question life, when the perfidiousness of those whom he has reason to believe the best of mortals, is so cruelly obtruded no his notice. Having had his theories of life founded on mediaeval and pragmatical conceptions, he now loses that subtle something which impels persons to go on in the ordinary currents; specifically, he loses the conviction that the usual motives & pursuits of life are more than empty illusions or trifles. Now this is not *"madness"*—I am sick of hearing fools & superficial critics prate about "Hamlet's madness". It is really a distressing glimpse of *absolute truth*. But *in effect*, it approximates mental derangement. Reason is unimpaired, but Hamlet no longer sees any occasion for its use. He perceives the objects & events about him, & their relation to each other & to himself, as clearly as before; but his new estimate of their importance, and his lack of any aim or desire to pursue an ordinary course amongst them, impart to his point of view such a contemptuous, ironical singularity, that he may well be thought a madman by mistake. He sums up this position himself when he says:

> "How weary, stale, flat, & unprofitable
> Seem to me all the uses of this world!
> Fie on't! ah, Fie! 'tis an unweeded garden
> That grows to seed. Things rank & gross in Nature
> Possess it merely."[14]

Now comes the ghost business—which (leaving out Marcello's, Bernardo's & Horatio's sight of the ghost) ought to be taken allegorically as the growth of a terrible *suspicion* in Hamlet's mind. He now hath an object in the world— Revenge!! Rrrevenge!!! His devotion to this object is necessarily enhanced by the absence of all other objects. He seizes it as his one guiding motive in a life devoid of all other motives; it sustains, energises, awakens, & perhaps even *comforts* him. In his assumption of madness, he gains verisimilitude from the lightness with which he regards life. Stolid critics fancy no man could think up such extraordinary grotesqueries & incoherencies as Hamlet's, were he not somewhat deranged; indeed, a very prosaic & dignified personage of strict sanity *would* have a hard time doing so. But we must remember that to Hamlet *all the world* & its pitifully inconsequential doings are just as grotesque as any fantastical babbling can be. Having so slight an estimate of human dignity, Hamlet delights in pseudo-idiotick satire, through which even ivory-skull'd old Polonius can glimpse enough light to mutter:

> "Tho this be madness, yet there's method in't."[15]

As the Prince himself saith; 'when the wind is southerly, he knoweth an hawk from an hand-saw'![16] All this grim phantasy is intensified by Hamlet's intense temperament.

Throughout the action of the play the attitude of Hamlet is clearly shewn. In the artless grace & affection of Oleary—I mean Ophelia—he sees but delusive & superficial qualities. His killing of Polonious affords him merely an opportunity to vent more cynicism—"how a King may go a progress thro' the guts of a beggar."[17] In the churchyard scene Hamlet's contempt of man is the central theme. In skulls & rotting flesh he sees the end of all humanity. What is the use of life? Alas, poor Yorick!

> "Imperious Caesar, dead & turn'd to clay,
>     Might stop a hole to keep the wind away;
>     Oh, that that earth, which kept the world in awe,
>     Should patch a wall t' expel the winter's flaw!"[18]

It is in consonance with this nature, that Hamlet always drifts. Not even his dire purpose causes him to do anything save when circumstance directs. His detachment from human motives destroys the correlation of will & action, & makes him dependent upon circumstance. Whatever he does actively, is brought about by causes or situations outside himself—a fact that makes "Hamlet" a true tragedy, wherein Fate is the impelling power. Hamlet's is the poetic, visionary, semi-irresolute mind. He recognises his limitations in the speech beginning "Oh, what a rogue & peasant slave am I".[19]

---

But let me bore you no longer with these disjointed & probably unoriginal observations. Probably a thousand writers have said the same thing—perhaps you have yourself, in the essay which prompted your interest in the unfortunate Prince. Let me see your theme when copied; it may not be too long for some amateur journal, after all. You will do well to study Shakespeare more detailedly than in school. He is certainly a splendid exemplification of genius, & the most natural reproducer of Nature & mankind in literary history. In variety & range he stands alone. However—I could never be such a Shakespearite as your Hypatia. The freedom, irregularity, & anachronisms of the great bard weary me when administered in too great doses. For purely pleasant reading, I seem to sink back into my favourite age of Pope. I can sympathise a trifle with Mr. Dryden, who writ of Shakespeare, albeit admiringly & sympathetically, that he was

> "Untaught, unpractis'd, in a barb'rous age."[20]

I shall be interested to see just what you substituted for the "nameless vagueosity" previously designed for the *Pippin*.[21] I am glad you are taking to *heroicks*. The editor informed me that you had contributed to the magazine "a poem which will give it the necessary high & abstract quality", but I know not whether she referred to the original effusion, or to the hastily substituted heroicks. I am sorry Father Mo was so iconoclastic—though I had an idea there was some room for improvement in the lines, despite your expressed conviction that you would never do better work. Unless you object, I think I shall send the piece, with a title & under an absolutely unrecognisable pseudonym such as "Cyril Fitz-James Grosvenor" or "Percival Byron Flanagan", to the *Tryout*—just to see what comment it may elicit from the publick. Keep on with versification, and do not let any amount of criticism dampen the poetick feeling to which you allude. As your style grows increasingly clear, your work will become more & more manifestly meritorious.

Last Sabbath Day I mailed to you a couple of *Amateur Journalist* files—one for you and t'other for your Delia-Margarita. As I said before, you ought to have the opportunity of making the benefaction in person. I am surprised to hear that the wingèd Eleanora[22] takes second place in your young affections. Pray do not fracture the sweet Hypatia's heart, or drive her to suicide! The 4th V.P. saith that the Lady Eleanora is quite a pote-ess, & intendeth to become an English teacher. I advise you to wed her in preference to the Delia person. Never mind Delia's looks—they will soon fade! Probably she will make a hideous-appearing old woman fifty years from now, whilst Misses Hypatia and Eleanora will be distinguished old ladies, either or both of whom would do you credit as spouses. You interest me in Mr. John Ingold, Jr. Try to secure him for the United! I hope the additional man-power in the Press Club may not be quite so mediocre as you fancy—at least, I hope some of it may become interested enough to join the United. I fear, though, that the Hon. Silas Buchman, or to put it classically, C. Silius Bucmanus Saltator, would hardly be desirable. We are in no need of dancers or other frivolous folk. Was it not my old friend M. Tullius Cicero who said in some oration or other, "Nemo fere saltat sobrius, nisi forte insanit!"?[23] I trust Ericson[24] may issue your *Pippin* by 1919 or 1920. He will never acquire the cognomen or agnomen of *celer*[25]—though to do the man justice, I believe he hath reform'd enough of late to print the Hon. Jno. Milton Samples' *Silver Clarion* on an approximately monthly schedule.

I am astonished to hear that der *Staats-Zeitung* iss allowedt in der ☾ office.[26] Ach! I thought Mr. Meyer vass giving avay Lipperty Loan posters mit der paper—dot he vass all conferted to Amerikanism yet alretty! At least, such was the semi-impression I received from your poetick friend Mrs. Arnold. By the way—that good lady recently sent two pieces for revision at professional rates, & one of them was a really splendid albeit simple lyric— better than anything from her pen which I had previously seen. The metre was all tangled up, but when unravelled, the result was surprisingly good.

Speaking of clients—you & Miss Durr will be satisfied at last. I am a real labouring man! In other words, I have undertaken to make a thorough & exhaustive revision of Rev. D. V. Bush's long prose book—now called "Pike's Peak or Bust", though part of my job is to find another name.[27] Rev. David is now Religious Director of the Central Y.M.C.A. of St Louis. I do not see how the fellow manages to get on so in the world. He is, literarily, such a complete d—— fool!

I have decided not to alter the name of *The Conservative*, though it does incense me to find the title preëmpted. Has your *National Amateur* arrived? I asked Cook to be sure to remember you regularly.

I hope Mo *is* working on the *Gallo'mo*. Otherwise I should fear he has dropped me altogether. Deep broods the silence o'er the templed hills of Madison!

      VALE.

## L. METADIVS. CAELO.

*Notes*

1. This letter was written 18 or 19 October.
2. "In the consulship of M. Rinartius Clina and A. Galpinius Secundus." Kleiner and Galpin were president and first vice-president of the UAPA for the 1918–19 term. In mid-September 1918, HPL wrote a mock drama about Galpin's high school romances, called *Alfredo* with Rheinhart Kleiner as King Rinarto and himself as Teobaldo.
3. The standard opening of a Latin letter: "L. Metadius Caelo sends greetings to A. Galpinius Secundus. If you are well, it is good; I am also well." Caelo is imaginary.
4. HPL was first Vice-President in 1915–16, when he wrote the recruiting pamphlet, *United Amateur Press Association: Exponent of Amateur Journalism* (1915).
5. Raymond B. Nixon of Tallahassee, whose paper was the *Capital City News*; John Ingold of Appleton, WI.
6. *Browning's Magazine* (1890–1922) had a department called "Beta Kappa Beta," where boys eighteen and older could exchange views on sports and other interests.
7. The 4th Vice-President of the UAPA in 1918 was Margaret Abraham, Appleton, WI, the 3rd Vice-President in 1918–19 was Mary Henrietta Lehr, Redlands, CA.
8. Ida C. Haughton, an amateur living in Columbus, Ohio, and editor of the *Woodbee*, was at this time Western Manuscript Manager. She would later become involved in a bitter dispute with HPL over the administration of the UAPA; in response, HPL wrote the vicious satirical poem, "Medusa: A Portrait" (1921).
9. I.e., Margaret Abraham (HPL's Hebrew is the masculine form of the word meaning "intelligent").
10. Fred W. Cheney of Georgetown, IL.
11. Anne Tillery Renshaw of Washington, DC, later to become Offical Editor of the UAPA (1919–20).
12. *Hearts of the World* (1918), directed by D. W. Griffith, starring Lillian Gish, Dorothy Gish, Robert Harron, and Adolphe Lestina. A propaganda film about World War I.
13. *The Birth of a Nation* (1915), produced and directed by D. W. Griffith, starring Lillian Gish, Mae Marsh, Henry B. Walthall. A celebrated film about Reconstruction.
14. *Hamlet* 1.2.133–37.
15. *Hamlet* 2.2.204.
16. *Hamlet* 2.2.374.
17. *Hamlet* 4.3.31.
18. *Hamlet* 5.1.203–6. HPL quotes the first two lines in "The Materialist Today" (1926).
19. *Hamlet* 2.2.538.

20. John Dryden (1631–1700), "Prologue" to *Troilus and Cressida*, l. 7.

21. A journal produced by the Appleton High School Press Club. See HPL's two poetic tributes to the *Pippin* (*AT* 346–47, 350–52).

22. Presumably Eleanor Evans Wing of Appleton, WI.

23. Cf. *SL* 1.35. HPL there maintains that he said this ("Scarcely any sober person dances, unless by chance he is mad") to his mother at the age of 8 when she wished him to take dancing lessons. The sentence comes from Cicero's *Pro Mureno* 13 (not the Catilinarian orations, as HPL declared).

24. E. E. Ericson of Elroy, WI, for many years the Official Printer of the UAPA.

25. Swift. *Celer* is an actual Roman cognomen.

26. Apparently a reference to the *Volkszeitung*, a German-language newspaper published in Appleton under the aegis of the *Crescent*. In his autobiographical notes, Galpin reports that it "soon disappeared as a war casualty."

27. The original edition was *'Pike's Peak or Bust''; or, The Possibilities of the Will* (Webster, SD: The Reporter & Farmer, 1916). There is no record of a revised edition.


[6]   [To the Gallomo]   [AHT]

Providence, R.I.,

Tuesday, September 30, 1919

Concerning l'art cinematographique and the sundry idols of Galmo therein, I may say that I find nothing outrageous in their taste; though I can't say that I see anything particularly brilliant in the eternal Mary of the Movies.[1] In my judgment her art consists mainly of a certain gelatinous saccharinity which is not at all hard to achieve—chance and press-agenting doing the rest. She has not even the originality of Chaplin[2]—who is at least master of a number of effective ideas and essentials of comicality which would not have been despised by the mimes and buffoons of Graeco-Roman days. Klei, though, thinks otherwise, and says he hath her framed picture in his room! I formerly attended the cinema quite frequently, but it is beginning to bore me. My interest lay more in the plays than the players, and I have no special enthusiasm for any of the artists of the shadow. If I have ever singled out any stars above the rest, it has been a pair about one whom relatively little— Henry B. Walthall[3] and the Japanese Sessue Hayakawa.[4] The latter was my late young cousin's favourite.[5] Walthall possess tragic potentialities all too seldom utilised on the screen. His part in the "Birth of a Nation", though a leading one, failed to do him justice. He could create a sensation if some of Poe's tales were dramatised—I can imagine him as Roderick Usher or the central character in "Berenice". No one else in filmland can duplicate his delineation of stark, hideous terror or fiendish malignancy. Hayakawa excels in tragical pathos, and would soar high if he were a white man. I would not be surprised if he had a dash of white blood somewhere. Both Walthall and Hayakawa are too good for films—they ought to be known more widely.

As to Rabelais—he is to me unexplored territory, and is likely to remain so till the day of my demise. I cannot seem to acquire any enthusiasm for French things, and the quality of coarseness would be enough to deter me anyway. I suffered all the horrors of P. Ovidius Naso[6] because he was a classick author and could not be skipped, but I'll be gracioused if I'll repeat the experience for any gracioused Frenchman! Cook and McDonald[7] are trying to get me to read de Maupassant and Flaubert, who are by me untouched, but I'll tell them to go to O. Dear! If I ever become more Gallick than Victor Hugo and Jules Verne makes me, it will be through M. Anatole France, who seems to be such a Galpinian favourite. The only furriner I've read lately is Vicente Blasco Ibanez, whose "Four Horsemen of the Apocalypse" was sent me by a correspondent who evidently wanted to take no chances about my absorbing it.[8] It was disappointing—all the characters but one were damned scoundrels. The one worthy thing about the book was its absolutely faithful picture of the Hun beast in all its native ugliness.

This neighbourhood is quite honoured today, His Eminence Cardinal Mercier of Belgium[9] being entertained in the McElroy mansion only four houses west of Castle Theobald on Angell St. My aunt is now there at the reception being given in his honour. The extensive grounds are all fenced off to deter curious crowds, and awnings cover the long drives whereby the mansion is reached from the street. His Immanence will sleep there tonight, then depart for the lawless town of Bosting. I should like to see the Cardinal, but feel too confoundedly miserable today to breast any bustle, formality, or excitement. I am saving my strength for H. R. H., the Prince of Wales, whom I intend to see or die in the attempt. The McElroy home is the only local stronghold of Hibernianism. It was built by the late Joseph Banigan, sometimes called "The Rubber King", who was Mrs. McElroy's father. He was a poor Irish peasant who succeeded in business and lived to found a family whose innate good qualities gave them a definite social standing hereabouts. He married an American lady, and gave his children the best education obtainable, so that they are rather influential in the community. One of our principal skyscrapers—where my grandfather had his office the last two years of his life—was named the "Banigan Building"—though Providence pride has led to its recent renaming as the "Grosvenor Building"[10] (some change from peasantry to aristocracy, eh, what?). My mother and aunts knew the daughters of Joseph Banigan from childhood, and found them really worthy in every respect. The grandchildren were my earliest playmates, though it made me shudder in my British soul to know "Dicky Banigan", "Robert McElroy", "Edmund Sullivan", etc!! However, there is some consolation in the fact that Dick, Joe, and John Banigan, who lived nearest me (next house to #454 Angell) were only a quarter Irish. Their father had followed the example of his own father and married into an old American family. Still, I wished they could have been solidly Saxon! The Banigan heirs are the recognised leaders of Catholic circles here, and have entertained all the visiting Popish dignitaries such as Cardinal Sartori of Italy, Gibbons of Baltimore, and now Mercier. Mercier, by the way, is rather Galpinesque in altitude. My aunt went to the college exercises this morning to see him obtain his LL. D., and says that the tallest professor was selected to confer upon him his academic cap. The registrar (whose wife told my aunt) is supposed to perform this ceremony, but is such a pygmy that he felt he could not do it gracefully, so called in more suitable assistance! The Banigan or McElroy Mansion, where Mercier is now receiving the homage of local society, is one of the "show places" of the neighbourhood, and excited Klei's vast admiration when he was here. It is a Gothic manor-house of brick and stone, such as its peasant builder may have seen and admired at a distance in his boyhood in Ould Oireland. The grounds are extensive and beautifully kept, with hedges, trees, and stables of pleasing architecture. It lies almost exactly half way betwixt the house where I was born, and that which I inhabit. Altogether, I fancy the Irish have helped rather than harmed the locality!

Concerning the posthumous publication of epistles, I sincerely hope that no one may ever be fatuous enough to embalm my folly thusly! Never have I entertain'd the Galpinian hope of such a thing—and I trust that I may never have to acquire a Lollian dread of it. For heaven's sake, Galba,[11] permit posterity to observe me in relaxed moments such as the present one! You must realise that the Gallomonistic Tibaldus is not the stern ascetick whom the rest of the world knows. Shew one of these Gallomoes to anyone save five or six intimate correspondents, and they wou'd vow I never writ it! For one thing—no one but Galmo ever beheld a word of profanity from my pen. The Klei-comolo is frankly written with a view to semi-publicity, but not this closer document—Gawd, no! I can't kick if Galba wants to keep these outbursts of microcephaly, but I can at least adjure him to keep 'em private. I've had one experience with Galloian publicity! (Vide chronicles of A. H. S.)

I am sorry the respected P. G. W. K.[12] falls for the "league" bunk.[13] The matter of the six British votes is simple—if voting in the league means anything, which it doesn't. It provides that Britain shall have a better chance to control decisions than otherwise—which is well and good. The veto power of the U.S. is a Wilsonian jester, a Congolese Bantu in the stack of fuel—for no country votes where its own affairs are concerned! Having no vote on its own affairs, the U.S. could do nothing to stay decisions affecting it. What Johnson, Borah,[14] and those other objectors want, is an equalisation of votes so that on general questions the U.S. can have an equal chance with the Motherland to sway decisions. As one of the articles—the 15th, I think, shews, disputes referred to the assembly are decided by majority voting. As you must know, there will be sharp competition amongst the larger powers to control the votes of the lesser powers. England will control Persia, Hedjaz, etc., whilst America will control Hayti, San Domingo, Cuba, etc. Johnson and his ilk want to be sure that England controls no more than America. Now this merely makes me tired. The fortunes of both Anglo-Saxon nations run side by side, and it matters not which one has the votes—but if it will help defeat the whole chimerical league plan, let Johnson talk! The voting would only affect minor matters. When a nation is in earnest, it will break through all the flimsy league paraphernalia. It would take force to break out of the league if that body were a reality and most of the members opposed withdrawal. Keller says that any nation could withdraw on two years' notice. That is plain error. All such questions would have to be submitted to the council for arbitration and decision. The covenant is full of little jokers that riddle the Wilson claims. Heaven knows, I haven't time to look them all up, for the scheme amounts to nothing anyway! By the way—I shall not try to answer Galba's sophistical defence of that fellow Wilson in a previous GALLOMO, but will enclose a bit of verse copied from a Western paper. Read it and pass on to Mocrates, little one. (N.B. Lapsus calami—I meant KLEICOMOLO when I said GALLOMO, but I will send the verse just the same.) The most infernally silly thing that league advocates say, is that the opponents of their plan are pro-German. That is not so. The only shady characters on our side are the Sinn Feiners, and Gawd knows we're ashamed enough of them. Germany knows that the league amounts to nothing, and is placidly indifferent as to what becomes of it. But allee samee if Allied folks no lookee out, German get much dangerous again! It behoves the publick to regard the future attitude and opportunities of this unrepentant and far from weak enemy. Despite the taking of territory from Prussia, the Balkans again lie open for Hun exploitation. Sooner or later Austria will either join Germany or reëstablish the dual monarchy with Hungary, in any case being on the German side. The best thing would have been to let Roumania take Hungary, as suggested a few weeks ago. Bulgaria—but we all know Bulgaria. And if we continue to mistreat Italy, she will be against us in the next war. The Dago loves not the gentle Boche, but he will hate us a great deal worse than he will hate Germany if we permit the Fiume blunder of the Paris council to be perpetuated. As to Russia—if it stays Bolshevik, Germany will exploit it and wax corpulent upon it. If it regains sanity, it will hate us with a cold, steely hate for our neglect in its hour of need. At this moment French, English, and American troops ought to be helping Kolchak and Denikine, for Russia was our ally whilst it lasted. When these elements triumph, if they do, they will have small reason to forgive us, and will in all reasonable probability align with Germany. I am no diplomat, but I am quite sure from what I read that a little common sense could turn the future course of two great nations—Italy and Russia. These hang in the balance—will they go with us or with the Hun? Our best possible ally in the event of Russo-German hostilities with us is Poland. This new nation has an undying hatred both of Russia and of Germany. If helped by us to the limit of our ability—given every stimulus for development into a great nation, and bolstered up commercially and financially—it will be no mean influence in our favour in the years to come.

Of Japan I have not so far spoken, because I think it a certain enemy of the future, which no plan can permanently make a friend. It demands free access to Anglo-Saxon soil for its citizens, and this can never be given. Orientals must be kept in their native East till the fall of the white race. Sooner or later a great Japanese war will take place, during which I think the virtual destruction of Japan will have to be effected in the interests of European safety. The more numerous Chinese are a menace of the still more distant future. They will probably be the exterminators of Caucasian civilisation, for their numbers are amazing. But that it all too far ahead for consideration today. The next war, I think, will see England, America, France, Spain,? Greece, Scandinavia,? Holland, Switzerland, and the South American countries, against Germany, Russia, Austria, Italy, Japan, Mexico, and Bulgaria. I forgot to add Poland to our side—also Belgium, of course. Italy and Russia might be doubtful—might even be friends if treated properly in time. Also, future German colonisation might make enemies instead of Allies in South America. But at any rate, it is a duty to maintain the solidity of the Anglo-Franco-American *bloc*, and to win to it as many friends as possible; all bound by ties of substantial self-interest. This Anglo-Franco-America is the only real league of nations. These three nations have no diverse aims, and can bear triple harness infinitely. I once thought Italy could make a fourth, but see that the other three are not sufficiently considerate of its interests. Anyone fostering disunion amongst these three countries ought to be shot—which means the many Irish curs who go about the United States preaching Anglophobia. It will be best to keep up Saxon dominance until the final crash—and it is not extravagant to hope that the English ideal can be kept through the new Dark Ages to blossom forth again after the next Renaissance—just as the Roman influence reappeared in European culture. But it is too late to talk of any separate destinies for America and England. They must stick together for the advancement of their common culture.

Concerning a reading course 1600–1800, stressing minor poets—let me lean back in my chair for a moment and think! I should hardly advise stressing minor poets, but if thou'rt determined, here goes: Of course, 1600 finds us in the heyday of the Elizabethan aera. I don't have to tell you to read the w. k. author of *Hamlet, Macbeth,* and other popular melodramas and comedies, but I will drop a word in behalf of my fat old friend Ben Jonson, whose *Catiline, Sejanus, Volpone, Alchemist, Silent Woman,* and *Cynthia's Revels*—plus of course *Every Man in his Humour,* ought to receive the o. o. from your penetrating O.K. Glimmes. Nor should Messrs. Beaumont and Fletcher be scorn'd. Doubt has been expressed as to their authorship of *Alfredo,* a Tragedy,[15] but you may accept as their genuine and meritorious work such things as *The Maid's Tragedy, Faithful Shepherdess, Knight of the Burning Pestle,* etc. Read 'em. And now for your poets, minor and otherwise. We come at this point upon a group called by Dr. Johnson the "Metaphysical Poets", of whom I shall first mention a favourite of Klei's—George Wither. George hath a sort of pastoral cast, hence he appealeth to me also. Read "The Shepherd's Hunting", one passage in which would be appreciated by the new romantick poet whom Mistress Hoyt[16] likes so well:

> So, my WILLY, shall it be
> With Detraction's breath and thee,
> It shall never rise so high,
> As to stain thy poesy.

Well, who's this? That celebrated old fellow Dr. Donne, about whom our former Chairman of Private Criticism, W. F. Melton, Ph.D.,[17] hath writ a book! Read as much as you can stand of old John—it won't hurt you. And at this point note how the old Elizabethan luxuriance of fancy is petering out in the artificial *conceit.* 'Tis an aera of transition, plain to see. Minor bards come thick and fast—Dick Corbet, Dr. Henry King, Sir J. Beaumont, Tho. Carew, a gallant like Waller and Klei, Phineas and Giles Fletcher, Francis Quarles— pious old duffer—George Herbert, another pious gink some of whose verse my aunt had to learn when she was even more of an infant than thou, O Galba. Sir J. Suckling, the arch-gallant, Robert Herrick, a really meritorious lyrist, Richard Lovelace—the "stone walls do not a prison make" fellow, Bill Davenant, the playwright, who was so unscrupulous for fame that he used to hint at being a left-handed son of Shakespeare, Dick Crashaw—pious guy— Edmund Waller, the Kleiner of his age, first of the neatly correct writers—

> "He caught at love, and fill'd his arms with bays"

Abraham Cowley, quite some poet—writ all sorts of junk including an epick, the "Davideis", which though writ in the Heroic Couplet hath met with unac- countable oblivion—Sir John Denham, author of "Cooper's Hill", wherein occurs the famous comparison of an author's work to the Thames:

> "Oh, cou'd I flow like thee, and make thy Stream
> My great Example, as it is my Theme!
> Tho' deep, yet clear; tho' gentle, yet not dull;
> Strong without Rage; without o'er flowing, full."

But I mustn't forget the prose artists in spite of your preference. Could you stand Burton's *Anatomy of Melancholy?* If not, try Sir Tho. Overbury or Sir Tho. Browne. I suppose you already know Walton's *Compleat Angler* by heart, to say naught of the diaries of Sir J. Evelyn and Saml Pepys. Therefore I turn to verse again, and hail the mighty name of MILTON. Read him through. Skip not Andrew Marvell, nor for thy life overlook the hilarious Samuel Butler, whose Hudibras is a text-book of wit and enchiridion of humour. John Phil- ips' *Splendid Shilling* is a rather good light diversion—a parody upon Miltonick style. We are now arriv'd at the Restoration aera, and faced with the illustrious name of DRYDEN. His contemporaries who deserve a reading are John Oldham the satirist,[18] Sedley, the gallant poet, Wentworth Dillon, Earl of Roscommon, rhetorician and didactick poet, and the brilliant dramatists. Of the latter you must not miss Otway, author of Venice Preserv'd, Nat Lee, Dryden's enemy Shadwell the Laureate, Nicholas Rowe, and (since you are a devotee of Rabelais) the comical authors Wycherly, Vanbrugh, Farquhar, Etherege, and Congreve. Congreve brings us down to the age of Pope, but belongs to the Restoration school so far as technique is concern'd. He writ not only comedies but tragedies, of which the most famous is *The Mourning Bride*, containing the celebrated couplet:

> "Heav'n has no rage like love to hatred turn'd,
> Nor hell a fury like a woman scorn'd."

By the way, it is this same play which contains "Musick hath charms to soothe the savage breast". Coming back to prose, miss not the philosophical Hobbes, Locke, and perhaps Boyle, nor the essayist Sir W. Temple.

Now hail to the dawn—Aetas Augustana! Poets in profusion await thine eye—John Sheffield, Duke of Buckinghamshire, the immortal Prior, Thos. Parnell, ADDISON, Tickell, Gay, Somerville, POPE, SWIFT, THOMSON, Ikey Watts, Ambrose Philips, Collins, Dyer, Garth, Shenstone, Young, Akenside, Allan Ramsay the Scotchman,—but stay—we are quitting the Augustan age for that later period of romantick beginnings. GRAY, the Churchyard Man, Falconer, author of the *Shipwreck*, Beattie, Blair, Percy's Reliques, COWPER, Dr. Darwin of Botanick Garden fame (grandfather of the immortal Charles), Wolcot—Peter Pindar, the biting satirist, Churchill, Anstey of the New Path Guide, poor Chris. Smart, Elizabeth Carter, the learned old maid, Macpherson, the Ossian faker, Goldsmith, the brothers Warton, Matt. Green, Sheridan, Rogers, Crabbe, Burns,—but we are getting rather near the present! To go back—I forgot to mention the Restoration burlesque on Dryden—*The Rehearsal*, by George Villiers, Second Duke of Buckingham, which perhaps furnished Mr. Sheridan with a model for *The Critick*. Prose writers from this age downward are Sir R. Steele, Addison, Swift, Budgell, Hughes, Arbuthnot (read his *History of John Bull*), L^d Bolingbroke (*Letters, Patriot King*) Lady Mary Wortley Montagu, (*Letters*) Mandeville, utilitarian moralist, Smollet, Sterne,—the philosopher and historian Hume, who exploded a great deal of theistic nonsense—EDWARD GIBBON, SAMUEL JOHNSON, Mr. Burke, Jimmy Boswell, "Junius", P. D. S. (Philip Dormer Stanhope, Earl of Chesterfield), Beckford, author of *Vathek* in French and English, Miss Burney, afterward Mme. D'Arblay, Gilbert White, author of the *Nat. Hist. of Selborne*, Horace Walpole,—but we are getting close to the end. The nineteenth century is near, and we now see new and strange authors publishing their first works, who will be better known a quarter of a century later. Campbell, Southey, Wordsworth, Coleridge—all are above the horizon, but still partly obscured by the thick vapours of that region. A great age is closed—an age in which men saw that reason is the paramount quality, and that emotion and passion are mere secondary things unworthy of serious treatment. Verse was then what it should be—a light tinkling amusement of the idle—for men's minds were on greater things. Hume was brushing away the clouds of miraculous superstition; Gibbon was re-creating the declining Roman world; Johnson was refining the publick morals as Addison did before him. Prose and verse had attained their utmost elegance of form, and were tottering on the brink of decline. Science was arising—that young giant later to carry everything before it. Probably my survey has been but imperfect. I have doubtless omitted in this hasty catalogue many writers who ought to be read, and included many who are scarce worth perusal—but tired as I am today it is the best I can do. Let me express the hope, O Galba, that thou mayest extract at least a grain of help or amusement from what I have writ.

Great was my delight to behold the Mocratic domicile in pictured majesty. Verily, Sir, thou art well off both materially and aesthetically. The place is exceedingly attractive both inside and out, and the views are thoroughly delightful. The sweep of lake horizon would delight my astronomical soul. The roof of 598 Engelstrasse is approximately flat, and in the days of my youth I had a set of meteorological instruments there. Hither I would sometimes hoist my telescope, and observe the sky from that point of relative proximity to it. The horizon is fair, but not ideal. One can see the glint of the Seekonk through the foliage of Blackstone Park, and the opposite bank is quite clearly defined. With a terrestrial eyepiece of fifty diameters on my telescope, I can see some of the farms in the heart of East Providence, and even Seekonk, Mass., across the river. One in particular delights me—a typical bit of ancient agrestick New England with eighteenth century farmhouse, old-fashion'd garden, and even archaic well and well-sweep—all this bit of primitive antiquity visible from a roof in the prosaic modern town!! One of the houses within range is a seventeenth century structure—1650 or thereabouts—but this is not nearly so picturesque as the more recent one above mentioned. A good telescope, or even a binocular glass, is a great pleasure when one has a wide vista. I am fortunate in having an almost ideal battery of optical aids, including a Warner and Swasey—hell, no, I mean Bausch and Lomb—prism binocular which cost me $55.00 about twelve years ago. Ah, them golden days when I didn't have to worry about what I spent! I'd like to see meself buying a $55.00 plaything today!!! Well, if Mocrates can make a lit'ry success of me, maybe prosperity will bless me humble hearth once more! The Gay Bldg. is attractive, as is the view therefrom and I congratulate Mocrates upon his good fortune in having so thoroughly pleasant an atmosphere to work in. Providence has some excellent skyscrapers, the newest and tallest of which is the Turk's Head Building—sixteen stories.[19] The dominant view from Providence tall buildings includes the state capitol on the north, and the attractive bay on the south. Into this bay used to come the shipping of all the world, and about a century ago it was a veritable forest of masts. The great storm of 1815 caused the bay to overflow and inundate the whole waterfront. Full-rigged ships were cast up on Market Square, and one schooner was driven some distance up Westminster Street—past the corner known as Turk's Head, above hinted at. Never hath so great a storm lash'd the shore since. The shipping has sadly fallen off during the last fifty or sixty years, but the bay is still beautiful—as it will always be in spite of decadence and Bolshevism. The eternal sea is the one thing which the degenerate creature man can never mar! But Oh, the deuce, what sort of senile rambling is this!

I am, Gents, yr obt &c

M. LOLLIVS

*Notes*

1. I.e., Mary Pickford (1893–1979), who, with Charlie Chaplin, was the first "star" of the film industry.

2. Charlie Chaplin (1889–1977), British-born actor. HPL countered Rheinhart Kleiner's poem "To Mary of the Movies" (*Piper*, September 1915) with "To Charlie of the Comics" (*Providence Amateur*, February 1916).

3. Henry Brazeale Walthall (1878–1936), silent film star in D. W. Griffith's Biograph stock company, whose work includes *Judith of Betthulia, Avenging Conscience*, and *Birth of a Nation*.

4. Sessue Hayakawa (1889–1973), Japanese stage and film actor who was featured in many Hollywood films from 1914 to 1962.

5. Phillips Gamwell (1898–1916), son of HPL's aunt Annie E. P. Gamwell.

6. HPL alludes to Ovid's *Ars Amatoria, Remedia Amoris,* and other works notable for their sexual explicitness.

7. Philip B. McDonald, an amateur journalist and contributor to HPL's *Conservative.*

8. Vicente Blasco Ibáñez (1867–1928), *The Four Horsemen of the Apocalypse* (*Los cuatro jinetes del Apocalipsis*), trans. Charlotte Brewster Jordan (New York: E. P. Dutton & Co., 1918), a popular but lurid novel about a Frenchman who returns from overseas to fight in World War I. It reveals a violent hatred of the Germans.

9. Désiré Joseph Mercier (1851–1926), Belgian theologian and philosopher. He became Archbishop of Mechelen in 1906 and thus leader of the Catholic church in Belgium.

10. The 10½-story Banigan Building (later Grosvenor building; now AMICA Building), constructed at 10 Weybosset Street in 1896, was the first tall, fireproof, steel-frame building erected in Providence.

11. It is not clear why HPL referred to Galpin as Galba (presumably alluding to the Roman general who was emperor for less than a year in 68–69 C.E.).

12. Evidently a reference to someone named Keller, perhaps a friend of Galpin's or Moe's. See further letter 8 (p. 80).

13. The reference is to the League of Nations, the brainchild of Pres. Woodrow Wilson. The U.S. Senate rejected U.S. participation in it in March 1920.

14. Hiram Johnson (1866–1945), U.S. senator from California (1917–45), and William Edgar Borah (1865–1940), U.S. senator from Idaho (1907–40), two Republicans who led the fight against U.S. entry into the League of Nations.

15. The play (1918) is by HPL, and is signed "By Beaumont and Fletcher." It involves Galpin, Moe, HPL, and others as characters.

16. Unknown. In 1927 HPL wrote a poem, "To Miss Beryl Hoyt," on her first birthday, but her identity is similarly unknown.

17. Wightman Fletcher Melton (1867–?), *The Rhetoric of John Donne's Verse* (Baltimore: J. H. Furst Company, 1906).

18. See HPL's "John Oldham: A Defence" (*United Co-operative*, June 1919). The poem was written in response to Rheinhart Kleiner's "John Oldham: 1653–1683," published on the same page as HPL's poem.

19. The seventeen-story V-shaped Turks Head Building (1913, 1978) at 7–17 Weybosset Street, dominating the intersection of Weybosset and Westminster streets, has a high-relief sculpture of a Turk's head in the frieze above the third story.

[7]   [To the Gallomo]   [AHT]

Providence, R.I.,

December 11, 1919

## BELLS[1]

I hear the bells from yon imposing tower;
    The bells of Yuletide o'er a troubled night;
Pealing with mock'ry in a dismal hour
    Upon a world upheav'd with greed and fright.

Their mellow tones on myriad roofs resound;
    A million restless souls attend the chime;
Yet falls their message on a stony ground—
    Their spirit slaughter'd with the sword of Time.

Why ring in counterfeit of happy years
    When calm and quiet rul'd the placid plain?
Why with familiar strains arouse the tears
    Of those who ne'er may know content again?

How well I knew ye once—so long ago—
    When slept the ancient village on the slope;
Then rang your accents o'er the starlit snow
    In gladness, peace, and sempiternal hope.

In fancy yet I view the modest spire;
    The peaked roof, cast dark against the moon;
The Gothic windows, glowing with a fire
    That lent enchantment to the brazen tune.

Lovely each snow-drap'd hedge beneath the beams
    That added silver to the silver there;
Graceful each col, each lane, and all the streams,
    And glad the spirit of the pine-ting'd air.

A simple creed the rural swains profess'd;
    In simple bliss among the hills they dwelt;
Their hearts were light, their honest souls at rest,
    Cheer'd with the joys by reas'ning mortals felt.

But on the scene a hideous blight intrudes;
    A lurid nimbus hovers o'er the land;
Demoniac shapes low'r black above the woods,
    And by each door malignant shadows stand.

The jester Time stalks darkly thro' the mead;
    Beneath his tread contentment dies away.
Hearts that were light with causeless anguish bleed,
    And restless souls proclaim his evil sway.

Conflict and change beset the tott'ring world;
    Wild thoughts and fancies fill the common mind;
Confusion on a senile race is hurl'd,
    And crime and folly wander unconfin'd.

I HEAR THE BELLS—THE MOCKING, CURSED BELLS
    THAT WAKE DIM MEMORIES TO HAUNT AND CHILL;
RINGING AND RINGING O'ER A THOUSAND HELLS—
    FIENDS OF THE NIGHT—WHY CAN YE NOT BE STILL?

—H. PAGET LOWE

Before quitting the subject of Loveman and horror stories, I must relate the frightful dream I had the night after I received S.L.'s latest letter. We have lately been discussing weird tales at length, and he has recommended several hair-raising books to me; so that I was in the mood to connect him with any thought of hideousness or supernatural terror. I do not recall how this dream began, or what it was really all about. There remains in my mind only one damnably blood-curdling fragment whose ending haunts me yet.

We were, for some terrible yet unknown reason, in a very strange and very ancient cemetery—which I could not identify. I suppose no Wisconsinite can picture such a thing—but we have them in New-England; horrible old places where the slate stones are graven with odd letters and grotesque designs such as a skull and crossbones. In some of these places one can walk a long way without coming upon any grave less than an hundred and fifty years old. Some day, when Cook issues that promised *MONADNOCK*, you will see my tale "The Tomb",[2] which was inspired by one of these places. Such was the scene of my dream—a hideous hollow whose surface was covered with a coarse, repulsive sort of long grass, above which peeped the shocking stones and markers of decaying slate. In a hillside were several tombs whose facades were in the last stages of decrepitude. I had an odd idea that no living thing had trodden that ground for many centuries till Loveman and I arrived. It was very late in the night—probably in the small hours, since a waning crescent moon had attained considerable height in the east. Loveman carried, slung over his shoulder, a portable telephone outfit; whilst I bore two spades. We proceeded directly to a flat sepulchre near the centre of the horrible place, and began to clear away the moss-grown earth which had been washed down upon it by the rains of innumerable years. Loveman, in the dream, looked exactly like the snap-shots of himself which he has sent me—a large, robust young man, not the least Semitic in features (albeit dark), and very handsome save for a pair of protruding ears. We did not speak as he laid down his telephone outfit, took a shovel, and helped me clear away the earth and weeds. We both seemed very much impressed with something—almost awestruck. At last we completed these preliminaries, and Loveman stepped back to survey the sepulchre. He seemed to know exactly what he was about to do, and I also had an idea—though I cannot now remember what it was! All I recall is that we were following up some idea which Loveman had gained as the result of extensive reading in some old rare books, of which he possessed the only existing copies. (Loveman, you may know, has a vast library of rare first editions and other treasures precious to the bibliophile's heart.) After some mental estimates, Loveman took up his shovel again, and using it as a lever, sought to pry up a certain slab which formed the top of the sepulchre. He did not succeed, so I approached and helped him with my own shovel. Finally we loosened the stone, lifted it with our combined strength, and heaved it away. Beneath was a black passageway with a flight of stone steps; but so horrible were the miasmic vapours which poured up from the pit, that we stepped back for a while without making further observations. Then Loveman picked up the telephone output and began to uncoil the wire—speaking for the first time as he did so.

"I'm really sorry", he said in a mellow, pleasant voice; cultivated, and not very deep, "to have to ask you to stay above ground, but I couldn't answer for the consequences if you were to go down with me. Honestly, I doubt if anyone with a nervous system like yours could see it through. You can't imagine what I shall have to see and do—not even from what the book said and from what I have told you—and I don't think anyone without ironclad nerves could ever go down and come out of that place alive and sane. At any rate, this is no place for anybody who can't pass an army physical examination.[3] I discovered this thing, and I am responsible in a way for anyone who goes with me—so I would not for a thousand dollars let you take the risk. But I'll keep you informed of every move I make by the telephone—you see I've enough wire to reach to the centre of the earth and back!"

I argued with him, but he replied that if I did not agree, he would call the thing off and get another fellow-explorer—he mentioned a "Dr. Burke," a name altogether unfamiliar to me. He added, that it would be of no use for me to descend alone, since he was sole possessor of the real key to the affair. Finally I assented, and seated myself upon a marble bench close by the open grave, telephone in hand. He produced an electric lantern, prepared the telephone wire for unreeling, and disappeared down the damp stone steps, the insulated wire rustling as it uncoiled. For a moment I kept track of the glow of his lantern, but suddenly it faded out, as if there were a turn in the stone staircase. Then all was still. After this came a period of dull fear and anxious waiting. The crescent moon climbed higher, and the mist or fog about the hollow seemed to thicken. Everything was horribly damp and bedewed, and I thought I saw an owl flitting somewhere in the shadows. Then a clicking sounded in the telephone receiver.

"Lovecraft—I think I'm finding it"—the words came in a tense, excited tone. Then a brief pause, followed by more words in a tone of ineffable awe and horror.

"God, Lovecraft! *If you could see what I am seeing!*" I now asked in great excitement what had happened. Loveman answered in a trembling voice:

"I can't tell you—I don't dare—I never dreamed of *this*—I can't tell—It's enough to unseat any mind————wait————what's this?" Then a pause, a clicking in the receiver, and a sort of despairing groan. Speech again—

"Lovecraft—for God's sake—it's all up—Beat it! *Beat it!* Don't lose a second!" I was now thoroughly alarmed, and frantically asked Loveman to tell what the matter was. He replied only "Never mind! Hurry!" Then I felt a sort of offence through my fear—it irked me that anyone should assume that I would be willing to desert a companion in peril. I disregarded his advice and told him I was coming down to his aid. But he cried:

"Don't be a fool—it's too late—there's no use—nothing you or anyone can do now." He seemed calmer—with a terrible, resigned calm, as if he had met and recognised an inevitable, inescapable doom. Yet he was obviously anxious that I should escape some unknown peril.

"For God's sake get out of this, if you can find the way! I'm not joking—So long, Lovecraft, won't see you again—God! Beat it! *Beat it!*" As he shrieked out the last words, his tone was a frenzied crescendo. I have tried to recall the wording as nearly as possible, but I cannot reproduce the tone. There followed a long—hideously long—period of silence. I tried to move to assist Loveman, but was absolutely paralysed. The slightest motion was an impossibility. I could speak, however, and kept calling excitedly into the telephone—"Loveman! Loveman! What is it? What's the trouble?" But he did not reply. And then came the unbelievably frightful thing—the awful, unexplainable, almost unmentionable thing. I have said that Loveman was now silent, but after a vast interval of terrified waiting another clicking came into the receiver. I called "Loveman—are you there?" And in reply came a *voice*—a thing which I cannot describe by any words I know. Shall I say that it was hollow—very deep—fluid—gelatinous—indefinitely distant—unearthly—guttural—thick? What shall I say? In that telephone I heard it; heard it as I sat on a marble bench in that very ancient unknown cemetery with the crumbling stones and tombs and long grass and dampness and the owl and the waning crescent moon. Up from the sepulchre it came, and this is what it said:

"YOU FOOL, LOVEMAN IS DEAD!"

Well, that's the whole damn thing! I fainted in the dream, and the next I knew I was awake—and with a prize headache! I don't know yet what it was all about—what on (or under) earth we were looking for, or what that hideous voice at the last was supposed to be. I have read of ghouls—mould shades—but hell—the headache I had was worse than the dream! Loveman will laugh when I tell him about that dream! In due time, I intend to weave this picture into a story, as I wove another dream-picture into "The Doom that Came to Sarnath". I wonder, though, if I have a right to claim authorship of things I dream? I hate to take credit, when I did not really think out the picture with my own conscious wits. Yet if I do not take credit, who'n Heaven *will* I give credit tuh? Coleridge claimed "Kubla Khan", so I guess I'll claim the thing an' let it go at that. But believe muh, that was *some* dream!![4]

Well, God rest you, Merry Gentlemen, may nothing you dismay.

Your affectionate Grandfather,

M. LOLLIVS. TIBALDVS

*Notes*

1. "Bells" (*Tryout*, December 1919; as by "Ward Phillips").
2. "The Tomb" did not appear in Cook's *Monadnock Monthly*, but in Cook's *Vagrant* (March 1922).
3. The reference is to HPL's being declared "totally and permanently unfit" to serve in the U.S. army in December 1917.
4. HPL soon afterward wrote the dream into the story "The Statement of Randolph Carter" (*Vagrant*, May 1920).

[8]    [To the Gallomo]    [AHT]

[April 1920]

It is seldom, O Gentlemen, that I have anything new to write ye of. So uneventful is my career that a trip to Boston is the occasion for four or five closely typed pages. But I now have another slightly out of the ordinary incident to relate—albeit one which hath not taken me out of my secluded study. To come to the point—I have been spending all my time since Monday correcting arithmetic papers for pupils in the two upper grades of the Hughesdale, R.I. Grammar School, and in concocting examples and problems and laying out work for them to do! Behold Theobaldus the long-distance pedagogue! The explanation? Simple and lucid! One of the still semi-rural branches of my maternal family inhabit the township of Johnston, wherein lies the village of Hughesdale. They are by nature scholastically inclined, and are largely represented on the school board. Last week there was dire need of a substitute teacher to take the place of the grammar-school principal, whose vacation is due; and in view of the amazing energy and versatility of my aunt they decided to keep the job in the family, so to speak. They are aware of the rather tenuous state of local finances, and rightly guessed that the unexpected emolument might not prove unacceptable. Now be it known that my aunt has never before taught school a day in her life. Though fond of children, and very capable and tactful in managing them, she has known schools solely from the pupil's point of view; and has been a stranger to all the educational novelties which have sprung up since her graduation from Miss Abbott's fashionable seminary for refined young females. Can you imagine such an one guiding the destinies of a village grammar-school? No? But then—you don't know my aunt! As a person of ample culture and general education, there was of course no difficulty for her in directing the classes in the non-mathematical subjects. With amazing skill she seized on the complicated routine, and kept her classes busy at reading, reciting, writing exercises, and the like. But then arose the grim spectre—the hated, damned thing—ARITHMETIC! Fancy for a moment a person out of schoolbooks since the early 'nineties, endeavouring to grapple with the fad-ridden arithmetic of the day—the absurdly pedantic science wherein such terms as "common denominator", "plus", "minus", etc. are, or seem to be, abolished, and wherein it is deemed treason to tell a child to divide fractions by inverting the divisor and proceeding as in multiplication! Such was the thing faced by my aunt, who candidly confessed her inability to attend to all the insistent needs of those two restless upper classes, and to explain to them each step of every example as scrawled on their daily exercise papers. They worked much of the time according to methods new to her, and to follow and correct their attempts in itemised fashion was practically impossible. All her evenings, anyway, were obviously to be taken up with the correction of other papers. But here behold the mighty redactor of amateurdom! All is well, for is not Tibaldus the Great at hand? Ecce homo! It is not alone bad verse with which my mighty talents can grapple! Which means that I offered my assistance, and have undertaken to be the Power Behind the Throne in the mathematical department of the Hughesdale Grammar School! Now I suppose Gahal-Bah, the Wonder, and Mocrates, the Superman, will marvel that the mere correction of 7th and 8th arithmetic should be any sort of task. But suppose, O Great Ones, ye were like unto me, who do abhor 'rithmetic with all the loathing of an ethereal nature? Most of the methods are as new to me as to my aunt, and the text-book is a crime—the work of a local dignitary who has a pull with the school board. But natheless the principles of mathematicks are through all the ages unvarying, and brains were made to use; so I mastered the damned thing Sunday night and have now set up as a pedagogue of the new school; albeit I will on my knees praise the Creator Friday, when I can dismiss it as a bad dream and go back to my old ways whenever ill fortune compels me to make mathematical computations! My aunt says she *could* not today do some of the complicated problems in the back of the book. I wishtagawd I could say the same; that my conscience might enable me to slide over them lightly—but unfortunately I still remember enough to do them, detest them as I do! Therefore picture me last night, waist deep in papers covered with everything from vulgar fractions to cube root, and tinkering at stupid mistakes as if I were patching up D. V. Bush's latest metrical misdemeanour. Oh, Boy! Yuh'd orter see Grandpa marking up examples with a real red pencil, austerely, just as reg'lar teachers do! In the old days I used to long for the authority represented by one of those forbidding red pencils—but now I perceive that the authority is dearly purchased in the coin of fatigue and headache! And Holy Pegāna! The mistakes those kids make! Much as I loathe arithmetical pursuits, I'd have been ashamed in my grammar school days to turn in such work! Some of them do fairly well on the plain sailing—but the problems knock 'em all down! Yuh hafta go after 'em wit' a diagram! Sometimes I find certain blunders strangely duplicated—and I smile to think of the slips of paper exchanged in classroom behind my aunt's back. I know, because I have myself been a scholar—in my day I used to revise my class's work about as I do the United Amateur today—though of course without pedagogical sanction. I hope that the stuff I furnished my youthful clients in those days was not as bad as some of the suggestions passed around by these Hughesdale hopefuls—if so, my aid was not of much value! What would you think of a seventh-grade class in which not a single member can tell how to find the depth of box when the length, breadth, and cubical contents are given? They have had all this, but the least jar in the routine throws their little brains all helter-skelter. Just now the trouble is coming from a mistake which the regular teacher made in her haste to escape vacationwards. At the last moment she put a problem on the board in which she must have written cu. in. when she meant cu. ft. Not one in the school could see any light, and the theory above outlined is due solely to Theobaldian deduction. But there is another good one on my aunt! In devising problems yesterday for today's papers, and putting them on the board, she was distracted by the incessant chatter of an amiable and friendly-intentioned fellow-teacher; and made a question asking how much profit a farmer would make if he bought 3¾ bu. apples at $3.00 per bu., and sold them at 5¢ per quart. D'ya get it? *Profit?* The poor kids were all at sea—they knew something was the matter, but not just what! I am taking pity on them, and explaining very kindly that the apples got rotten or worm-eaten or something, so the unfortunate swain hadda sell 'em at a bargain! Yuh'd laff tuh see the bluff some of the kids made—and yet not one seemed to remember the second term of the common expression "profit and ———". It taketh not much to puzzle the faculties of infancy, and there are no Galpinii in Hughesdale! The racial composition of the school is appalling. Dagoes exist in amazing numbers—children of the thrifty peasants who settle on little farms and shun the congested urban Italian colony. My aunt says that they are much superior in conduct and appearance to city Italians, and I can testify that the brightest kid in the institution is named Joe Merluzzo! By the way—devising problems ain't the easiest work this side of Cleveland! If yuh'd don't watch out yuh'll make some absurd condition which the eye of youth will demur at. I hope I have escaped all pitfalls, making examples that come out well and fairly evenly. It is hard to tell just how hard or how easy the work should be made, and how to differentiate betwixt the 7th and 8th grade intelligences; but anyhow—'tis but for a week! To my mind, a teacher's job is no job for one person. Teamwork is needed—one to hold down the youngsters through the day, and another to wrestle with the papers at night. My aunt says she positively could not manage the thing without aid, and I am sure I don't see how anyone else can! She wants to give me a share of the financial spoils, but I scorn remuneration for labour performed in the cause of upholding the family's scholastic honour! The house is now a veritable branch office of the school. Arithmetical paraphernalia abound in my room, whilst my aunt has set up another table in the library to hold her linguistic, orthographical, geographical, historical, etc. matter. At this point I am going in there to get one or two of the freak exercises handed in, which I shall copy in these columns! Ah! Here's a good grammar one:

### JOHN HUNSPERGER 6B

Parse "I thought the school bell was broken".

    *I*, pronoun; *thought*, verb; *the*, l. adj.; *bell*, noun; *was*, adverb; *broken*, noun.

"Boys should be very brave."

    *Boys*, noun; *should*, adj.; *be*, prep.; *very*, adj.; *brave*, noun.

What a fine crop of Millars etc. is growing up to replace those who pass from our midst! Ah, well! Probably inefficient tuition is to blame for some of the dulness in rural schools. I'll wager the regular teacher of the higher grades has been monstrous remiss in explaining arithmetical matters to her young charges. I am having to make copious marginal notes on their papers, explaining principles they should have known ages ago. In short, gents, Grandpa Tibaldus is getting to be quite some schoolmaster! If only I could keep up and about longer at a time, I should take my rattan in hand and seek an appointment in some institution of l'arnin—after I had tried everything else and failed! Congrats, O Sage, on getting out of it! I should "need more beefsteak" too, if I were to do a millionth part of what thou didst. If nocturnal home correction is to me such a burthen, you can fancy what sort of a classroom despot I would make. I'd last just about ten to fifteen minutes!

But my new and evanescent professional pedagogy is not my only contemporary care—would that it were! The United is bound for trouble again, this time because of the idiotic way some members have been nagging Cook about the lateness of the official organ. They ought to know that he is practically giving them this de luxe thing as an act of charity—but they don't; and instead of being grateful they ask for more! Such is mankind. These naggings, coupled with his scant sympathy (which I share) for the professionalism of the present editorship, have caused the worm to turn at last—and Cook has just sent me the rough draft of his resignation, as he means to forward it to Miss D. and Mrs. R. DAMNATION! Kin ya imagine the result? The year's programme ruined, and that nasty wretch Dowdell gloating and triumphant![1] I have written Culinarius a note of ultimate appeal, imploring him for the sake of old and hallowed memories not to desert the flag in time of need. Will he heed? I hope so! If not, back to Ericson—higher rates, less intelligent work, and just as much delay after all. It is that filthy Cleveland sewer-rat and that disgusting Columbus hippopotamus-jellyfish who have done all the malevolent work by their raucous howls, and I fervently wish them both a swift and rough passage to the abode of Beëlzebub.

B/t/w—I s'pose youse geezers have saw the new BEARCAT.[2] What an odd contrast—essay by Martin and poem by Loveman—and that damned fool editor's own mouthings! Dowdell amuses me when he does not anger me. So he thinks his poor old Grandpa Lollius is boss of the United does he? Well, well, ain't it a shame! If I really were, you can wager that Dowdell would have been kicked out long ago—as he may be yet! "What will hold the recruit?" sneeringly quotes young William. "A rope!" He cynically replies. Well, Willie, I notice they ain't throwin' many ropes out in your direction! The only way the United will ever use a rope on that little thief is to give him a necktie party beneath the spreading sycamore or the genial telegraph pole! Oh, hell! But I must not sour my angelic nature by thinking of that unwashed brat. It'll make me cross with my pupils when I correct their mistakes! Let's turn to poetry—no, I mean my verse. I have really sworn off, but t'other day I received a touching request from young Nicol, out in dreary Saskatchewan (that's almost as dreary as Alberta, where Al Fred Willie lives!), who wants a few lines for his crude SARDONYX. I am a kind-hearted soul when I ain't mad, so within ten minutes I had scrawled off the following:[3]

### ON READING LORD DUNSANY'S BOOK OF WONDER

The hours of night unheeded fly,
And in the grate the embers fade;
Vast shadows one by one pass by
In silent daemon cavalcade.

But still the magick volume holds
The raptur'd eye in realms apart,
And fulgent sorcery enfolds
The willing mind and eager heart.

The lonely room no more is there—
For to the sight in pomp appear
Temples and cities pois'd in air,
And blazing glories—sphere on sphere!

H. PLANTAGENET LYTTLEWYT

This reminds me of Gahal-Bah's postcard request for information on the 'tendencies of modern verse'.[4] Gracious! What do I know about modern verse? I should say, at a guess, that poetasters are striving after formlessness, obscure rhythm which is not rhythm at all, commonplaceness and colloquialism in language and imagery (naturalness, they call it!), introspectiveness, subjectivity, and merciless realism. Half with and half against the current is imagism—which is a species of idiocy wherein sensation replaces reason. I am mightily glad I have ceased to cultivate poesy. It's going to the dogs, and it would pain me to see it go if I were a poet. Let me see thy collegiate theme on the subject, O Parvule! And b.t.w.—congratulations on appointment to the debating team! Now Lawrence will win every contest of wits in sight! Happy will be the U. of Wis. next year!

Speaking of the "Carter" story, I have lately had another odd dream—especially singular because in it I possessed another personality—a personality just as definite and vivid as the Lovecraft personality which characterises my waking hours.

My name was Dr. Eben Spencer, and I was dressing before a mirror in my own room, in the house where I was born in a small village (name missing) of northern New York State. It was the first time I had donned civilian clothes in three years, for I was an army surgeon with the rank of 1st Lieut. I seemed to be home on a furlough—slightly wounded. On the wall was a calendar reading "FRIDAY, JULY 8, 1864". I was very glad to be in regular attire again, though my suit was not a new one, but one left over from 1861. After carefully tying my stock, I donned my coat and hat, took a cane from a rack downstairs, and sallied forth upon the village street. Soon a very young man of my acquaintance came up to me with an air of anxiety and began to speak in guarded accents. He wished me to go with him to his brother—my professional colleague Dr. Chester—whose actions were greatly alarming him. I, having been his best friend, might have some influence in getting him to speak freely—for surely he had much to tell. The doctor had for the past two years been conducting secret experiments in a laboratory in the attic of his home, and beyond that locked door he would admit no one but himself. Sickening odours were often detected near that door . . . and odd sounds were at times not absent. The doctor was aging rapidly; lines of care—and of something else—were creeping into his dark, thin face, and his hair was rapidly going grey. He would remain in that locked room for dangerously long intervals without food, and seemed uncannily saturnine. All questioning from the younger brother was met with scorn or rage—with perhaps a little uneasiness; so the brother was much worried, and stopped me on the street for advice and aid. I went with him to the Chester house—a white structure of two stories and attic in a pretty yard with a picket fence. It was in a quiet side street, where peace seemed to abide despite the trying nature of the times. In the darkened parlour, where I waited for some time, was a marble-topped table, much haircloth furniture, and several pleasing whatnots covered with pebbles, curios, and bric-a-brac. Soon Dr. Chester came down—and *he had aged.* He greeted me with a saturnine smile, and I began to question him, as tactfully as I could, about his strange actions. At first he was rather defiant and insulting—he said with a sort of leer, "Better not ask, Spencer! Better not ask!" Then when I grew persistent (for by this time I was interested on my own account) he changed abruptly and snapped out, "Well, if you must know, come up!" Up two flights of stairs we plodded, and stood before the locked door. Dr. Chester opened it, *and there was an odour.* I entered after him, young Chester bringing up the rear. The room was low but spacious in area, and had been divided into two parts by an oddly incongruous red plush portiere. In the half next the door was a dissecting table, many bookcases, and several imposing cabinets of chemical and surgical instruments. Young Chester and I remained here, whilst the doctor went behind the curtain. Soon he emerged, bearing on a large glass slab what appeared to be a human arm, neatly severed just below the elbow. It was damp, gelatinous, and bluish-white, and the fingers were without nails. "Well, Spencer", said Dr. Chester sneeringly, "I suppose you've had a good deal of amputation practice in the army. What do you think, professionally, of this job?" I had seen clearly that this was not a human arm, and said sarcastically, "You are a better sculptor than doctor, Chester. This is not the arm of any living thing." And Chester replied in a tone that made my blood congeal, *"Not yet, Spencer, not yet!"* Then he disappeared again behind the portiere and emerged once more, bringing another and slightly larger arm. Both were left arms. I felt sure that I was on the brink of a great revelation, and awaited with impatience the tantalisingly deliberate motions of my sinister colleague. "This is only the beginning, Spencer," he said as he went behind the curtain for the third time. *"Watch the curtain!"* And now ends the fictionally available part of my dream, for the residue is grotesque anticlimax. I have said that I was in civilian clothes for the first time since '61—and naturally I was rather self-conscious. As I waited for the final revelation I caught sight of my reflection in the glass door of an instrument case, and discovered that my very carefully tied stock was awry. Moving to a long mirror, I sought to adjust it, but the black bow proved hard to fashion artistically, and then the whole scene began to fade—and damn the luck! I awaked in the distressful year of 1920, with the personality of H. P. Lovecraft restored! I have never seen Dr. Chester, or his young brother, or that village, since. I do not know what village it was. I never heard the name of Eben Spencer before or since. Some dream! If that happened to Co, he would be surely seeking a supernatural explanation; but I prefer actual analysis. The cause of the whole is clear—I had a few days before laid out Mrs. Shelley's "Frankenstein" for re-reading. As to details— Ambrose Bierce supplied the Civil War atmosphere, no doubt; whilst it is easy to trace in Dr. *Chester* and his brother—facially, I mean—the likenesses of my boyhood friends *Chester* and Harold Munroe; those brothers of whom I spoke in one of my ancient KLEICOMOLOES. I am not sleeping much this week, but last night I had a promising fragment of a dream that was cut short by premature awakening. I was alone in a black space, when suddenly, ahead of me, there arose out of some hidden pit a huge, white-robed man with a bald head and long snowy beard. Across his shoulders was slung the corpse of a younger man—cleanshaven, and grizzled of hair, and clad in a similar robe. A sound as of rushing wind or a roaring furnace accompanied this spectacular ascent—an ascent which seemed accompanied by some occult species of levitation. When I awaked, I had an idea for a story—but queerly enough, the idea had nothing to do with the dream!

At the recommendation of James F. Morton, Jr., I am perusing the works of a modern imaginative author named Algernon Blackwood—but Hell! I mentioned that before, didn't I! I can't say that I am very much enraptured, for somehow Blackwood lacks the power to create a really haunting atmosphere. He is too diffuse, for one thing; and for another thing, his horrors and weirdness are too obviously symbolical—symbolical rather than convincingly outré. And his symbolism is not of that luxuriant kind which makes Dunsany so phenomenal a fabulist. Just to see what he's like, youse fellers might read "Incredible Adventures", a collective of five very long "short" stories.[5] It ain't half bad, and if the first one tires you out, you are not compelled to swallow the remainder.

As to my friend Ed Plunkett—I am sorry to hear of the way the Middle West has treated him—not that the effete east was any too courteous. Rascoe[6] of the CHITRIB sums the case up well when he speaks of the discrepancy betwixt the writings and personality of an author. But really, the publick should shew more tact. The only reason why an author leaves his privacy is because the morbid curiosity of the rabble about his face, figure, and favourite breakfast food drags him out. He does not wish to parade on a platform for two bucks a look! If the crowd like him not, the crowd alone is to blame for its disappointment. If left alone, he would never have come before it. Critics, expecting so much, sadly exaggerate the awkwardness of Dunsany. In absolute fact, he is a very tall, thin man with just a touch of awkwardness— and it is an engaging, boyish sort of awkwardness which does not offend the eye at all. His voice is *not* of the "mush-in-the-mouth" sort, but is merely a bit mellow and throaty after the British pattern, rather than thin and nasal after the Yankee style. Perhaps there is a slight lisp, but it appears only at rare intervals. Obviously he has been at pains to correct it. The only trouble with Dunsany as a public speaker is that he makes no pretence of *stage presence*. As a successful dramatist, one expects him to have a bit of the actor about him, but he is essentially of a non-dramatic type. His striving for dramatic effect is an intellectual one—exercised when he *writes,* not when he *reads* his plays. He addresses his audience not as a performer declaiming to a crowded pit, but as a gentleman entertaining friends in his own drawing-room. He is at home with his audience—he mingles with them in spirit, as it were, and is not conscious of the platform and the gulf it is supposed to create between reader and auditor. He makes no effort at bodily pose—he is merely himself. Accordingly he seats himself and crosses his long legs when he chooses, and occasionally resorts to the water-pitcher. But he does not do this in an absurd or ungraceful way. There is not a trace of the clown in his acts. As to that "dumping a pitcher of ice water over his head"—I rebel at the callous remark of a half-baked reporter who probably knows nothing of headaches. When he lectured at Boston I heard him remark after the address, in speaking to a friend, "I have a fearful headache". Now I know *all* about headaches. All there is to be known. Some of mine seem impossible to live through. And I know that if Edward J. M. D. Plunkett's are anything like mine, he *must* put water to his head when they are near their climax. He did not do so the night I saw him—in fact, he did not even rub his brow until after he had descended from the platform. But it takes no great amount of deduction to infer that in Chicago he was more sharply afflicted whilst on the platform. Instead of descending, he stuck it out like a stoic to please his audience—and in return a writer jests about his antics with the water-pitcher! I am eloquent about headaches tonight, because I have just emerged from a veritable "killer", contracted by working half the forenoon and all the afternoon on Bush junk. *I* have been using water on my forehead, and I give not a river-regular on what any critick on reporter says of me!

I wonder that some of these journalists do not speak of Dunsany's face and expression—but they are obviously concerned only with things about which they can find fault. Dunsany is really handsome, and has one of the most kindly, winning, wholesome expressions I have ever beheld. Whether serious or whimsically humorous, his blue eyes are alight with an indefinable quality which makes one sure that he is a very good and very generous man. Dunsany left in my mind an exceedingly favourable impression—an impression which made me wish that he were a personal friend of mine. He is, I think, a trifle *unworldly*—if such may be said of a man who has travelled all over the globe and served through two wars.

Next on the programme is the Einstein theory, which I must confess at the outset that I cannot discuss authoritatively. I have as yet seen no really coherent account, and many of the articles by professors in local papers admit freely imperfect comprehension on the part of the respective writers. Einstein himself says that only twelve living men can fully comprehend his theory. I am intensely interested, and at the very beginning of the present publicity wrote McDonald for a key to the mystery. As you may or may not know, he teaches the history of science and mathematics as well as "Engineering English". His answer was—zero! Evidently he is not sure himself, and did not wish to let Grandpa see his deficiency. In such matters he is my very opposite—when I don't know a thing, I never try to cover up my lack. But now for my puerile observations. Einstein has two distinct theories—one relating to the nature of light, gravitation, and ether; the other relating to time and space. One of the two may be correct whilst the other is erroneous; and personally I think he is partly right on light and gravity but at sea on infinity and eternity. Coming down to the simple things I can comprehend—Einstein believes, and has apparently proved fairly well, that the direction of light can be changed by gravity. Not that light tends to follow anything but a straight line, but that gravity can act as a deflecting agent like refracting and reflecting media. Now the significance is this: if gravity can affect the course of a luminous ray, *then light does not consist of ether waves!* Think of the significance of this fact, if fact it be: All our basic theories of optics must be revised, and perhaps all our conceptions of radiant energy revolutionised. We are thrown back to my own beloved periwig days, when my old friend Ikey Newton held out for the old emission theory in spite of the undulatory doctrines of Huyghens and Euler! Back to the Queen Anne period! And woe unto Ambrose Bierce—his "Damned Thing" is altogether out of the running! Einstein is cautious—he confesses himself unable to explain the nature of light. He shows merely that the commonly accepted wave theory is improbable if not impossible, and shows this on a solid experimental basis—but further than that he is unable to go. It is worth noting that Einstein denies altogether the existence of the ether. For him there is no substance whatsoever in interplanetary and interstellar space; radiant energy being something substantial projected through utter nothingness. So far I have been speaking of Einstein's first and simpler theories. I cannot state my own position yet, for I am bewildered by the conflict of evidence. Eclipse observations certainly have shown a strange deflection of light rays by solar gravity; yet on the other hand, the mass of accumulated evidence in favour of ether-wave light is certainly immense. The conflict is baffling—no foot hath trod the new trail opened up. For mine own part, I am wondering whether or not some compromise theory cannot hit the truth. Perhaps there is an universal ethereal medium susceptible of waves, but perhaps wave-effect is only *for the conveyance of material particles susceptible of gravitational deflection.* I am slow—extremely slow—in relinquishing a theory which fulfils so many varied conditions as well as the wave theory fulfils them. Whatever of Einstein's may be true, it does not seem possible that the older doctrines can be utterly void of foundation. As with the periodic system in chemistry, we seem to be almost on the verge of some universal truth which eludes us! Lest I seem too reactionary in clinging somewhat to the older theories of light, let me say that the Einstein theory is not without its contradictions. In one point it fails to agree with observed phenomena, this being the displacement of the lines in the solar spectrum. So far the rapid displacement required by the theory has not been detected. This point, however, would positively disprove the larger and more complex relativity theory, but would not disprove the possibility of a material light affected by gravitation. The presence of one flaw makes it still possible to accept all of Einstein's work on a purely probational basis. Einstein has certain original ideas on the nature of gravitation itself; ideas partly conflicting with the law of Newton. These, however, have never been clearly explained in any article which I have yet seen. They seem to be involved inextricably in the theory of light, but to be independent of the general relativity theory—which scientists are slow in endorsing.

As to relativity on the whole, the commentator must proceed with extreme caution. As I said, I do not fully grasp the key to Herr Einstein's mode of thought; but so far as I can piece out his meaning from the unsatisfactory and fragmentary articles I have seen, I am inclined to think that he is falling into that most reprehensible habit of theorists—running ahead of experimental and practical science with speculations *for which observed phenomena and accepted hypotheses make no demand.* In other words, I think he is dipping into metaphysics and constructing some ingenious notions which *might* account for observed phenomena, but which are not *required* by the known conditions. This I deem a practice not to be encouraged. Such things as "dimensions" are merely terms invented to describe and define observed things. When we let the nomenclature run away with us and try to imagine conditions with one, two, three, four, five, or six "dimensions", we approach the borderland of sophism and fallacy. Now, O Galba, be not as glib as usual in calling Grandpa "dogmatic". (How youse two guys do overwork that woid in speaking of

Theobaldian ideas—as if there *were* such a thing as "dogmatism" in science!)
What I am trying to convey is this: that so far I have not seen any account of
any natural phenomena which call for explanation by an hypothesis as extravagant as Einstein's. Is it not just possible that the personal equation and
the desire of the individual enter in, as in religion? That is, is it not possible
that Einstein has been influenced by a certain instinctive reaction against the
starkly realistic conception of infinity and eternity? He may be right—I am
not fighting yet—but how doth it look to thee, O Gahal-Bah? Remember, I
judge from imperfect data. I may change my mind after reading some really
authoritative article on the question. W. r. m.—for Pete's sake, Kid, send me
anything you find about it. If it's something you don't wish to spare permanently, remember that Grandpa treats books and papers very carefully, and
will pay the postage with pleasure for the sake of enlightenment.

If Einstein minimises the importance of present systems on the ground
(O what familiar ground!) that human perception and conceptions are imperfect, he must be prepared to have the same objections levelled against his
own doctrines. He contends, I seem to gather, that Time is a sort of motion
in a hitherto unknown time-dimension. According to him, a clock runs
slower when in motion, because it is bucking up against the current of Time
itself. Now with all due respect to metaphysics and to Herr Einstein, and with
due knowledge that the super-mind of Gahal-Bah will accuse me of "dog-
maticism" (where t'ell didya get that spellin', kid?), I will venture the calm
opinion—(mindya I said only *opinion*) that all this talk about Time and Space
is damned nonsense. Whatever evidence there is for the relativity of Time and
Space, I feel sure that the evidence for their absoluteness is vastly greater.
Take Time, for example. Time is a definite thing. A planet revolves around
the sun once—twice—thrice—and so on. There is a difference between one,
two, and three. If its rate be uniform, something different has happened between the first, second, and third revolutions. What is the difference? It is
Time—which is not an entity but a condition. At an uniform rate, two separate bodies always cover the same distance if they move in one direction simultaneously from a given point. Why does not one move farther than the
other? Or in other words, there is a certain relation in Nature which causes
certain things to occur concurrently, and which establishes a definite quality
in certain processes whereby they occur in a fixed manner presenting them to
our perception at a time when we are not perceiving corresponding stages of
parallel processes. All this is the detached and abstract way of saying that
there is such a thing as absolute *Time*—that some things are more swift than
other things, and that the quality of swiftness is a definite one. Certain phenomena are evolutional, being characterised by continuous change. Such is
the growth and development of an organic being or race of organic beings.
We know that there is an absolute relation between this organic change and
such changes as that of our planet's position in space, or of the place of some

known star. We know that this organic change can be ranged by the side of other phenomena and found to conform to certain laws of uniformity. When the birth of two children reaches our perception simultaneously, we know that no matter what the subsequent conditions attending each, the future steps of their development will exhibit a correspondence. We know that there are no conditions whereby one will present himself to our perceptions as a child side by side with the presentation of the other as an adult. In other words, the development of organic beings is measured by a certain inexorable law of duration which we must call something—and might as well call *Time*. If our senses are not reliable in informing us of the various time-relations; if there is no such thing as order and precedence as we know it, then our perceptive apparatus is strangely out of harmony with that regularity which seems omnipresent in the cosmos. Einstein tears down more than he realises! For my part, I cannot say that my conception of Time is at all shaken. The contrary evidence cannot outweigh the vast bulk of perfectly consistent and intimately correlated evidence in support of the generally accepted notions.

Much the same thing applies to space. We know that there is such a thing as distance. No matter how unreal the evidence of our senses may be, it is positive that the relation of Providence and Pawtucket is different from the relation of Providence and Appleton. No geometrical scheme can make it possible for a man to journey from Providence to Appleton with the same amount of energy which takes him from Providence to Pawtucket, or to reach Appleton with a perception of as little change in the position of the sun and stars as that experienced in reaching Pawtucket. In other words, it takes more time and energy to get to Appleton than to get to Pawtucket; shewing that Providence and Appleton have a fixed relation which is different from the fixed relation of Providence and Pawtucket. Nothing can controvert this—the evidence of the human senses cannot be made to vary, so that even if they are delusive, a true difference exists in the same ratio as that which appears to exist. Now what applies to this small globe applies as well to outer space. By methods as definite and conclusive as those which demonstrate terrestrial relations, we have established a knowledge of certain celestial relations. We know, for example, that we are nearer the sun than Saturn is; and we know that this relation is of exactly the same sort as that involved in terrestrial distances. The solar system is positively no illusion—its dimensions exist in *exactly* the same absolute manner as those of a small orrery standing on the neighbouring table. As the ball of the orrery representing Jupiter is to the ball of the orrery representing Mercury, so *in every respect* is the actual planet Jupiter to the actual planet Mercury. There is positively not the least ground for denying this exceedingly obvious and overwhelmingly supported truth. So far, so good. Of course, the facilities for measuring siderial space—parallax and spectrum displacement, are less direct than those available for measuring the solar system. In the latter case, there are means of confirming the parallax results, and the conditions for noting parallax are much more favourable. But the perfect consistency of the results which have been attained, and the prodigiously great probability—practical certainty—that all known laws are not arbitrarily and abruptly broken off at some definite point at the artificial "boundary of the solar system", make it impossible for us to doubt seriously the reality of space and magnitude as universal, cosmical things. That a definite order which holds good so far as we can see should break off just beyond our perception, is inconceivable. How odd that the limit of familiar nature should coincide so exactly with the limit of our perception! Altogether, no really open mind can conceive of any boundary to space. Space and distance are proven to be real things, and this having been proved, it is impossible to limit them. The relation of Providence to Appleton has a positive analogue in the relation of the earth to the sun, and to deny that the analogy cannot extend to the relation of the solar system to Canopus would be puerile. So while freely conceding Einstein a place among real scientists, and eagerly looking for truth in his observations upon light, I must respectfully decline to take seriously his attack upon the fundamental structure of all things. He has not shewn us, or at least the prevalent articles on his system have not shewn us, any definite thing about our sense which justifies our substituting for recognised perception some equally uncertain and much less probable alternative series of perceptions. I await further light.

As a closing word on Einstein, I will add that many scientists reject his speculations *in toto*, believing that even the observed deflection of starlight during solar eclipses is due to refraction by some hitherto unsuspected outer atmosphere of the sun. This may prove the end of all the perplexity—an end reached by the complete rejection of Einsteinism.

I cannot resist taking a fling, at this point, at Galba's too hasty mode of jumping at conclusions. (Pardon the awkwardly repeated *at's!*) He confidently states that Grandpa cares no more for astronomy because no mention has been made in these epistles of the silly maunderings of "Prof." Porta.[7] Really, Child, I thought better of yuh! It never occurred to me to mention something which by its extravagance and baselessness is altogether excluded from serious thought, and I am honestly surprised that one with Galba's vast store of information should accept anything like the Porta farce as being in any way connected with sober astronomical matters. To be blunt, there was nothing in Porta's outburst to capture the attention of a real astronomical student for so much as a second. It was pure amateur charlatanry, since anyone having a primer knowledge of plaentary motions realises that combinations almost as "ominous" as that of Dec. 17 are of constant and un-disastrous occurrence. Searching history for precedents; one can easily see that no conspicuous weather perturbations have attended these groupings of the planets. Moreover, the large planets move so slowly, that the practical effects of the "pull" would have been manifest long before December in this particular case.

Hadst thou been exercising thy usual alertness, O Babe, thou couldst have detected the earmarks of charlatanry in the extravagant *language* of the "Professor". (Who is an unknown amateur with a little home-made tin telescope and a few old almanacks, out somewhere on the Pacific Coast.) Pipe this "give-away" flourish—cheap stuff:

> "Owing to a strange grouping of six mighty planets, such as has not been seen in a score of centuries, the United States (why only the U.S.?) next December will be swept by the most terrific weather cataclysm experienced since human history began.
>
> It will be caused by the hugest sun-spot on record—a sun-spot that will be visible to the naked eye. (How wonderful!)
>
> Since men first began to make a record of events, no sun-spot has been large enough to be seen without the aid of instruments. (Haw! Ya damn liar, there have been dozens! I've seen one myself, and such things have been announced in the papers scores of times within the past decade.) This one will be.
>
> The sun-spot that will appear December 17, 1919, will be a vast wound in the side of the sun. (Ya fathead, sun-spots never appear suddenly, in one day—they form gradually, developing in intensity like cyclonic storms.)
>
> It will be a gigantic explosion (sic) of flaming gases, leaping hundreds of thousands of miles out into space. It will have a crater large enough to engulf the earth, much as Vesuvius might engulf a football. (Ya poor boob, any ordinary sun-spot is like that! I knew as much when I was eleven years old—wonder how *old* you are, Porta old sport?)
>
> Such a sun-spot will be rich enough in electro-magnetic energy to fling the atmosphere of our planet into a disturbance without precedence (spose ya mean *precedent*, ol'scout!) or parallel." (O mother, shoot me while I'm happy! If every spot that size could do all that harm, we'd be havin' cataclysms 'bout every year!)

Well, Kid, is this enough nonsense to quote? An' tuh think you expected Grandpa to discuss this seriously in the GALLOMO! Only one person ever mentioned this thing to me—a mediocre correspondent who sent me the clipping of the prophecy wherefrom I quote. I replied in explanatory vein, but never thought of mentioning it to a guy of Mogal's mental calibre! Later I saw some clever spoofin' about the thing in the papers, but no one took the affair to heart. The best comment I saw was in the CLARION—young Keller gave the event a witty write-up. It seems that some sensationalist must have magnified the Porta prophecy to a prediction of the end of the world—though I never heard that till I saw the CLARION. One word more, O Boylet. Not long ago I saw an item about Porta's claim that present weather conditions had verified his raving. Haw! We've had some weather, all right, but Porta said it was coming from a sun-spot—and *there ain't been no big sunspot!* Porta's claim of "verification" is about as sound as the claim of the average charlatan!

I can imagine that B. L. T.[8] and his contribs may have had a good time about the joke, and wish I had seen some of the colyum matter published during the crucial period.

Speaking of astronomical things—is either of youse guys interested in (a) the supposed new trans-Neptunian planet, (b) the talk of telegraphic communication with Venus or Mars, and (c) the Goddard plan for sending a rocket to the moon? If so, just speak up! Grandpa has heaps to say about all these things!

T'anks fer de remarks on "Dagon", kid! I rather liked that thing myself. It was written in 1917, and is the second tale I wrote after resuming my fictional pen after a nine years' lapse. I think I told youse ginks that I quit writing fiction in 1908, despairing of my ability to shape anything with the grace of a Poe. I went over all my old MSS., bade most of them a last farewell, and saved out only two—"The Beast in the Cave", written in April, 1905, when I was 14 years and 7 months old, and "The Alchemist", which I had just finished. Thereafter I sent in "The Alchemist" for a credential; thinking that in an immature organisation stories might be better appreciated than verse or essay matter. I never expected to see that published, but later the chance came, and I tinkered with it a while, preparing the slightly revised version which appeared in 1916. So far I had never thought of resuming my old pastime. But then I chanced to send Culinarius "The Alchemist", and he immediately told me that fiction is my one and only province! Mildly amused, I sent him the "Beast", which he snapped up as though it were worth printing.[9] My stock of tales was now quite exhausted, but Cook kept urging me to improve my supposed gift for weird tales, so I decided to revive the old atmosphere. For a long time I was too indolent to do anything, but one June day in 1917 I was walking through Swan Point Cemetery with my aunt and saw a crumbling tombstone with a skull and crossbones dimly traced upon its slaty surface; the date, 1711, still plainly visible. It set me thinking. Here was a link with my favourite aera of periwigs—the body of a man who had worn a full-bottom'd wig and had perhaps read the original sheets of *The Spectator*. Here lay a man who had lived in Mr. Addison's day, and who might easily have seen Mr. Dryden had he been in the right part of London at the right time! Why could I not talk with him, and enter more intimately into the life of my chosen age? What had left his body, that it could no longer converse with me? I looked long at that grave, and the night after I returned home I began my first story of the new series—"The Tomb". My narrative pen was very rusty—believe me, boys, very rusty indeed! To drop back into the forms of fiction was exceeding hard after nine quiescent years, and I feared that the result would be the limit of absurdity. But the spell of the gruesome was upon me, and I finally hammered out the hideous tale of Jervas Dudley. At last—a Poe again! Honestly, I was afraid to send the deuced thing to Cook—especially afraid because he had himself just begun to write stories again after an eleven year lapse, and said he had lost all his talent. I really felt that the new attempt was inferior both to the "Beast" and "Alchemist". Meanwhile I had been reading Poe again—for about the ten millionth time. The new or rather revived mood was hard to dismiss, and after limbering up my style a bit with practice work I perpetrated "Dagon" in August. To me it seemed better than "The Tomb"— smoother, less halting and angular. I felt that my practice had done me a bit of good. Meanwhile Cook paid me a personal call—in September. We talked about everything under the sun, and in observing some little rusticities and plebeianisms in his dress and demeanour, I lost some of my awe for his fictional greatness. Before he bade me a reluctant farewell, I had placed the manuscript of "The Tomb" in his hands—not being quite ready to part with "Dagon", which I was still polishing in places. With eagerness I awaited Cook's verdict on my revived art—and fancy my delight when he wrote enthusiastically, saying my new tale immeasurably surpassed all my juvenile attempts, and declaring he would print it in his de luxe MONADNOCK at some indefinite future date! Tickled, I at once began work on "Psychopompos"—as yet unable to cast off my beloved heroicks altogether, even in fiction. Duties pressed, and I worked slowly. "Psychopompos" was abandoned midway, and not resumed till the summer of 1918, when I sent it to Cook and received a glowing acknowledgment. My egotism was now becoming almost Galpinian again, and I hustled with a new yarn—"Polaris"—which you fellers saw before anyone else. That really was an important milestone in muh brilliant career—for its unconscious resemblance to the work of Dunsany is all that finally led to my acquaintance with that then unknown source of inspiration. My next job was more mechanical. A singular dream had led me to start a nameless story about a terrible forest, a sinister beach, and a blue, ominous sea. After writing one paragraph I was stalled, but happened to send it to Mrs. Jordan. Fancy my surprise when the poetess replied that she had had a precisely similar dream, which, however, went further. In her dream a piece of the shore had broken off, carrying her out into the sea. A green meadow had loomed up on the left hand side, and horrible entities seemed to be hiding among the trees of the awful forest behind her. The piece of earth on which she was drifting was slowly crumbling away, yet this form of death seemed preferable to that which the forest things would have inflicted. And then she heard the sound of a distant waterfall and noted a kind of singing in the green meadow—at which she awaked. It must have been quite some dream, for she drew a map of it and suggested that I write a story around it. After a little consideration I decided that this dream made my own proposed story a back number, so I abandoned my plan and used my original opening paragraph in the new story. Just as I was speculating how I should infuse a little life and drama into the rather vague fragment, my mother broke down, and I partially broke down as a result of the shock. For two months I did nothing—in fact, I can hardly remember what I even thought during those two months—I know I managed to perform some imperative amateur work mechanically and half-consciously, including a critical report or two. When I emerged, I decided to add piquancy to the tale by having it descend from the sky in an aerolite—as Galba knows, for I sent the thing to him. I accordingly prepared an introduction in very prosaic newspaper style, adding the tale itself in a hectic Poe-like vein—having it supposed to be the narrative of an ancient Greek philosopher who had escaped from the earth and landed on some other planet—but who found reason to regret his rashness. As it turned out, it is practically my own work all through, but on account of the Jordanian dream-skeleton I felt obliged to concede collaboration, so labelled it "By Elizabeth Neville Berkeley and Lewis Theobald, Jun." I sent it to Cook, who will soon print it.[10] Then came "Beyond the Wall of Sleep"—written spontaneously after reading an account of some Catskill Mountain degenerates in a N. Y. TRIBUNE article on the New York State Constabulary.[11] By this time I was beginning to hear Dunsanian urgings, but I paid them scant attention. My next—"Juan Romero"—was written merely as a reaction from copying a dull yarn by Phil Mac. He had made such a commonplace adventure yarn from such a richly significant setting, that I yearned to shew what ought to be done with such a setting. Youze gazinks have seen both Mac's and my yarns. And then, having been told so often that my "Polaris" was exactly like Dunsany, I idly began to read "A Dreamer's Tales"! The rest is history—or would be if I amounted to anything. I had a new interest in life—EDWARD JOHN MORETON DRAX PLUNKETT. A week before I had wished to die—now I had something to live for! In succession have appeared "The White Ship", "The Street", "The Doom that Came to Sarnath", "The Statement of Randolph Carter", "The Terrible Old Man", and "The Tree"—this last being the living tree yarn which I choked off when I thought The Boy was going to publish his Bog-Batty without spoiling it with a realistic ending. In a word, Dunsany has restored my lost childhood, and I am again spinning stories for the pure fun of it—just as I used to do from 1897 to 1908. Viva Plunkett!

Well My Gawd—wot a lotta space I ben wastin' on muhself!! Galba, your introspection and autobiographical fluency is ketchin'! By the way—my Dunsanian library is getting enlarged. My mother has just given me "The Gods of Pegana", and as a token of gratitude for lending her the "Dreamers' [*sic*] Tales", Miss McGeoch has just ordered Little Brown & Co. to send me the Bierstadt biography—"Dunsany the Dramatist"![12] That's wot I calls high int'rust for merely lendin' a small book, believe muh! Now I'm gonna lend the Tales to Cook—wonder if he'll print me a CONSERVATIVE for the favour? As to professional publication of the fabulae Theobaldianae as a book—ferget it, kid! Upstarts and nobodies have to financc their own books—I know, because Sherman, French & Co. made me what they called an "offer" after reading my ode for Jul. 4, 1917, in the NATIONAL MAGAZINE.[13] And I hain't so anxious to squirm into the publick eye that I'd risk six hundred iron men on a damn fool scheme that would never pay. No, gents, I ain't got no ambition whatsoever! The older I grow, the more futile life seems to me. What does fame mean? What would I do with it? Would it make any difference to me if my work were mentioned in the ATLANTICK and the leading reviews? It would be fun at first, but I'll wager I'd be tired of it all in two weeks. Life is an empty thing, and if one can keep reasonably contented, and dismiss thoughts of suicide, he ought to be satisfied. I write what I feel like writing because I feel like it. The writing is all the fun—I am even getting less eager for amateur publication. To think out a plot and raise in fitting language some image of horror or fantasy—that is now my favourite indoor sport. To prove that my words are true—I have not even tried to place "Sarnath" anywhere![14] If I can extract a good word from a few gazinks—Mogal, Loveman, Cook, or Morton, my egotism is entirely satisfied. For the publick I have only profound contempt—dear, dear, how theatrical that sounds! Oh, b.t.w.—at the repeated nagging of my aunt I sent "The Tomb" to THE BLACK CAT, and received it back in a month with nothing but an insulting printed rejection slip. I am not sorry for the incident, for after this I can with clear conscience turn a deaf ear to all who urge me on toward publicity!

Concerning radicalism—I see no excuse for tolerating it in any form. The more radicals are allowed to utter both orally and in print, the quicker their nasty doctrines will spread. Cut off their advertising, and a good work is done. I wished to suppress the Wahlstrom article in THE CREDENTIAL, but Mrs. R. insisted on its retention with a footnote—and that footnote has aroused Campbell.[15] Another time I would withdraw all support from THE CREDENTIAL unless the offending article were removed. As it is, I am going to have a word to say about Campbell's position—am going to tell him he ought to be ashamed of himself. This reminds me—I have recently joined the Loyal Coalition of Boston, which is fighting the Sinn Fein movement in America, and wish youse guys would join also.[16] Any contribution of a dollar or more makes you a member. The object of the Coalition is to combat with propaganda the deadly and insidious campaign of Irish hyphenates to intimidate our venal and vote-craving politicians into recognising the mythical "Irish Republic" and thereby committing an international crime against that friendly power and motherland whose continued friendship means more to civilisation than anything else. Few realise the perilous nature of the agitation which criminals like that mongrel wretch De Valera are conducting against Anglo-American harmony. The passage of such a thing as that infamous Mason bill providing for diplomatic recognition of a seceded Ireland would be an indescribable calamity—it has been said that it would cause the British ambassador to withdraw. These Irish malcontents, with their vast power to "swing the Oirish vote", must be killed off or throttled somehow, and to do this the Loyal Coalition is leaving no stone unturned. Its battles with Hearst's slimy BOSTON AMERICAN are refreshing to read of. I have promised the Coalition to circulate their printed matter widely through the United, and intend to mail a judicious selection with every issue of the UNITED CO-OPERATIVE, besides having an anti-Irish editorial in that paper. I enclose one of the booklets—Gal to Mo, Mo to Lo. I am asking for its return because I have relatively few of these, and cannot get them at less than a nickel apiece. I wish the contents to reach as many amateur eyes as possible. Later I shall send both of you more matter—to keep. I suppose Galba will have a sneer ready—but these Micks have got to be crushed despite the sneers of all the 18-year-olds in or out of the nursery! If either or both of you can find time to help in distributing Coalition matter and fighting the Sinn Fein, let me know; and I will see that you receive a goodly supply of printed matter, including the booklet I am now asking you to return. I first heard of the organisation from Mrs. Jordan, who is so devoted to the cause that she does secretarial work at the offices two or three days every week without remuneration. I later heard of it from Miss Hamlet,[17] whose aunt is equally active in its behalf. It certainly deserves all the support anyone can give it, for the Sinn Feiners in this country are a devilish force; with dangerous opportunities to influence politicians. A word of advice to those who take Sinn Fein propaganda lightly: remember the German propaganda, and how some adjective-adorned fools laughed at it at first, and then kicked themselves when they found out how real a menace it was! As to prohibition—I doubt if any gradual process could have equalled the eighteenth amendment in real efficacy. If anything is too drastic it is not the amendment, but the Volstead law. Undoubtedly some of the provisions for drastic enforcement are excessive and troublesome to the medical profession; but when one reflects on the abuse of privilege sometimes practiced by that same profession, one is less sympathetic. I doubt if any reaction of dangerous strength could ever develop against the amendment, because the whole question is so infinitely less grave than other matters confronting the country—matters involving the existence of all civilisation. There will never be harmony during the present generation, but when a new generation, largely unused to drink, grows up, I fancy that pro-liquor sentiment will sink to a minimum. Galba's rage and disgust at the prohibition of bibulous idiocy in the individual seem to me ill-founded. The number of drunken men must be reduced, irrespective of principle. O Principle, how many sins are committed in thy name! A man who gets drunk is not merely an idiot but a potential menace to society. Drink has turned law-abiding men to murderers many times before, and will many times again. Let there be as few as possible of these cases. Of course, the manufacture and traffic is the great thing to strike at, but if you allow home brewing and distilling, and free possession of liquor, you will have a good-sized share of drunkenness left. For that matter—we still have. But the more firm the law the less we shall have. Remember that all the object of this prohibition reform, however the movement may assume various aspects in its various phases of operation, is this: *to keep men from becoming intoxicated.* Anything tending toward this is proper. Anything tending in an opposite direction is mere sophistry.

I was afraid those disjointed things bored you, but since they seem not to have done so, I will give you a few more, as I have recorded them for future fictional development in my commonplace-book. Remember, gents, that these crude sketches are the mere dreams themselves, not the stories. I relate only exactly what I dreamed, not what I am going to build up around the dreams.

## I

I was walking or rather wading through a seemingly interminable and treeless marsh, under a leaden sky. My companion was an old man—a man so old that he frightened me, although I felt that I knew, or had once known him. His white hair streamed about his shoulders, and his beard nearly trailed the ground. Despite his age, he was stronger than I, for he set a pace that fatigued me. Then suddenly I saw a lonely house upon the horizon ahead. It was a very ancient house—a New-England farmhouse of the type built from 1640 to 1680, with a peaked and exceedingly steep roof, and shingled over all its surface. It appeared to be rotten—in the last stages of decay. As we approached the house, the old man said to me, "It has not changed". I did not reply. Then he said, "For two hundred years it has not changed". I remained silent. Then he said, "You were foolish to wait and be re-born; I am wiser, and have lived all along." As he said this, I fancied I remembered him. He was now clad in a garment so discoloured and nondescript that I could not analyse it—it may have been a mere robe made of old burlap sacks sewed together—but as I have remembered him he was young, clad in high boots and red coat, and having a black full-bottomed wig and three-cornered hat. His face in this vague memory was smooth, although bluish from the shaven roots of a prodigious growth of beard. Then I said "It has not changed". We approached and entered the house, finding the interior a mass of fallen plaster and general ruin. Up a rotting staircase we began to climb, and the old man said, "We shall find it just as before". And I said, "The thing is still the same after two centuries, we shall find it above". Still we climbed. The house had but two stories, but the top of the ancient staircase seemed no nearer. Up, up, up—until the walls about us melted into mist and swirling cloud—yet ever on and up—on and up—"We shall find it as of yore—it has not changed".—on and up—on and up—and there ended the dream!

## II

I was in an ancient castle at the foot of a damp stone staircase. All about me were men-at-arms—every churl of them fast asleep! I seemed enraged, and shook several of them, yet could not rouse them. The castle seemed to be my own. I then clanked interminably up the staircase—for I had on armour and a heavy sword—until sounds from the plain below arrested my attention. Peering down through a narrow window I beheld our men of England, mounted, and with red tabards bearing the golden lions of Britain over their armour, in mortal combat with an unknown foe. The foe was also mounted and armoured, and wore tabards of yellow with red dragons depicted thereon. The fight grew demoniacally furious, and I experienced a wild desire to get into it. Then the leader of our men rode out before the army and challenged the leader of the foe to single combat. The challenge was accepted and the two armies drew back, leaving an open space between. The leader of the foe was a mighty figure in his heavy armour, and the fight was fierce. Finally the foeman was unhelmeted by our leader—*but beneath that helm there was no head.* At this moment the whole force of the enemy seemed to melt from sight, and I also felt a change. No longer was I at the window, but on an horse before the ranks of our men, a gigantic sword unsheathed in my hand. At this point I remembered the window on the staircase, and recalled with a start that the face of our leader had been the exact replica of my own. I glanced about, and on my left saw the form of a vast and interminable castle whose turrets reached up into the clouds beyond visibility. Then the dream abruptly changed, and though I did not awake, was conscious of drifting down some hideous stagnant river in a rotting boat, between terrible overhanging cliffs of basalt. There was no wind, and I wondered why I moved down so still a stream. The insects were of strange form, and made me shudder as their numbers increased and they began to light all over me—I had been sleeping at my table, my head resting on my arm.

### III

I was in a museum of antiquities somewhere in Providence, talking with the curator, a very old and very learned man. I was trying to sell him an odd bas-relief which I had just modeled myself from clay. The old man laughed at me, and asked me what I meant by trying to sell a new thing of my own workmanship to a museum of ancient things. I answered him in words which I remember exactly—a rare thing for me. Usually I recall no exact words beyond isolated sentences from my dreams. I said:

"Why do you say that this thing is new? The dreams of men are older than brooding Egypt or the contemplative Sphinx, or garden-girdled Babylon, and this thing was fashioned in my dreams."

Then the curator bade me shew him my product, which I did. It was of old Egyptian design, apparently portraying priests of Ra in procession. The man seemed horror stricken, and asked in a terrible whisper—"WHO ARE YOU?" I told him that my name was H. P. Lovecraft—adding that I was the grandson of Whipple V. Phillips, who I thought would probably be better known to a man so old. He replied "No, no,—*before that!*" I said that I had no memories before that save in dreams. Then the curator offered a high price, which I refused; because I saw from his face that he meant to destroy my sculpture as soon as it was his—whereas I wished it hung in the museum. My refusal clearly perturbed the man, who asked me to name my own price. Humorously, I cried "One million pounds sterling!" (currency mixed up!), when to my amazement the old man did not laugh, but looked only more deeply worried. He had taken me seriously! Then he said in a perplexed, baffled, frightened tone, "I will consult with the directors of the institution—please call a week from today." I do not think the dream ended there, but I recall nothing beyond. My remembrance of dreams is often affected by a sort of sense of unity—I can recall only things which have a connected sequence, hence my narratives stop as soon as the main subject is exhausted. Dream II in this letter is exceptional in this regard.

But enough of dreams. When the weather is hottest, and I am therefore at my best, I shall weave many of these nocturnal phantasies into short stories, though I am aware that the amateur press can never accomodate them all, especially now that Culinarius hath failed us. And speaking of stories— Mocrates, never mind about Mocraftising that "Beyond the Wall of Sleep" of mine. The comparative comment of Loveman, Morton, and other authorities places it so much below "Dagon" that I am sure you could not possibly have any success with it. Try "Dagon", if you want a story to experiment on. My British recruit, James Hull Goss—who is a teacher—says that he has taken the liberty to try to place "Beyond the Wall of Sleep" in some British professional magazine without securing my permission. Nice fellow, Goss, but he doesn't know what a hopeless task he hath undertaken!

Some diary! Well, I got news this trip, fellers! EDWARD JOHN MORETON DRAX PLUNKETT, 18th BARON DUNSANY, is the 1920 Laureate Judge of Poetry for the United Amateur Press Association! Yep—'s true! I thought of the thing a month or two ago, but did not dare write Ed. Then I decided that he might prove kind if the letter came from one with whom he had previously corresponded, so I asked Miss Hamlet to write him, which she did c/o the J. B. Pond Lyceum Bureau. For a long time no answer came, and we gave him up for lost. Miss Durr[18] asked me to find another judge, and I wrote a Capt. Fielding-Reid of Baltimore, one of the Bookfellows. But Friday Miss Hamlet received a telegram from Ed accepting the post!! The letter had chased him all around the British Isles, finally reaching him at his mother's place, Dunstall Priory, Shoreham, Sevenoaks, Kent. So the 18th Baron is ours!! Think what it will mean to have Lord Dunsany's name at the head of our Honorary Membership list all next year!! And that gives us an excuse to send him papers and the like!! I vow, I shall get out a CONSERVATIVE some time soon if I have to blow a safe to cop the coin—just for the sake of having something to send Dunsany.[19] I will take care that one of my Dunsanian tales, plus some critical puff of Dunsany himself, shall appear therein. At least, that is my momentary dream—probably I shall do nothing of the sort in reality! I hope the Convention will frame a nice resolution of thanks to send him. But amidst this burst of felicity I am not unmindful of the lowlier writers. A week ago I asked Fielding-Reid to serve, so the question naturally arose: what the hell shall I do if he accepts? I hate to offend any person who has graciously consented to perform a favour, and to shelve Fielding-Reid after asking him seemed rather awkward. To relieve this embarrassing situation I devised the following simple plan: to resurrect the obsolescent short verse class, enter the requisite number of "pomes" without the respective authors' consent, and send it to Fielding-Reid as if nothing had happened—he'd never know the difference, and would fancy he was doing just what we asked in the first place. I had said "short poems" anyway, so that he would not be discouraged from the task—providential adjective! So I have notified Miss Durr, and sent the list of entries to Mrs. Campbell,[20] requesting both to deal with Fielding-Reid as they would have originally. Thus if he accepts, we shall have an extra Laureate Class this year; though if he does not accept, the thing can be dropped. But believe muh, boys, I sure am tickled at Dunsany's acceptance. A damn good fellow, if ya ask me! Vivat Dunsanius!

Anent the Rt. Hon. Samuel Langhorn Clemens, I read the Bradford critique in the ATLANTICK,[21] and now have from the library both "What is Man?" and "The Mysterious Stranger". I never read any of his work before, on account of a sort of instinctive doubt of the solid worth of native American authors aside from those of the Atlantick Coast, but from considering the depth of philosophical reasoning in "What is Man?" I am coming to believe that Clemens was a genuine genius. Really, the old fellow agrees with me to a surprising extent regarding the human ape, which at once proves his greatness! I think I shall like Marcus—I may even read his humorous works.

As to any especial "creed of speculative scepticism", as Gahal-Bah describes his present need, I would advise Epicureanism as a base. That old geezer had the right idea, and drew from the right sources, largely my old friend Democritus. Read Lucretius' "De Rerum Natura" for the best possible exposition of this unsurpassed philosophy. There are many reasons why moderns can never surpass Epicurus, among them racial inferiority. We are certainly as far below the Greeks as, for example, the Mongolians are below us. That Pelasgian stock which gave rise to the dominant qualities of the Greeks and Romans alike has no parallel today. As to a creed of pure and absolute selfishness, O Child, I should have to ascertain exactly what you mean before criticising it. Certainly, selfishness is the only strong motive force in human life, but it must be restrained and guided. It is on this point that poor Nietzsche loses track of reason. The general tranquillity of that part of mankind which is most highly organised and sensitive is the logical aim of life. This really means the general tranquillity of the whole, for to concede unusual privileges to lower and coarser elements would not give them enough happiness to make up for that taken from elements which are more capable of feeling pleasure and pain. In order to establish this general tranquillity, everyone must sacrifice a little for the general good. If no one made sacrifices, no harmonious existence would be possible; if only a few made sacrifices, to benefit the majority, they would soon tire of it and revert to primal selfishness. And if the majority made all the sacrifices to benefit the few, the equilibrium would be equally unstable. A civilised order can be maintained only by the sacrifice of power by the ignorant and coarse, and the sacrifice of superfluous emotion by the educated and refined. The animal-like labourer must refrain (if he can be made to do so) from using his physical strength to overturn his superiors and rise to the leadership of a savage state, whilst the man of position must sacrifice the natural impulsiveness which if unchecked would cause conflict and wreck the cultural fabric which his mind has evolved. Neither, for purely selfish reasons, can afford to be selfish! If actually pays, in the end, to make the necessary small sacrifices. The Old Man in "What Is Man?" speaks the purest wisdom when he tells the Young Man: "Diligently train your ideals upward and still upward toward a summit where you will find your chiefest pleasure in conduct, which, while contenting you, will be sure to confer benefits upon your neighbour and the community." Yes, Sir—Clemens was a deep, realistic, and accurate thinker—I have done him injustice in neglecting him heretofore. These are the hard, cold, practical facts which the Christian twist to suit themselves, enshroud with a cloak of idealistic nonsense, and metamorphose into a code of abasement and self-inflicted misery. They scorn pleasure and speak of the "sanctity" of sacrifice. We exalt pleasure, but know that the greater pleasures are obtainable only by the sacrifice of the lesser; so that we recognise sacrifices as plain common sense rather than sanctity. And we know—or ought to know—that the greater pleasures are not hectic or animalistic things, but delicate aesthetic perceptions and unemotional tranquillity. Those are the only pleasures that last, and that are not conducive to subsequent pains which more than neutralise them. The hedonist, following Aristippus and Gidlow-Mills,[22] believes in seeking the wildest delights of sense, and in accepting all the consequences both to the individual and to society. That is what he calls "living"—the poor fish! He thinks the calm and unemotional Epicurean is only half alive; that he actually misses something in avoiding the violent alternation of emotional exaltation and depression. But it would not take long to demonstrate that the Epicurean loses less pleasure and escapes more pain in the long run, thus ending up with a better balance than the hedonist. And if the hedonist shall say to him that he has missed "life" by his even course, he can fling back the unanswerable reply—"Well, what the hell of it?" Pleasure is purely relative and measured by the attitude and emotional and intellectual organisation of the individual. Probably the sensual hedonist secures very little more pleasure at any time than the delicate and finely organised Epicurean who lives his calmer, more ethereal life; whilst of course he is continually subject to agonising emotional reactions and depressions which the colder man escapes altogether. As a matter of fact, the hedonist does not "live" any more than the Epicurean. He merely lives differently and on a less highly evolved plane. The hedonist has much more in common with the religious man than with the rational Epicurean. The crude emotional attitude of the Christian toward what he calls deity, and the spasms of sloppiness into which he goes about what he calls "universal love" are mere perverted manifestations of the same physical and psychic forces that drive the hedonist to his riot of apparently opposed but actually analogous sense-gratification. Above all this mess of emotional overdevelopment stands the Epicurean rationalist; his emotions educated down to insignificance, and his higher qualities cultivated for the benefit of himself and of society. I am aware that these candid opinions of mine are not very well calculated to pleasure either of my readers, but must enunciate them in the interest of truth and unprejudiced investigation. Galba will see that I am not likely to favour his plan of 'developing his emotional senses more strongly'. Believe me, kid, emotion is a false will o' the wisp. There is only one quality in man or for that matter in all the cosmos that calls for anything like worship. Only one quality which represents really exalted evolution and finely organised complexity of structure—and that quality is REASON. If thou wouldst know what is God, I answer thee, REASON!

## Notes

1. The reference is to William J. Dowdell of Cleveland, whom HPL had opposed for Official Editor of the UAPA in the election of July 1919 (see the essay "For Official Editor—Anne Tillery Renshaw," *Conservative*, July 1919).

2. I.e., *Dowdell's Bearcat*, Dowdell's amateur journal. The issue in question is that of December 1919, containing Loveman's poem "A Song of Chamisso's."

3. John R. Nicol. It is not known if HPL's poem appeared in the journal. The poem did appear in the *Silver Clarion* (March 1920).

4. See Galpin's "Some Tendencies of Modern Poetry" (*Philosopher*, December 1920; rpt. herein, p. 239).

5. Algernon Blackwood (1869–1951), *Incredible Adventures* (London and New York: Macmillan, 1914). In later years HPL revised his opinion of the volume, regarding it very highly.

6. Burton Rascoe (1892–1957), journalist, critic, and editor who was literary and drama editor of the *Chicago Tribune* (1912–20) before going to New York to work on several newspapers there.

7. Albert Porta, a seismologist and meteorologist, announced that the conjunction of six planets on 17 December 1919 would "cause a magnetic current that would pierce the sun, cause great explosions of flaming gas and eventually engulf the Earth." His announcement resulted in worldwide panic, isolated outbreaks of mob violence, and several suicides.

8. "B.L.T." refers to Bert Leston Taylor (1866-1921), American journalist and author of the "A Line o' Type or Two" column in the *Chicago Tribune* (1909–21).

9. "The Alchemist" appeared in the *United Amateur* (November 1916) and "The Beast in the Cave" appeared in the *Vagrant* (June 1918).

10. HPL and Winifred V. Jackson, "The Green Meadow"(*Vagrant*, Spring 1927; as by "Elizabeth Berkeley and Lewis Theobald, Jr.").

11. "Beyond the Wall of Sleep" (*Pine Cones*, October 1919). The article HPL referred to is "How Our State Police Have Spurred Their Way to Fame" by F. F. Van de Water, *New York Tribune* (27 April 1919): Sec. VII, pp. 2–3.

12. Edward Hale Bierstadt (1891–?), *Dunsany the Dramatist* (Boston: Little, Brown, 1917; rev. ed. 1919 [*LL* 91]).

13. HPL's poem "Ode for July Fourth, 1917" (*United Amateur*, July 1917) had been reprinted in the *National Magazine* (July 1917).

14. "The Doom That Came to Sarnath" eventually was published in the *Scot* (June 1920).

15. Evidently a reference to the *Credential* (April 1920), an amateur journal of which Anne Tillery Renshaw was editor and HPL assistant editor. It featured the "credentials" (proofs of literary ability) of new members. HPL refers to an article by Emil C. Wahlstrom of Dillon, Colorado.

16. On this subject see further HPL's "Lucubrations Lovecraftian" (*United Co-operative*, April 1921).

17. Alice M. Hamlet, an amateur living in Dorchester, MA, had introduced HPL to the work of Lord Dunsany.

18. See letter 3, n. 13.

19. HPL did not in fact issue a *Conservative* between July 1919 and March 1923.

20. Eleanor Barnhart Campbell of Ridgefarm, IL, who was Laureate Recorder for the UAPA in 1919–20.

21. Gamaliel Bradford, "Mark Twain," *Atlantic Monthly* 125, No. 4 (April 1920): 462–73.

22. See letter 2 n. 25. Gidlow had written an article, "Life for Life's Sake" (*Wolverine*, October 1919), advocating a hedonistic attitude to life. HPL responded with "Life for Humanity's Sake" (*American Amateur*, September 1920).


[9]    [To the Gallomo]    [AHT]

Friday, Sept. 3, 1920

ON A GRECIAN COLONNADE IN A PARK[1]

From the green shore the gleaming marble towers
        Against the dusk and verdure of the trees;
Beyond, there rise the odours of rare flow'rs
        To swell the fragrance of the Eastern breeze.

That breeze, which o'er Hymettus' slopes hath play'd,
        Finds beauty here, like that it fondled there;
And to these scenes, in classic semblance made,
        Adds the old magic of the Grecian air.

In the calm twilight, as the hush'd wood
        Darkens the mystery, obscure and deep,

Forgotten shadows come to dream and brood,
　　Wak'd for a moment from Elysian sleep.

The dim past beckons thro' the marble gate,
　　Stately and silent, distant and divine,
While the still pool reflects a duplicate
　　Within its depths—a shadowy ocean shrine.

Once in the gloom beyond that porch of white
　　I heard a murmur of ethereal sound,
And seem'd to see, as by some eery light,
　　A shimm'ring band, with woodland myrtles crown'd.

The waters, too, a strange enchantment breath'd,
　　And old, old thoughts rose spectral from the grave;
I saw Leucothea, in damp blossoms wreath'd,
　　And young Palaemon from his coral cave.

That shrine of white, deep in the glassy mere,
　　Upon my soul a charm resistless cast;
The dark gate lur'd, as to my straining ear
　　Came voices, calling from the cherish'd past.

And now at eve there lingers in my soul
　　The haunting mem'ry of that placid scene;
While in my dreams I strain to reach a goal
　　Where Glaucus waits me, clad in kelpy green.

The portal calls; beyond that wat'ry door
　　Lies all the bliss my heart hath ever known;
The past is there—yet I stand on the shore
　　In the cold present, alien and alone.

So as pale forms by sunken altars praise
　　Deserted gods of years remote and blest,
I, too, shall tread again those ancient ways,
　　And in the templed deeps sink down to rest.

HENRY PAGET-LOWE

I am interested to hear of the Mocratic experiments in road construction, an art dear to the Romans, and invaluable in the extension of empire through easy communication. I am myself no viafactor, though I have in winter made efforts to qualify as a nivicide; and next to making a road, I fancy it is a good distinction to be an effective clearer of roads. My days of manual exertion were in my youth—what pride I took in my little world in the vacant lot next the house! When I was very small, my kingdom was the lot next my birthplace, 454 Angell St. Here were trees, shrubs, and grasses, and here when I was between four and five the coachman built me an immense summer-house all mine own—a somewhat crude yet vastly pleasing affair, with a stair-case leading to a flat roof from which in later years I surveyed the skies with my telescope. The floor was Mother Earth herself, for at the time the edifice was constructed I had a definite purpose for it. I was then a railway man, with a vast system of express-carts, wheelbarrows, and the like; plus some im-mensely ingenious cars made out of packing-cases. I had also a splendid en-gine made by mounting a sort of queer boiler on a tiny express-waggon. The new building, therefore, must needs be my grand terminal and roundhouse combined; a mighty shed under which my puffing trains could run, even as the big trains of the outside world ran under the sheds at the old depots in Providence and Boston—depots long since razed to the ground to make way for the Union, Back Bay, and South Stations of today! So the building became in familiar household parlance "The Engine House"—and how I loved it! From the gate of our yard to the Engine House I had a nice track—or path—made and levelled for me; a continuation of the great railway system formed by the concrete walks in the yard. And here, in supreme bliss, were idled away the days of my youth. As I grew older, I took the road and its buildings more and more under my personal management. I began to make repairs myself, and when I was six I constructed many branch lines. Once I carefully laid track with wooden rails and sleepers—forgetting the trivial detail that I had nothing to run on it! But it looked nice, anyway! Then came changes—one day there was not any coachman to help me, whereat I mourned; but later on I had compensation—the horses and carriages were sold too, so that I had a gorgeous, glorious, titanic, and unbelievable new playhouse—the whole great stable with its immense carriage room, its neat-looing "office", and its vast upstairs, with the colossal (almost scareful) expanse of the grain loft, and the little three-room apartment where the coachman and his wife had lived. All this magnificence was my very own, to do with as I liked! Many were the uses to which I put that stable. The carriage room was now the main terminal of my railway, whilst in other parts were my office, theatre, and other institu-tions. But the call of the pastoral could not be resisted! Despite my new pos-session, my interest in the vacant lot and the Engine House was unflagging. One day I decided to alter my scheme, and instead of a railway system my domain became a pastoral countryside. I invited all the boys of the neigh-bourhood to co-operate in building a little village under the lee of the high board fence, which was in due time accomplished. Many new roads and gar-den spots were made, and the whole was protected from the Indians (who dwelt somewhere to the north) by a large and impregnable fort with massive earthworks. The boy who suggested that fort and supervised its construction was deeply interested in military things and followed up his hobby. Today he is a Lieutenant-Colonel in the U.S. Army, having attended West Point and served brilliantly as Captain and Major through the World War, being twice wounded. My new village was called "New Anvik", after the Alaskan village of "Anvik", which about that time became known to me through the boys' book "Snow-Shoes and Sledges", by Kirk Munroe.[2] As you see, I then read juvenile matter as well as the classics, and liked it! As the years stole on, my play became more and more dignified; but I could not give up New Anvik. When the grand disaster came, and we moved to this inferior abode, I made a second and more ambitious New Anvik in the vacant lot here. This was my aesthetic masterpiece, for besides a little village of painted huts erected by myself and Chester and Harold Munroe, there was a landscape garden, all of mine own handiwork. I chopped down certain trees and preserved others, laid out paths and gardens, and set at the proper points shrubbery and ornamental urns taken from the old home. My paths were of gravel, bordered with stones, and here and there a bit of stone wall or an impressive cairn of my own making added to the picture. Between two trees I made a rustic bench, later duplicating it betwixt two other trees. A large grassy space I levelled and transformed into a Georgian lawn, with a sundial in the centre. Other parts were uneven, and I sought to catch certain sylvan or bower-like effects. The whole was drained by a system of channels terminating in a cesspool of my own excavation. Such was the paradise of my adolescent years, and amidst such scenes were many of my early works written. Though by nature indolent, I was never too tired to labour about my estate, attending to the vegetation in summer, and shovelling neat paths in niveous winter. Then I perceived with horror that I was growing too old for pleasure. Ruthless Time had set its fell claw upon me, and I was seventeen. Big boys do not play in toy houses and mock gardens, so I was obliged to turn over my world in sorrow to another and younger boy who dwelt across the lot from me. And since that time I have not delved in the earth or laid out paths and roads. There is too much wistful memory in such procedure, for the fleeting joy of childhood may never be recaptured. Adulthood is hell.

Valete—

LO.

*Notes*

1. Published in *Tryout* (September 1920, as by "Henry Paget-Lowe").
2. Kirk Munroe (1850–1930), *Snow-shoes and Sledges* (1895).

[10]   [To the Gallomo]   [AHT]

Wednesday, August 31, 1921

Well, Gents, I can't tell youse how it delights yore Grandpa's heart to get back to the old GALLOMO mode of expression! Nevermore let the thought of dissolution cross the threshold of our minds, but let us remain for ever the Three Musketeers of amateur philosophy—one for all, and all for one!

Where shall I begin? I left Mocrates in the grey of the morning before I departed on that trip to Boston to meet Mrs. Renshaw, and Galba a few days later, just as I had received an urgent invitation to repeat my Hampstead-Haverhill visit. Verily, my mail records more of social activity than in the old days; though I shall soon plunge once more into the unbroken solitude of former years. It is strange to move among mankind—I smile sardonically as I mingle with the race of which I am only nominally and physically a part; for is not my spirit of the cold aether and the far spaces beyond the Milky Way? And yet I shall open my missive with more social chronicles—beginning with a simple event which pleased me more than any elaborate convention, yet which took me no more than twenty miles from home.

I have frequently lamented in my accounts of travel, the absence of that carefree kind of activity to which I was accustomed in youth. Amidst the formal and heterogeneous gatherings of amateurdom, I have longed for a return to boyish life; and for a mingling with crowds of youths only, bent on crude song and innocent merriment. You will recall that in describing my Allston-Boston walk of July 2, with Morton, Kleiner, and Dench,[1] I compared its songful stagness with the atmosphere of those older, happier walks with "the fellers" back in 1906, '07, '08, or '09, when I was young and all the world was gay. And now I am able to record a brief return to just that youth, with promise of occasional repetitions in the future! Truly, the hand of time is not proof against all the artifices of mankind!

On Monday, August 8, as I was splashing in the bathtub about 9 a.m., I was summoned on the telephone by my best of all boyhood friends—Harold Bateman Munroe, with whom I played joyously through long years of primary, grammar, and high school experiences or their chronological equivalents. Not for any mortal other than Harold, youse guys, and perhaps Klein, would I have stirred out of that refreshing thermal tide; but H. B. M. is H. B. M., so I made shift to conquer the difficulties of the situation as best I might. Attaining the instrument at last, I was rewarded for my fraternal devotion; for what should Harold propose but a trip through our boyhood play-scenes— East Providence, Seekonk, and Rehoboth—in his camouflaged Ford! Was I on? I'll enlighten the universe! In less than an hour we were spinning over the old Taunton Pike, drinking in the sights on which we had once gazed with the eyes of youth. Much was changed—green fields had here and there become tainted with the sties of foreign canaille, white houses had turned red and red houses white, and one old mill through whose rotting timbers we had played had collapsed from sheer old age,—but the spirit of rock-ribbed and immutable New-England was unconquered, and among remembered vistas we were boys once more. I had not been there for eight or nine years, and the happy sequence of old panoramas was paradise to me. There lay antique Rehoboth Village beneath its centuried canopy of giant oak branches, dreaming stilly in the green twilight it has known since Queen Anne sate on the throne; its simple houses ever the same, and its soul lingering in the past. There too lay the hills and the woods where Indians and Englishmen once fought, and where in our time we too fought showy frays; happy legions with the blood-thirstiness of boy-barbarians. Our ride took us to sleepy Taunton, a city un-changed since the forties, where a boy who had run away to Civil War might return and find nothing strange save the trolleys on the old horse cars. And as we returned, we resolved to visit the most sacred shrine of all, that spot on Great Meadow Hill where we had made a clubhouse by enlarging an old wood-cutter's shanty, and where we had for years assembled for rites of juve-nile fellowship. At Wheeler's Corner we turned from the level pike to enter the familiar rutted road and feel the familiar bumps—almost as bad in the Ford as on our boyhood wheels. Not a thing was changed—one might dream that scarce a leaf had fallen, and that the whole country had lain quiet under a spell until the coming of the old crowd to waken it. Up the long slope we jolted, past the last farmhouse—the mournful old Moore place where even the young children seemed old and wan with strange solitude—and finally attained the entrance to the forest that marks the neighbourhood of the summit. Leaving the Ford, we plodded along the stony path between the oaks and maples, marvelling at the new growth of trees which had been cut down in our time. The clubhouse, we soon realised, would no longer stand bleakly under the sun commanding a vast horizon; but would hide its old age in a leavy covert of young saplings. We speculated on how much of the edifice we should still find—Harold believed that only the fireplace—built with the aid of old James Kay the Civil War veteran—would be left standing. That was of great stones, and James Kay was a splendid mason who had worked on Caro-lina fortifications during the war. He died long ago, God rest him, but we felt that his work would survive his body. I, on the other hand, maintained that we might find some of the newer walls; not indeed the original woodman's hut, but the portion of new pine boards that we had added. And so, still speculating, we rounded the bend in the path and prepared to see what the monster Time might have left for us—when behold! Our youth came again upon us a flame. For there amidst the growing trees in awkward grace stood the symbol of our old days in wonted wholeness—*the boyhood clubhouse, erect in its tar-papered grotesqueness, and intact in every part through all the years!!* There was neither vandalism nor decay—the lock was gone, but that was all. Even the old pictures hung on the walls of this haunted place; this little world of the past, where even Time had eased his scourging in the absence of any human audience. What shadowy companies, moreover, could we picture about the grey cement heart where the pebbled initials G. M. C. C. still lay fixed as we had stamped them when it was new and wet! We seemed to see the old gang as it was—Ron, and Ken, and Stuart,[2] with the fresh faces and clear eyes of youth. They are not dead, but the boy in them is dead, so that their ghosts appear only in this silent and forgotten place. And as we gazed about, Harold conceived the idea of regaining for brief snatches the youth that we have lost. If all goes well, we shall refit this house of miraculous preservation, and bring back to it the men who were once the old gang; and perhaps on some nights in the golden autumn when the logs burn red in the stone fireplace the ghosts may pass back into the aging bodies to which they belonged of old, and the gang will live once again. And perhaps we shall sing in the olden way, and teach the birds of autumn the songs known to the birds of other autumns, and awake the old trees to memories of strains that stirred leaves now fallen. Then as we drive home in the late night the long road will echo as of old, and the voices of men shall sing the songs of boys—the songs of fifteen years ago—"In the Golden Autumn Time, My Sweet Elaine", "When the Mocking Bird is Singing in the Wildwood", and all the others that we learned with such care, and taught with such care to J——— S———, who was a trifle dull and who was our mascot. And perhaps we may some day have J——— with us at a session, and chide him as we go back for his slovenly dress, and straighten his tie and re-crease his felt hat as we approach East Providence Six Corners, where we are ashamed to be seen with him under the strong electric lights. Who the deuce says we are over thirty? He's a liar! But we shall be careful to include only such boys as have not imbibed too strongly the persistent delusion of having grown up. Only these shall gather as of old around the hearth and plan for the still distant years of adulthood. To others we shall seem odd—but what the hell do we care? Who would not be odd, if he might thereby re-enter the sealed door of his youth? But I'd better turn off the wosh.

My next trip, that of Wednesday, August 17, was of prosaic modernness. On account of the innumerable feuds amongst the Boston amateurs, Miss Hamlet insisted that I make a call at Dorchester separately from the main event of meeting Mrs. Renshaw. I missed two trains through the delay of a beastly headache, arrived just as Miss H. had departed on a trip to see poor old Mrs. Bell, and though I gave not a damn about it, was forced by an over-hospitable family to promise to make a special trip another day, lest the disappointment quite break their hearts! Gawd, what a lot of fuss over a poor old nobody—flattery is the universal order of things around Boston. What moved me to promise was the sight of my own work saved and pasted in a scrap book. It is not everywhere that Grandpa can pose as a great man! After I broke away from the cordiality of Elsinore, I made for the Curry School of Expression, where Mrs. Renshaw was holding forth, and there found the great leader, attended by her inseparable satellite Miss Crist. Mrs. R. was about as her pictures shew—stout and homely, but highly cultivated and as urbane an arguer as James F. Morton Jr. We departed immediately for Newton Centre, where Mrs. R. is visiting a sister of Miss Crist, arguing violently on the way about Haeckel, Hegel, Kant, Schopenhauer, Nietzsche, cosmogony, and other pleasant things. Mrs. R. is still an idealist, but I think she is waking up gradually. Geology has radically modified her formerly bland theism, and within a decade she ought to be a thorough materialist. She is not one to stand still—the only trouble is that she may move in a circle like Morton. The argument was civil throughout, and interrupted only during the wait at Trinity Place Station, where occasional passing trains would cut one or the other off just as the fate of the universe was being decided. At Newton Centre the first stop was made at the Wurtz household where Mrs. R. is visiting. Here Miss Crist was temporarily dropped, whilst the Renshaw-Theobald arguing team forged onward to Mortonstrasse 53, where Mrs. McMullen[3] had invited us to dinner. Here came quite a surprise for me, for despite the new feuds I found Mrs. Miniter there! She was very cordial, and just as flattering as ever. At dinner were Mesdames Renshaw, Miniter, & McMullen, to say nothing of Grandpa. I had the honour of telling Mrs. McMullen of her new laureateship, and she was vastly pleased. Later there arrived the Crist-Wurtzes and the Aonian W. V. J.,[4] the latter having an interesting tilt with Mrs. Miniter in cattishly civil dialogue whose iciness was delectably veiled with politeness. Afterward, I am told, Mrs. Miniter decided to introduce fiction into her account of the meeting; and has been telling the world that "W. V. J. did not speak to her for over an hour after she arrived". Hell, how the cats fight! But I am outside it all—a cosmic being apart, as 'twere. Although I am of course on the United or Jackson-McMullen side in any real warfare, I shall be civil to Mrs. Miniter as long as she is civil to me, despite the view of W. V. J. that I ought to observe a more marked coolness as a mark of United loyalty. No mere poet can tell me anything about United loyalty! Hell—who is the United anyway? (toot-toot!) But speaking of cats—the best one present was the real thing, a tiny grey kitten, part Angora, that a neighbour brought in at Mrs. McM's suggestion—Mrs. McM being aware of my predilection for the (genuine) feline species. He was a good double handful, with an inexpressibly pretty face and eyes, and a collar with tiny bells that tinkled as he cavorted with the innocent sprightliness of youth. Most of the time he sat in his Grandpa Theobald's lap, chewing either my waistcoat buttons or my fingers according to his juvenile taste. This neighbour also brought in twin collie dogs—an interesting pair, which completed rather a quaint menagerie. Conversation ranged from the grave and scholastic to the gay and humorous, and was diversified by songs by the two musical members—Mesdames McMullen and Renshaw. I was asked to sing, but knew enough to refuse. Among the subjects broached was a commercial arrangement whereby I might revise English themes for Mrs. R.'s classes at Research University—by mail, of course. That would not, perhaps, be as bad as Bush work if the pay were adequate. A wilder suggestion of Mrs. R.'s was that I write a text-book of rhetoric![5]

The riot broke up at 11:10, and I departed for my usual night train. The next evening Mrs. R. was to meet the Hub Club (whom W. V. J. and Lilian Middleton will no longer meet), and Mrs. Miniter invited me to stay over at 20 Webster, but I was wretchedly tired and decided to omit the sequel. I reached home at 1:20, drenched by a sudden shower which caught me just before I attained the portal. Mrs. R. later said she was surprised at my aspect. She had expected something conspicuously awkward, eccentric, and hermitish.

On the following Friday I received still another invitation, as Galba already knows. This time Hampstead and Haverhill again, by request of the super-hospitable Littles,[6] who so delightfully approximate the state of England's rural gentry. It was for a longer time than the other visit, but I compromised on two nights, and arranged to use the final evening on my homeward trip to discharge the debt of courtesy by calling at the Hamlet Castle. Leaving Providence Thursday morning at 11:00, I arrived in Haverhill at 2:15, and was met with a horseless carriage containing Miss Little, her mother, and a bearded and pleasant uncle whom I had not seen previously but whom I liked at once. In describing these rural magnates I am happily able to discard that tone of sarcasm with which I describe certain more urban amateurs; for verily, they are of the wholesome Saxon gentry that needs no apology or allowances. In a word, they are all right; of one's own sort, as it were. We first proceeded to 408 Groveland, where we found no visible Smithy.[7] We thought he was out, but later learned he was merely asleep. After that we visited picturesque Winnikenni Castle, a mock-chateau of ivied stone that crowns a noble steep. Here, in certain angles of the hoary wall, one's mind is wafted magically back to the tenth or eleventh century; and it should not surprise one to behold the wraith of some armoured knight or retainer pacing silently up and down the platform. Haverill is some town, we'll tell the world! After a long drive over gentle hill from parts of which spread wondrous panoramas of steeple-studded valley, we attained Little Manor once more, and I made at once for the crowded library. Later I saw strawberries growing for the first time in my life, and even condescended to soil my hands by picking some. In the evening I produced the binoculars, planisphere, and astronomical handbook I had brought with me, and sought by a flashlight's aid to ascend the neighbouring "Pinnacle" for purposes of celestial observation. It was a wild climb through the spectral wood in the dusk, the light gleaming fitfully, and the sentient boughs reaching out to claw at the faces of the travellers. And finally when the summit was attained, fancy my curses at discovering that the god damn sky had clouded up too much to permit of observation! The descent was accomplished by another route, including strange shadows where goblins danced in the shadow. Though the expedition was a failure, the climb itself may perhaps furnish an idea or two for a story. Next day I read some of my new hideous yarns aloud at the hillside camp, and received one good suggestion from the audience regarding the improvement of "The Outsider". Not that I hadn't thought of the point before, but I was not sure. In the afternoon an Haverhill trip was planned. First came Smiffkins, who had received the note I had put in his mail slot the day before, and who was ready and waiting under a gnarled tree. How I like that queer old cuss! He is in truth a wild woodland thing—a real faun if there ever was one—and if I were an artist I would draw him with goat's feet, or half merged into the trunk of some gigantic and shadowy tree. Among other things, he told me of a coming split in the National, engineered by the vindictive Hyde-Outwater gang[8] who were so beautifully licked at the Boston convention. Not that I relish seeing the enemy suffer—but this thing will not hurt the United any! Now who will call us the "Divided Amateur Press Association"![9] After Smithy came the big event—a trip through the museum of the Haverhill Historical Society. This is not supposed to be open Fridays, but the influence of the Littles is far from Little, and it was opened for the special benefit of the present expedition! Of all fascinating places, this comes near the top of the list. In its nucleus it is still a private Colonial mansion of brick, inhabited by the original family, whose head is the director of the museum. This family dates from the early eighteenth century, and its natural accumulation of rare furniture is more vital and time-annihilating than any formal collection in a more formal museum. Not least pleasing of the items is the lord of the manor himself, Leonard Smith, Gent., in whose blood is combined all the best strains of the land. In him we behold the true British Colonial—the purest of the ancient stock—and I found his conversation a delight; later telling the Littles that I like all Haverhill Smiths, both patrician and plebeian. I took a picture of Mr. Smith in his entrancing old-fashioned garden, and will shew you a copy if it turns out well. He is venerable, white-headed, and white-bearded, and a true artist in soul. His landscape gardens are a joy, and his interior decorations something to admire. Annexed to the old mansion is the new museum building, where repose a multiplicity of Merrimack Valley antiquities. One could stay in this paradise indefinitely, but other attractions called. On the premises, not far from the main buildings, stands a small white house of one story and loft. This is the ancient Ward house, built in 1640, and the oldest edifice of any kind I have ever beheld. The musty odour of the place is appalling, but deters no one from entering—for who would not like to stand within walls that were reared but a decade after the Massachusetts-Bay Colony was founded, and but a score of years after the first white pilgrim landed at Plymouth? On the wall was a framed copy of the MERRIMACK ADVERTISER for some date in 1815. There is nothing new under the sun—I noted a poet's corner with verse almost as bad as some of the stuff I revise! But who could tell in one letter—even a GALLOMO—of all that such a museum contains? It amused me to note that despite their influence none of the Littles had ever visited the place before. Only Miss M. A. Little made this trip, but now they are all going! It was now evening, an after a detour to the business section to pick up the younger Little sister the party returned to Little Towers. After dinner the family again demanded that Grandpa amuse them with some of his theatrical impersonations—and believe us, you'd never know the old man in some of the things they made him put on! In my acting days I went in for the heavy villainous stuff; but the Hampsteaders seem partial to the Julian Entinge stuff, and could not be satisfied till they had Grandpa laced into a hoop-skirt outfit with bonnet and parasol to match! Though it was hard to think of dialogue for such a makeup, they seemed satisfied with my improvisations; and compensated by prolonged applause for the injury inflicted upon my patriarchal dignity. The evening concluded with an attempt to solve a new checkerboard puzzle of Mr. Little's; and here I must confess that I failed as miserably as all the rest. I have asked them to let me know if they ever solve it. On the next and final day there was a morning session at the camp, during which I used my binoculars to sweep the valley below—to sweep yet not clean it, for what could need cleaning in a region like Hampstead? Believe Grandpa, but that panorama of spires and roofs amidst foliage is something which would make anyone but a hardened modern write heroick couplets indefinitely! I was surprised to note that the Littles had no telescope or binoculars, and that the younger sister had never used any before—strange are the lacunae of rural life. The noontide period was occupied in the construction of a cake by Miss Little for our friend Tryout—a masterpiece designed to outdo the one sent him some time ago by honest old Mrs. K. Leyson Brown. There was a large cake for Smiffkins himself and several little cakes for his grandchildren; and I am sure that poor Mrs. Brown's eclipse was complete! We took it to him on the trip which carried me to my train, and I had the honour of carrying the main cake and handing it to Tryout, thus obtaining an infinitesimal spark of reflected glory at the achievement. He seemed transported, and has evidently decided to immortalise the whole Little gens in his next TRYOUT, for he has just written me asking the name of the father—which is Albert, as I shall presently tell him. After the presentation I was whirled to the station and duly dumped, later puffing southward on the uncertain Boston & Maine amidst many courteous invitations to come again and often. Some hospitality! I am convinced that I am by nature a simple rustic, whose genuine aesthetic sympathies are excited only by rural virtues and scenery, and to whom the pastoral is therefore the only authentic medium of expression. My urbanism and sophistication are but an intellectual cloak assumed academically through philosophical conviction, and touching no spring of real creative art. I shall never really care for modernistic expression, no matter how long I try, for I am of the old order, with every perceptive faculty attuned to the old and simple images. After the country, the city seems cheap and tawdry to me—I can sneer loftily and intellectually at the ecstasy of a Nature-poet over a sweep of hill, but damn it all, that same view will move me to admiration when the alleged emotional stimuli of the modern and disillusioned poet leave me cold! I must stay in my room and keep my eyes from Nature if I expect to become truly sophisticated. Otherwise, I shall be strongly moved by things which are too simple to move a true poet of today. But stay! I must not display prejudice—and after all, the rural landscape would probably bore me to death after a week or two. Everything is a bore in the end.

And speaking of bores—as I puffed out of Haverhill the Hamlet call still lay ahead of me. I had given a forewarning that I might be "unavoidably" delayed till evening, and hoped my prospective hosts would not do anything elaborate—but Gawd 'elp us! When I finally reached there via B. & M., elevated, and surface car, I found that they had a near-convention staged for me! There was an ambitious dinner of lamb and sundry fixings, and many reproaches at my "unavoidable" tardiness. As a local delegate Miss Hamlet had unearthed a literary protege of hers—the Mildred LaVoie whose name has lingered inactively on our lists since 1916, and who is a young person of undistinguished aspect and ancestry; not uncomely, but more suggestive of the artless nymph than of the fictional titan. This quiet and unassuming individual writes stories, but is afraid to send them anywhere—even to TRYOUT—for publication; hence has remained an amateur nonentity for five years despite the efforts of Miss Hamlet to bring her genius to the world's notice. I was not very enthusiastic about the process of LaVoian assimilation till after the maid in question had departed, and Miss H. produced a story of hers which she had secured surreptitiously. Then I perceived that the work was not half bad in its way—shewing at least clear observation, command of detail, and a keener picture of the subject matter than mere words. It is surely worth printing, and I shall accomodate Miss Hamlet by placing it somewhere where its appearance will duly surprise its over-modest creator—Lawson's WOL-VERINE ought to stand for it.[10] But after all, I was paid for my politeness in making the Dorcastrian detour. Just before I beat it for the 11:45 I was given the loan of a new book which I am told is the most horrible collection of short stories recently issued! It is called "The Song of the Sirens", and is by one Edward Lucas White, who claims he dreamed all the ghoulish things described.[11] I have not yet had a chance to peruse it, but am expecting a fine time when I get around to it. Returning to the trip—I returned to the South Station via Andrews Sq. subway, and was home at the usual 1:20. I slept till the next evening, and am still drowsy from the three days unwonted exertion.

This ought to be enough of a social programme to hold me for a while—but Gawd 'elp us! when one gets to be a social butterfly the thing gets beyond one's control! Am now notified that I must act as an host next Saturday and Sunday or Sunday and Monday, when there will descend upon Providence no less a whirlwind than Galba's new friend and admirer, Mrs. Sonia H. Greene, the Champion Long-Distance talker of Muscovy and Lands Adjacent! What can one do to entertain such a human dynamo and phonograph combined is beyond me, but I must think of something lest a $50.00 Fund contributor be offended into financial sterility. Galba, yuh'd orta hear what she says about you in her latest 12-pager! If your ma don't watch out, she'll kidnap yuh! Galpinitis? We'll spill it to the solar system! I never before saw a nut quite like Mme. Greenevsky—it must be Slavonic blood! For pure hot air she may have rivals, but the joke is that there is sound sense and profound literary erudition beneath all the nonsense. So she thinks Grandpa is egotistical? Hell! That's what she told me at the convention—and then added that she never would have wasted her valuable time in trying to convert me if I were not an unusual specimen, or something like that. Her worst trouble is an absent sense of humour—the poor fish thought it was serious egotism when I told her that I despise all mankind and consider myself a cosmic intelligence aloof from the race. In letters Mme. G. is not at all egotistical—I was surprised at the Uriah-Heepness[12] of her written as distinguished from oral arguments. But Holy Yahveh, what floral rhetoric! However, let me not libel an honest and learned thinker, who is really the most remarkable accession which amateurdom has had for some time. Klei likes her, and calls on her often, though that may be partly due to her possession of a beauteous daughter who scorns the sedateness of our bookish Brooklyn bard, and who must therefore be a tantalising object to a professional heart-breaker like the rhythmic Rheinhart. Mme. Greenevitch is nothing if not generous—Monday I received from her a present of a new book, Shaw's latest emanation, yclept "Back to Methusalah".[13] Surely gratitude will impel me to forget the charge of egotism and be as courteous an host as possible—besides, philosophy and its great Appleton exponent will furnish an unlimited variety of topics for rational discussion. And despite the surface, there is no denying that Mme. G. *is* rational and highly cultivated to boot. I have just read proofs of my RAINBOW article, which consists of some cynical aphorisms culled from two letters of mine.[14] I fear this stuff will shock friend Mocrates—but it may help prepare him for the fuller shock of my "Confession of Unfaith" in Campbell's next LIBERAL.[15]

Friday, Sept. 12, 1921

Oh, Boy! Gents, yuh'd orta see Grandpa today! Am I a beauty? I'll tell the woild! From underneath my hair to a point perilously close to my left eye there stretches a beautiful and gory welt acrost me marrble brow, adding to muh classic features the one charrm they lacked beforre—the devilish scarriness of the pirate or Heidelberg duellist. What's the trouble? Some experience, boys! I'll hev ta write it up into a story—earthquakes, avalanches, and all that sort of thing. At about 6 a.m. yesterday morning, as I was concluding an all-night literary session at my desk, I stopped in the kitchen to secure my solitary second meal. Perhaps you know that I am a singularly light eater, taking but one full meal and one self-prepared cracker-and-milk lunch each day. Well, as I was a-sayin', this was the light second meal. I had sot muhself down at the table and was daintily toying with my epicurean repast, when I seemed to hear a sort of crackling sound, and saw a fine grey dust gathering on the board before muh. Before I could rouse my sleepy head to connected thought, something else happened to the aforementioned cranium—for suddenly and without further warning the roof of the cosmos busted up and fell on poor Grandpa!! Gawd, wot a cataclysm to spring outa nothin! Some last days of Pompeii! It knocked me flat down against the table, burying me and the latter in one indistinguishable heap of lava and scoriac chaos. Were I not possessed of a record-breaking shock of hair, which just now needs cutting at that, the moon would be laying pale lilies of light on dead Grandpa!!! As it was, I sure was sanctified with dust, albeit not star-dust. To lay all mystery and symbolism aside, what really happened was this: the plastering of the ceiling had perversely loosened and fallen from a point directly above the grey head of the lone diner! It was some wreck, take it from me! The room looked like devastated Belgium as I surveyed it through the curtain of blood trickling from my injured dome. But I managed to dig out, shake off the worst of the dust and debris, and finally free myself from the fine grains of plaster which had sifted all over me. Today I am very comfortable, relatively speaking. The wound is healing, but it sure is a thing of beauty! And soon a gang of plasterers will be at work—not on me, but on the room.

The Hampstead-Haverhill pictures are now done, and I will enclose some for Gallomonistick inspection—Lo to Mo, Mo to Gal, Gal to Lo. They will, I think, bear out my narrative in convincing you of the scenick beauty of southern New-Hampshire. The upper story windows of the "ell" of the house, as shewn in the picture, are those of the antique room I occupied—a room with not a fitting changed for 150 years. The vertical scenic view is that of the willow lane forming the subject of Miss Little's poem in a recent TRYOUT. In the next GALLOMO I shall probably enclose another set of pictures taken during the coming Greenevsky visit; pictures of more interest to Galba because of his acquaintance with their subject. I shall dodge the camera this time unless my gashed forehead returns to something more like normalcy. It would take a pirate's costume to give that scar an appropriate setting!

But enough of Grandpa's social whirl! As to the Galpinian satire about the fanciful kingdom—go to it, kid! You can make something of it if anyone could! I am getting too damned cynical to appreciate satire lately—I am so disillusioned about the institutions of mankind that the ridicule loses its point— why the hell should anyone *expect* the shams of statecraft and society to be true? Is it not a trifle naive to *ridicule* pomposity and pretence when there is nothing else in the world? It becomes, methinks, only the outer gods to judge man—and then may not the outer gods as well be hypocrites and fools? I dismiss life with one contemptuous "bah" and shrug of the shoulders—let the fools stew in their own lies and puerilities! "It is good to be a cynic. It is better to be a contented cat. It is best not to exist at all."[16] Boy, the cyanide!

This leads me—the subject, not the cyanide—to consideration of our little friend's code of philosophy as outlined on the 8½ × 13 GALLOMO sheet. I am asked to criticise it—but I can't, for it expresses mine own present views so closely that the difference is negligible. I can only endorse, and express my pleasure that once more the Galban and Lollian orbits should intersect. One cannot get beyond these simple assumptions and preferences without leaving behind the solid data of fact and experience. More elaborate and dogmatic systems may be beautiful, but they rest on thin aether. Like Galba, I have sympathy for reformers—and indeed, in my youthful simplicity I once had reforming tendencies myself. But lately I see the huge futility of it all, and must needs mix pity with my admiration. The world is a beastly mess, and will never be anything else. All that one may do is to train down the worst crudities for the same of smoother existence. As to the relative value of love and contempt, I am undogmatic. In me liking springs from two distinct sources—admiration for intellect, which is personal admiration, and admiration for picturesqueness, which is akin to aesthetic admiration. I like only great minds, or minds which are beautiful, picturesque, or individual in any way—even a comic way. The two kinds of liking are very distinct—the first is intense and fixed, and regards the object as a human being with dignity. I save this for a very few persons, most of them dead and famous, but a few living and acquainted with me, as Galba and Mocrates. The second kind is whimsical and impersonal—I do not instinctively recognise these non-great but picturesque minds as wholly human, and do not take them seriously; but am fond of them in a pictorial way—as I am of a landscape or a cat. My liking of this kind is variable, and more or less mingled with tolerance and even kindly contempt. I think of such minds as toys to amuse my fancy. Still, such likings are sometimes strong—it is thus, for instance, that I cherish my old pal Smiffkins of the TRYOUT, and poor Jawn Samples[17] of the austral backwoods. They are pleasingly quaint, and I like them because they please me and add to my sense of importance. They are like the grotesque vignettes in certain old books, or the gargoyles upon some antique cathedral. But the real article in liking is that which I possess toward Galmo, in whom I perceive the evolved minds that spell superiority, which is the only absolute value in the cosmos.

I perused with much interest the Galbanian "In Memoriam" and allied phenomena. Surely it is some hoax, and I am strongly tempted to use it despite an undeniable lack of enthusiasm concerning "The Decline and Fall of the College Library". Not that I fail to appreciate the excellence of that masterpiece—but the author is so great that it is overshadowed by his other and more titanic performances. Gimme more time to appreciate it, boy. My taste may clarify, and my point of view alter. I like the distinctly memorial part vastly—and the pome as well. I'll hold on to it a while and do some deciding—perhaps Gahal-Bah will find some Hastingian specimen even more clever than the "Decline". I have no cut appropriate for the thing, but if in his h. s. and college experience Galba has acquired any freakish looking half-tone from CLARION, LAWRENTIAN, or some such publication, I would be glad to use it. B. t. w.—"The Gods in the Gutter" is rather good—I never read much of Service,[18] but deem him very capable in his chosen field of ostentatious virility.

About the U. of Wis. course—Gawd, kid! D'ya wanta lap up the whole damn college? I tykes off me 'at to a bloke as can tackle a course like that! As to advice—who the deuce am I—a non-collegian—to pass judgment upon the studies of my betters? However, I should choose (in the order of the table) Jastrow's Psychology to French Poetry, Divine Comedy and Contemporary Philosophy to Genl. Survey French Lit., English Philology to Cont. Drama and Rise of Russia, Human Traits to Abnormal Psych.—and I guess this is all, the two other points being the same in both second year semesters. My main method of advising is to promote diversity and to minimise studies of a general literary nature which a mind like Galba's would hardly need in addition to his exhaustless general reading. But since all this pertains to an intellectual world far in advance of my meagre attainments, I would advise Gahal-Bah to go ahead and do as he damn pleases without listening to Grandpa's senile twaddle.

And now, Mawruss, mein knabe, I'm gonna get after you for an hasty judgment! Hee-haw! So Mocrates thought his Grandpa wrote "The Eye Above the Mantel"!!!![19] Sage, the only thing I did to that thing was to straighten out one split infinitive and improve one fanciful name. Otherwise the thing stands verbatim as written by its real author—a genuine human being without a pseudonym; a real, live boy of nineteen, about to enter his sophomore year at New York University—Frank Belknap Long, Junior, son of Frank Belknap Long, Esq., a prosperous dentist of 823 West End Ave., New York City. Young Frank is the latest of my adopted grandchildren, and is some kid, albeit hardly in the exalted Galpinian sense—or even the Spoerrian[20] sense. He is a true artist, and a devotee of Poe and America's older literature, and I think he is about to become a leading amateur. He is, moreover, our new First Vice-President. Yes, my son, Frank is no empty cloak for his Grandpa Theobald, but is a highly independent youth, wholly responsible for his own stories. I like "The Eye Above the Mantel" very much—so much so that I snapped it up for the Official Organ the moment Long sent it to me; but pray do not fancy I wrote it. There may be crudities— even Mocrates' objection may be partly valid, though that kind of "sensibility" belongs more to the languid effeminacy of Cowper than to the vigour of a Nietzschean,—but the whole is certainly a good job. Yes, a damn good job for a kid of nineteen!

And whilst I am in the mood for literary disavowals, let me chide Father Mocrates for a second hasty guess—that concerning "The Crawling Chaos".[21] Brudder, although I had a hand in that job, I swarta Gawd I didn't do more than half or three quarters of it. I thought I told you all about that composite piece work, but I must have been thinking of the earlier "Green Meadow". It is true that I once used the pseudonym of "Elizabeth Berkeley" in conjunction with its more rightful owner W. V. J.—in 1916 the name covered certain verses by both authors, in an effort to mystify the public by having widely dissimilar work from the same nominal hand.[22] But that is past history, and today Elizabeth ain't me at all, but exclusively my eldest daughter Winifred. Since Loveman rates "The Crawling Chaos" ahead of all my strictly original stories, and since Mo's friend thinks the author must be a real snowbird or hop-hound, it may be worth while to clear up the constituent elements once for all—so here goes, with documentary evidence 'n' everthin! The enclosed fragment of a Jacksonian letter, written late in 1918 or early in 1919, is the nucleus of the story. As you will perceive, the whole bizarre setting comes from an actual dream of the poetess whilst in the clutches of influenza. This element of illness may account for much of the fantastic colouring, though in actual truth no drug was administered. I have, I think, mentioned before, that the genius of W. V. J. can produce hideous conceptions far outdoing any of mine, and remaining ineffective solely because of their creator's singular helplessness in prose. This is one of them—others you will see in the remarkable CONSERVATIVE I am trying to get out. I kept this dream outline a long time without utilising it—for being basically egotistical, I put mine own work first. Finally, last December, the authoress became impatient about it, so I threw the story together in a hurry. The colouring impressed me as opiate, so I supplies the dopy prologue. Then in analysing the nature of the dream, I found that the dominant points were a hellish pounding and an encroachment of the sea upon the land. Using these two latter "starters", the denouement was fairly inevitable to me; so that although everything after the ninth line of page five in the printed version is my own, it is only broadly so; the impulse having been supplied by the original data. When I sent the finished story to W. V. J. I was amused by her idea that I must have actually seen the same supernal sights that she saw in the dream. Her overpowering imagination, conjoined to very scanty scientific attainments, makes her vaguely credulous of the supernatural; and she cannot get rid of the notion that there may be an actual region of dream and vision which can be independently and objectively seen by different individuals. In this case she declared that I had described details of the strange interior, and of the architecture of the dream-house, which she had plainly noticed but had not described to me; which to her is proof that a common dream experience must underlie the work of both collaborators. She does not realise that imagination can seize on new things and subconsciously project them backward into association with past things—just as all prophecies are written after the occurrence of the things prophesied. In the case of "The Green Meadow" I related to her a dream of mine, and she claimed to have had exactly the same dream, with a subsequent development which mine lacked. This was certainly her honest belief, yet I could swear that she had no such dream till she had seen my account. Then, doubtless, she did have the dream in its amplified form; automatically putting it backward in time when later thinking of it and repeating it. I will send the epistolary extract to Mocrates, who seems most interested in the tale. He can return it either directly to me, or to me via Appleton. And by the way—don't mention to W. V. J. that I sent the thing. She has a fad for destruction, and wishes all her epistles burnt without exhibition, though they are in truth far less slanderous than the presumably preserved GALLOMO. I usually comply with the wish, though in this case had to save this one sheet for the sake of the story. One more point—about that woshy paragraph which Mocrates cites. Here I plead guilty and have not the least excuse to offer. It is all in my own part of the story, and was slung in purely for verbal effect. Tinsel ornament pure and simple. I wanted something poetic and bizarre, and since the story wasn't mine, neglected to be particular. I am a damnably selfish cuss—don't ever expect me to be conscientious in a collaborated work! I'll write any old rot if I can escape responsibility for it, and frankly, I didn't think the "Crawling Chaos" was going to make such a hit that anyone would notice it. When I did that job my egotism was at its height over Loveman's praise of my "Nyarlathotep",[23] and I failed to see the real superiority in W. V. J.'s richly and exotically ornate dream nucleus. I looked down upon something to which I should have looked up! But Loveman took down my pride in short order!

I perused with much interest the account of Mocratic vacation activities, and congratulate our Sage upon his natatory exploits. Mocrates could be me awright—d—n me if I can swim a stroke! I always hated sea bathing, and have not voluntarily indulged in it since the age of nine. The only time I have been in bathing since is once when I was about 16 or 17—when I had to merge with the waters of a crystal lake in order to prove to the gang I was with that I was not afraid of the cold ripples. I leaves the beach to them as likes it—mine be the warmer billows of the bathtub! I am, very literally, a *poor fish!*

About them new United rates—forget the four bucks, Mocrates! If you are two years overdue, merely renew for one—it is just as well to have been technically a non-member for one year—what the devil do you care so long as you are paid up a year ahead? Call it a reinstatement and let Grandpa be your sponsor—I'll send ya a blank an' get the credit for a splendid new recruit!

But Oh, Boy! Mebbe I ain't got a fight on my hands in the United! Ida[24] has just written me that she and her Columbus henchman expect next year's UNITED AMATEUR to be conducted in a more commonplace and democratic manner; with less of the purely artistic and more of the chatty and plebeian. Only on such conditions, she implies, will the Columbus purse strings be liberally open. I have been dreadfully polite in replying, and have courteously ladled out wosh to the effect that I'll see her in hell first. As long as I'm editor, the organ will be exactly as it is now—exactly as good a thing as I can produce. If they don't like Grandpa they can get another boy—and that will be some job just now.[25] They can keep their money if they wish—I had rather edit a good four-page leaflet than a 20-page mess of Columbus junk. But anyhow, I think hell's gonna break loose somehow. Either they will try to starve me out and leave me to struggle on in my own way without support, or they will fire me and set up some Woodbee bonehead for editor. If the latter, I shall get out a UNITED CO-OPERATIVE as a rival official organ if I can scrape up the cash—ridiculing the administration's bourgeois foibles, and making 'em sorry they ever tried to monkey with the boss. If they expect to depend on me, they've gotta take things as I hand 'em out! I have long been patient with Columbus, but now that I've made up with Cleveland I simply must fight somebody or something else. A pug gets stale if he doesn't get into a mill once in a while—me an' Dempsey is lookin' for a brisk match!

I look forward with eagerness to future APPRENTICES—especially illustrated ones. Them's the stuff amachoordom needs! The present one will certainly win vast favour—I have already heard it complimented in no uncertain terms. Let's have a contrib, O Sage, as soon as ya get something nontheological. What we're lookin' for is less the didactic than the essay of belleslettres type. I noted with interest the Palaestina essay and the sundry jests and howlers. How Mocrates can remember speeches verbatim is beyond me! If I can carry all the ideas I feel proud enough—the words are too much for Grandpa in his old age! I will forward the items to Galba.

Well, I gotta quit. If you could see the hopeless mess of unanswered mail before me, you would realise what Gallomonistic devotion prompts these eleven pages just now. My Bush work is going to the devil, and I am ashamed to write Mr. Hoag till I can shew him something in the way of accomplished work.[26] My nerves are in a chaos this year—I seem better and more active outwardly, but I am getting to be an old man, fonder of dozing by the fire than of exerting myself. Life is such a beastly bore—I shall have to get hold of that laudanum some day soon. But until then, I shall remain, as ever, Gentlemen,

Yr most obliged and obedient Servant,
HENRY PAGET-LOWE

*Notes*

1. Ernest A. Dench, an amateur living in Sheepshead Bay, NY. HPL saw him frequently during his residence in Brooklyn (1924–26).
2. The references are to HPL's boyhood friends Ronald Upham, Kenneth Tanner, and Stuart Coleman.

3. S. Lilian McMullen ("Lilian Middleton"), an amateur poet. See HPL's unpublished essay, "The Poetry of Lilian Middleton" (1922).

4. Winifred Virginia Jackson (1876–1944), amateur poet with whom HPL was rumored to have had a romantic involvement during the period 1918–21.

5. Late in life HPL revised just such a treatise for Renshaw, *Well Bred Speech* (1937).

6. Myrta Alice Little and her mother, who lived in Hampstead, N.H.

7. Charles W. Smith (1852–1948), editor of the *Tryout*.

8. I.e., the amateur journalists Edna Hyde and Marjorie H. Outwater of the NAPA. Nothing is known of this "split."

9. Members of the NAPA were fond of referring to the UAPA in this manner because in 1912 it had split into two factions because of a disputed election.

10. Horace L. Lawson was editor of the *Wolverine*, an amateur paper for which HPL was conducting the "Zoilus" column.

11. Edward Lucas White (1866–1934), *The Song of the Sirens and Other Stories* (New York: E. P. Dutton, 1919; *LL* 944).

12. Uriah Heep is a (falsely) humble clerk in Charles Dickens's *David Copperfield* (1849–50).

13. George Bernard Shaw (1856–1950), *Back to Methusaleh: A Metabiological Pentateuch* (New York: Brentano's, 1921; *LL* 791).

14. "Nietscheism [*sic*] and Realism" (*Rainbow*, October 1921).

15. "A Confession of Unfaith" (*Liberal*, February 1922).

16. The quotation is from "Nietzscheism and Realism."

17. John Milton Samples, editor of the *Silver Clarion*.

18. Robert W. Service (1874–1958), "Gods in the Gutter," in *Ballads of a Bohemian* (1921), a poem attacking Baudelaire, Wilde, and Verlaine.

19. Frank Belknap Long (1901–1994), "The Eye Above the Mantel" (*United Amateur*, March 1921). Long was a fiction writer, poet, and one of HPL's closest friends and colleagues.

20. J. Fuller Spoerri, an amateur living in Washington, D.C.

21. HPL and Winifred V. Jackson, "The Crawling Chaos" (*United Co-operative*, April 1921; as by "Elizabeth Berkeley and Lewis Theobald, Jun.").

22. HPL's poems "The Unknown" (*Conservative*, October 1916) and "The Peace Advocate" (*Tryout*, May 1917) were published as by "Elizabeth Berkeley."

23. HPL, "Nyarlathotep" (prose poem) (*United Amateur*, November 1920).

24. Ida C. Haughton, president of the UAPA (1921–22). The feud between her and HPL became so bitter that HPL wrote the vicious satire "Medusa: A Portrait," directed at her. HPL sent the poem through the Gallomo (see letter 12).

25. In fact, HPL was ousted as Official Editor of the UAPA in the election of July 1922, Leo Fritter taking his place; but the official board for 1922–23 proved ineffective, and HPL and his associates were returned to office in 1923.

26. Jonathan E. Hoag (1831–1927), an aged amateur poet. HPL's comment suggests that he was doing revision work for Hoag.

[11]  [To the Gallomo]  [AHT]

Providence, R.I.,

October 6, 1921.

Concerning Ireland, I would ask Gahal-Bah what he means by "rights". What "right" exists on earth, save that of strength? If the Irish had the "right" to independence they would possess it. If they ever gain it, they will possess it—until they lose it again. England has the right to rule because she does. When she ceases to rule it will be time to talk of "rights" of others. It is not chance, but racial superiority, which has made the Briton supreme. Why have not the Irish conquered and colonised the earth if they are so deserving of regard? They are brainless canaille. Galba asks why he should worry about how hard a time the powers of Europe have. I will answer, because their overthrow would mean the overthrow of art, science, literature, and civilisation. If Galba respects the one, he must respect the other. Personally I agree that neither nations nor civilisations matter ultimately, but I do think it contributes to our immediate comfort to maintain the status quo. If Galba were truly cynical he would leave college, spend what money he has in drink and pleasure, and then commit suicide. The fact that he continues to live and waste time in reading and study proves that he cares for civilisation, and he who cares for civilisation had best be on the side of the Empire which alone sustains it. What if we are hypocritical? Is there either good or bad in the cosmos? What works, is best. Shew me another modern nation capable of keeping as much order as the British Empire keeps, and I will listen to drivel about our decadence. The decadence is not in Britannia but in all mankind—of course we know that man is now on the down-grade. As to the coming supremacy of the Prussian and Slavonic world, I should not be surprised at another challenge from Germany, but do not think any Slav nation will rise even to semi-civilisation. Whatever the Slav conquers will be lost to civilisation, for the race-stock is deficient. Slavs are emotional and irrational—the leaders of their nations are mostly non-Slavs with a veneer of Slavic culture. The ruling classes of the Slav nations are mainly Teutonic—clearly dolichocephalic Xanthochroi.[1] The brachycephalic masses are incurable peasants incapable of governing themselves or anyone else—they constitute part of the dull peasantry of many nations outside their nominal linguistic boundaries, including the characteristic South-German with his stupid face, broad head, and wholly non-Teutonic qualities. Germany may have a chance for leadership toward the end of the civilised period, but I hope that the Anglo-Saxons can prevent it. It is a free fight, with the strongest entitled to victory. Cosmically it does not matter, but I am an Englishman and have the healthy instinct of the animal to see its own pack win. I am not in the least uncynical about it, but certainly do not see what use there is in doing anything save stand by the old order. We are in the saddle now, and will prevent the maximum of chaos most easily by keeping there. If we cannot, all very well—it does not matter much—but so long as we have such vile things as lives the best we can do with them is to dedicate them to the service of Old England, whose influences gave us all we have. GOD SAVE THE KING!

I would like to disillusion Galba regarding his "brilliant and downtrodden" Ireland. So far as any evidence goes, the majority of men who have brought eminence to Ireland are nearly or wholly Anglo-Saxon by blood. Lord Dunsany is frankly an Englishman, with not one drop of the Celt—a Cheam School, Eton, and Sandhurst man whose voice and accent are as Londonese as any I have ever heard, and whose sympathies are ardently with the Empire. Even the self-conscious "Irish" intelligentsia are nine-tenths Anglo-Saxon, including Yeats, Synge, and everyone of any reputation. The ancient Irish civilisation is an ephemeral vision of the past, dead long before Britannia brought to the accursed island the only enduring culture it has ever possessed. That English culture in Ireland has certain local modifications no one wishes to deny. They are pleasing and appropriate, like the local variations of other cultures. We have Scottish, North-of-England, South-of-England, Welsh, Irish, American, and perhaps Australian variants of our English root-culture; but it is all English at the fountain-head, for none of it would have existed if our ancestors had not invaded the abandoned Roman province, driven out the Celts and Gallo-Romans, and founded the most solid and powerful civilisation since the Roman age. I will stand or fall with "fat John Bull", for he is mine own.

"England, with all thy faults I love thee still".[2]

In the NEW YORK TRIBUNE for last Sunday is a review which should interest our youthful sceptic; an account by Burton Rascoe, Esq. of the CHI-TRIB, of a striking fictional portrait of the modern bloodless intellectual: "Erik Dorn", by Ben Hecht, G. P. Putnam's Sons $2.00.[3] I believe that if I have a little more energy I shall try to obtain this work for perusal, for it seems to describe the modern with almost scientific comprehensiveness. I advise Gahal-Bah to peruse it at any cost. In commenting upon it Mr. Rascoe observes:

"Modern artists and aestheticians are rapidly eliminating from art all emotions which are not concerned with abstract form, and are thus helping to minimise sentiment in the life of the sentient being. The tendency is toward a biological atavism, highly intellectualised. A philosopher has said that we have lived emotionally beyond our means, and that we are reaping a harvest of complexes and neuroses which cripple the nervous system and weaken the body. Perhaps Erik Dorn is a prototype of the not unusual man of tomorrow."

The discussion on modernism hath served to confirm me in my belief that, so far as I touch art at all, I am not only a non-modern but a violent anti-modern. Intellectually I believe in nothing; aesthetically I believe only in the irradiate dreams of childhood. Sophistication I loathe and abhor with all the venom inherited from aeons of reptile and saurian ancestors in palaeolithic abysms of terrestrial history, and I even despise intellect when not directly concerned in the process of philosophical and scientific intellection. By this latter paradox I mean that I see nothing of beauty or pleasure in intellect, but only the hideous fascination of the forbidden Golden Door for the miserable Agib who stands before it. All reality is a putrid mess, and whilst an intellectual negation of it is a stigma of inferiority or senility; I deem an aesthetic negation of it not only justified, but perhaps the only true art as well. It is not, however, romanticism which I deem art. In the negation of the obvious, whether intellectual or aesthetic, there is only puerility and absurdity. It is in a more subtle, conscious, and phantastick way, that the mind must seek its momentary surcease from the hell with which it is normally environed. The evolution of art during the coming half-century will be worthy the study of philosopher, scientist, and aesthetician alike. Decadence or reaction are the two obvious alternatives; with a parallel development of both as a not impossible third course. Progress I deem impossible—reason has dealt healthy emotion its death blow.

Concerning the question of Hibernia, and of the Britannick race, I need say no more than that Galba is misled by a false species of analysis whereby the observer cannot behold the wood for the trees. The fact remains that our race alone hath founded the circle of culture embracing all the elements which Galba is sophistical enough to class as non-English. But for England, there would be no Irish or American civilisation, and if at the present moment the Mother Isle chances to be below its normal degree of intellectual fertility, the circumstance is of no ultimate significance in the appraisal of the entire civilisation. If the Empire be decadent, it but shares the general decadence of this age; a decadence inevitable to all civilisations in the end, and detracting nothing from the historical merit of the nation itself. We do not respect Rome the less because she fell; indeed, any man had rather be an antique Roman, though the republick be dead, than a modern Italian, though the kingdom be shakily living. Of modern races the Britannick is so indisputably the greatest that argument is futile. I am not even disturb'd by the cries of those who challenge it. That the Gauls are the most uniformly artistick and cultivated of peoples, I do not dispute; but as I grow older I respect art the less, and power the more. It is not improbable that all art is merely an unsatisfactory substitute for physical supremacy; the imaginative gratification of that will to power which is frustrated in the objective attainment of its objects. It may be that the finest work of the aesthetick fancy is but a poor makeshift for the victory of one vigorous tribe or individual over another. Were I stronger, I might have gone to West Point, adopted a martial career, and found in war a supreme delight which scribbling can but faintly adumbrate. At heart I believe I despise the aesthete and prefer the warrior—I am essentially a Teuton and barbarian; a Xanthochroic Nordic from the damp forests of Germany or Scandinavia, and kin to the giant chalk-white conquerors of the cursed, effeminate Celts. I am a son of Odin and brother to Hengist and Horsa . . . . Grrr . . . Give me a drink of hot blood with a Celtic foe's skull as a beaker! Rule, Britannia . . . GOD SAVE THE KING!

Concerning my pessimism, it is well to differentiate betwixt the general and the personal. The general is of course theoretical, and subject to change as evidence warrants; being merely a present conviction that the pains of life overbalance the joys. The personal, to which I fancy Galba alludes, is based on my own mind and condition; and is a sentiment of inferiority rather than superiority. I have not the energy to study with that vigour and pleasure which mark the researches of Galba, and while freely granting that better men have put on paper a pleasure which hath cheered multitudes, must simply affirm with regret that I am unable to extract sufficient pleasure to make consciousness preferable to oblivion. From study I derive pleasure, but not so much as I could derive from non-existence. As to the depising of mankind, surely Galba realises that all despising is necessarily relative and empirical. In the cosmos there are no values whatsoever, so that the vilest insect is ultimately equal to the most magnificent spiral nebula. When I say I despise man, I do not mean to single him out as the one most loathsome object in creation, or on the other hand to differentiate him from myself in a spirit of assumed superiority. Indeed, I despise myself fully as much as the average fellow-louse; having what amounts to a positive personal dislike for the fellow called H. P. L. I despise man as compared with his own prevailing opinion of himself, that is all. There is no such thing as absolute beauty; what is called beauty is purely subjective and variable. Galba argues well that the quest for beauty forms as profitable a pastime as any, but he does not explain how one can avoid being bored by it ultimately, when he realises that it is all no more than a matter of fortuitous molecular, atomic, and electronic arrangement. The cosmos is a mindless vortex; a seething ocean of blind forces, in which the greatest joy is unconsciousness and the greatest pain is realisation. It is useless to point to the trivial pleasures of existence as justification for the numberless pains thereof—that they are truly pleasures, none disputes; yet how fleeting and how satiating! It is my present conviction that one must be either a downright pessimist or a complete dupe of mythology and religious delusion. Real extasies exist only in the fancies of the poets and priests. But after all, how absurdly trivial is the whole controversy on pleasure and pain—for what does it matter whether we suffer or not? Our feelings are the most trivial of incidents in the unending cycle of existence.

Concerning materialism, I believe that all ultra-modern objections to it arise from mere reaction and confusion in nomenclature. The resolving of the atom is interesting, and to chemical and physical science quite revolutionary, but that it constitutes any affirmation for the silly idea of permanent cosmic evolution in one direction, or for the notion of human personality as something apart from physical organisation, is quite unthinkable and certainly unwarranted by the least particle of genuine evidence. It is not for the philosopher to quibble over the exact definitions of matter and energy, or their possible identification. The minutiae of the operation of the blind infinite vortex are quite immaterial. Vitalism is a pleasing fad, but it cannot overcome the evidence for determinism or establish so absurd a doctrine as one-direction progress in an eternal universe. If Galba hath more evidence to present in these matters, I shall be pleased to hear it; though perchance he will not care to discuss the question till I have perused Santayana. I have now finished "Back to Methuselah", and deem it vastly clever. I knew about the struldbrugs before Galba was born, and can see the resemblance, though it is not great. The struldbrugs were examples of the futility and misery of old age, whilst the ancients of Shaw are examples of the virtues of that condition. What Shaw does suggest, is the glowing oration upon struldbrugs which Gulliver deliver'd to the Luggnaggians before he had seen those pitiable creatures. Shaw, I think, is by no means so great a man as Swift; he is too much preoccupy'd with trivial questions of society, and doth not perceive to the full the tragedy of existence. He is too humorous—the truly great pass beyond humour, and retain only a terrible admixture of infinite disgust and soul-rending pity.

Well s'long,
H. PAGET-LOWE.

*Notes*

1. The racial terms are derived from various essays in Thomas Henry Huxley's *Man's Place in Nature* (1894), referring to "long-headed blond-haired" peoples; i.e. descendants of the "Nordic" barbarians in Europe.

2. William Cowper (1831–1800), *The Task* (1784), 2.206.

3. Ben Hecht (1894–1964), *Erik Dorn* (New York: G. P. Putnam's Sons, 1921), a novel concerning a jaded intellectual. HPL apparently later read the work, for in later years he continually regarded it (along with T. S. Eliot's *The Waste Land*) as a landmark in modernist literature.

[12]   [To the Gallomo]   [AHT]

Providence, R.I. Tuesday, November 29, 1921

MEDUSA: A PORTRAIT[1]
By Theobaldus Senectissimus, Gent.

TO THE HON. IDA COCHRAN HAUGHTON, VISCOUNTESS WOODBY————
MY LADY:—

I shou'd be but a Cheater, and unworthy of the poetick Art, were I not to acknowledge to you by this Dedication the Indebtedness I bear you. For 'tis plain that I may my self claim but partial Credit for a Picture which, without so illustrious a Model, wou'd never have been drawn with any Sort of Fidelity. Truly, the Satirist desiring to shew certain Traits of Mind, wou'd be hard put to it, had he not before him some Sort of living Example; and I am in Candour forc'd to concede, that of the Qualities I here seek to pourtray, no human Being cou'd display so great and flourishing an Abundance as your self. I shall ever count it a Piece of the greatest good Fortune, if my Satire proceed, that your Hatred of me mov'd you to slander and vilify me behind my Back; for lacking that Provocation I shou'd have neither had the Temerity to expose your Failings, nor possesst so compleat a Fund of Lies and Calumnies from which to draw a Picture of such Venom as I never thought before to exist upon Earth.

Conscious, therefore, of my Debt, I will commend this unpretentious Effort to your well-known Graciousness, and beg leave to subscribe my self,

> MY LADY,
>> Your Ladyship's most obedient,
>>> most devoted, humble servant,
>>> THEOBALDUS SENECTISSIMUS, ARMIGER.

> Soak'd in her noxious venom, puff'd with gall,
> Like some fat toad see dull MEDUSA sprawl;
> Foul with her spleen, repugnant to the sight,
> She crudely whines amidst eternal night.
> From wit and sense by slothful brain debarr'd,
> And with the chains of age and sourness scarr'd,
> Her half-liv'd life one hateful wish reveals:
> To give to others all the pain she feels!
> Unschool'd in youth, unchasten'd by the years,
> Grotesque with ignorance, absurd with fears;
> Shunn'd for her ugly face and fretful mind,
> She crawls alone, at war with all mankind.
> In her black heart no love or kindness dwells,
> But hate that shocks, and malice that repels;
> Her narrow thoughts an equal vileness shew,
> For there but envy and suspicion grow.
> Blind to the truth, by jealous passion fann'd,
> She slanders all she cannot understand,
> And with loose tongue the sinner and the saint
> Alike befouls in one inclusive taint.
> Slow to see goodness, quick to smell a fault,
> She scours the earth for victims to assault;
> With what strain'd words she doles her lagging praise!
> With what glad force her instant hatreds blaze!

Sluggish of wit, her loathsome bulk attests
One spark alone—a rage that never rests!
But not content to be an open fool,
Or candid knave, she seeks to cheat by rule;
Her want of sense in quoted saws she cloaks,
And with trite pelf a double laugh provokes,
Whilst all her cruelty must candour seem,
Tho' doubly evil for the strategem.
So lurks MEDUSA, scourge of all around,
With hate, spleen, vanity, and dulness bound.
Anxious the wretch that courts her tardy smile,
And hapless he that knows her sneers and guile;
For since her envy flays all greater minds,
In ev'ry one alive a foe she finds—
Save for a little band of kindred sort,
In torpor mighty, but in wisdom short.
Void of all humour but the sly grimace,
She sees a challenge in each smiling face,
And spreads with twofold zeal her net malign,
Since she as injur'd innocence may shine.
From such a pest what rescue may we gain?
What spell may crush her hypocritic strain?
Her human form (perchance 'twas human once)
Forbids us smother the offending dunce;
Besides, we hesitate to smother such
A reptile thing, repellent to the touch.
A musket-ball but little harm could do
Where there's no brain or heart to hurtle through,
So still the monster heaves and puffs and rolls,
The toothless tearer of a thousand souls!
So must she fume, insatiate, sour, and wild;
Deaf, stupid, blear'd; by ev'ry tongue revil'd:
So must we wait, till Heav'n the curse revokes,
And the swoln snake in her own poison chokes!

Sweetly yours,
GRANDPA.

*Notes*

1. "Medusa: A Portrait" (*Tryout*, December 1921; as by "Jeremy Bishop" and lacking the introductory letter).

[13] [ALS]

[. . .]

30th June [1922]

Pray send the preceding two sheets, writ yesterday, to our Presbyterian pal Mocrates. He likes the travelogue stuff,[1] as I have before intimated. I now have your more recent cards & letter, & am infinitely delighted to learn with how great felicity the Galpinio-Lovemanick meeting was effected. I was quite certain that you wou'd be surpris'd with the scholastick attainments & engaging manners of S L, since I am so well aware alike of their vast extent & of S L's custom of systematically underrating & understating them. The modesty of the great one is almost incredible. Your coming will be a tremendous boon to one who is not only lonely & unappreciated, but singularly susceptible to the pangs caused by that condition. I had already gather'd that his family are out of sympathy with him—you must teach him to regard them as mere inconsequential parts of the landscape; beyond the radius of worriment, as it were. That so vast a scholar & genius shou'd regard me & my works with favour, is indeed a source of gratification to me. Dulce est, saith an old proverb, laudari a viro laudato![2] I hope he realises, in return, the vast esteem & admiration in which I hold him & everything connected with him. Certainly, there is no one of any degree of taste who knows him, but shares this high opinion. Small Belknap hath just sent Mme. G.[3] an acknowledgment of the new *Rainbow*, & most of his text consists of an extended rhapsody on the arts & graces of the distinguish'd author of the "Letter to G. K." Pray tell this to S L in case Mme G. does not send him the epistle.

This reminds me that said Belknap is indeed a tantalisingly infrequent correspondent. I must limber the child up—at least to the extent of letting him know that he is on the particularly favour'd list. A great boy—I hope I can persuade him to stop off a day in Providence whilst on his way to the summer camp at Lebec Lake, Maine.

I wish that I might get to Cleveland—Aedepol! how I wish it! But apparently any serious attempt would rend #598 with a civil war of no mean proportions. Poverty—ugh! how I hate it! Ask Sam what it's like! My best hope of seeing you lies in a possible Lovemanic move to N.Y.—faintly shadow'd forth in a recent epistle of his to Mme. Greenevna. That might lure you thither to see him—& then Grandpa'd get there if he had to be a stowaway on the New-York Boat!

*Monday—night before the Fourth*

'Sh no ushe! Jesh shimply can't get zish letter done! One thing after another comesh up! This time it was a campaign matter. Campbell's sister-in-law, Miss Eliz. Barnhart, is planning an anti-Woodbee paper—a mock *United Amateur* as Fritter[4] would edit it—& asked me to contribute the "credentials" in a hurry so that the thing can be hustled out before convention. I concocted three spoofs like your old *Clarion* wheeze—the Knutzenel prize-winning Ford essay—representing the sort of stuff Fritter would accept & publish. One is a "poem"—"The Wonderful Hills" by Hiram N. Good. Another is a social-amateur "essay"—"A Day in the Country" by Otto Nobetter. The third is a "story"—"Uncle John's Legacy",* by Bella Dumm. I don't know how funny they really are, but they were at least funny enough to convulse Mme. G. with mirth. I guess they'll give the Won't-Bes a reasonably *mauvais quart d'heure*. Miss Barnhart is going to print the thing herself on Campbell's press, with intentional misspellings & misprints.[5]

My aunt tells me that the Gallic stuff has safely arrived at #598. Thanks, O Tiny Hyacinth-Bud! Shall be damn glad to see it when I get home. All right about the amateur stuff—any time—no hurry—n'importe.

Thanks for the kind words anent that first attempt at Baudelairian translation.[6] It was merely a piece of luck, though, if it was any good. Perchance I'll try the second again, using your literal translation, when I get home & see the original again. Sure I'll do some more if they'll do ya any good, Kid! But don't expect anything worth anything.

This region is not as near the Haverhill section as I thought, so I shall not be able to drop in on the Davis kid.[7] When I get home I'll send you his 18-pager, so that you can judge him more fully even if you don't care to adopt him as a literary grandson. By the way—it looks as though the Galpinian cast-asides are going to found a scholastic salon of their own, for this a.m. there blew into the Magnolia P.O. two bulky duplicate letters for Mme. G. & myself, from good ol' Mocrates in Madisonium. He calls the new circle the *Gremolo*, & doubtless intends it as the standard refuge for rejected second-raters. Well, I'm glad something waked the old sport up—I like him.

About that Carlylean puff for the Old Gent's stories—t'anks, Sonny! Glad you can speak well of 'em! Shall read the completed work with interest. Mme. G. has just taken to this sort of composition—has written one & planned two more—& I'm damned if they don't look like good stuff! The first one, "Four O'Clock", has some images noxiously Poe-esque—I shall polish it up for use in the U.A. or something else.[8] The others pertain to the sea, attesting to the inspiring effect of the wild Magnolian coast & the colourful (& odourful) harbour of antique Gloucester.

*The Glorious 4th—9 a.m.*

Some day I guess I'll give the immortal Remy the once-over—he sounds interesting.[9] That crack about fire is a wise one—my uncle-in-law Dr. Clark once made a very detailed study of the "descent of fire" & legends appertaining thereto, even going so far as to make an excellent translation of an es-

---

*If it doesn't beat "Aunt Minerva's Ku Klux", I'm a damn liar!

pecially apposite article in your favourite lingo—an article in the *Revue des Deux Mondes*.[10]

About "Arcady"[11]—I'll follow your instructions when I get home & have the lines before me. It is a riotous intoxication of aesthetic magnificence—who gives a damn what it's about? But Sam's obscurity will, of course, always tend to baffle the academic mind. Mo gives a cruel anecdote in the new *Gremolo*, which you must not repeat to SL on pain of death. He had shew'd the "Letter to G. K." to an English professor at your delightful alma mater, & asked him what he thought of the line

"The red Lustration of a Soul that dies"[12]

—whereupon the literate one responded: "Sounds like a hemorrhage!" I hope the guy wasn't your friend Bill Ellery.[13]

Now that you & Sam are together, I trust you can synchronise the "Hermaphrodite" & the critique for inclusion in July U.A. copy.[14] The May issue is still in press, & there is no hurry. *I will omit Bingville Bugle Notes* from the Loveman issue. I hope you will change your mind about poem—it ought to appear, & it's too late for the (May) issue with the Saturnian critique.[15]

Well, I'd better shut up. Lemme hear from ya as often as ya care to sling the new quasi-Lovemanick violet ink or pound the newly beribboned Corona. And give my most abundant regards to your illustrious companion; urging, encouraging, entreating him to drop a line to his aged grandfather!

Yr obt Servt

M. LOLLIUS

*Notes*

1. The first two sheets of this letter presumably contained an account of HPL's trip through New Hampshire in early June 1922 (cf. *SL* 1.183–85).

2. "It is sweet to be praised by a man who has been praised."

3. Sonia H. Greene, the second number of whose *Rainbow* was published in May 1922. Among other contributions, it contained Loveman's poem "Letter to G—— K——," addressed to George Kirk. See n. 12.

4. Leo Fritter of Columbus, OH. He ousted HPL as Official Editor of the UAPA in the election of July 1922.

5. It is not clear whether this paper was ever published.

6. Evidently a reference to HPL's attempt at "translating" a poem of Baudelaire (presumably from *Les Fleurs du mal*) based upon a literal prose translation by Galpin.

7. Edgar J. Davis of Haverhill, MA, with whom HPL made a trip to Newburyport in April 1923.

8. There is no known publication of Sonia H. Greene's "Four O'Clock" prior to its appearance in *Something about Cats and Other Pieces* (1949). Greene maintained that she wrote it entirely herself at HPL's suggestion, but HPL implied he revised the story.

9. Remy de Gourmont (1858–1915), author of *A Night in the Luxembourg* (1906; Eng. tr. 1912), read by HPL in the autumn of 1923 (*SL* 1.250).

10. The *Revue des Deux Mondes* is a leading French journal, founded in 1831 and still being published.

11. A poem by Samuel Loveman (*National Amateur,* March 1908).

12. Samuel Loveman, "A Letter to G—— K——,"*Rainbow* No. 2 (May 1922): 15, l. 6.

13. William Ellery Leonard (1876–1944), poet, classical scholar, and professor at the University of Wisconsin.

14. The *United Amateur* for July 1922 has not been located.

15. Samuel Loveman (1889–1976), *The Hermaphrodite: A Poem,* preface by Benjamin De Casseres (Athol, MA: W. Paul Cook, 1926; *LL* 549). Loveman's amateur magazine, *The Saturnian,* ran for three issues. Galpin commented at length on the third issue in "Department of Public Criticiam," *United Amateur* 21, No. 5 (May 1922): 54–55.

[14]   [To Galpin and Frank Belknap Long] [AHT]

[Early February 1923]

To my dear Grandsons, Alfredus and Belnapius;
Children:—

If you will gather close to Grandpa's knee, the Old Gentleman will tell you all about his late trip to Boston, and other parts of the Province of the Massachusetts-Bay.

I left these plantations on Thursday, the 14th of December, arriving at Boston late in the afternoon, where I was met by my genial and scholastick host, the Hon. Edward Cole, of Cambridge. Convey'd by him to his house, a pleasing domicile in the best part of town, near a church, I was regaled by an excellent meal. The better I know Mr. Cole, the more pleas'd I am with him; and the more I regret the lack of earlier acquaintance. His household consists of himself, his wife[1] (an excellent tho' unliterary person), his son by his first wife, (ag'd four and three-quarters) and a daughter by his present wife, ag'd one and three-quarters. The precociousness of both infants is extreamly amazing, and without doubt inherited from their illustrious common parent. The daughter, for example, can at her early age walk and run with perfect vigour, to say naught of playing continually, and talking with much fluency and intelligence. By these children I was greatly reminded of yourselves, who so far surpass all ordinary babes of your years.

After dinner, my host and I set out for Maplewood, in Malden, where I was bespoken to address the Hub Club upon my favourite author, Lord Dunsany.[2] The gathering was bright and numerous, most of the feuds of local writers having been tolerably compos'd; and my remarks were attended with flattering diligence and encomiums. I followed my address with a reading of Dunsany's work, and induc'd several auditors to pledge themselves to a future perusal of him. I am of an opinion, that Lord Dunsany's manner is the only artistick manner possible in this aera of decadence. Scientifick learning having rendered obsolete all the illusions of our youth, and realistick expression having become perforce a chaotick mess like Mr. Eliot's "Waste Land",[3] it behoves the lover of beauty to create an artificial pattern amidst the meaningless desert of Life; and what pattern can be more appropriate to his purposes than that body of mythical thought and fable which Time hath invested with so many priceless associations? After my reading, and the social period which follow'd, Cole and I return'd to his house, which we did not reach till 2 a.m. on account of the snowfall and wretched tram service.

On the following day, my host being occupy'd with the labours of scholastick instruction, I perform'd despite a head-ache a careful tour of the more antique parts of Boston. Chusing the North-End as my seat of travel, I walk'd up Hanover-Street, view'd the home of Paul Revere, Esq. in North-Square, and branched off thro' Prince and Salem Streets to Christ-Church, built 1723, commonly call'd the Old North Church, tho' that edifice was really burnt for firewood during our occupation of Boston at the time of the Yankee rebellion. It was in the steeple of this church, that Mr. Revere display'd the traitorous lanthorns which warn'd the rebels of our coming in 1775. At Christ-Church I was confronted by a curious small boy, of Italian blood, who began without looking directly at me to recite in a mechanical monotone the history of the region. The effect was highly comick, since the urchin scarce knew what he was repeating. I believe he had learnt it by heart, and used it as a means of earning stray pence from travellers. I was later told, that this region abounds in such diminutive and acquisitive ciceroni. From Christ-Church I went to Sheafe-Street, where was born the grandfather of our good friend and companion Mortonius; the Rev. S. F. Smith, author of the Yankee version of "God Save the King".[4] A tablet marks the house where he saw the light in 1808. Thence I proceeded to Hull-Street, and up the steps to that fascinating necropolis which thro' some singular fate I had never before seen—the Copp's Hill Burying Ground.[5] Here are interr'd some of the most illustrious Colonial dead of the Province, including the Mathers, who are interesting to me from my possession of Cotton Mather's "Magnalia Christi Americana".[6] But the chief charm of the scene is in the entire broad effect; the bleak hilltop with its horizon of leaden sky, harbour masts, and Colonial roofs. In sight are many houses of the early 18th century, to say nothing of the rebel frigate "Constitution", which defends the harbour from attack. Over the sod was a thin coat of snow, thro' which the slabs peer'd grimly whilst black leafless trees claw'd at a sinister lowering sky. In fancy I could conjure up the Boston of the late 17th century with its narrow, hilly, curving streets and quaint wooden and brick houses. At present this part of the town is abominably squalid, and inhabited by peasant Italians of the filthiest description.

From Copp's Hill I proceeded to the corner of Park and Tremont Streets, where I had agreed to meet my host; but my journey was interrupted by a stop in Cornhill, where at an old shop I purchas'd the compleat works of Ch: Lamb, Esq. for two shillings.[7] This collection, in one thick volume, is precisely like the one at Eglin's, in Cleaveland, which was sold to Clarence Wheeler, Esq. It is well to recall, that this Cornhill is not Boston's original Cornhill, but meerly Hillier's-Lane renam'd. Cornhill was originally the name of part of Boston's main street, other parts being call'd Newbury and Marlborough. After the lamented rebellion, the whole thoroughfare was joyn'd, and invested with the patronymick of the illustrious Genl. Washington; whilst the former individual names were elsewhere plac'd. Cornhill, as mention'd, was apply'd to Hillier's-Lane; whilst Newbury and Marlborough were given to new streets later made when the Back-Bay was fill'd in; a circumstance reminding us that much of modern Boston stands on artificial land. The Old Boston of my day was but a slight peninsula, almost an island, containing the North End and Beacon Hill, and linkt to the mainland by a narrow isthmus. Amongst the streets named for illustrious men I was pleas'd to note a Belknap-Street, commemorating the Revd. Jeremy Belknap, minister of a church in Federal-Street, and founder of the Boston Historical Society. The name of this street hath since been chang'd to Joy-Street, and I am sure that no reader of my small Belknap's phantasies can deny that Belknaps invariably afford joy!

Having met Cole, I proceeded with him to the State-House, completed in 1798, whose golden dome was by a poet call'd "The Hub of the Universe". I had often seen, but never enter'd, this distinguished edifice; hence I was glad of expert guidance on this occasion. The modern wings and additions I did not stop to observe. Cole next usher'd me from the rear door, and shew'd me the antique Beacon-Hill district, which also I had never before seen. Here I was mov'd to speechless admiration by the numerous memorials of better days; whole blocks of 18th century brick houses, magnificent Colonial doorways, and an unending succession of picturesque panoramas along the steep narrow streets leading down the hill. The climax was Louisburg-Square, nam'd from our glorious victory over the French in 1745 under Col. Pepperrell, later Sir W: Pepperrell, Bart. This is a perfect Georgian Square in perfect preservation, still decent in population, and quaintly situated on the side of an antient hill. Many literary persons have dwelt therein, and I am sure their work hath gain'd thereby. The hour being now late, Cole and I threaded our way thro' many narrow thoroughfares and down many steep hills, till at last we reach'd the North-Station and travell'd to Cambridge (across the Charles River) by a steam route not often available. That evening was spent at the home of Denys Myers, Esq., an international lawyer of pleasing parts, tho' afflicted with idealistick delusions and a love of universal peace. Mrs. Miniter, the Coles, a colourless couple named Johnston, and myself were the guests; Mr. and Mrs. Myers doing honours in the traditional Boston manner.

On Saturday, the following day, Mrs. Miniter, Cole, and myself, made an exhaustive tour of historick sites. Cole and I, before meeting Mrs. Miniter, took lunch at an ordinary call'd the Georgian Cafeteria; which interested me as a perfect replica of the typical Cleveland cafeteria—a type not found in New-York nor in Providence. In fancy I was transported back to August days—to Mills', or Chapin's, or the Statler; and I was several times on the point of addressing my companion as "Sonny", fancying him that small boy with whom I sate on those earlier and Mid-Western occasions! I wish'd, indeed, that I might step out to 105th and Euclid and purchase fresh fruit salad sundaes for the company! At the Transcript office we stopt to obtain the small free guide there publisht; a copy of which I enclose for each of you children. Then we met Mrs. Miniter at the Old State House, and proceeded to explore that edifice. You, little Belknap, have no doubt seen this pleasing pile; but to you, small Alfredus, I must some day shew it. I remov'd my hat whilst gazing at the golden lion and unicorn symbolick of His Majesty's authority over the Province, (they were pull'd down by the rebels in 1776, but subsequently restor'd) and thereafter enter'd the building and noted the remarkable collection of antiquities. It was with a family pride that I noted some possessions of John Phillips, Esq., first Mayor of Boston, with whom genealogy remotely connects me. I am, by the way, told, that at Watertown there still stands the brick 17th century house occupy'd by my lineal ancestor, the Rev. George Phillips, who was among the settlers of that place in 1630. This fact I have not verify'd, but I design to do so at some future date. From the State-House we proceeded to Faneuil-Hall, and thence to the Paul Revere house built in 1676, one of the three remaining 17th century buildings in Boston proper. This house was much spoilt by modern change, but was restor'd in 1908 to the condition it had when inhabited by Mr. Revere the goldsmith from 1770 to 1800. How can I do justice to the ineffable charm of this hoary dwelling? Tho' my proper century is the 18th, I am peculiarly fascinated by memorials of the century before; and to me there is something alluringly sinister in these massive, low-pitch'd, heavy-beam'd, diamond-window'd remains of the first Puritan times. The odour of them is alone sufficient to awake dark speculations—I found it most pronounc'd in the antient Ward house in Haverhill, the oldest part of which was built in 1640. The cavernous fireplaces, too, add to the macabre grotesqueness. In this house were many relics, including old maps of Boston (1728) and papers containing Mr. Revere's advertisements. There were on sale replicas of the old 18th century lanthorns which Revere fashioned, as well as pewter spoons newly struck from his own well-preserv'd moulds. I obtain'd a lanthorn for myself, and a spoon apiece as Christmas presents for my aunts, who share my fondness for New-England antiquities. I am enclosing for each of you boys some printed matter which I obtain'd at Mr. Revere's; and hope it will interest you during your holiday vacations. From Revere's we went to Christ-Church (where I mounted the pulpit and gesticulated in ecclesiastick fashion unseen by the sexton) and Charter-Street, where I shew'd Mrs. Miniter the only two 17th century houses besides Revere's—structures of which despite her antiquarian erudition she was previously ignorant. They are ill-kept, and in frightful slums; some society shou'd reclaim them.

[*The rest of this letter has been lost.*]

Notes

1. Mildred Cole. Cole's first wife, Helene Hoffman Cole, died in 1919, giving birth to E. Sherman Cole.
2. "Lord Dunsany and His Work" (*MW* 104–12).
3. T. S. Eliot (1888–1865), *The Waste Land*, first published in the U.S. in the *Dial*, November 1922 (*LL* 238).
4. Samuel French Smith (1808–1895) wrote the song "My country, 'tis of thee" in 1832. The tune is based upon "God Save the King."
5. Four years later HPL would incorporate this burying-ground in his tale, "Pickman's Model" (1926).
6. Cotton Mather (1663–1728), *Magnalia Christi Americana; or, the Ecclesiastical History of New-England, from Its First Planting in the Year 1620, unto the Year of Our Lord, 1698* (1702; *LL* 598).
7. Charles Lamb (1775–1834), *Complete Works in Prose and Verse*, ed. with a preface by R. H. Shepherd (Boston: De Wolfe, Fiske, [1874]; *LL* 510).

[15]   [To Galpin and Frank Belknap Long]  [AHT]

[mid-February 1923]

Alfredus and Belnapius:

[. . .]

Accordingly I embark'd upon the Medford coach, with the purpose of viewing the mansion of the late Col. Isaac Royall, which was built around the walls of an older house in the year 1737.

Grey thro' the trees I saw the old manor-house from afar; with its brick ends, tall chimneys, and extensive slave quarters. Its aspect was of the freshest, and I was hard put to it not to fancy Colonel Royall standing in the doorway, in his short full-bottom'd periwig, to extend me the welcome which in these days of Yankee sedition one loyal King's man owes another. My welcome, however, was given by a venerable person of the yeoman class: one George Fuller, who acts as curator of the estate. Upon admitting me, he shew'd me a vast hall with arches and pilasters of the finest classical carving; the work of such honest artisans, with a true eye for beauty, as cannot be found in these days of rabble degeneracy, trade guilds, and such like monstrosities of an evill aera. You, little Belknap, will comprehend the beauty of these decorations when I tell you that they surpass the finest carvings in the parlour of the Van Cortlandt Mansion;[1] but you, small Alfredus, must behold a Colonial dwelling before their merit can justly impress you. 'Tis sufficient to remark, that in the panelling of the walls, the arching of the windows, the framing of the doors, and the designing of the mantelpieces, our mansions of the eighteenth century surpass'd every other sort of edifice before or since for pure grace and loveliness of outline and proportion. The architects and decorators of that time, amongst whom Saml: McIntyre of Salem[2] takes a prominent place, and had an eye for beauty which the uniform good taste of the eighteenth century marvellously develop'd; and I am truly of an opinion, that their creations and carvings are just as genuine poesy as anything ever writ in lines and rhymes. Their age had in it some subtle stimulant to their particular sort of genius, which subsequently vanish'd, and will not return till after another age of barbarism. If we wish to shine in the building and adornment of houses, we can but copy these predecessors with fidelity; the which I am well-pleas'd to see some of our architects doing. I was on this occasion shewn about by Goodman Fuller, who prov'd to possess a singular amount of intelligence and information. He permitted me to overlook nothing; and upon my displaying interest, stay'd an hour after the usual closing time to converse with me about the past. His age is above eighty, and his memory of Old Boston phenomenally distinct. He can recall, for instance, the best days of Louisburg-Square; when old gentlemen in white, bell-crown'd beaver hats and swallow-tail'd coats with brass buttons used to bow low to prim old ladies with large bonnets and hoop-skirts, who would courtesy profoundly in return. When I purchas'd the customary post-card pictures, (for I am collecting views of all the antique places I visit) my honest friend was so generously amicable as to give me a slightly aluminum card tray with a picture of the mansion thereon; an object which I shall treasure as a symbol of that antient good-will which ought to exist betwixt the yeomanry and the gentry. Of everything in the house, aside from the architecture and carving, I think I lik'd most the sign of an old tavern own'd by Col. Royall and once standing in the publick square of Medford-Village. It had finely painted upon it His Majesty's arms, but was marr'd by a wanton musket-ball shot into it by straggling rebels on the night of April 19, 1775, when the scoundrels defied the authority of our regulars. Next to this, I most liked the painting of the younger Col. Royall at the age of 22; a finely bred young fellow in scarlet coat and neat periwig of the fashion of 1741. Poor man, he liv'd to see foul treason stain these rural shades, and in 1775 went to the Mother Land; dying at Kensington in 1781. He was a man of unquestion'd virtue and extensive ability, serving the Province in many important military and political capacities. In 1763 he gave to Medford the first fire-engine it ever possess'd, and upon his death (notwithstanding the secession of the Province) bequeath'd a valuable tract of land to Harvard-College. He was born in Antigua, in the West-Indies, where his father was for some time a planter. In faith he was sincerely attach'd to the Estáblish'd Church, holding a pew in King's Chapel, Boston, (which I have seen) and being foremost in works of philanthropy and publick spirit. I shou'd have felt honour'd by his acquaintance; and indeed took pride in spending three hours under his hospitable roof.

Upon quitting the Royall House, which I did with much reluctance, I repair'd to an ordinary in Boston, where I procur'd a meal of the same sort which you and I, small Alfredus, used to obtain at Clark's Taverns in Cleaveland. Thereafter I call'd a chair and proceeded to the meeting of the club; which was held in Huntington-Chambers, near Copley-Square. I here found the usual numerous assemblage, including Mr. Cole, Mrs. Miniter, and Mr. Nelson Morton (brother to my bosom friend in New-York), whom I vastly respect; Mr. Sandusky, whom I vastly like; and Mr. Michael White,[3] whom I essay'd to snub throughout the entire evening with no success—for truly, he seem'd dispos'd to take offence at nothing I cou'd do without causing a publick riot.[4] The speaker of the evening was one Osborne (not him who Sam: Johnson knock'd down) who edits the National Magazine,[5] and who told the company how to write salable short stories. Upon the matter of literature he touch'd not; doubtless recognising the taste of most of his auditors. All was over by midnight; at which time I accompanied the Parker-Miniter delegation[6] home, but not before promising to meet Mr. Cole for dinner the following night, at the Copley-Square Tavern. Arriv'd with my hosts at their Maplewood home, I sat up conversing with them till half past five in the morning; at which time all retired. I awaked at nine, was treated to an excellent breakfast, and after bidding suitable adieux to the six cats and numerous human beings, set out for my next important goal—the antique and daemon-haunted town of SALEM.

Arrived at Salem, I determin'd to spare no effort to learn the town from end to end; even better than I learnt New-York during my stay of many weeks. I therefore flouted fatigue, and proceeded to follow the long general itinerary prescrib'd in the excellent guide-book of the Essex Institute. This took me first to the Grimshawe House (where Mr. Hawthorne not only courted his wife but laid the scene of a weird tale),[7] and the antient Charter-Street Burying Ground adjacent. And what a scene delighted my eyes in that story'd and venerable necropolis! Picture, my children, an extensive undulating tract cover'd with snow; the blacken'd slabs peering thro' like the helmets of a crop of daemons got by sowing dragons' teeth.[8] On the north is Charter-Street, above which it broods over a bank wall. On the northwest the Grimshawe House (now sold to Jews, and the finely carv'd doorway remov'd to the museum) abuts; with its fence looking on the graves of Justice John Hawthorne, Dr. John Swinnerton, and young Nathaniel Mather, the Belknap or Galpin of his age, whose stone reads: "an aged person that had seen but nineteen winters in the world". Nathaniel died on the 17th of October, 1688, amidst universal mourning; and is accounted one of the most learned individuals in the Province; in theology, philosophy, Latin, Greek, and Hebrew alike. Farther from the fence is the simple but dignify'd sepulchre of the mighty SIMON BRADSTREET, twice Governour of the Colonie, and a man of magnificent parts; born at Horbling, in Lincolnshire, in the last yeare of our blessed sovereign ELIZABETH.

> Majestick here on ev'ry Hand arise
> BRITANNIA'S Glories, mounting to the Skyes!

On the south is a bluff, which formerly overlookt an inlet from the harbour, but beneath which is now the made land of recent times, containing an extension of Derby-Street. Still lofty in position, the graveyard is swept by the winds of heaven by day and the winds of hell by night. Out of its terrible soil crawl vast funereal willows; one of gigantick size and curious convolutions occupying the exact centre. This tree hath so expanded, that its bole now infolds the greater part of an antient slate slab; growing solidly around it so that in time it will be wholly swallow'd up. The slab is one dating from the reign of Charles the Second, which is by no means old for a place whose earlier interments reach back to 1637. (I have, tho', seen older graves in Boston, where some reach back to 1630.)

From the graveyard I went down to Derby Street, observ'd the Custom-House where Mr. Hawthorne work'd, and once more inspected the House of the Seven Gables in Turner-Street on the harbour. This scene is one which no man but an artist cou'd rightly describe, hence I can meerly suggest the bolder parts of it—the narrow street with no house visible of later date than 1700, and with two of the antient Gothick houses in sight; houses of the peaked sort that preceded our familiar "Colonial" architecture, and whose diamond-paned lattice windows, exposed beams, and overhanging gables are of a school of construction extending back into the Dark Ages and seen on every towne streete in England when Richard the Lion-Hearted sate on our throne. Boston and Salem were once fully built up with this sort of houses, copy'd directly from those of London; but by 1690 they were largely replac'd by the gambrel-roof'd type out of which evolv'd the "Colonial" style. That style itself (tho' I have heard no one else remark it) is palpably the result of an anomalous fusion peculiar to New-England and later to the Colonies; namely, the superposition of *manor-house* architecture upon *town-house* architecture; the whole later embellish'd by that Greek and Roman classical influence which distinguisht the eighteenth century. To go back to the Gothick houses: I know not any which fully preserv'd its antique aspect thro' the centuries. All were to some degree modify'd by succeeding generations; so that such as we now see are largely the result of expert restoration. This restoration is one of the great works of the famous Essex Institute of Salem; an institution which of its kind is surpass'd by nothing in the United States. In Salem there are many of the Gothick houses; in Boston only one: that of the late Paul Revere, Esq. Overhanging gables are more common, having been used in the earlier gambrel-roof'd houses; though there is no record of one later that 1700. In Boston there are but three houses with such a feature, but in Salem and Marblehead innumerable specimens exist. This feature was the occasion of a dispute betwixt myself and Mrs. Miniter last December, when that learned lady insisted that the overhang was an American device for protection against the Indians. How so proficient an antiquarian cou'd fall into so great an error, I know not; unless it be that her erudition does not extend back across the ocean; for in truth, the overhanging gable was not meerly mediaeval, but existed in many of the RO-MAN houses, even unto the early times of the republick. (Tho' in the GRE-CIAN houses, the upper storey not only did not overhang, but seldom cover'd so much space as that below it.) Amongst the Romans, the overhanging storey was called a *maenianum,* and many have been found in Pompeii. In later Imperial times they were forbidden because of the narrowness of the streets, an edict against them being pass'd in A.D. 368, tho' it soon fell into obsolescence. The ban was reviv'd by Imp. Honorius (he that abandon'd Britannia and play'd with poultry) and Imp. Theodosius II., tho' exemption was granted in case of an open space of 10 or 15 feet before the maenianum in question. When the Goths destroy'd the empire, all Roman customs slowly decay'd away; and we find the overhanging gable prominent in the new Gothick architecture, from whence it pass'd to the early towns of America.

But I digress. This scene, at the foot of Turner-Street, is one of the most impressive in existence. Landward we behold the seventeenth-century scene just describ'd; seaward we behold the deserted harbour, deep and nobly landlock'd, yet holding only the ghosts of the ships that once made known the name of Salem on distant shoars of Ind. It is a terrible sight, for as I lookt I saw a spectral train of galleons and frigates, barques and brigantines; sailing, sailing, sailing, with tatter'd sails distant by no breeze, and with seaweed and barnacles on the wormy hulls and high sterns.

I turn'd away and went inland, mourning to see the antient houses on Derby-Street fill'd with loathsome Polacks. Crossing to Essex-Street, I breath'd better; for here are the old Salem folk unchang'd, and lineally descended from the pioneers of Mr. Winthrop's colonies of 1626. After looking at the Narbonne-House (1671), I cross'd to the region of Washington-Square, or Salem-Common; where (God be devoutly thank'd) dwell some of Salem's old aristocracy in their fullest pristine splendour; inhabiting the houses in which their forbears entertain'd Sir William Pepperrell[9] and Genl. Washington. I look'd at the stately rows of mansions with their sublime doorways and shining brass knockers; and cou'd not but remove my hat out of respect to the genius of our ENGLISH nation, which planted this colonie and rais'd it up to the summit of taste, dignity, and elegant simplicity. GOD SAVE THE KING! I now went to Mall-Street, where Mr. Hawthorne for some time dwelt; and doubling around venerable Bridge-Street, essay'd to return to the Common down Williams-Street. (So named from Rev. R. Williams, founder of the Providence-Plantations, who dwelt in Salem before 1636.) Here I was destin'd to encounter a very agreeable shiver of spectral horror, for I had not walkt far when I came upon a very antient house of unknown date, but certainly standing prior to the witchcraft of 1692. It was now abandon'd and condemn'd, and when I went up to one of the tiny, small-pan'd windows to peer into the black interior, I saw that the main floor had mostly fallen thro' into the cellar, whilst the second floor was sagg'd down nearly to where the main floor shou'd be. There were doors leading farther into the interior, and amidst the dusk I cou'd see fallen plaster, gaunt walls, empty doorways, and quantities of mould, discolouration, and water in stagnant pools. It was not a nice place to peer into late in the afternoon, for it is not good to look upon midnight and death when the sun shines. None the less I peer'd again and again; till at last I saw more than I had seen before, being aided by the eye of sinister fancy. From every door-frame hung a corpse in some state or other of decay; a few skeletons, and a few with purple putrescence left. They were all aged, and drest in rags, and were both men and women. And when I lookt down toward the floor I saw there was not any floor, but only a black unfathomable abyss, into which straggled vainly the lurid phosphorescence of the corpses. And I stared in fascination till a workman passing by on the sidewalk brush'd against me and reminded me of the proper dignity of an old gentleman, who shou'd not be standing in a publick street staring into bleary windows and subject to the passing contact of plebeians. And I saw a cat on that street. A tiger cat.

Thence I proceeded to Brown-Street, where I was determin'd to buy some marvellous bas-reliefs of antique Salem and Marblehead places, that I had two months before seen in an art shop window. In December I had been penniless but for coach fare; this time I was (for me) fairly well supply'd with money. The shop in question was that of one Sarah Symonds, a spinster of elderly years and unquestion'd genius; of the oldest Salem stock, and an artist of much local celebrity. Her sole specialty is the brown or tinted bas-relief of ancient and weird places; and in the shop windows all of Salem, Marblehead, and Old Boston stare at the passenger with curious magick. It was, indeed, the haunting placque of Marblehead there, which induc'd me to make those enquiries last December which resulted in my visiting that singular town. This placque I was resolv'd to buy, together with one of the Salem Witch House, brooding under its horrible overnourished oak tree. I can scarce convey in words the sentient terror or antiquity in those placques for it is too subtle for human expression.[10] It broods . . and leers . . I am convinc'd that no medium is equal to the bas-relief in expressing such peculiar gradations of fear and age as Salem and Marblehead possess; and believe that Mistress Symonds hath made a master stroke in its selection and exclusive use for the purpose. The execution is of the highest order; with just the proper balance betwixt impressionism and realism—and my judgment is confirm'd by the discriminating

publick, whose purchases make of the shop a thriving institution. On this occasion I was tempted to buy all the contents of the shop, for truly, the spirit
of antiquity was captur'd in all the objects hanging about; but I confin'd myself to the two I had originally wisht, together with two small witch placques
(a shilling each) as souvenirs for my aunts. The artist was out, and I was
waited on by a young nymph of much intelligence and loquacity anent Salem
antiquities; who directed me to several places not in the guide book, but who
finally did up the wrong placques thro' negligence, so that I was that night
disappointed when I sought to shew them to Edw: Cole, Esq. From the shop,
bearing (as I thought) my precious placques, I proceeded to East India Marine Hall, (which wou'd make you, little Belknap, think of the India-House in
Hanover-Square, New-York) now the property of the Essex Institute and
housing the Peabody Museum of Marine and Oriental antiquities. There I
revell'd the time away; browsing amidst models, relics, and memorials of antient New-England shipping, till I feel I cou'd now write as good a sea story
as Arthur Gordon Pym;[11] and afterward delving into the Japanese collection
so deeply that time became a myth. There is no collection half so good elsewhere: even the New-York Metropolitan Museum is infinitely behind this
special horde of Japanese curiosities; whose fulness is due to the long years of
active trade betwixt Salem and the Orient. My New-England blood leapt at
the thought of this former maritime glory; and I swell'd with the pride of a
Nordick, a son of uncounted generations of blond-bearded men of power
and adventure . . . . conquerors, . . . . . slayers . . . . a master-race!

From Marine Hall I went to a shop and bought the cards which I sent
you children. Then I started out, by a winding route, for Gallows Hill. Ascending St. Peter Street, I stopt at St. Peter's Church (a place for all the world
like an old parish church in England) to view the graves. They are scatter'd
about in all angles of the hoary edifice, even straggling in single file along the
narrow plot of grass separating the north wall from the flagstone walk beside
it. One stone, in a southwest angle of the church, contains a name used by
Mr. Hawthorne in connexion with one of his novels: reading "Here lyes buried ye body of Jonathan Pue, Esq., Late surveyor and searcher of his Majes-
ties' customs in Salem, New England".[12] He died in 1760. I was now at the
corner of Federal Street, site of the town gaol of 1692 where the suspected
witches were confin'd. One wall of the gaol is still standing, built into a house
now number'd 4 Federal St. Being yet at liberty I paused not here, but walkt
along Federal St. westward, following the route prescribed by the book and
my later informant. I beheld some of the most famous mansions of the town,
including the Pierce-Nichols House (1782), into which I could not get till the
following day, tho' it is own'd by the Essex Institute. I several times paused to
stroke cats, which abound in all parts of the town; whether or not left there
by witches, none may say. At last I reached bleak Boston-Street on the western rim of the town, and walkt north toward Gallows-Hill. Here the houses

were greyer and more uncommunicative, and the cold wind made sounds I had not before notic'd. A very old man told me where to find the approach to Gallows-Hill, and hobbled beside me a while as if knowing that I was, like himself, in some way strangely linkt to the spectral past. When the ascent became steep he left me, but not without hinting that Gallows-Hill is not a nice place to visit at night. On and on I climb'd, crunching under my heavy overshoes the crushed, malignant snow. The wind blew and the trees tossed leafless branches; and the old houses became thinner and thinner. Some were not over a century and a half old, but others had overhanging gables and latticed windows which told me that they had been standing there when the terrible carts rattled with their doomed load from the gaol in Federal Street. Up . . . . up . . . . up . . . . Damn that wind—why *can't* it sound less *articulate?* At last I was on the summit, where in the bed rock still lurk the iron clamps that held the witch gallows. It was getting on in the afternoon, and the light was reddish that glow'd over all the outspread town. It was a weird town in that light, as seen from that hill where strange winds moaned over the untenanted wastes on the westward. And I was alone on that hill in that sepulchral place, where the allies of the devil had swung . . . and swing . . . and hurled out curses on their executioners and their descendants. I recall'd a witchcraft judge (Major Bartholomew Gedney) in mine own maternal ancestry, and thought of certain imprecations of the dead in fact and fiction. . . . . "God shall give them blood to drink."[13] And at that moment, as God is my judge, I heard faintly but distinctly the clanking of chains in the wind . . . . the chains of the gibbet which had not stood since 1693 . . . . and from that accursed wind came a shriek that was more than the shrieking of wind . . . . . a malignant, daemoniac sound that left in my ears the hideous echo of a syllable . . . "-ire" . . . . which in turn brought up as if in shocking memory a crude couplet I never heard before or since:

> "We swing higher,
> You feed the fire!"

And so I hung around Gallows Hill so long that Marblehead became out of the question for that day. Silently I descended past the leering houses with their centuried small-paned bleary windows, and as I did so my fancy brought vividly to my eyes a terrible procession going both up and down that hill beside me—a terrible procession of black-cowled things bearing bodies swathed in burlap. And so ample were the cowls, that I could not see the face of any of the things . . . . or whether they had any faces. And as I neared the bottom of the hill they faded silently away, leaving me to pick my way back to Chestnut Street, the most exclusive part of the town, where in palaces of Colonial architecture still reside the aristocratic descendants of the captains and merchants who planned so well. The street is a veritable boulevard with its rows of antient chestnuts and its stately and opulent mansions; it is the London West End of George the Third's time, transplanted to these colonies. The hour was now late, and I hasten'd past the Old Pickering House (built in 1660, the year of his Majesty's glorious restauration) to the Broad-Street Burying Hill, where I trod under cypresses on grave-snows which held no print but mine. It was cold on Burying Hill. Thence a tortuous walk to the station through slums of Greeks and Italians—slums that were standing when the usurper Cromwell spread treason through our Kingdom. In one filthy Greek alley I found the house where the father of the architect McIntyre liv'd, early in the 18th century, and where the artist John Singleton Copley[14] liv'd for a time . . . . a true loyalist, who went to England in 1775, and whose son became the Lord Chancellor Lyndhurst. After that the station, a coach-ride to Boston, and a meeting with the Hon. Edward Howard Cole.

Dinner at the Copley-Square Hotel . . . but a skeleton at the feast! Politics! To make a long story short, Cole pleaded, wept, and got down on his knees in an effort to make me run for the *National* presidency next July.[15] Sancta Pegāna! He said that if I had any friendship for him, or any solicitude for the amateur cause, I would not leave my work uncompleted; and lugubriously assur'd me, that if I shou'd retire in July all my former work wou'd be lost. It was a piteous spectacle—Cole was Morton with a quarter of a century knock'd off . . . . these Harvard men are frightful entreaters! I pacify'd him as best I cou'd, remain'd non-committal, bade him sleep well, and departed for the Brunswick. Meanwhile I had tried to shew him my new placques and found the wrong ones. Damn.

On the following day I started again for Salem and Marblehead; this time with a programme more carefully plann'd. I first visited the Essex Institute, view'd again the collection I had admir'd last December, including the scarlet-coated PEPPERRELL before the walls of Louisburg, and obtain'd a card of admission to the Pierce-Nichols house. Thence I visited the Symonds Shop in Brown-Street to exchange the placques, and by rare good fortune discover'd the artist herself in charge. Mistress Symonds is a plain, stoutish, elderly person who brilliantly refutes the fallacy of some little boys I know, that artists must be decadent, bohemian, hecktick, dissipated idiots; for to a genius of the most undoubted sort, she adds the homely and wholesome personality of an old New-England conservative aristocrat. She has dwelt always at Salem in the conventional manner of an old Salem gentlewoman, and lives in a house that knew the tread of an ancestor's buckled shoes. When I enter'd the shop she knew who I was, for her clerk had describ'd me as one who not only admir'd the bas-reliefs but loved all things old and weird. And thereupon I struck an ideal fountain of antique Salem lore, for Mistress Symonds has hunted up every ghost and ghoul in the town, and is on familiar terms with most of the daemons. In 1692 she wou'd have been hung as a witch, but in 1923 she is safe in expressing an undying devotion to Poe and all that is antient and sinister.

From her I learnt of new sources of wild tales, and incidentally obtain'd a note of introduction to John Gauss, Esq., brother to the H. E. Gauss whose free-verse poem on Salem I quoted in my last joint letter to you children. The Gausses are old Salem stock. And I also receiv'd a card of introduction to Mr. Dowe of the Soc. for the Pres. of N. E. Antiquities, which will help me enter the old Cooper house (1654) in Cambridge. In turn I describ'd to Mistress Symonds many of the antiquities in Providence which she had not seen, and shew'd her pictures of the Royall House, which so imprest her that she decided to go at once and model certain parts of it. Mention of art led to mention of Clark Ashton Smith, Esq., and she was anxious to see his work—of which I regret I have not better specimens to shew her. Thence conversation inclin'd toward weird tales, and I mention'd that I had written some. Interested by this, she ask'd to hear some of the plots; and these having been related, she desired me to lend her the manuscripts as soon as I reach'd home—which I will do, subject to the usual temporal aberrations of confirm'd indolence. And as a final courtesy, the generous dame presented me free of charge with a most attractive placque of the Salem Town Pump—nor did she forget to exchange the placques I had bought. All now adorn my walls, and I gaze with a shudder at that Witch House glowering under its terrible oak—horror stalks there. And beside it rise the mad maze of gables, vanes, and chimney pots that form hoary Marblehead! Truly, my travels have come home with me, for the scenes live poignantly in those vividly fashion'd bas-reliefs.

I now crost over past the old church to Federal Street, and sought the Pierce-Nichols House. This is a poem in white wood and magic carving, the masterpiece of that SAMUEL MC INTYRE whose name shou'd live for ever in the annals of art. 'Tis still inhabited by descendants of the Salem Nichol-ses—two pitiful old maids nearing eighty, who a few years ago ran wholly out of money and were forc'd to put their house on the market. Salem, having a dignify'd and proper respect for its antient and honourable families, cou'd not suffer a NICHOLS to be in want, or even in penury; so that in the end the Essex Institute bought the house as a triumph of Colonial architecture, but gave it back to the poor old ladies with only one proviso: that on Wednesdays and Saturdays they admit to three rooms on the ground floor such visitors as have a card from the institute and desire to see the wonderful interior panelling and carving of the illustrious McIntyre. I struck thrice on the knocker (for no Salem aristocrat wou'd tolerate a doorbell—such things are unknown to the finer mansions) and was admitted by a serving-wench of plain but respectable appearance; who conveyed the sad information that one of the poor old ladies was ailing and like to expire. Naturally, I made to withdraw at once, but as I did so the other old lady call'd the wench from within and bade her ask me to view the rooms; for such is the pride of a true old aristocrat, that the shirking of a duty of honour, such as was imply'd by the Institute's purchase of the house, wou'd seem abhorrent. Accordingly I adopted that course prompted by tact, and went perfunctorily thro' the parlours and dining-room shewn by the wench; noting as I pass'd the breathless beauty of the carvings, panels, and cornices, and the shining brass latches and stately Colonial furniture. Then, having no doubt satisfy'd the poor old gentlewoman on the stairs that she had done her duty by the Institute, I departed in decent haste, saying (that the old lady might overhear) 'that I was grateful for having seen a dual monument of Salem's taste: a decoration that bespeaks a master designer, and a furnishing and atmosphere what bespeak a life of culture and nobility.' Today that stately mansion may be a house of death, where Salem ghosts in full-bottom'd wigs waft wistfully away with them the poor shrivell'd soul of their next the last daughter. But I hope that it is not, and that the antient sisters may float away together a long time hence, when the time comes, so that their dying will be scarce distinguishable from their living. Then there will be a funeral, and pompous people will say things they do not mean, and the house will become a museum under the efficient guidance of the Institute which is destroying one by one (to the vast disgust of Mistress Symonds) the more tenuous and nebulous myths of the antient town. Mayhap the shadowy Misses

[*The rest of this letter has been lost.*]

*Notes*

1. The Van Courtlandt House is located at Broadway and 242nd Street in the Bronx; it was built in 1748.
2. Samuel McIntire (1757–1811), a leading sculptor distinguished for his carving of portals and architectural decorations.
3. These all are fellow amateur journalists: Edward H. Cole (1892–1966); Edith Miniter (1867–1934); Nelson G. Morton, brother of James Ferdinand Morton (1870–1941); Albert A. Sandusky (d. 1934); and Michael Oscar White.
4. HPL alludes to his dispute with White over the latter's attack on Samuel Loveman in the article "Poets of Amateur Journalism" (*Oracle*, December 1922). HPL responded to White in "Bureau of Critics" (*National Amateur*, March 1923) and "In the Editor's Study" (*Conservative*, July 1923).
5. The *National Magazine* was a professional periodical that years before had reprinted several of HPL's poems first published in amateur journals, and published for the first time "On Receiving a Picture of the Marshes at Ipswich" (January 1917).
6. Charles A. A. Parker. At this time he and Edith Miniter were sharing quarters at 30 Waite Street in Malden, MA.
7. Nathaniel Hawthorne's *Doctor Grimshawe's Secret* (written 1861, published 1883) is set in a house next to the Charter Street Burying Ground in Salem.
8. HPL alludes to the myth of Cadmus.
9. Sir William Pepperrell (1696–1759), colonial American merchant, politician, and soldier who in 1745 commanded land forces that, with a British fleet, captured the French fortress of Louisbourg (now in Nova Scotia).

10. See HPL to Elizabeth Toldridge (5 October 1933; ms., JHL): "I have a very attractive bas-relief of the old Witch House hanging above My table—together with a companion piece depicting the ancient gambrel Roofs of Marblehead; both the work of the ingenious sculptor Sarah Symonds of Salem. . . ."

11. A reference to Poe's tale of nautical adventure, *The Narrative of Arthur Gordon Pym of Nantucket* (1838).

12. Jonathan Pue is a surveyor who has preserved the tale of Hester Prynne, as related by Hawthorne in the preface (titled "The Custom House") to *The Scarlet Letter* (1850).

13. This is the curse uttered by Matthew Maule upon Col. Pynchon in *The House of the Seven Gables* (1851) ("him" for "them" in Hawthorne). HPL cites it in his discussion of the novel in *Supernatural Horror in Literature* (1927).

14. John Singleton Copley (1738–1815), American painter of portraits and historical subjects; generally regarded the finest artist of colonial America.

15. HPL had become interim president of the NAPA in December 1922, taking over for William J. Dowdell, who had resigned. Although HPL served the remainder of the term (till July 1923), he did not run for re-election.


[16]   [To Galpin and Frank Belknap Long] [TLS]

598 Angell St., Providence, R.I.

May 1, 1923

To Belknap and Alfredus:

My dear Little Grandchildren:—

Tho' long delay'd by the vicissitudes of labours and distempers, I will at last take my pen in hand to tell you of my late travels in the Province of the Massachusetts-Bay.

I quitted Providence on a late afternoon coach Thursday, April 12, arriving in Boston shortly before the time of the Hub Club meeting to which I had been invited, and which form'd the excuse for the trip. This meeting lack'd the intellectual vigour which Edw: Cole, Esq., or Nelson Morton, Esq. wou'd have brought to it, but was amply enliven'd by the presence of my learned young friend Albert Sandusky, Esq., whose piquant additions to our English speech have earn'd him so just a celebrity in his native province. To employ his own diction, Bimbo Sandy[1] was there with bells on—you tell 'em, kid!—and ladled out enough spoonfuls of 190-proof syncopated socony to cop the fleece-lined electric fan for bulging brows. Sizzling sausage! but that egg sure did knock the other goofs west for a row of Aethiopian aeroplane hangars! We have no bananas today! Torrid atmosphere of less scholarly nature—but assaying a darned sight more C.P. egotism to the cubic centimetre—was provided by Al's bosom friend (they park their automatics outside when forc'd into the same room) Joseph Bernard Lynch, Esq., who seen his duty an' done it good, tipping off the empyrean at some length how he, and he alone, built up the new Hub personnel—and how the other guys has gotta come acrost wit' de kale if they expects he's gonna keep it up. Deep stuff, Joe—deep stuff! However, the principal speaker of the evening, George Brinton Beale, editor of the BOSTON SUNDAY POST MAGAZINE, was no flivver; and slung a pernicious line of gab on story writing and magazine requirements in general. Snappy stuff—except that he paus'd not to touch upon so trivial a concernment as artistick composition. He's one of them bozos what wants a spiel to be real uplifting and wholesome, and couldn't think of enough cuss words to lam at Eliott Paul, Esq.,[2] Boston's one realist, who from all accounts (I ain't read nothin' of his) is the Ben Hecht of New-England. Beale thinks Paul is just too awful and horrid for anything—an opinion which fossilised Boston shares, and which Paul recently reciprocated by telling Burton Rascoe, Esq. 'that he found it more interesting to live in Boston than in a civilised community'. Well—the meeting rolled along so-so. Michael White, Esq. endeavour'd to prove a pleasing and sociable talker, and inform'd me, that he lik'd my criticism in the NATIONAL AMATEUR![3] My gawd—the smelling-saults—quick! The bally dumbbell *liked* it, after I spent an hour trying to make it as subtly stinging as possible! No use—ya gotta bean that bimbo wit' a sledge-hammer afore he'll get wise that ya ain't pattin' him! Good night!

The meeting dispers'd without overt violence at about 11 p.m., and I accompany'd the Parker-Miniter delegation to their modest abode. There, after a conversational session with my joint hosts which lasted nearly till morning, I retir'd early and slept soundly; dreaming mainly of "Victory", the six-weeks-old kitten who had sat, squirm'd, or scratch'd in my lap during the entire period. Victory was born March 1st, and is the most engaging mite I have beheld in years. He climb'd over the entire area of his aged and adipose Grandpa, and finally settled on the back of the Old Gentleman's neck as an ideal sleeping-porch. But I digress. In the morn I greeted the natives, consum'd a moderate breakfast, and set out for my favourite antique Salem region. This time I went on the electrick coaches, twice having to change (at Revere Beach and at Lynn) before attaining Salem. 'Tis a ride of extream attractiveness, and must have form'd a diversion of prime magnitude in the days when open cars ran direct from Boston to Salem. But all things decay, and nothing more so than the rural tramways of New-England. The country is not what it was when I was young, and only the gods know what we are all coming to!

Arriv'd in Salem, I stroll'd a while through the venerable streets, and finally embark'd for Danvers—call'd "Salem-Village" in the 17th century, and forming the seat of most of the witchcraft cases of 1692. The coach ride was delightful, giving frequent glimpses of ancient houses in a fashion to stimulate the antiquarian soul. Suddenly, at a graceful and shady village corner which the coach was about to turn, I beheld the tall chimneys and ivy'd walls of a splendid brick house of later Colonial design, and espy'd a sign which proclaim'd it open for publick inspection. Captivated by the sight, I signall'd the driver and alighted; determin'd to add an item to my Colonial itinerary. Inform'd by the sign that this was the Capt. Samuel Fowler house, built 1809, accessible for eightpence, and the property of the Society for the Preservation of New-England Antiquities, I loudly sounded the knocker and awaited developments. Nothing develop'd. I then knock'd at the side door, but with equal futility. Then I noted a door half open in a miserable "ell" at the back of the house; and believing the place tenanted, made a third trial there.

My summons was answer'd simultaneously by two of the most pitiful and decrepit-looking persons imaginable—hideous old women more sinister than the witches of 1692, and certainly not under 80. For a moment I believ'd them to be Salem witches in truth; for the peculiarly sardonick face of one of them, with furtive eyes, sneering lips, and a conspicuously undershot lower law, intensify'd the impression produc'd by their incredible age and gauntness, and the utterly nondescript bundles of brownish rags which form'd their attire. The "ell" in which they dwelt was in a state of indescribable squalor; with heaps of rags, books, cooking utensils, and the like on every hand. One meagre wood stove fail'd altogether to heat the barren room against the cold of that sharp afternoon. The smaller, and probably older, of the two spoke first—in a hoarse rattling voice that dimly suggested death, and that was occasionally halted by a curious guttural impediment. This was the crone who did not have the corpselike sneer—but what a study they wou'd both have made for a Poe, a Baudelaire, or a Goya! If, however, their weird aspect and hideous squalor were sinister; what can one say of the *contrast* involv'd when the guttural salutation of the speaker became intelligible? For despite the omnipresent evidences of a slatternly decadence beyond words, this ancient witch was mumbling forth a courtly and aristocratick welcome in language and accents beyond question bespeaking the gentlest birth and proudest cultivation! The witch apologised for the unfavourable conditions prevailing, and lamented that she had not heard my knocking at the front door of the mansion proper. There was, she coughed in explanation, not enough fuel to heat the mansion; so she and her sister had to dwell in the wooden "ell" once used as a shed and storehouse. But in summer, indeed, they dwelt in the mansion—for was it not their own by inheritance, and had they not been born in one of its upper rooms? Yes—it was the old, old New-England story of family decay and aristocratick pauperism—a case like that of the poor Salem Nicholses, but infinitely worse. These tatter'd ancients were the Misses Fowler, own granddaughters of the proud seafarer and fighter who in his dashing prime had built that house for the comfort, dignity, and splendour of his descendants. Short-sighted man! Had he but foreseen the depths to which those descendants wou'd be driven! To think of their rags and kennel, and of his fastidious elegance in demanding the best French wallpaper, the finest brass latches, the choicest carved mantels, cornices, and wainscoting, and the most delicate silver, china, and ornaments that both Europe and America cou'd furnish! 1809–1923—one hundred and fourteen years of slow, insidious decay. In the veins of those horrible wrecks—last of their line—flows the mingled blood of all that was proudest in the Salem region—Endecotts who boasted the first Colonial governor, Fowlers who were known the seven seas over, Pickmans who bowed only to those whom they thought worthy, Ropeses whose halls were portrait-galleries of great ancestors, Pages who live in history . . . . . . the great-grandmother of these poor relics was that sprightly Mrs. Page who, at the time of the Colonial tea agitation, serv'd her guests with the beverage *on the roof* after her husband had forbidden her to serve it *under his roof.* Such is the dying New-England of today—a whole section's tragedy was epitomised when these unfortunate survivors paus'd beneath an oaken frame and amidst their tatters hoarsely call'd attention to the coat-of-arms which bespoke the haughty gentility of the Fowler blood. The house is finely preserv'd and restor'd, having been purchas'd from the aged sisters at their frantick request by the Society for the Preservation of New-England Antiquities. The Society hath given them the care of it for the pitiful remainder of their lives—as is the custom of such societies when dealing with such cases—but it has not money enough to keep them in food, fuel, and clothing. Still—it is better than the almshouse. The lives of the sisters is not wholly dull, for many intelligent persons come to see the house and its marvellous interior. The day before I was there, an architect from New-York had been over the place, and had copy'd many of the priceless Colonial designs for modern use. Fallen New-England! And yet how great were thine ancient glories! Who today cou'd create such things of beauty as the carvings of Salem craftsmen, the plate of Boston silversmiths, or the designs of classick architects all over the several provinces? Golden 18th century! It is not in jest that I hail thee as the age of universal taste and vigour! Led by the Sibylline wraiths of decay'd gentry, I explor'd the house from cellar to attick. Its decorations are of unrivall'd beauty, and its furniture, ornaments, china, and silver, are beyond description. Fine ancestral portraits, old garments of great richness, priceless laces and other Colonial remnants of domesticity—all these recall uncannily a bygone prosperity which the present mocks. I was allow'd to don a cap which Capt. Fowler wore in the War of 1812, and a civilian swallow-tail coat of the same period—a cream-colour'd dress garment which fitted me finely, and shew'd that the good captain was as stout an old gentleman as your grandpa. Finally I left—pressing upon my pathetick hostesses the admission fee which they sought to refuse in a last gesture of reminiscent aristocracy.

The afternoon was now well along, and I wish'd to visit two other places before leaving the region. Walking a mile to Danvers Square, I visited the old Page house (1754), where the great-grandmother of the Fowlers had once serv'd tea on the roof, and where now the Danvers Historical Society holds forth. The contents of the house did not prove of extream interest, but the building itself did. I examin'd the architecture with unaffected joy, and climb'd to the gambrel roof where the tea-party was held.

I now put the aera of Colonial refinement behind me, and hark'd back farther still to an age of darker and weirder appeal—the age of the dreaded witchcraft. Leaving Danvers, I struck out along the roads and across the fields toward the lone farmhouse built by Townsend Bishop in 1636, and in 1692 inhabited by the worthy and inoffensive old widow Rebekah Nurse, who was seventy years of age and wished no one harm. Accused by the superstitious West-Indian slave woman Tituba (who belong'd to the Rev. Samuel Parris and who caus'd the entire wave of delusion) of bewitching children, then denounc'd blindly by some of the hysterical children in question, Goodwife Nurse was arrested and brought to trial. Thirty-nine persons sign'd a paper attesting to her blameless conduct, and a jury render'd a verdict of "not guilty"; but popular clamour led the judges to reverse the verdict, (as was then possible) and on July 19, 1692 the poor old grandam was hang'd on Gallows Hill in Salem for a mythological crime. Her remains were brought back from Salem and interr'd in the family burying-ground—a ghoulish place shadow'd by huge pines and at some distance from the house. In 1886 a monument was erected to her memory, bearing an inscription by the poet Whittier.

As I approach'd the spot to which I had been directed, after passing thro' the hamlet of Tapleyville, the afternoon sun was very low. Soon the houses thinn'd out; so that on my right were only the hilly fields of stubble, and occasional crooked trees clawing at the sky. Beyond a low crest a thick group of spectral boughs bespoke some kind of grove or orchard—and in the midst of this group I suddenly descry'd the rising outline of a massive and ancient chimney. Presently, as I advanced, I saw the top of a grey, drear, sloping roof—sinister in its distant setting of bleak hillside and leafless grove, and unmistakably belonging to the haunted edifice I sought. Another turn—a gradual ascent—and I beheld in full view the sprawling, tree-shadow'd house which had for nearly 300 years brooded over those hills and held such secrets as men may only guess. Like all old farmhouses of the region, the Nurse cottage faces the warm south and slopes low toward the north. It fronts on an ancient garden, where in their season gay blossoms flaunt themselves against the grim, nail-studded door and the vertical sundial above it. That sundial was long concealed by the overlaid clapboards of gothick generations, but came to light when the house was restored to original form by the memorial society which owns it. Everything about the place is ancient—even to the tiny-paned lattice windows which open outward on hinges. The atmosphere of witchcraft days broods heavily upon that low hilltop.

My rap at the ancient door brought the caretaker's wife, an elderly unimaginative person with no appreciation of the dark glamour of the ancient scene. This family live in a lean-to west of the main structure—an addition probably 100 years less ancient than the parent edifice. I was the first visitor of the 1923 season, and took pride in signing my name at the top of the register. Entering, I found myself in a low, dark passage whose massive beams almost touched my head; and passing on, I travers'd the two immense rooms on the ground floor—sombre, barren, panell'd apartments with colossal fireplaces in the vast central chimney, and with occasional pieces of the plain, heavy furniture and primitive farm and domestick utensils of the ancient yeomanry. In these wide, low-pitch'd rooms a spectral menace broods—for to my imagination the 17th century is as full of macabre mystery, repression, and ghoulish adumbrations as the 18th century is full of taste, gayety, grace, and beauty. This was a typical Puritan abode; where amidst the bare, ugly necessities of life, and without learning, beauty, culture, freedom, or ornament, terrible stern-fac'd folk in conical hats or poke-bonnets dwelt 250 and more years ago—close to the soil and all its hideous whisperings; warp'd in mentality by isolation and unnatural thoughts, and shivering in fear of the devil on autumn nights when the wind howl'd through the twisted orchard trees or rustled the hideous corpse-nourish'd pines in the graveyard at the foot of the hill. There is eldritch fascination—horrible bury'd evil—in these archaick farmhouses. After seeing them, and smelling the odour of centuries in their walls, one hesitates to read certain passages in Cotton Mather's strange old "Magnalia" (which you, little Belknap, shall see when you come to visit your old grandpa) after dark.[4] After exploring the ground floor I crept up the black crooked stairs and examin'd the bleak chambers above. The furniture was as ugly as that below, and included a small trundle-bed in which infant Puritans (even as you, children) were lull'd to sleep with meaningless prayers and morbid hints of daemons riding the night-wind outside the small-paned lattice-windows. Poor little creatures! No wonder there were very few Alfredi or Belnapii amongst them—what artistick or intellectual mind cou'd survive so stultifying an environment? It was the somewhat more civilised class in the larger towns, and the newer colonists from Mother England, (GOD SAVE THE KING!) who in the next century burst forth into that sublimation of beauty which is Colonial architecture and decoration. That was New-England's one gift to the fine arts—and a magnificent gift it was. But still the old Rebekah Nurse house broods and leers on its ancient hill. I saw old Rebekah's favourite chair, where she used to sit and spin before the Salem magistrates dragged her to the gallows. And the sunset wind whistled in the colossal chimney, and ghouls rattled ghastly skeletons from unseen attic rafters overhead. Tho' it was not suppos'd to be open to the publick, I persuaded the caretaker to let me ascend to that hideous garret of century'd secrets. Thick dust cover'd everything, and unnatural shapes loom'd on every hand as the evening twilight oozed through the little blear'd panes of the ancient windows. I saw something hanging from the wormy ridge-pole—something that sway'd as if in unison with the vesper breeze outside, tho' that breeze had no access to this funereal and forgotten place—shadows . . . . . shadows . . . . .

shadows . . . . . And I descended from that accursed garret of palaeogean arcana, and left that portentous abode of antiquity; left it and went down the
hill to the graveyard under the shocking pines, where twilight shew'd sinister
slabs and rusty bits of fallen iron fence, and where something squatted in
shadow on a monument—something that made me climb the hill again, hurry
shudderingly past the venerable house, and descend the opposite slope to
Tapleyville as night came.

After that I rode uneventfully back to Danvers, (where I mail'd cards to
you children) Salem, Boston, and Maplewood. Partaking of dinner with Victory on my lap chewing my watch-charm, I again participated in conversation
till the small hours, and retir'd to await the dawn which wou'd usher in my
Merrimack and Newburyport excursion. Victory was with me to the last—
after he became tired of chewing his grandpa's fingers and watch-chain, he
scrambled up to his favourite place behind the Old Gentleman's neck and
there slumber'd peacefully whilst discussion wax'd high amongst the meer
human beings present. Blest atom of happy life! Wou'd that all the world
might be as thou! And yet are not thy cousins the subtle sphinx, and the insatiable lion of Libya and Numidia?

Dawn of Saturday! I was up betimes, and ate breakfast with Victory
climbing sportively all over me. Near the close of the meal, my young friend
essayed a journey from the floor up my leg and chest to his chosen perch behind my neck; but as he near'd the summit he unwisely chose the lace ruffles
of my shirt instead of my brocade waistcoat or velvet coat as a hand-hold.
Unponderous as he was with his meer month and a half of terrestrial entity,
the dubious fabrick of the too-often-launder'd garment was not enough to
sustain him—and down he went, leaving an aching void in my aged bosom!!
Not that he was hurt—bless my soul! . . . the mite was kicking and rolling
about gleefully in my lap before I knew what had happen'd—but that aching
void was in a place which neither suit nor cravat cou'd cover, and in my attempt to "travel light" I had provided no other shirt! Eheu! And when I
sought to bunch the place and fix it with pins, my fingers made new rents!
No use—the old rag had reach'd the end of its rope—and it had to choose a
place like Malden for the grand finale! Well—the only solution was a new
shirt, so after bidding my hosts adieu, and running off a page of the new
HUB CLUB QUILL on Parker's press, (it took three trials to shew me the
knack of feeding and pedalling the confounded thing) I beat it for Boston,
where I stock'd up at a linen-draper's and threw the old outfit away. I could
not find anything antient enough exactly to suit me—the new shirt hath chev-
iot fabrick and turn'd-back soft cuffs—but any port in a storm. So, duly
garb'd, I took the coach for Haverhill and was there by mid-afternoon.

Transferring to the Merrimack coach, and speeding toward the abode of
my great-grandchild Davis, whom I was to visit, I pass'd Whittier's birthplace
(built 1688 by his ancestor Tho: Whittier, inhabited by the poet till 1837, and

scene of "Snow-Bound") and beheld a region of delightful scenery. The trip was not long, and I soon alighted by the large early Victorian house in sleepy Main-Street which shelters the youthful near-Galba and his family. Edgar himself answer'd the door, and lo! I found him in his first suit with long trousers! How you children do grow! His 15th birthday occurr'd a week ago last Friday, and he is consuming the second year of high-school as a pure pleasure. When, recently, intelligence tests were apply'd to all the pupils in the Merrimack High-School, Edgar came out with a rating conspicuously highest! He has a reputation to live up to, and I predict that he will fulfil every expectation—even tho' you, small Alfredus, scorn to honour him with your epistolary communion. I trust that you, little Belknap, will be less haughty; and will take the time to give the infant a general stimulus in the direction of art and voluminous reading. Remember his abode—16 Main St., Merrimac, Mass. Name, Edgar Jacobs Davis.

After briefly greeting such of the family—mother and sister—as were present, I departed with Edgar for the ancient shades of Amesbury; it having been decided that Newburyport shou'd be saved for the morrow. The coach took us thro' some of the choicest scenery of New-England, for in this northerly region the hills are gentle and graceful, and unexpected vistas of old village roofs and spires are frequent. Commerce and manufactures have not destroy'd the Arcadian simplicity of the inhabitants, and they still dream the years away amidst scenes but little alter'd by the passing centuries. We alighted at the ancient graveyard where Whittier lies bury'd, and marvell'd in the sombre pines and willows, slabs and monuments. Edgar reveal'd an imagination of high quality, and upon one occasion call'd my attention to the inimitably *Babylonian* effect of a certain granite memorial of pyramidal outline, as glimps'd thro' distant trees against the iridescent sunset. The older part of this necropolis is on a hill, and as we wander'd among the hoary slate headstones we feasted our eyes on many a gigantick elm or incredibly antient house. As the sun sank, we rambled on past the "Captain's Well" mention'd in Whittier's poem, and finally attain'd the actual village of Amesbury, which holds much of its primitive quaintness despite a ridiculously metropolitan traffick sign at one of the central junction points. Strolling along Friend St., we sought the later home of Whittier; finally pausing to ask an aged man its whereabouts, and discovering to our chagrin that we had made the inquiry directly in front of it, so that the old villager had only to point to the conspicuous tablet which we had wholly overlook'd. One, so to speak, on us! Tarrying briefly, we sought the coach; and were soon whirling thro' the mystick loveliness of old New-England toward the Davis mansion.

That evening I met the entire family, including William, the aged and dignify'd cat who thereafter spent much of his time in Grandpa's lap. Another interesting object was Herman F. Davis, Esq., head of the house and father of the prodigy, who tho' of excellent ancestry was born in the district of Maine, and retains a rustick love of citizenly practicality which makes him lamentably unsympathetick with his civilised son. Despite his provincial and commonplace ideas, and dogmatick way of arguing, he is intelligent and hearty; and I took considerable pleasure in verbal warfare with him. I try'd to make him realise that his "lazy and dependent" child is not to be criticised too sharply; and that he shou'd be proud of being the parent of so superior an individual. Edgar's mother is sympathetick toward his aspirations, but distinctly Victorian in her own literary activities and appreciations. The sister—now in college—is a conscientious and undistinguish'd "grind"—learned but not gifted. On this occasion a college friend of the sister's was present—an unimaginative encyclopaedia of the same type; about to win a Phi Beta Kappa key, yet essentially provincial and commonplace. Amidst this dull-grey environment small Edgar hath sprung up and blossom'd like an exotick plant—dimly admir'd yet never understood. He is a true 12 o'clock feller in a 9 o'clock town—or I might say a 2 a.m. feller in an 8 o'clock town! Critical, cynical, iconoclastick, unsentimental, tolerant, civilised—he belongs around B'way and 116th St. rather than on Merrimack's Main Street.* But the future beckons him, and he is sufficiently independent to map out his own course . . . . even tho' his father complains that he's unpractical to the extent of sitting and shivering rather than fetching wood for the fire. His general type is just now perhaps a trifle more Galpinian than Belnapian; but he is by no means one-sided, and only an authentick prophet cou'd justly presume to define his course thro' the farce call'd life. The Davis home is of the solid type of two generations ago, opulently clutter'd with the hideous black-walnut of the 1850 period. I was assign'd an immense room—perhaps even larger than my old room at my birthplace—in which was running water . . . . . an archaick marble set-bowl just like those at good old 454 Angell! In these homely if rococo surroundings I dropt peacefully to sleep, to be awaken'd on the morrow by the gentle tap of my great-grandson.

Sunday morning was spent in general discussion, the entire household sitting like a Roman audience at the Amphitheatrum Flavianum whilst Davis' father and I good-naturedly tore each other to pieces. It was so spirited a fight, that Edgar and I were late in starting for Newburyport; but finally we contriv'd to board a coach at the village square. We had wish'd to take honest Tryout along with us, but he writ that he was nervously ill, and cou'd not bear even so much as a caller at his Plaistow hermitage. Poor, amiable old faun! Here's hoping the warm weather gives him new vigour and calls him forth to disport with Pan and the satyrs and dryades of his native groves! He's around 72 now, but still a gentle, unspoilt boy at heart. I wish I cou'd have seen him.

Changing electrick coaches twice—once because of a broken bridge and the other time just because—we sped along the old Colonial river country in

---

*He now lives in Boston.

delight. Crossing Chain Bridge over the Merrimack—the oldest suspension bridge in America—we approached the suburbs of Newburyport and began to get whiffs and glimpses of the neighbouring sea, and to descry the ancient houses and chimney-pots of the famous town which, tho' said a century and a quarter ago by John Quincy Adams to possess a social life more cultivated and brilliant than that of Washington, is today locally known as "The City of the Living Dead".

Up the narrow street we rattled—deciding to stick to the one-man coach for a preliminary panorama, and to defer the pedestrian exploring till later. Ineffably quaint and archaick are those Georgian streets which we saw from the windows—fascinating hills lin'd with venerable dwellings of every description, from 200-year-old hovels huddled together in nondescript groups with rambling extensions and lean-to's, to stately Colonial mansions with proud gables and magnificent doorways. One feature possess'd in common by nearly all the houses, great and humble alike, especially held our attention; this being the curious old-world abundance of *chimney-pots*, here more prevalent even than in mysterious Marblehead. All at once the coach reach'd a spacious square, lin'd on every side with the quaint brick mercantile buildings of the Revolutionary period. It was a sight such as we had never seen before—a city business section of the 18th century, preserv'd in every detail. As the coach pass'd on, entering again a delicious maze of ancient streets and turning almost every corner in sight, we wonder'd when we shou'd reach the modern business section; but after a time the houses thinn'd out and we found ourselves speeding past the shanties (shantih shantih shantih)[5] of fishermen toward the salt marshes of the open country to the south, with the sandchoak'd harbour on our left, and the long stretch of Plum Island in the distance beyond. Then we question'd the driver, and discover'd the truth of a suspicion which had cross'd our minds but fleetingly before. It was really so—that Georgian business section was in fact the business section of today as well! You children have seen it on the cards Edgar and I sent—can you imagine it? Fancy, little Belknap, the New-York of 1780 still surviving—with Broad and Pearl Streets lin'd with the principal shops and counting-houses, Wall Street distinctly northerly, the City Hall Park too far uptown to be a good land investment save for dwellings. Grotesque? Yet the commercial Newburyport of 1780 still stands . . . truly, a City of the Living Dead!

There are only three restaurants, two of which are Hellenick dumps frequented only by the peasantry, and the third of which is the cafe of the Adams House—an hostelry over a century old which keeps its original sign. This eating-house wou'd (small Alfredus) make any Cleveland Clark's Lunch look like the main dining-room of the Statler, or (little Belknap) any upper Broadway cafeteria look like the Plaza,—and yet it is Newburyport's only civilised place of refection! But what prices! Cheap? Say! 65 cents bought a bigger dinner than I could eat; tho' Edgar managed to stow his away.

Upon alighting from the coach, at the end of its route, we stroll'd back thro' the maze of picturesque streets; ecstatically drinking in the antique houses of wood, brick, and stone, with peaked, gambrel, or flat roofs, massive or graceful chimneys, quaint chimney-pots, and artistick Colonial doorways. It was the past brought to life—flashes of 18th century bye-streets, silhouettes of Christopher Wren steeples, kaleidoscopick etchings of old-time skylines, snatches of glistening harbour beyond delectably rambling and alluringly ante-diluvian alleys that wind lazily down hill—a true paradise of the born antiquar-ian! Once we walk'd the whole length of a ramshackle alley without losing for a second the illusion of the Colonial age of sea-power. Thro' a cross-alley we saw the splendid facade and columns of a stone mansion in the distance—engaging vista! Thoughts of the past well'd up—here were the lodgings of ad-venturous sailors who knew the far Indies and the perfum'd East, and there dwelt a solid, periwigg'd captain whose skill had led many a sturdy barque around the Horn, or thro' Magellan's tortuous strait, or past the Cape of Good Hope. Then we went down to the rotting wharves and dream'd of old days, and in fancy saw the heaps of cordage and bales of strange Asian wares, and the forest of Yankee masts that reach'd half across to Plum Island. Ah, me—the days that were! After this we return'd to the business section, bought some cards at one of the two visible chemist shops, (the other was clos'd for Sun-day!) and set out for famous and opulent High Street, where stands the old mansion of the celebrated eccentrick Timothy Dexter.

Timothy Dexter—or Lord Timothy Dexter, as he lov'd to be call'd—died 117 years ago, but is still the principal topick of interest in Newburyport. His fame, indeed, went far beyond his native shoars; and you children have probably heard of him as the man who was jested into buying warming-pans to export to tropical Cuba, yet who made a fortune with them because the Cubans eagerly bought them as molasses ladles; who was trick'd into buying some useless whalebone, yet who made another fortune with that because of the rise of a new fashion which put the commodity in demand; who stock'd his cellar with needless provisions in expectation of a visit from the heirs of the murder'd Louis XVI, whom he had spectacularly invited to live in his mansion; yet who sold those provisions at an handsome profit when the visit fail'd to materialise. "Lord" Timothy is a semi-legendary figure, and New-England will never forget him!

Timothy Dexter was a common and ignorant leather-dresser, born in Malden Jany. 22, 1747. Later moving to Charlestown, he made a very sub-stantial fortune by marrying a rich widow and increasing her prosperity thro' shrewd investments such as "cornering" necessities in a small way, and buy-ing up the depreciated continental currency which ascended spectacularly when Mr. Hamilton put the U.S. finances on a solid basis. The close of the 1780's found Dexter quite wealthy, but with a grotesque temperament which made that wealth the source of unprecedented vagaries. His first step was to try to gratify his extravagant social ambition, and to seek equality with the Hancocks and other rising mercantile families of Boston. This, quite naturally, was rather a joke; since he could not even speak or write grammatically; but his failure caus'd him to quit Boston for ancient Newburyport, whence his wife had come, and whose society he erroneously deem'd more accessible than Boston's. Settling in Newburyport, Dexter bought the finest mansion in the town, and proceeded to embellish it in what his ignorant mind conceiv'd to be the best European taste. Within a month he was a general laughing-stock; for aside from his clumsy social advances, he had begun to evolve around his house a bizarre chaos of absurdity and grotesqueness such as New-England had never seen before. Flamboyant carvings bedizen'd the mansion—carvings which violated every aesthetick principle—and ridiculously laid-out gardens offended the eye on every hand. Erecting a high fence with massive posts, and within it a variety of conspicuous arches and pedestals, Dexter topp'd each post, pillar, and arch with hideous wooden statues of celebrities, clumsily wrought by a young ship-carver named Joseph Wilson, whom he later underpaid and abused. The statues had no resemblance to their purported subjects, and when Dexter tired of one hero he wou'd have him alter'd to another . . . . thus Genl. Morgan soon became the rising soldier Buonaparte, whose future majesty the eccentrick shrewdly forecast. Other statues were of the American presidents, added one by one as they were elected; sundry Indian sachems; Benjamin Franklin; Horatio Nelson; the goddesses of Fame and Liberty; and chief of all, Timothy Dexter himelf, with the self-assum'd title of Lord, and the following modest inscription—which Joseph Wilson spell'd out for him:

> "I am the First in the East, the First in the West, and the Greatest Philosopher in the Western World."

Dexter, failing to enter Newburyport society, contented himself with perpetual drunkenness, dissipation, and ostentation. He liv'd in the utmost disorder, mussing and tearing the valuable books which an expert had purchas'd for him, (and in which he only try'd to spell out the obscene passages) and breaking half of his elegant French furniture. He had a splendid coach with a coat-of-arms (taken at random from a book) painted on it, and bought a country house in Chester, N.H., afterward styling himself "King of Chester". Sometimes he wou'd go afoot thro' the streets, drest in rich cloathes and well-powder'd periwig, carrying a gold-headed cane and follow'd by a curious little hairless dog. The more aristocratick children wou'd mock at him, but common boys wou'd follow him and hail him as "My Lord", which ever bought a shower of money from his capacious pockets. He affected to be a great lover of nobility, and had the church-bells toll'd when the French mob kill'd King Louis XVI, whose heirs he invited to share his mansion. He hired a sort of

David V. Bush to be his poet-laureate—a miserable ex-fishmonger who produc'd stanzas like this:

> "Lord Dexter like King Solomon
> Hath gold and silver by the ton,
> And bells to churches he hath giv'n
> To worship the great King of Heav'n."

This "poet"—whose name was Jonathan Plummer[6]—he drest in a most gorgeous livery. Dexter had a magnificent coffin prepar'd for himself, and like
the late Mde. Bernhardt sometimes slept in it.[7] Once he publickly rehears'd
his funeral, and afterward beat his wife because she did not weep enough. His
half-wit son Samuel, a debauch'd gamester, and his almost wholly idiotick
daughter, he educated expensively; having special masters since they cou'd
learn nothing in any school. Later he marry'd the daughter off to an Englishman of much refinement, who divorc'd her as soon as he perceiv'd the extent
of her imbecility. But all the while Dexter kept his business shrewdness. He
speculated wisely, and was interested in the building of Chain Bridge across
the Merrimack. Some have even believ'd that part of his eccentricity was assum'd for advertising purposes. His wealth was probably overrated, however,
for he left only $35,027.39 in his will. His superstition was extream, and he
not only kept an aged negress as household soothsayer, but frequently con-
sulted the celebrated Moll Pitcher of Marblehead; a "witch" then living in
Lynn at an advanc'd age.

In 1796, stung by the ridicule of the publick, Dexter publish'd what was
probably America's queerest book—Bush's "Peace Poems and Sausages" not
excepted. This hilarious pamphlet, intitul'd "A Pickle for the Knowing
Ones", consisted of odd scraps of Dexter's views on everything under the
sun; together with some sharp rebukes of the inquisitive Newburyporters
who gossip'd about how he made his money. It is here that he told the
warming-pan and whalebone stories which are so famous, yet which are set
down by modern criticks as meer fabrications of Dexter's odd ironick humour. Among the subjects discuss'd by "Lord" Timothy are the folly of separating Newburyport from the town of Newbury, the value of bridges, the
world situation, and such like. In one place he singularly anticipates that other
fool Woodrow Wilson in the "League of Nations" matter—listen, children, to
this specimen of his genius, copy'd *verbatim et literatim* from his "Pickle" as still
preserv'd in the publick library at Haverhill:

> "I Command pease and the gratest brotherly Love and Not fade be
> Linked to gether with that best of troue Love so as to govern all nasions on
> the fass of the gloub not to tiranize over them but to put them in order if
> any Despout shall A Rise as to boundreys or Any maturs of Improtance it is
> Left frense and grat britton and Amacarey to be setteled A Congress to be

allways in france all Despouts is to be there settled and this maybe Dun this will balless power and then all wars Dun A way there-fore I have the Lam to Lay Don with the Lion Now this may be Dun if thos three powers would A geray to Lay what is called Devel one side and Not Carry the gentlemen pack hors Any longer but shake him of as dust on your feet and Laff at him."

Is this not truly Woodrovian—aside from spelling and punctuation? By the way—people complain'd that Dexter's "Pickle" was unpunctuated, so when he issued a second edition he added a full page of assorted punctuation marks at the end—though again failing to punctuate the text—and explain'd himself in the following note:

> "mister printer the Nowing Ones complane of my book the fust edi-tion had no stops I put in A Nuf here and thay may peper and solt it as they plese."

Of this book Dexter gave away thousands of copies, so that it is fairly obtain-able today by collectors with the requisite finances. Edgar says he feels akin to Lord Timothy—but I have not yet seen the likeness.

Drunken, revelling, cursing—Timothy Dexter died on Octr. 26, 1806, and was cheated of interment in the garish mausoleum which he had built behind his house—since the Newburyport Board of Health forbade it! He rests obscurely in a churchyard—the yard of a church which refus'd the gifts he once offer'd on condition of having a statue set up to him in an alcove. Vain to the last—an object of ridicule—he is still the best known feature ever connected with the dead city whose people so thoroughly repudiated him. After his decease, the grotesque mansion was inhabited by his idiot daughter and her own small daughter—also an imbecile,—till the two died, about the same time. The son surviv'd his father only a year. Later, in the absence of any legitimate heirs, the place was sold by the town; and is now restor'd to sanity, nothing but some columns (which are hard to remove and not very conspicuous) and the gilt eagle on the cupola (which is not at all ugly) re-maining today of all the gewgaws affix'd by the erratick "Lord". In our family there is an old print of the place as it look'd in 1810—four years after Dex-ter's death—and the scene is indeed grotesque!

Having found and gaz'd at the Dexter mansion, Edgar and I proceeded to explore other parts of stately High Street. It is a splendid thoroughfare, and remarkably alive considering the deadness of the business section; tho' it must be less gorgeous than when Talleyrand prais'd its beauty. I wou'd not think of comparing it to Chestnut St. in Salem. The reason for its vitality as compar'd with that of the anaemick "downtown", is that most of the resi-dents are very wealthy, and keep in touch with Boston thro' their coaches. When they wish to buy or see anything, they make for Tremont St. rather than their own village square; thus being practically Bostonian & leaving

Newburyport commerce to the small fry—or such of them as do not trade in Haverhill. High St. boasts even a traffick watchman!

The day was now advancing. As we stroll'd south from Dexter's mansion we notic'd the antient churchyard and the new church going up within it. That edifice will mark Newburyport's awakening to the great aesthetick truth which Salem hath always realis'd—namely, that every old town hath its fixt architectural atmosphere, to which all new buildings must conform. In the hideous Victorian age of tastelessness, nearly every old town but Salem was ruin'd by the construction of ugly nondescript buildings like New-York's Post-Office, Providence's City Hall and Butler Exchange, Boston's City Hall and Post Office, etc. Salem alone knew the need for harmonious congruity, and stuck to classical and Colonial models. But just now Newburyport is waking up, and is trying to reclaim its heritage. In this old churchyard, where once a Colonial belfry saluted the sky, an ugly neo-Gothick church was built some time in the 19th century when the original structure decay'd or burn'd. It was horribly out of place in Newburyport—but what cou'd be expected of Victorian times? Now—Pegāna be prais'd—taste hath reappear'd; and the Gothick monstrosity hath been torn down to make way for a beautiful new stone edifice on the simple and classical lines of the original Georgian fane. Gloria in excelsis! Once more the ancient slabs will look up to noble walls in harmony with their atmosphere, and the quiet corner—where a venerable bye-street slopes shadily and beckoningly down from the travell'd way—will outdo the Church and Flatbush Ave. intersection where you and I, little Belknap, have often ponder'd on the faith and mortality of the New-Netherland burghers. In this churchyard Edgar found the graves of some of his ancestors of 200 years ago—Adamses and Jacobses. His great-great-great-grandfather once spent a night in gaol in Newburyport—arrested for travelling on Sunday! Who says the times are not improv'd? Here we were doing the selfsame thing, yet chatting amicably with the watchmen instead of shunning their gaze!

Still farther south we went, admiring the stately mansions of old captains, with the tall cupolas where they used to scan the sea with spy-glasses. Good old days! Providence has some of these cupola'd houses—on the old hill overlooking the bay, which I shall shew you children when I can lure you to this village. Salem has many, but Newburyport probably has the most of all. On a side street we found an old house whose lower floor was in process of conversion to a shop. The new shop-window, with its glassless frame and broad seat, invited us; and we sate down for a long rest, gazing at ancient houses—one fully 250 years old—and stately, gigantick elm-trees. But time was flying, and it was growing cold. We had now reach'd a point which involv'd a retracing of those quaint, narrow streets and alleys we had first explor'd; and delightedly we set about it, pausing now and then to admire some particularly picturesque scenick effect—whether of quaintness, magnificence, or antique decay. Reaching the central square, we partook of the meal before mention'd—veal, potato, peas—coffee—coffee jelly with whipt cream—all for 65¢ apiece! Finally fill'd, we took the coach back to Merrimack; spending the evening in heated tho' friendly discussion—with Davis Senior and myself as prime antagonists.

Monday dawn'd rainy, and I barely had time to greet and breakfast with Edgar before his departure for school. I had intended to leave soon after, visiting Marblehead (which haste had excised from my programme) if the weather improv'd; but Mr. and Mrs. Davis prov'd such interested arguers that I did not get away till after dinner, when Davis Sr. took me into Haverhill in the family Ford. He's a good chap, for all his dogged commercialism and opinionatedness; but I'm infernally sorry he doesn't appreciate his son more. If Edgar were my boy, I'd consider myself damn'd lucky; but Davis merely mourns the child's absence of practicality and business sense. It is a vague ambition of Edgar to be a lawyer, and thus employ his strong *analytical* sense; but Davis Sr. can't see anything but the hardware business. At that, though, I guess he's a good hardware man—the leading one of Haverhill. I had Davis drop me at the Publick Library, where I spent the rest of the afternoon reading up on Timothy Dexter, whose picturesque eccentricity awak'd the responsive chord of eccentricity within myself. Among other things, I swallow'd the entire "Pickle for the Knowing Ones"! Haverhill hath a live and excellent library, which publishes a regular bulletin—I enclose a copy to each of you children, touching upon a man who help'd to make the 18th century the most artistick in history.

The city itself is quite delightful in its way—extremely vigorous and prosperous, as strikingly contrasted with Newburyport. The one lack is *picturesqueness,* for although Haverhill is an old town—settled in 1640 and incorporated in 1645—its large size and prosperity date only from the dawn of the boot and shoe industry of the last century. Accordingly, whilst a few Colonial houses of the original village remain—including the delightful edifice of the Historical Society which I think I describ'd to you boys a year and a half ago—most of the present city was built up since 1870, and is correspondingly modern. There are no truly ancient districts, as in Providence and Boston, or even New-York, and no comparison whatsoever can be made with such places as Salem and Newburyport. What distinctive features there are, are of modern origin. Among these is Winnikenni castle, a true replica of mediaevalism constructed some years ago by a wealthy man, and crowning a wooded hill whose slopes are a delightful publick park. I visited it last year. Another is the new country-club—the second in the town, and not yet finished—which reproduces perfectly a maediaeval Gothick abbey. Apparently Haverhill, lacking Georgianism, is determin'd to go back to the Dark Ages! The population of this place is nearly 54,000, and constantly growing. Tryout misses it in his Plaistovian retirement, and has half a mind to return next winter. In the

evening I climb'd the gentle slope to the station, and took the Boston coach.
Once more in the Hub, I dined at a classically Hellenick dump across the
street from the North Station (have you seen it, Belknap Sonny? The proprietor is one of those few neo-Hellenes who are conscious of the past, and
has actually covered the walls with fine ancient Greek designs!) and hit the
trail south. Instead of rattling to the South Station on the elevated, I chose
the subway, (I am exceedingly fond of all things dark and subterranean, and
miss the rides up to 96th!) taking a train to Washington-Summer and there
transferring to a S.S. train. The trip was uneventful, as was the later Providential trip, and midnight found me back at the old shebang.

It was a great trip, but fatigued me prodigiously. Since then a sort of modify'd grippe hath claim'd me, and I am at this moment nearly stone deaf! But
my trust is in the Lord, and I am confident of better things to come. Your visit,
small Belknap, will work wonders in bracing the Old Man up, and if you, little
Galba, cou'd but join the conclave, I am certain I shou'd be cur'd forthwith!

Well, boys, the clock advanceth, and my aunt is reminding me that I must
prepare to go to the matinee, after which I shall have a fitting of my new
summer suit of sober grey. The outside world seems quaint to my deaf ears—
I was vastly amus'd a week ago, when I ventur'd forth with the novel deafness so stably fixt upon my aged head.

Well—be Grandpa's nice boys, and don't let your French novels corrupt
your native English taste! Remember the honour and dignity demanded of a
man of the world's master-race, and learn a lesson from the robust old captains of Newburyport, and the simple-hearted wood-carvers of ancient Salem,
whose sincerity and devotion builded an art which shall outlive all the fad-
dishness and indecency of modern, degenerating Gaul and Italy. Grandpa's
getting old, childish, and rambling these days, but remember what he tells you
and let it influence you sometimes after he is dead and buried in an old New-
England churchyard. Be good children, and you will know a tranquillity which
is better than all the hectick anticks of drunken Frenchmen.

Yr most aff: ancestor and obt: Servt:
GRANDPA THEOBALD

*Notes*

1. Sandusky regaled HPL with his use of contemporary slang. HPL dedicated his
poem "The Feast" (1923) "To Wisecrack Sandusky, Esq., B.I., M.B.O. (Bachelor
of Intelligence, Massachusetts Brotherhood of Owls)."
2 Elliot Paul (1891–1958), journalist whose early novels, *Indelible* (1922), *Impromptu*
(1923), and *Imperturbe* (1924), were hailed by highbrow critics as landmarks in realism.
3. See letter 15, n. 4.
4. Long did not visit HPL in Providence until July 1927.
5. HPL mockingly repeats the final line of T. S. Eliot's *The Waste Land* (1922).

6. Jonathan Plummer (1761–1819), American poet whose work included *The Awful Malignant Fever at Newbury Port, in the Year 1796: An Elegaic Epistle to the Mourners, on the Death of Forty-four Persons Who Died of Malignant Fever . . . in the Summer and Autumn of the Year 1796.*

7. French stage actress Sarah Bernhardt (1844–1923) was said to have slept in a coffin.

[17]   [To Lillian M. Galpin]   [ALS]

169 Clinton St.,

Brooklyn, N.Y.,

August 16, 1925.

Dear Mrs. Galpin:—

Your gifted young husband having informed our local circle of aesthetic dilettanti of your impending arrival on the S.S. *Majestic*, & having delegated to us the agreeable responsibility of showing you such sights & salient points of interest as you may care to inspect here, I herewith take it upon myself to facilitate your location & identification of the circle in question. Mr. Galpin tells me that you will call me up by telephone, but it occurs to me that I may not have given him the number of this haven of remunerative guests; in which case you will look in vain through the book for a telephone in my name. Let me, therefore, here state that the correct number is *MAIN 1401*, at the Brooklynward end of which a proper sentry will be posted during the day of your arrival as estimated by the White Star offices—Tuesday, Aug. 18.

It furthermore occurs to me that, since you have met none of our local contingent in person, you may have trouble in identifying whomever of us may be first to meet you. To obviate this difficulty, I herewith enclose the rudiments of a portrait gallery in which the physiognomies of the two representatives likeliest to be on hand are rather explicitly treated. You will not, I think, find it hard to pick out either one or both of these individuals—Mr. Samuel Loveman & myself—when you observe them at any designated point in attitudes of expectancy. I must, by the way, request the return of these modest likenesses—each being the only one of its kind in my possession.

Pray consider our unassuming group most entirely at your service as guides & expositors—so far as those of us still in town are able to act adequately in that capacity. We all hold your spouse in the most abounding esteem as a favourite adopted grandson; & anything we can do to enhance the pleasure of his accomplished consort will afford us the keenest delight. We regret that our only youthful member—the meteoric Mr. Frank Belknap Long, Jr., of whom you must often have heard Mr. Galpin speak,—is now sojourning at the Thousand Islands; so that he will be unable to add the zest of modernity to the welcome which we antiques & fossils shall extend. On Wednesday evening, the 19th, our group holds its hebdomedal meeting at the abode of one of the members; & should you care to participate in the session you would not only do honour to the hostess, but confer distinction upon a coterie to whose lips the name of Galpin is no stranger.

And may I not add, as an individual, that my wife & I are both very anxious to meet the bride of our young prodigy-friend? Since my wife will be called imperatively West on business by Wednesday at the latest, she bids me ask you if you will not favour us with your company at dinner on Tuesday evening—at a restaurant, perforce, since we are this year existing in a rented room instead of housekeeping.

Such, then, are the essential features of the reception committee. Be assured that the telephone MAIN 1401 will be competently manned, & that the sentinel will be empowered to make whatever arrangements for meeting & guidance you will find most convenient. Meanwhile my wife & I trust that you may not have formulated any previous plans for Tuesday evening, when we should be so delighted to act as your hosts.

With renewed expressions of pleasure at your prospective arrival, & heartiest regards to yourself & your scintillant husband,

I have the honour to remain, Madam,

Yr. most ob$^t$ humble Servt:

H. P. Lovecraft

[18] [ALS]

Thor's Day—May 15, 1930[1]

Son:—[2]

Gad, Sir, I swoon! I swoon with the conscious contemplation of compleat & culminant beauty! I can't begin to describe it—for I am without breath & without words—but just look at this folder & at the accompanying postcard. They may faintly suggest, tho' they can never fully reveal. For Pegāna's sake chuck Peterborough & come down here at once! This is something to see & dream about all the rest of one's life! I am sure I shall think of very little else during my few remaining days! It is Poe's "Domain of Arnheim" & "Island of the Fay" all rolled into one—with mine own Cathuria & Gardens of Yin[3] added for good measure. It *must* be a dream, after all. I stumbled on it yesterday afternoon, & have come out today to enjoy it from 11 a.m. to the closing hour of six, bringing some revising work with me. Ædepol! But it wholly eclipses the upheaved Wade Park of Birchdale days[4]— & my erstwhile favourite Japanese Garden beside the Brooklyn Museum is as nothing to it!

You are perhaps sensible, from many olden observations of mine, that to me the quality of *utter, perfect beauty* assumes *two* supreme incarnations or adumbrations: one, a mass of mystical city towers & roofs & spires outlined against a sunset & glimpsed from a fairly distant balustraded terrace; & the other, the experience of walking (or, as in most of my dreams, aërially floating) thro' ethereal & enchanted gardens of exotick delicacy & opulence, with carved stone bridges, labyrinthine paths, marble fountains, terraces, & staircases, strange pagodas, hillside grottos, curious statues, termini, sundials, benches, basins, & lanthorns, lily'd pools of swans & streams with tiers of waterfalls, spreading gingko-trees & dropping, feathery willows, & suntouch'd flowers of a bizarre, Klarkash-Tonick pattern never beheld on land or beneath the sea . . . . . .

Well, Son, call your Grandpa an aged liar or not—*I have at last actually found the garden of my earliest dreams*—& in no other city than antient Richmond, home of my beloved Poe! How I wish it cou'd have been here in his day! I doubt if there is another such realm of faery open to the publick in these American colonies! ¶ Shall probably have to begin my reluctant northward trek tomorrow. Eheu! ¶ Hope to see you in 3 weeks or so.

Yr obt Grandsire

Θεοβαλδος

P.S. "The Rivals" was great Tuesday night.[5]

*Notes*

1. Written from Maymont Park, Richmond, VA.

2. This is the earliest surviving letter of many using this appellation. Note that the son of the narrator Delapore of "The Rats in the Walls" (1923) is named "Alfred."

3. Cathuria is mentioned in "The White Ship" (1919). "The Gardens of Yin" is sonnet XVIII of HPL's *Fungi from Yuggoth* (1929–30).

4. I.e., 1922, when HPL stayed with Galpin at 9231 Birchdale Avenue, Cleveland, during a visit with Samuel Loveman.

5. HPL saw a performance of Richard Brinsley Sheridan's *The Rivals* in Richmond at the Lyric Theatre on 13 May 1930.

[19] [ALS]

Tuesday [c. September 1930]

Son:—

Your pre-autumnal exodus caused you to miss my travel postcards—directed to Appleton—at the time your much-appreciated epistle was sent. By this time you doubtless have them, through forwarding, & are aware that the Old Gentleman has at last set foot on soil still loyal to our rightful Sovereign, to say nothing of inspecting the quaintest & most exquisite relique of antiquity in the western hemisphere—the venerable & beautiful fortress town of *Quebec.*

Quebec! Can I ever get it out of my head long enough to think about anything else? Who cares for Paris or Antipolis now? Never have I beheld anything else like it, & never do I expect to! In due time you will see a travelogue on it[1]—but for the present I am wholly inarticulate. All my former standards of urban beauty are superseded & obsolete. I can scarcely believe that the place belongs to the waking world at all. A mighty headland rising out of a mile-broad river & topped by a mediaeval fortress—city walls of cyclopean masonry scaling vertical cliffs or towering above green table-lands—great arching *city gates* & frowning bastions—huddles of pointed red-tiled roofs & silver belfries & steeples—archaic lanes winding uphill or lurking in the beetling shadow of precipices—horse-drawn vehicles, & all the vestiges of a mature, leisurely civilisation—these things are only a fraction of the marvellous totality that is Quebec. The trip was amazingly unpremeditated. I was just back from Cape Cod with Belknap when I saw the advertisement of the $12.00 excursion from Boston. This, I decided at once, was an ideal last fling of summer—& what a fling it turn'd out to be! The weather favour'd me miraculously—& as for Quebec, it outdistanced my wildest expectations. I had only 3 days there, but my sightseeing was so continuous & assiduous that I really form'd a surprising acquaintance with the place. I threaded virtually all the antient streets of both upper & lower towns, made a compleat circuit of the old city wall,—in some places walking on top—[unlike the walls of your precious Paris, Quebec's wall is *all standing in good condition* except for 3 gates removed & 1 partly removed] ascended to the citadel & obtained various views therefrom, crossed the ferry to Levis & climbed the cliff there for a sunset view of the Quebec skyline, & in general assimilated the aspect & atmosphere of a region whose linkage with our age & continent is truly of the feeblest & most nominal sort. Quebec is really a part of old Bourbon France—a Norman hill town of the year 1700 or thereabouts. In retrospect the whole thing is a fantastick dream. On the way back—as you doubtless know by this time from a postcard—I stopped off at Boston for an all-day boat trip to Provincetown, at the tip of Cape Cod. This village (which I did not reach by land during my Belnapian journeyings) I found to be somewhat overrated, but the sail—my first experience on the *open sea*—was well worth the price of the excursion. To be on limitless water out of sight of land is (as the Atlantick hath doubtless taught you) to have the fantastick imagination stimulated in the most powerful way. The uniformly blank horizon evokes all sorts of speculations as to *what may lie beyond*, so that the sensations of Columbus, Madoc, Arthur Gordon Pym, the Ancient Mariner, & all the other voyagers of song & story are rolled into one & sharpen'd to expectant poignancy. Who can tell what strange port or temple of the sea will loom suddenly ahead? To approach Boston Harbour at sunset from open water is something one can never forget. Grey headlands—monolith-like lighthouses—low-lying, cryptical islets—what vespertine realm of mystery is this which rises mirage-like from vapour-shrouded vacancy? Phaeacia—Avalon—Tyre—Carthage—Alexandria—Atlantis—the City of Never—The net effect is some sort of mystical defeat of the intolerable limitations of time & space & natural law—

some burst of escape (or hint of a possible burst of escape) from known conditions & dimensions, & passage through strange, inconceivable sunset gates to realms of beauty & wonder which one has formerly known of only darkly, in hints & touches of pseudo-memory that are strong in childhood but dead in adult years except among those few who have not forgotten how to live.

I rejoice to hear of the improved milieu you have achieved, & of the prospect of bringing it within the radius of financial safety through judicious management. I hope the new furniture is of 18th century design—at least, I hope it is not of that stiltedly artificial & irrelevantly unmotivated sort which laboriously pretends to express the present age & goes under the popular appellation of "modernistic". Ugh! Too bad you have to wait for the new paradise in such semi-squalid quarters—but after all, the interregnum is brief, & will give you all the keener zest for the ultimate haven. You seem very well situated as regards neighbours, & I trust you may be able to make the spot a fixed & permanent headquarters—punctuated, of course, by such excursions into the varied outside world as circumstances may permit.

No—you hadn't previously mentioned the relay'd greetings from the quondam Mme. Theobald;[2] an incident which prompts the usual platitude concerning the microscopic dimensions of this planetary spheroid. My messages from that direction during the past two years have been confin'd to Christmas & birthday cards, but if occasion arises to exchange more verbose greetings, I shall assuredly add your respects & compliments to my own.

I am glad that your youthful law-kinsmen enjoy'd my tales, even tho' it was but a renewed acquaintance in one case. Up to the present writing, the assortment has *not* been return'd to Rhode-Island waters—but there is not the least hurry so long as the MSS are safe. You might make diplomatick inquiries when next you converse with the sprightly twain—always taking care not to express an impatience which I wou'd be the last to transmit.

The cutting you enclosed was my first intimation—& so far as I know, active amateurdom's first intimation—of the passing of Alfred L. Hutchinson.[3] I am sending the news to Tryout & to young Spink[4]—the National's official editor—in the belief that they will wish to make items of it. Poor old duffer—I didn't know he was ill, & it seems to me I recall his having written or telegraphed greetings to the recent Boston convention. An amateur to the last! He had his crude spots, from all accounts, (I hardly knew him myself, & doubt if I ever exchanged five letters with him) but I guess he meant well enough basically. An odd character; short on formal education & long on egotism, but gifted with a salty horse sense & general gregariousness which gave him a rather good time in the world, all told. His *Trail* was a naive & spicy addition to the amateurdom of its day,[5] & I doubt not but that his dearly cherish'd tome "The Limit of Wealth" (which I am urging the amateurs to mention in their obituary items) was much less silly than I imagined it to be in those days of my own relative youth & narrowness. I recall your meeting with him at the Dells convention[6]—indeed, I have more than one group photograph of that event which includes you both. He would scarcely have been a fount of congenial conversation for a young philosopher already far removed from mundane commonplaces—but it is to his credit that he recognised juvenile genius when he saw it. I am glad the local press gave him a final publicity commensurate with the ample exploitation he liked. Poor old Hutch—but after all, he probably got as much out of the empty mockery of existence as most do.

I am glad to hear that your magnum opus has attained something like a definitive shape, & hope its orchestral production will prove a conspicuous triumph. Too bad so much rearranging of "West Wind" is necessary—but I suppose one cannot begrudge pains expended in bringing a work of art to perfection & presentability. I can imagine the labour which must go into all this part copying—hence can fervently thank the Creator that inclination & ability did not combine to make me a musician! Still—when it comes time to reap rewards, the rewards of a successful & conscientious composer are undoubtedly very great.

I hear frequently from good old Moe, & am daily expecting to hear of the acceptance of his poetry-appreciation textbook[7] by some standard firm. This book—whose MS. I looked over last year, & for which I furnished many metrical exercises—is really a marvellously fine thing, & ought to do more than any other influence to teach mediocre minds to distinguish betwixt real poetry & hackneyed sentimentalism. Mocrates is the same amiably orthodox soul of yesteryear, & in time his faithful plodding ought to gain him the comfortable niche in paedagogical pantheon which probably forms the apex of his ambitions. By the way—he has just looked up our bizarre & piquant old pal Co—Ira A. Cole, the one-time Kansas poet & present Colorado theologist. Poor Co has never recovered from his 1917 attack of pentecostal religion, & throws forth impressive hints of having suffer'd strange martyrdoms for his faith; but for all that he sounds like a reasonably contented agrestick soul, whose messianick responsibilities neither bow his shoulders nor hamper his digestion.

I just had quite an echo of marine adventure in the form of a letter from the young New Zealand amateur Robert G. Barr. Stampless, watersoaked, & marked with a rubber stamp—

Salvaged from S.S. Tahiti
Lost at sea.

In its unspoken drama it makes me think of the letters I used to receive from the British amateurs during the war, with their stickers of government censorship & their occasional salty marks of oceanick mishaps.

Well—if I don't get to work I'll never clean up the pile of junk which my Quebec truancy allow'd to accumulate. Here's wishing you a speedy transfer to your new & palatial quarters, & a successful term of Gallicising a fresh generation of more or less Anglo-Saxon youth.

With customary expressions of grandparental esteem, & sincere regards uxori fratribusque, I have the honour to subscribe myself

Ever y[r] most oblig'd, most ob[t] Serv[t]

Theobaldus Avus[8]

P.S. Our old fellow-amateur Paul J. Campbell is now living in Chicago. Address, 7528 Honore St.

*Notes*

1. HPL eventually wrote *A Description of the Town of Quebeck, in New-France* between October 1930 and January 1931.
2. Sonia H. Greene, formerly Mrs. Lovecraft.
3. Alfred L. Hutchinson (b. 1859) was the author of *The Limit of Wealth* (New York: Macmillan, 1907).
4. Helm C. Spink, Official Editor of the NAPA (1930–31).
5. HPL published "On a New-England Village Seen by Moonlight" in the *Trail* for Summer 1915; his "The Crime of the Century" and "A Rural Summer Eve" appeared in the January 1916 number.
6. The UAPA convention at the Wisconsin Dells occurred in July 1918.
7. *Doorways to Poetry* (never published). Cf. *SL* 2.253, 255; 3.10, 13, 55, 129.
8. "Theobald the grandfather."

[20] [ALS]

Aug. 28, 1932

Son:—

Well, well, Sir! Grandpa is glad to welcome the wandering Consul Hasting back to regions of familiar impressions & more certain postal communication! Sorry the retrograde path was beset with costly obstacles—but all's well that ends well, & the roar of the Fox River dam again resounds on the ear of the return'd native. I hope you will not fail to bring Felix-Charles-Pierre Baudelaire[1] from Chicago—how has he thriven under the care of your quondam-Charlestonian acquaintance?

The card from antique Londinium duly came, & filled me with envy at your opportunity to behold civilisation's capital, if only for a single full day. If I were in Europe, I would devote not less than 2 or 3 weeks to London—& might not get outside of Britain at all. The British Museum card surely reveals one of my (or Klarkash-Ton's or Sonny Belknap's) extra-human monsters in disguise—indeed, I am positive that this entity reached Java as a relique of sunken Mu, or of the still more monstrous & fabulous R'lyeh! Thanks!

I don't envy you your semi-arctic voyage—except for the glimpse of whales, icebergs, aurorae, & other terrestrial marvels—but I would envy you your Quebec-Montreal vistas if it weren't that I expect to see both of those antient cities a week hence. You don't mention stopping in Quebec . . . . . is it possible that an inhuman steamship company denied you landing privileges in this, the most interesting & exquisite town on the North-American continent?

Sorry so many practical responsibilities awaited you on home soil, & hope all the various difficulties may presently be adjusted without too nerve-racking a series of ordeals. Before long, I dare say, your duties at the Methodist Seminary[2] will begin; & I trust that these may not prove irksome beyond endurance. Alas, that good old Mocrates is not on the job at A.H.S. to give your youthful charges some preliminary enlightenment before they tread the classick Laurentian shades!

I appreciate very much your expressions of sympathy concerning my recent bereavement—an event which indeed aggravates the barrenness of existence, despite one's recognition of its inevitability.[3] Shall be glad to get your post-Hispanick epistle if it turns up, & am eager to hear more of your impressions of London. Meanwhile the Majorcan travelogue, with its graphick map & pleasing rotogravure illustrations, afforded me the keenest delight—& will no doubt duplicate the performance with Little Belknap & Fra Samuelus.

I had no idea that the charm & quaintness of the Balearick Islands was so great, tho' in truth I suppose all the less frequented parts of Europe are full of such unchanged deposits from the past. Such richness in visible history is almost dizzying to a native of the western world, where 300 years forms the limit of architectural age. I must some day get at least a momentary glimpse of the old world with its piled-up accumulations of centuries & millennia, & its curious survivals not only of tangible edifices but of modes of life. The Baleares, I believe, have a civilis'd history extending back to the days of Carthage (as indeed your folder mentions), & were esteem'd for the skill of their inhabitants in the warlike use of the sling—Balearick slingers being valued in all the armies of antiquity. Besides the Punick settlements, there were less vigorous ones establish'd by the maritime Greeks. One of the present towns of Minorca—Mahon—is of Punick origin & perpetuates the common Carthaginian name of *Mago.* It is my impression that the islands kept their Punick culture till after the fall of Carthage proper, being brought under the dominion of ROMA only in 121 B.C., when the piracies of their denizens induced our Senatus to despatch against them the younger Q. Caecilius Metellus. Q. Metellus, having subdued them, colonised them with 3000 settlers from Italia & Hispania, introduced the classick olive which so much impress'd you, (& which I wou'd give my eye-teeth to behold!) founded the towns of Palma and Pollentia on Balearis Major, & assum'd the title or agnomen of Balearicus in honour of his exploits. The isles became part of the province of Hispania Citerior—tho' toward the decline of the empire they form'd a separate administrative unit till overrun by the

Vandals in A.D. 423. Tho' you have not mention'd any ROMAN remains, I am inform'd that such do indeed exist—notably an aqueduct at Pollentia—or Pollenza, as I believe the modern inhabitants call it. This, however, is in the northern part of the island, which you did not visit. The Moors took the Balearicks from the Vandals in A.D. 790, & in 1009 they split off from the Emirate of Cordova as a separate Saracen kingdom—notable (as in Punick days) for piratical exploits. These piracies made the islands the object of a crusade dictated by the Romish Pope; & in 1232 (or 1229 as your folder gives it) Don Jaime, El Rey de Aragon, conquer'd them & made of them a Spanish kingdom under one of his sons. In 1439 they were united to Aragon. In modern times, in the war of the Spanish Succession during the glorious reign of Her Majesty Queen ANNE, whom God save, our troops under Gen[l] STANHOPE took Minorca (1708) & temporarily added it (under the treaty of Utrecht in 1713) to the BRITANNICK Dominions; tho' the cursed French seiz'd it from 1756 to 1769. About 1770 Minorca's history joins to that of the American colonies by reason of the great number of peasant labourers exported thence to Florida (now gain'd by us in 1765) by Dr. Andrew Turnbull, to work his great plantations at New-Smyrna, below St. Augustine. Dr. Turnbull so mistreated his Minorcan bondmen that the indentures were cancelled by His Maj[ty's] Governor at St.-Augustine in 1776; whilst the Minorcans themselves settled around St. Augustine, where their descendants may be found to this day. Minorca was re-taken by the Spaniards in 1782, temporarily restored to ENGLAND in 1798, & finally ceded back to Spain in 1803.

It is indeed difficult to imagine anything more fascinating than Majorca with its ancient towns, frowning castles, terraced hills, & rugged coast-line. Your long walk was assuredly a notable event, & I trow fatigue and footsoreness were none too great a price to pay for it. Bañalbufar sounds like a fragment of a dream, whilst all the scenick suggestions inspire one with a wish to emigrate thither. All this would have transported Little Belknap's Spanish soul in the pre-1932 days before he went Bolshevik. Incidentally—I am sending your travelogue to the child, with instructions for trans-shipment to Samuelus. (who is now home visiting in Cleveland, tho' financial reverses have forced his family to leave the familiar shades of 1537)

I myself have taken advantage of phenomenally cheap boat rates (50¢ round trip) & have visited ancient Newport repeatedly this summer—thus not being wholly out of touch with either venerable streets or rugged cliffs. On Tuesday I start for Boston, & Wednesday W. Paul Cook & I will (weather permitting) view the eclipse from some point (either Newburyport or Portsmouth) north of there—incidentally stopping at Haverhill to see good old Tryout Smith, who will be 80 in October. On Friday, Sept. 2., I shall start from Boston on an incredibly cheap rail excursion to both Montreal & Quebec (whole thing *$12.00!*)—seeing Montreal for the first time. It won't give me much time in either city, but it's all I can afford—and a glimpse is better than nothing. I *could* make it all-Montreal & have more time—but it would break my aged heart not to see Quebec as well. You will receive postcard echoes of this brief & hurried Odyssey next week.

And so it goes. Hope home won't seem too tame after the picturesque antiquities of Europe. More later.

> Thy obt Servt
> Grandpa

*Notes*

1. Galpin's cat.
2. Galpin's term for Lawrence College in Appleton.
3. HPL's aunt Lillian D. Clark had died 3 July 1932.


[21] [ALS]

> Theobald Grange—
> Oct[r] 27, 1932

Son:—

I am consum'd with appropriate envy upon hearing of your new sable charge. Bless my old bones, but what an elf of darkness the little Spinx (to use Sonny Belknap's pronunciation, which he insists is good Manhattanese) must be! But I mourn, simultaneously, at the unmistakable reference that M. Felix Baudelaire has evaporated into his native shadow. Rex mortuus est—vivat Rex! I am sure that there cou'd be no worthier heir of the departed than this sprightly emissary from the nighted gulphs of Dis. In matters of nomenclature I am sure you have observed the precepts of good sense, & I trust that mounting years may never cause the lively creature to belie the dual implications of his title. Your account of his ancestry I have perus'd with the utmost interest & attention, & I wish I might behold the singular household of decay'd gentry where so many of his kind are bred & harbour'd. I assume that the family of Grignon is descended from the earliest French pioneers of the region—trading posts & missions having existed there since the 1660's. It seems to represent the sort of picturesque & pathetick decline which so much appeals to the increasing realistick genius of another young Wisconsin friend of mine—August W. Derleth of Sauk City, whose work is now beginning to appear in magazines like *Pagany* & *The Midland*, & who was three-starr'd by O'Brien in this year's "Best Short Stories."[1] Cats & curiosities—what better accessories to attend the fading of a great house? Wou'd that my own last years were thus appropriately environ'd! The late founder of the feline dynasty assuredly had the right idea regarding the place of the cat in domestick œconomy, & I regret that his venerable relict does not echo his attentive devotion to the species. That nocturnal search for the future skipper must have been an event of pleasing & mystical weirdness, & I am glad that its result was so eminently fortunate. I trust that the later & undiscover'd brood turn'd out to be equally attractive. In the Dutch Nieuw Nederland this latter group wou'd have been call'd *stubbletje* cats because of their late summer birth at a time when the mown fields bristle with stubble. Such a brood was tradition-ally held to be of inferior quality, tho' I doubt if many kittens were banish'd because of birth-date alone. My friend Wilfred B. Talman—whom you may or may not have met during one of your Noveboracense[2] passages—is of the old Dutch stock & now lives again on his ancestral farm at Spring Valley. He last August inform'd me of the birth of some stubbletje kittens to the house-hold Sphinx; but so far has tradition declin'd, that each of the young arrivals was carefully cherish'd—one for permanent retention at the Talman bouwerie, & the other two for affectionate placement with pious & respect-able patroons elsewhere in the colony. I am glad that Skipper is maturing gracefully, & that he is not afflicted with the nervous irritability of the urban train. I have ever maintain'd, that large towns are not fit for gentlemen to live in, or for the young to be rear'd in; & rejoice that your charge will have an opportunity to grow up amidst the beechen groves that line the Vulpine stream. Happy the cat whose wish & care a few paternal acres bound! I hope that no rapid chariots course along the way where Skipper's nimble steps are like to stray; for perils lurk where ruthless haste attends, & furry wand'rers meet untimely ends.

"War & Peace", in two ample volumes, is among the paternally inherited section of my library;[3] & upon your enthusiastick endorsement I am almost tempted to consider its perusal. The fact that its text leaves are cut, plus the evidence supply'd by fly-leaves that they were originally uncut, leads me to the conclusion that my father must have surviv'd a voyage thro' it; tho' it is pos-sible that he meerly amus'd himself of an evening by running a paper knife thro' it. What I have read of Count Lyof Nikolaievitch's work has not filled me with enthusiasm. Both in him, & in M. Dustyoffsky's efforts, I have seem'd to discern an exaggeration of neurotick traits which, however true they may be for the brachycephalick, moody, & mercurial Slav, have not much meaning or relevance in connexion with the Western part of mankind. I will not deny the greatness of these authors in reflecting the environment around them—but I understand too little of that environment to appreciate its close pourtrayal. But since "War & Peace" is actually in the house, it is not impossible that I may at least begin it some day. (N.B. Having just taken a look at the *size* of the volumes, I'm not so sure!)

Glad you've been working toward the greater permanence of your natal rooftree. My native edifice still stands[4]—being now used as an office-building by 12 physicians. The rear part of the grounds, with the stable, was sold se-prately; & last year the venerable barn (whose cupola had long been succumb-ing to worm & fungus, & which had for years been vacant) was razed to make way for a smug mock-Tudor residence. Eheu—thus pass the landmarks of my youth. In the early days of decline, after we had given up our horses & carriages, that stable was my exclusive personal playhouse—a whole echoing building with shadowy, mysterious loft, cavernous carriage room, empty stalls, & trim, office-like harness-room all at the disposal of one tenant of ten years' growth! Ah, me—in those days it was a police station, theatre, army headquarters, car barn, railway round house, outlaws' rendezvous, fire station, house to be robbed, & everything else that youthful imagination could make it! And now it is gone! It was not so very old in reality—being the second stable on its site. My grandfather built it in 1880, & my surviving aunt,[5] then a small girl, put a tin box of records into the unfinish'd walls, to be exhum'd & studied by the archaeologists of a fabulous posterity. Alas that she shou'd live to see its destruction & reclaim the records herself! Last summer, when the workmen had it partly razed, she went over & looked in the place where she had put the records 51 years before. They were still there—Harsford's Baking Powder box rusted but intact, & the contents only slightly touched by the mould of intervening aeons. My aunt's tintype, & that of a youthful friend (now dead) quite decipherable, & their messages to a future civilisation legible in every part. She still has the box—but alas, we have no hope of erecting another family castle in which to reincorporate it with a XX century postscript! By the way—it must be pleasant for you to have a sprightly & altitudinous young brother-in-law about the house.

Glad to hear that the Methodist Seminary is improving since the days when a young intellectual titan, wearied with the puerilities of one Farley & other upholders of obsolescent illusions, fled in desperation to the more congenial shoars of crystal-blue Mendota. I hope your position there, aided by the better element, will grow more & more favourable—& that in time the giggling Hadrianus & his inexperienc'd Antinoüs may be put compleatly to rout! Meanwhile you are undoubtedly accumulating much useful influence through your extra-collegiate labours in cosmopolitanising the local patricians—& are, I trust, so firmly reëstablishing yourself on hereditary soil that you will not wish to quit it again without some uncommonly great inducement. There is no place for a man like the rural acres or village lanes from whence he sprang; & in my opinion any lack of brilliant conversation (easily palliated by reading, travels, & correspondence) is more than aton'd for by the ineffable harmony resulting from the sight of familiar roofs & spires & gardens, & from the presence of a million imponderable influences connected with one's earliest & most valu'd memories. I am acutely sensible of the pleasures of travel, & none likes strange, far climes more than I; but all their delightfulness is really dependent upon my knowledge that Old Providence is awaiting my return with well-rememberc'd hills & steeples & winding lanes. After all, there is no real life except that which allows for the natural relationship of the individual to the soil which produc'd him. If a mechanis'd modernity is to make of our descendants a rootless & nomadick race, it will certainly impoverish our antient English civilisation by subtracting a vital element whose place can never be adequately fill'd.

Musical creation, I trust, will in course of time enliven your moments of leisure. As for study—I have not perus'd the second volume of Spengler, tho' I believe it hath long been put into English. The original (&, I conceive, the most general & inclusive) volume I read some years ago[6] with much attention & a great degree of acquiescence, tho' I think the philosopher errs when he draws too close a comparison betwixt the life of a culture & that of a single biological organism. In effect, the parallel may indeed be close; for it is certain no civilisation can last more than a limited length of time without going thro' various typical phases of decline. But when one considers the nature of the interdependence betwixt the parts of an organick unit, & compares this type of indivisible union & inevitable development with the looser bonds linking the elements of a culture, it becomes plain that the case is one of *resemblance* rather than of *identity*. Whilst the ultimate senescence & extinction of a culture are virtually unavoidable, the degree & conditions of its aging are certainly much more variable through chance & calculation than are those of a living organism's aging. Spengler is probably right in his prophecies concerning Western Europe's decline, but he is probably less so in his attempts to assign a precise initial cause. Another philosopher who deals with the decline of the west is one Egon Friedell;[7] whose ultimate conclusions are marr'd by a kind of mystical optimism unjustify'd by any evidence he produces. I hope you have been able to make contemporary international relations clearer to your clientele than they are to the average person—including most statesmen. Do you attempt to account for the magnitude of the present depression? In surveying the effects of mechanis'd industry upon society, I have been led to a certain change of political views. Formerly I favour'd the concentration of resources in a few hands, in the interest of a stable hereditary culture; but I now believe that this system will no longer operate. With the universal use & improvement of machinery, all the needed labour of the world can be perform'd by a relatively few persons, leaving vast numbers permanently unemployable, depression or no depression. If these people are not fed & amused, they will dangerously revolt; hence we must either institute a programme of steady pensioning—panem et circenses[8]—or else subject industry to a governmental supervision which will lessen its profits but spread its jobs amongst more men working less hours. For many reasons the latter course seems to me most reasonable—especially since the vast accumulations of the commercial oligarchs are not now used to any great extent for cultural purposes. Therefore (deeming both democracy & communism fallacious for western civilisation) I favour a kind of fascism which may, whilst helping the dangerous masses at the expense of the needlessly rich, nevertheless preserve the essentials of traditional civilisation & leave political power in the hands of a small & cultivated (tho' not over-rich) governing class largely hereditary but subject to gradual increase as other individuals rise to its cultural level. How practicable such a programme could be, only Pegāna can say; but it seems to me at least a more rational ultimate goal—in a very general sense—than any other. Its approximation could be facilitated by a gradual modelling of the publick mood & standards in its favour, to be accomplish'd through the coöperation of various agencies in control of instruction & expression. The ideal of a benevolent monarchy & wise aristocracy ought to be revis'd & justify'd in practice—confirming the judgment of Claudian of old, when he writ (amidst another aera of decay much like our own) "Nulla libertas gratior, quam sub rege pio."[9] God Save the King!

As for my travels of August & September, as I writ you on a card, the eclipse was a compleat success for Paullus Culinarius[10] & me. Having fixt upon antient Newburyport as our post of observation, we repair'd thither on the stage-coach by way of Haverhill; where he stopt to converse with honest Tryout Smith. (he turned 80 last Monday, but is still as spry as a boy) We cou'd not persuade him to go with us, but he had a very good sight of the eclipse (tho' the totality did not last so long) from his own dooryard. Once in Newburyport, we chose an hilltop meadow north of the compact section as our station. Some clouds in the sky made us anxious, but the sun came out every little while & gave us long glimpses of every stage of the phaenomenon. The landskip did not change in tone until the crescent of the fading sun was rather small, & then a kind of sunset vividness became apparent. When the crescent waned to extream thinness, the scene grew strange & spectral—an almost deathlike quality inhering in the sickly yellowish light. At last the outspread valleys sank into unnatural night—Jupiter came out in the deep-violet heavens—ghoulish shadow-bands raced along the winding white roads—the last beaded strip of glitter vanish'd—& the pale corona flicker'd into aureolar radiance around the black disc of the obscuring moon. The earth was darken'd more deeply than in the eclipse of 1925, tho' the corona was not so bright. We absorb'd the whole spectacle with the utmost impressedness & appreciation—totality lasting a surprisingly long time (it seem'd nearly a minute) despite our distance from the central line of the eclipse. Finally the beaded crescent reëmerged, the valleys glow'd again in faint, eerie light, & the various partial phases were repeated in reverse order. The marvel was over, & accustomed things resum'd their wonted sway. I may never see another, but it is not everyone who has, like me, witness'd two solar eclipses.

My trip to New-France was also a decided success, tho' your own passage thro' the region will make my account seem less than novel. Montreal—which I saw for the first time—struck me very pleasantly; tho' of course it cannot compare with Quebec. I saw it with some thoroughness, taking several different motor tours (including Lachine Rapids) & exploring the antient waterfront sections on foot. The interiors I saw were the Cathedral, (1827) Chapel of Notre-Dame de Bonsecœurs (1771), & Chateau de Ramezay (1705)—aside from modern places. I don't need to tell you anything about the city & its suburbs, including the totally British *Westmount*. I had an excellent view of the whole region from Westmount Mountain. Montreal is much less French than Quebec—for as you have seen, the dominant language west of St. Lawrence Blvd. is uniformly English except for official bilingual signs like

DEFENSE DE STATIONNER

———

NO PARKING

(The *Quebec* idiom for this same sign is NE STATIONNEZ PAS, showing a distinct local difference in usage.) But I was glad to get to primaeval & mystical Quebec—of which you can have had but the most tantalising glimpse from the river. As in 1930 I revelled in the mass'd reliquiae of antiquity—the rugged cliff, frowning citadel, precipitous winding lanes & flights of steps, antient, crumbling facades & tiled roofs, magnificent scenick vistas, queerly robed priests & friars, centuried publick buildings of grey stone, beetling, cannon-lined ramparts, & the scenes of our glorious WOLFE'S victory over the Gallick foe. God Save the King! On this occasion I explor'd the neighbouring Isle d'Orelans (which you must have seen from the boat—& did you also see Montmorency Falls on the N. Mainland shore?), where the old French countryside remains in an unspoil'd state just as when WOLFE landed in 1759. There were endless brick farmhouses with curved eaves, wind & water mills, wayside shrines, & quaint white villages clustering around antient silver-steepled parish churches. Nothing but French is spoken, & the population—seigneurs & habitants—live where their ancestors have lived for 200 years & more. I hated to go home—& when passing thro' Bostonium eased the transition by making a side-trip to antient Marblehead. Since then I have been kept on the move by two successive visitors, after whose departure accumulated work compleatly ingulph'd me. I did pray truant, however, on warm & sunny Oct^r 9, when I took a farewell auto trip to archaick Salem & Marblehead. And now hibernating time draws near—alas!

Best of wishes—
Yr most obt
Grandpa.

P.S. Samuelus—now moved around the corner from Col. Hts. to *17 Middagh St.*—may pay me a visit before winter closes down. ¶ As to being a weird-fictional celebrity—if so, I've receiv'd very few reports of it! On the contrary, magazines were never more hostile to my stuff. I've about stopped trying to contribute. ¶ Here's an echo of my recent work in amateurdom.[11] Needn't return it. Can't quite shake the old associations!

*Notes*

1. Derleth's "Five Alone" was on the Roll of Honor in O'Brien's *The Best Short Stories 1933* (1933).

2. Adjectival form of *Novum Eboracum* (New York).

3. Probably a reprint of the first English translation of *War and Peace*, "translated into French by a Russian lady, and from the French by Clara Bell" (1886; rpt. New York: W. S. Gottsberger, 1887; 2 vols.; *LL* 888).

4. 194 (later 454) Angell Street; it was razed in 1959.

5. Annie E. P. Gamwell (1866–1941).

6. HPL read the first volume of Oswald Spengler's *The Decline of the West* (Eng. tr. 1926–28) no later than February 1927 (*SL* 2.103).

7. Egon Friedell (1878–1938), German historian and philosopher. HPL is evidently referring to Friedell's *A Cultural History of the Modern Age: The Crisis of the European Soul from the Black Death to the World War* (New York: Knopf, 1930–32; 3 vols.), the only work of his to be translated into English.

8. "Bread and circuses," the celebrated phrase from Juvenal, *Satires* 10.80.

9. "There is no liberty more welcome than under a pious king." Claudius Claudianus, *De Consulatu Stilichonis* (c. 400 C.E.), 3.114–15 ("Numquam libertas gratior extat / quam sub rege pio" in Claudian).

10. I.e., W. Paul Cook.

11. *Further Criticism of Poetry* (Louisville, KY: Printed on the Press of George G. Fetter Co, 1932). The ms. of the essay is titled "Notes on Verse Technique" (18 April 1932).

[22] [ALS]

Tenbarnes—

Jany. 20, 1933.

Son:—

"En Route" is indeed delightful, & I surely hope you will set it to music as you suggest. It has a profound, fundamental beat not unlike that of the ocean it celebrates; & ought to give you great opportunities for aural effects. The "Deep Sea Meditation" is sprightly & appealing—& full of the true speculative feeling proper to a philosopher. Many thanks for both—I shall keep them, since they are not attached to any part of your epistle which demands the confidence-keeping processes of combustion.[1]

Concerning the matter of emotion—I fancy about 3 or 4 rounds of an old-time Kleicomolo discussion would remove more than one point of difficulty & possible misconception, but whether it would leave you on the side of gawd & Mocrates or on that of the devil & Grandpa Theobald I don't yet know—not having kept track of all your philosophick mutations since the Golden Age of unstinted dialectick. Possibly you're coming around to the "spirituality"-recognising position of the Methodists—so that you & Lawrence's founders will be in utter harmony.[2] I may yet hear of your rolling around in the sawdust of a camp-meeting tent & begging the holy ghost's mercy for your sins! As for me—I don't see any reason for going beyond the possibilities indicated by the evidence around us. There is no ground for fancying the existence of other "spiritual" orders superimposed on the general order of which we perceive a fragment, & within this general order it is clear that all organick life, including human, is the merest temporary accident occurring now & then—that on any one planet being only a flash in galactick history, & leaving nothing behind to indicate that it has ever existed. Yesterday man did not exist; tomorrow there will be no trace of him, & the cosmos will be exactly as it would have been had he never existed. During the second that the race lives, it develops certain structural reactions to external conditions, which ramify & multiply as environment grows complex & as the organic substance becomes modified & specialised to meet various natural changes. The phenomenon of consciousness arises, & reactions become classified as they contribute to or detract from the sense of normal adjustment. Experience becomes complicated by the retention of impressions left on the tissue by former experience, & originally simple reflexes acquire distinctions & overtones depending upon memory, association, & suggestion. Sensations & judgments are built upon, & conceptions & feelings become more & more elaborate—both in directions leading to increased comprehension of relationship & environment, & in directions leading to fundamental misconceptions & fallacies. Whatever has been experienced is erroneously thought capable of isolation & intensified (even infinite) experiencing, whilst whatever exists is erroneously thought capable of existing on an intensified or even infinite scale. Analogously, the fulfilment of some desires (i.e., the production of normal adjustment after the perception of abnormal adjustment) is accepted erroneously as evidence that all desires can potentially be fulfilled, & that perfect states without any maladjustments whatsoever (impossible in view of the complex nature of the higher organisms & the consequent conflicts of impulse with impulse within a single organism—not to mention the instability & relative unmanageability of environment) are theoretically if not actually possible. Thus out of simple instinct plus experience, memory, association, & suggestion, there grows the tenuous yet powerful quality of *imagination*—which works both for & against the perception of reality. On the side of unreality we have the natural tendency toward illusion-formation & grandiose expansiveness which arises from the unreflective extension of principles & phenomena seen on a smaller scale, & from the application of false analogies in explaining the unknown. Gradually man comes to acquire a false & cosmically amusing sense of the supreme importance of certain things which may not exist at all, or which may be mere meaningless routine phenomena or fragments of phenomena that happen to suggest or symbolise (through steps of plausible though purely illusory linkage) non-existent but gigantic & impressive things or processes or conditions erroneously conceived through the misapplication of consciousness. Thus the impressive popular conceptions of "god", "righteousness", "sacredness", "love", "evil", "tragedy", "mystery", "humanity", & so on. All these things seem tremendously important to the organism which refrains (either through ignorance or through tradition) from analysing them—tied up as they are with certain real & elemental impulses, & inculcated as they are by facile illusions of reality & by countless generations of naive & often compulsory acceptance at face value. It is not remarkable that this is so, or that the force of these erroneous conceptions persists powerfully in the average organism's reflexes long after the conscious brain has grasped their actual unreality. But this does not alter the fact that the conceptions actually *are* unreal, & built up falsely through misleading associative processes. They may *seem* very real & potent in the history of the ignorant race, & their clutch on human sensations & actions may remain very strong despite the recognition of their nature by the thinking minority; but that is no evidence in favour of their actuality. And it follows that the minority who understand the *essential meaninglessness* of these grandiose fallacies, & of the emotions they have drawn into their service, will tend to be more independent of their capricious dominion than will the ignorant or wilfully unanalytical majority. The wise man will use the misconceptions decoratively & intelligently when he can get pleasure or stimulation thereby, but he will be able to *undermine their associated emotions* through reflection on their meaninglessness & triviality when such emotions tend to operate against his larger well-being . . . . i.e., either his physical welfare or his general emotional equilibrium. Thus Schopenhauer pointed out that the one way to circumvent the pain resulting from the will is to undermine the will through reflection on its actual place & function in the universe. When we grasp the fact that the emotions are nothing but tangled & misleading linkages of memory, association, symbolism, & suggestion with the eleven or twelve primary instinctive reflexes of protoplasm in the vertebrate stage, we shall find it less difficult to reconcile their elaborate imagery, ideology, subjective force & illusion of cosmic significance, & claims to importance & authority, with the actual physiological basis of glandular secretion & hormonic discharge underlying them. Of course the elaborate structure would not exist if the immediate secretion & discharge were not joined to a confused jumble of leftovers from other organic reactions; but conversely, it would not exist if the left-overs were not tickled by a fresh secretion & discharge—which may proceed from one of many different causes, some psychological (perception of images suggesting situations calling on the given gland for coöperation in the œconomy of the autonomick nervous system) & some purely mechanical or physical, & altogether irrelevant to the grandiose chain of sensations & conceptions resulting from accidental combination with the left-overs. It is merely *convention*, ignorance, traditional inhibitions, or mental indolence which finds anything remarkable or incompatible in the contrast betwixt the pompous & grandiose pseudo-significance—& the intense poignancy—of certain emotions as *subjectively* experienced, & the actual triviality & fortuitousness (for it is largely a matter of chance & caprice just what especial left-overs will happen to combine with any given hormonic impulse) of these emotions themselves, considered *objectively* in relation to the immediate environment & to the cosmos in general. There is no reason whatever to feel shocked or incredulous at Joseph McCabe's[3] assertion that the difference betwixt the cry of a dog & a symphony of Beethoven is purely one of *degree*, nor of *kind*. It is of course understood that the more impressive & elaborately illusory conceptions & emotions are peculiar to the more complex organisms—since only complex organisms generate enough left-overs to supply the associative structure of such things . . . . . . . but that does not make the things themselves any more really important or related to cosmic truth. They are very pretty as long as they can be used to advantage in embellishing our monotonous & accidental period of existence & consciousness (though Joseph Wood Krutch in "The Modern Temper"[4] believes that their field of effective use in this direction is sharply narrowing); but when they begin to get in the way of one another, & of the less elaborated & less exaggerated emotions concerned with more direct environmental adjustment, it is time to deflate & minimise the more intrusive & mischievous ones by exposing their real absence of cosmic significance & causing the independent part of the mind to withdraw its support from them. Of course, not everyone can profit by such an exposé. Even the most keenly intelligent persons are often so powerfully dominated by traditional inhibitions, primitive reflexes, & other anti-cerebral influences that their abstract intellection is locally retarded or nullified. But at least, everyone can try; & many may find themselves surprised by the degree to which they can win emancipation from troublesome emotional conflicts. The most useful question in the world, as concerns the moulding & harmonisation of the human personality, is "Well, what the hell of it?"

Your discussion of this point does not impress me as being of quite the old Consul Hasting acuteness, but haste & possible bias account for that. You ask whether it is more probable that glandular discharge causes emotion, or that emotion causes glandular discharge. In reply to this, one might ask what causes emotion if glandular discharge doesn't? It has long been recognised that emotion is the result of perceptions of physical impacts on the nervous system—the relationship being too repeatedly verifiable for doubt. All that I have said of the part played by instinct, memory, association, suggestion, symbolisation, &c. has been well understood; it being certain that nothing ever gets into the emotions or consciousness which does not come through the five senses. All this matter of the "significance" of emotion & of intuitive impressions was carefully threshed out *long before* the discovery of the part played by the ductless glands—with the result that no sober & impartial thinker could for a moment credit the existence of anything save chance & caprice behind such parts of man's subjective feelings as are not the direct expression of primary instincts. Thus glands & hormones need not enter into the matter at all. Everything was settled except the *exact physiological way* in which perceptions or physical stimuli became translated into the sort of autonomic nervous impulse which manifests itself as an instinctive reflex & (in the case of complex organisms with associative left-overs) as a psychological emotion. Discovery of the role of the glands & their secretions merely supplied the gap & settled this question—but did not change any major conception of independent biologists & psychologists. The facts about the cosmic insignificance & fortuitousness of human emotions do not rest in any way upon endocrinology . . . . . . so that it was simply as a *symbol* that I happened to choose gland-secretion as typical of the kind of thing really lying behind pompous & pretentious emotions. Getting back to the *order* of gland-discharge & emotion, it is certain that discharge comes as a result of some direct impression, either physical or psychological, which acts on the gland. If the impression is purely physical or chemical, no *need* for the discharge may exist—yet some emotion will result if the organism is sufficiently complex & if certain associative left-overs happen to be in the right position for combination. Thus glandular injections, as well as the Steinach operation (which renders an external secretion internal by making gonads wholly ductless), often cause complete changes in emotional life. If the impression is psychological, it is almost never originally an *emotion*, but simply the *perception of a condition naturally tending to demand this particular gland-discharge*. The primary product is an instinctive reflex—which becomes an emotion only after taking on certain associative factors. Clearly, the action precedes the emotion in the first place, although of course the exercise of the resultant emotion renews the original gland-exciting perception in such a way as to increase & prolong the hormonic discharge. An instinctive reflex precedes each emotion, but the latter strikes back & renews the excitation of the instinct. All this has been determined by various types of actual experiment explained in some detail in books on endocrinology. In ordinary life, the question is complicated by the fact that what we commonly regard as single emotions are in most cases very far from that—being complex & sometimes capricious or even contradictory groups of totally unrelated emotions, which change irresponsibly & imperceptibly before we can reach anything like a genuine analysis. The interaction of the components of these groups, as they strike back & influence the underlying instincts, is of tremendous & hopeless complexity—& well illustrates the capriciousness & essential meaninglessness of everything in the emotional field.

What I said some time back regarding the non-remarkableness of the elaborate sensations which come from purely capricious & mechanical causes v(top of sheet II, 1.) ought to dispose of your exaltation of "unfathomably rich emotional phenomena which alter characters, transform lives, & in the social realm occasion murders, marriages, procreation of the species, & incalculably more." Do not irrelevant trifles determine everything? Have not lives been changed by the missing of a morning train, or battles determined by what a general ate the night before? Many a man has married because he was drunk, & George Jean Nathan[5] once pointed out that most of the great philosophers probably thought or reasoned as they did because of such minor & overlooked factors as diet, digestion, wife's temper, debts, & so on. A stomach-ache may have just as much effect on the world, & almost as much on an individual's thought, as an ecstatic adoration of the Virgin Mary. What is more—you betray subjectiveness & conventionality in taking for granted the importance of such things as character, life, murder, marriage, procreation, & so on. What do these things really amount to in the cosmos? All things are merely incidents in a blind cyclic flux from nowhere to nowhere, so far as probability suggests. The fact that emotions cause great consequences in the lives of those not sufficiently strong or sufficiently on guard to resist them means absolutely nothing. A plain knock on the head or knife-thrust between the ribs can change a life to nothingness, while a bad tooth infection can completely alter a person's psychology, motivation, personality, social adaptability, & intelligence level. I don't see where your argument is. Even your climactic parallel fails to sustain it—for as a matter of fact even the greatest of the philosophers with his psychological problems **is** only the natural & inevitable result of two cells stuck together to form an egg. Of course there are many steps between the original egg-cell & the full-panoplied Galpinius or Democritus, but it is all a fixed mechanical process resulting from the structure of the universe. The full-blown & subjectively powerful & important-seeming emotion which moulds character is of course the product of a vast number of accidental association-processes superadded to a simple reflex— but that does not make it a whit more *truly* important or typical of cosmic design than is the itch of a flea-bitten hog. Such *virtual*, empirical, apparent, or relative importance as it may have is wholly artificial—to be gauged only by the thin & variable standard of effect on a certain variable personality under certain momentary conditions. Any really serious estimate of such pseudo-importance is a mockery. True, the emotion may operate powerfully on a given individual under a given set of conditions—but so may the kick of an army mule. There is nothing in all this to demand exaltation & bated breath. If the damn thing tickles pleasantly & doesn't do anybody any harm, let it alone. Certainly, some of our finest diversions & strongest non-primitive reasons for living come from *the intelligent manipulation* of such raw material. So also do fine things come from the intelligent manipulation of lumpish bronze, random bricks, aimless colours, & casual sounds. But if the damn thing tickles or grates *unpleasantly*, there's nothing "sacred" about it which needs to prevent our deflating & largely banishing it through a rational analysis of its purely biochemical irrelevance. Emotion is essentially *raw material.* It is a magnificent thing to harness & use, but a damned poor & inappropriate thing to obey as a master or worship as a god.

If you'll reflect on this you'll see a good many of your objections removed. No one wishes to dispute the value of *emotion well managed,* or to claim that as much aesthetic possibility resides in a dog's yelp as in a musician's symphony. One wishes merely to emphasise that the complexity of evolved emotion is nothing other *in kind* than the multiplication of simple biological reflexes, so that it has *no intrinsic cosmic value* whatever, & no relative value *except when it is used to advantage.* Grant that it is better *raw material* for something of subjective value than a hog's itch is—but that doesn't make it valuable *until* it is well used. The fact remains that it is merely a fortuitous result of bodily accidents, & that it does not mean in any way what it appears to mean in our illusion-blinded & unanalysing consciousness.

I don't think that a rational view of these matters is by any means peculiarly American, though it may be that certain American have used the basic facts as an excuse for depreciating aesthetically valuable imponderables. Actually, the fortuitous & meaningless nature of the emotions need not cause us to abandon their artistic use whenever they can be made to bolster up pleasing illusions of ego-expansion & liberation. Indeed, a vast number of exploded concepts are still capable of stimulating decorative use. Whatever is closely allied to basic animal instinct is imperishable, & the emotional & imaginative world grows so gradually out of the realm of instinct that the line will always be hazy. Despite what Krutch predicts, it is unlikely that the illusions of the fancy will be drained of their titillative value for some time to come—especially since all of us must live through a vividly impressionable childhood during which the fruits of disillusion are inoperative.

It is a mistake to try to isolate one form of truth-appraisal from another. When people talk of "science", "philosophy", & so on they are in danger of letting *nomenclature* interfere with genuine ideas. In looking over the universe it is possible to get many different sorts of perspective, & the separate investigations of the various sciences merge together in the correlative processes of philosophy. After all is said & done, there is really no trace of reason to consider organic life in general—or the human species in particular—as anything of importance or of more than momentary duration. All of the pseudo-importance felt by man himself before he surveys the wider field necessarily drops away—as does the illusion of a fly's giganticism when we remove the magnifying-glass through which we have been looking. It still remains a fact that man is the most complex organism in this immediate part of the universe—but *what of it?* Nobody tries to deny the obvious facts regarding man's consciousness & grasp on certain parts of the external world. His superiority to other immediate forms of matter is clear, & we can even get a hint at the precise structural reasons for that superiority. What the de-bunker attacks is merely the absurd & gratuitous (though natural enough as a result of early ignorance) assumption of the tradition-blinded part of mankind that the race is especially differentiated from the rest of molecular matter, especially endowed with ideas not coming through the senses, & especially important to the mythical consciousness governing the cosmos. And no de-bunking is too drastic for such puerility—into which I hope to Pegāna you are not falling! Don't join good old Mocrates & revive the defunct Biblical Alliance of 1918![6]

Life itself—the especial form of union betwixt carbon, hydrogen, nitrogen, & other elements in which certain unique processes & energy-forms develop—is probably a widely-scattered phenomenon; but there is no reason to think that its more complex forms of growth (dependent as these are upon environment) are even remotely similar in widely separated parts of the universe, or that the psychological attributes of any one highly complex branch are parallelled in any other. Such things as honour, beauty, love, &c. are by no means to be regarded as other than local to the momentary race of primates harbouring these conceptions. On the other hand, *hunger* is probably basic with all vital compounds. The number of bodies in the cosmos containing life-forms at any one time is probably vastly less than was commonly supposed prior to twenty years ago—since we now believe life-sustaining planets to be very rare accidents. However, even so, it is not likely that terrestrial man is the most complex of all things in the *totality* of the varied galaxies—or at least, it's only an even guess that he is. And in the endless history of time & space it would be foolish to fancy that he has not been vastly surpassed vigintillions of times.

As for your present perturbations—I think a year or so will find you much less agitated, since all amorous attractions are essentially transient. And of course, if you'd get outside yourself, take an objective & panoramick survey, & give some really serious thought to the fortuitous meaninglessness of all emotion, you would be greatly helped in the cooling-off process. That's the only process worth cultivating unless the other victim gets ashamed of accepting luxury from a deceived partner & coöperates toward putting the whole matter on an open & straight-forward basis. Meanwhile one may only advise that you "coast" as inconspicuously & indecisively as you can—with eyes open as to possible exits & solutions. Let us hope that your wife will have time in Chicago to think on the value of the prize that is slipping away, & that a renewed affection on her part may assist in toning down the new & capricious hormone-storm. But time & common sense will doubtless bring their own adjustments.

Little Belknap has had a bad spell of influenza since my visit, but is now adequately convalescing. ¶ Did I tell you in my last that Cook has presented me with a three-volume copy of "Melmoth, the Wanderer"?[7] Glad you're doing some congenial composing, & hope the folk-song comes out well. ¶ Heard a lecture on Schopenhauer Wednesday night[8] which made me think of many an old Gallomo discussion. ¶ There's a course of poetry readings in town which will bring hither our one-time debate-subject *T. S. Eliot.*[9] I expect to hear him . . . . Shantih, Shantih, Shantih! ¶ So you've had snow in your part of the world? None here—in fact, the winter has so far been as mild as last winter.

And so it goes. May Pegāna guide you in paths of only moderate feloniousness!

> —Yr obt hble Servt—
>
> Grandpa

*Notes*

1. A manuscript entitled "En Route (An American to Paris, 1931)" survives among HPL's papers at JHL. "Deep Sea Meditation" has not been found.
2. Lawrence College was founded by two Methodist clergymen in 1847.
3. Joseph McCabe (1867–1955) was a well-known philosopher, historian, and freethinker, author of such works as *The Evolution of Mind* (1910) and *The Story of Evolution* (1912). He also translated Ernst Haeckel's *The Riddle of the Universe* (1900).
4. Joseph Wood Krutch (1893–1970), *The Modern Temper: A Study and a Confession* (New York: Harcourt, Brace, 1929).
5. George Jean Nathan (1882–1958), drama critic and essayist. The comment referred to probably derives from *The Autobiography of an Attitude* (New York: Knopf, 1925): "A man's philosophy, his attitude toward the world, is very seldom found to be the result of carefully reasoned reflection, meditation and deduction. It is, on the contrary, generally the largely fortuitous end-product and sum-product of a hundred and one extra-subjective occurrences, adventures and phenomena that have figured in his life" (p. 3).
6. See HPL to Adolphe de Castro, 14 October 1934 (ms., JHL): "For years he [Maurice W. Moe] was associated with the late William Jennings Bryan (supplying the brains, perhaps, while poor old Bill supplied the wind & braying!) in some sort of scheme called the 'Biblical Alliance', for giving bible courses to students in state universities where such teaching is barred."
7. Charles Robert Maturin (1782?–1824), *Melmoth the Wanderer* (1820; rpt. London: Richard Bentley & Son, 1892; 3 vols); *LL* 599.
8. I.e., on 18 January, by a Prof. Baylis.
9. Eliot's reading occurred the week of 24 February See letter 23.

[23] [ALS]

> Tenbarnes—
>
> March 24, 1933

Son:—

I am very glad to hear that, in spite of distracting influences, you have been improving & solidifying your collegiate position, & laying the foundations for better conditions next year. After all, security & tranquillity are the foundations of all things—as I am alarmingly reminded by my own financial instability, which may soon force me to quit #10 for cheaper & accordingly less congenial quarters. A firm & comfortable foothold on one's native sod is assuredly something to be adhered to with utmost sedulousness. Which reminds me that Cook (who has, alas, just lost his job through the closing of his firm) lately sent me a picture of an extremely quaint Gothick masterpiece on your local campus—whose medium of construction, however, speaks rather forbiddingly of the climate from my tropick-demanding point of view. Were you (whose critical knowledge of St-Etienne de Mont & other ecclesiastical landmarks of the Old World might well make you an expert in such matters) by any chance associated with its construction? I enclose the view in question. And incidentally—whilst upon the subject of architecture & its accessories—let me enclose another cutting to shew how well Rhode-Island has resisted the degenerate tendency toward building & decoration of the modernistick sort. You may have a set of epigoni in the West; but by God, Sir, the true & authentick civilisation of white Englishmen still survives in antient New-England! God Save the King.

As for those matters of emotion lately under discussion—whilst I certainly do believe that the purely human & derivative emotions are richer in permanent satisfactions then the more primitive impulses, & therefore to be preferr'd to the latter; I wou'd not be thought of as unduly minimising the raw material, or implying that it is *always* oppos'd to the most superior processes of the personality. Rather wou'd I say, that it is to be ruled against only when it demonstrably interferes with some process of the higher sort, & thereby tends to reduce the personality to a lower level than it might otherwise attain. That, I conceive, was the position of the celebrated Spinoza; a lecture upon whom I last December describ'd to you. But in general my point was not so much a championship of the evolv'd over the unevolv'd, as a championship of the *balanc'd whole* over *any* hypertrophick or disturbing ingredient, be it of the human or bestial sort. It was—& is—my position, that a man's entire, coördinated personality ought to be the unimpeded arbiter of his destinies; that no irrational caprice, or isolated overdevelopment of some single impulse, be it high or low, ought to enslave him by defeating that rational course of action which the bulk of his impulses & faculties dictates, & which therefore is essential to his tranquillity & good adjustment to life. Such a position does not necessarily look down upon any particular impulse or set of impulses as compar'd with others. It meerly looks askance at *any* impulse which, by growing out of its proper proportion, conflicts badly with the general emotional equilibrium & total welfare of the possessor. 'Tis a case of prescribing the sound classical maxim of *nihil nimium*,[1] as over against the feverish & irrational mediaeval attitude summ'd up in the title of Mr. Dryden: "All for Love; or, the World Well Lost."[2] Conceiving, therefore, that the reduction or deflation of certain isolated & disturbing emotions is often of value in the development of the whole personality, & the tranquil governance of existence; it is but natural that I shou'd bring up the purely mechanical &

non-"sacred" character of all human feelings, in order to remove that superstition which allies them to the "divine" & resents any attack upon any of them. I claim, & I think not without reason, that the extream force of any emotion can very sensibly be blunted by a careful examination of all the trivial & fortuitous factors which go into its composition. More than one determin'd person has very successfully & advantageously modify'd his character by the rational & deliberate toning down of emotional predispositions which warr'd against balance, tranquillity, & social adjustment. This, indeed, I know from many concrete & verifiable cases—not excluding my own, wherein a tendency toward quick & violent anger, highly inimical to urbanity, has been vastly diminish'd since the hot-temper'd days of my youth. The important thing to fix in mind is *that no emotion is really worth anything in itself.* All that is of value is the pleasing *balance* brought about by the harmonious *correlation* of the various emotions. The emotions themselves are simply existing forces—not to be valued or worshipp'd in themselves, but simply to be accepted as natural phaenomena & manag'd to the greatest advantage of the whole personality. The *value* of a feeling depends altogether upon its adjustment to the fabrick compos'd of all the other feelings.

As to the emotional development of those persons distinguish'd in the arts—it is very possible that certain (but not all) types of creativeness are associated with a lack of balance otherwise unfortunate. That the keener sensitiveness demanded by art is often associated with uneven development & lack of rational control, can scarcely be deny'd—& did not the late Max Nordau[3] associate all genius with degeneracy? But that is no argument against every man's trying to be as well-balanced as he *can* be—& fortunately for society, not many of us are of the extream & irresponsible hyper-artistick type. Most persons, happily, are more or less capable of transferring a little of their artistick sense into the art of living itself; instead of pouring it all into specifick external enterprises & living with a loose & slovenly ugliness which they wou'd scorn to have associated with their professed work. I am an advocate of making life the chief of one's arts—of being a gentleman first & a specifick artist second if at all. All of which, I trust, even tho' it is not likely to accomplish any convincing or conversion, may at least remove a little of the aspect of error or inconsistency from my arguments.

Our enlivening discussions & diverting parodies of a decade ago were last month vividly recall'd to me by a poetick reading which I attended—the celebrity being none other than our old-time nucleus of debate, the eminent & incomprehensible Shantih S. (Waste Land) Eliot, now grown to be 45 & looking every year of it.[4] He hath pick'd up a strong Britannick accent thro' his long (& now naturalised) residence in London, & despite his love of symbolick chaos it is easy to picture him in his latterly announc'd role of 'royalist in politics, classicist in literature, & Anglo-Catholick in religion.'[5] His remarks were tinged with a pleasing infusion of humour, & it was perhaps not without an unobtrusive ocular scintillation that he asserted the essential *plainness* &

*simplicity* of his poetical emanations. He read from "The Waste Land", "Ash Wednesday", & other products made famous by his criticks, & appear'd to hold his surprisingly vast audience in that state of tense awe which only a combination of reputation & incomprehension can produce. After the lecture he held a kind of court in a hall adjoining the auditorium; his starry-eyed admirers filing past & introducing themselves with a deferential handclasp—a naive ceremony in which I did not think it necessary to participate. I enclose some accounts of the event, & of a rather comical interruption of it, from the pen of the columnist Bertrand Kelton Hart, Esq., literary editor of the local *Journal.*[6] I would appreciate the return of these at some time—to preserve betwixt the pages of that now-tatter'd copy of the Nov. '22 *Dial* which contains "The Waste Land." Shantih, shantih, shantih!

Another thing I shall send when I can find it (my files being in the worst possible state of disorder) is a cartoon of the syndicated "Metropolitan Movies" series (drawn by one Wortman)[7] in which our old friend George Willard Kirk & his Chelsea Book Shop are very plainly delineated. G K is shewn leaning against the wall in a very characteristick posture, & even his face is distinctly suggested despite certain departures from line-for-line realism. The Chelsea seems to have grown into something of an institution on the borders of Greenwich-Village.

My programme has of late been exceedingly crowded with annoying tho' doubtfully remunerative revisory tasks—& the correction of an 80,000-word novel MS. looms formidably ahead.[8] A fortnight ago a job took me to Hartford, in His Maj[ty's] Province of Connecticut, to assist a client in some research[9] at the Athenaeum there, & I took advantage of my sojourn to survey many picturesque memorials of the past. As I doubtless writ you in 1931, when another job gave me my first sight of central Connecticut, Hartford itself is not a town of especial interest; most of its antiquities (save the late-Georgian Bulfinch state house, now superseded for that purpose) having succumb'd to the venom of the years. On this occasion, however, I had time to explore the antient suburbs of Farmington & Wethersfield, & found them abundantly rich in my favourite kind of material. Farmington is one of the most beautiful of all the villages of this continent, lying 9 miles S.W. of Hartford in an exquisitely rolling countryside replete with adventurous vistas of hills beyond hills. Its vast elms are of a highly impressive aspect, & the well-kept plenitude of colonial houses—a few of the antique 17th century mode, with peaked gables & second-story overhang—impart an induplicable charm. The inn at which I stopt was a rambling composite with a nucleus dating back to 1638 (the year of Farmington's foundation) & with no part newer than 1790. The village church, white & steepled, was built in 1771, & many picturesque burying-grounds are present. Restrictions on the sale of land have kept the place in a state of great selectness. Wethersfield, 4 miles due south of Hartford, is likewise an absorbing repository of tradition, tho' vastly different from Farmington in aspect. It lies in a flat region, & has a wide village common shaded by the greatest elms east of the Rocky Mountains. Its abundant array of 18ᵗʰ century houses display the distinctive marks of Connecticut Valley architecture, & include the Webb house, where in May 1781 Genls. Washington & Rochambeau, & other damn'd rebels & foreigners, plann'd the crucially disastrous battle which took place the following October in York Town, in Virginia. The brick church, with a well-design'd spire, was built in 1763, being then accounted the finest church in New-England outside Boston. The view from its belfry is prais'd in the letters & diaries of all the French officers who pass'd thro' Wethersfield in 1781. This region was, & probably still is, fam'd for the growing of onions. It was at Wethersfield that the Pequot war started in 1637.

The winter here has, on the whole, been mercifully mild; tho' I am none the less glad to hail the advent of spring. I fear that bad finances will debar me from any long trip this year, tho' I hope to make the most of short ones. Best wishes—& may good sense guide you in all the departments of life.

Yr most obᵗ hᵇˡᵉ Servᵗ—

Grandpa

## Notes

1. Nothing in excess.

2. Dryden's play is an adaptation of Shakespeare's *Antony and Cleopatra*.

3. Max Nordau (1849–1923), *Degeneration* (1895); translated from *Entartung* (1892–93).

4. HPL wrote a parody of Eliot's *The Waste Land*, entitled "Waste Paper: A Poem of Profound Insignificance."

5. The quotation comes from the preface to Eliot's *For Lancelot Andrewes* (1929).

6. Bertrand Kelton Hart (1892–1941), was literary editor of the *Providence Journal* and author of the column, "The Sideshow." He discussed Eliot's lecture—given on 19 February at Faunce House, on the Brown University campus—in several columns, including those of 20 and 22 February 1933. In the latter column, Hart noted an interruption in Eliot's lecture when a janitor handed Eliot a slip of paper, at which point Eliot stated: "I am requested to announce that Mr. Greenwich Black is wanted on the telephone."

7. Denys Wortman (1887–1954), whose work appeared at the Armory Show in New York in 1913, worked for Metropolitan Movies for 30 years.

8. This work has not been identified. HPL mentioned to correspondents that he would be paid only $100 for his work.

9. Actually, he appears to have gone to Hartford at the urging of his ex-wife Sonia; see her *Private Life of H. P. Lovecraft* (West Warwick, RI: Necronomicon Press, 1992), 22: "I took a trip to beautiful Farmington, Conn. I was so enchanted with this beautiful Colonial city that I wrote to Howard at once to join me there which he did." It was their last meeting.

[24] [ALS]

Note & record. The sincerest          66 College St.,
form of flattery—though I            Providence, R.I.,
haven't gone so far as to ape the         June 24, 1933.
"Ave." or the 536 (or 726 E.)!

Son:—

    Well, Sir, the Old Gentleman is indeed glad to hear from you after all these silent weeks! As you will note from the above, the period has not been a quiescent one for Grandpa—& knowing the settled habits of advanced years, you can picture to yourself the cataclysmic magnitude—material & psychological—of the upheaval. I think I told you that the alarming state of our family finances was making it necessary for my surviving aunt & myself to embark on a series of radical retrenchments, & that the chief œconomy ahead was a consolidation of households in one cheap flat. This has now come to pass—so that we are sharing a 5-room-&-attick apartment at a cost no greater than that of my *one* room & alcove at good old #10. Thus I am once more, as in the youthful & middle-aged days of 598 Angell, part of a private family household instead of a mere roomer. But none of this tells the whole story; for as felicitous fortuity would have it, the present move is no ordinary one. Poverty being the spur, I was all steeled up to brave a plunge into a less congenial neighbourhood—when a streak of pure luck put us in touch with something not only cheap, but so incredibly desirable that our move *down* has all the externals of a move *up*. But before I describe the prize secured, let me narrate the current bad news—news of that which has completely spoilt the summer for my aunt—& indirectly, for me.

    On June 14, before the complete settlement of our new abode, my aunt broke her ankle through a slip on the stairs while descending to answer the doorbell during my absence. Doctors . . . . ambulance to R.I. Hospital . . . . . x-ray . . . . . setting under aether . . . . . plaster cast . . . . . room in Ward K . . . . . prospect of being in bed six weeks & on crutches several more . . . . . . . & a financial strain utterly ruinous to us at the present juncture! Such is life. Of course there is no danger or actual illness, but the restriction to bed is accursedly unpleasant & productive of backaches. After another week my aunt will probably be brought home with a nurse. She reads, writes notes, & eats fairly well—very well, in fact, today. I call at the hospital each afternoon. Naturally the disaster has kept me overwhelmingly busy—with the house in its unsettled state & everything in the air—& it is very unlikely that I can accompany W. Paul Cook to the N.A.P.A. Convention in New York (July 3–4–5) as originally planned. I was going to stay with Sonny Belknap—in fact, the Longs had postponed a contemplated trip to Asbury Park on my account—but I fancy I had better tell him not to expect the Old Man. The Convention promises to be one of more than average interest & activity.

But about 66 College St. The one overwhelming thing from my point of view—& you know what an architectural antiquarian & general 18th century relique your Grandpa is—is that the house *is a colonial one!*[1] All my long life I have been enthralled by the mellow old Georgian houses on Providence's ancient hill. Nothing else on earth has so deeply coloured my imagination or so persistently woven itself into my dreams. Never had I lived in one, yet always did I long to do so. And now, I *am* living in one! Pure luck. What we sought was cheapness plus practical convenience—yet through some fantastically fortunate miracle the cheapest & most practical thing *was colonial* . . . . the sort of place I'd pay any price for if I had the money. And, to complete the miracle, no sacrifice of neighbourhood quality was involv'd. The locality is predominantly collegiate, with the business district surprisingly close—yet far, far down the steep precipice which divides the city into two separate worlds. The main Brown campus with its great clock tower can be seen from our easterly windows, & a goodly quota of our neighbours are fraternity-houses.

The edifice itself—yellow & wooden—lies on the crest of the ancient hill in a quaint grassy court just off College St.—behind & next to the marble John Hay Library of Brown University (which contains the famous Harris Collection of American Poetry—greatest in the world), about half a mile south of 10 Barnes St. The fine colonial doorway is like my bookplate[2] come to life, though of a slightly later period (circa 1800) with side lights & fan carving instead of a fanlight. In the rear & on the western side there are picturesque, village-like gardens—those behind being at a higher level than the front of the house. In front there are some flower-beds, an hedge, & a row of old-fashion'd posts to keep off vehicles. The upper flat we have taken contains 5 rooms besides bath & kitchen on the main (2nd) floor, plus 2 attic storerooms—one of which is so attractive that I wish I could have it for an extra den! My quarters—a large study & a small bedroom—are on the south side, with my working desk under a west window affording a splendid view of the lower town's outspread roofs & of the mystical sunsets that flame behind them.[3] In general, the interior is fully as fascinating as the exterior—with colonial fireplaces, mantels, & chimney-cupboards, curving Georgian staircase, (would that no ankles had been broken thereon!) wide floorboards, old-fashion'd latches, small-paned windows (old style—innocent of cords & weights), six-panel doors, rear wing with floor at a different level (3 steps down), quaint attic stairs, &c.—just like the old houses open as museums. So like a museum is it that I keep fearing a guard will turn up to chase me out at 5 o'clock closing time! The sensation of *actually living* in such a place is indescribably fascinating—to come *home* through a carved colonial doorway & sit beside a white Georgian mantel looking out through small-paned windows over a sea of ancient roofs & sun-golden foliage. The proximity of many belfries makes each hour the occasion for a symphony of chimes—which even a musician like you cou'd not but approve. Our old family furniture fits in marvellously well—& we have rescued from storage many items belonging to the old home broken up in 1904 . . . things for which we've had no space since then. Naturally we play up the least Victorian pieces—& the colonial mantels in my study & my aunt's living-room are perfect throwbacks to the 18th Century. I have on mine an old clock, vases, & candlesticks, & above it a marine painting by my mother, newly fram'd in the authentick Georgian manner. Bookshelves actually play a large part in my furnishing scheme—I've had to get 4 new cases to replace the built-in shelves in my alcove at #10. It remains to be added, that the dominant antiquity in no way detracts from comfort & convenience in the most contemporary sense. All plumbing is modern, & steam heat & hot water are piped in from the adjacent college library—the house being own'd by Brown University. Appended is a plan of the Theobald-Gamwell flat—main (2nd) floor.[4] As you see, my quarters are perfectly distinct from my aunt's, so that each can have company without disturbing the other. The whole effect, though, is that of a single well-rounded household—my study answering to the family library, & my aunt's living-room to the parlour. I moved in May 15th—half a month ahead of her—& had my quarters (books & all) fully settled exactly one month ago to a day—May 24th. Right now my place looks as mellow & homelike as if six generations of the family had dwelt here! My aunt moved in June 1st, & had her living-room settled by the night of the 3rd. Her bedroom is partly settled, but the dining-room is still a chaos of piled-up crockery. We are going to hang over the fatal staircase a huge painting by my late elder aunt—the Rocks at Narragansett Pier. Something about the atmosphere of the place & its familiar furnishings reminds me curiously (in miniature) of my birthplace at 454 Angell St.—the old home broken up in 1904, & preceding #598. This quality does much to neutralise any homesickness I might otherwise feel for 10 Barnes. Now the desperate problem is how to hang on to it! My aunt has always been the family banker, but now that she is down I have charge of all papers & accounts, & can see in stark plainness the utter desperateness of our financial situation. With the bottom completely out of revision, & with no knack whatever for commercial fiction, I am certainly up against a stone wall as to how to get the cash to keep alive. No one ever had less instinctive aptitude or experience in the cryptic & devious ways of money-making . . . unless it be Little Belknap.

I am glad to learn of your debut as a gentleman-agriculturist, & trust that a rich harvest may crown your ploughing & sowing. The eternal soil & its immemorial ways have ever form'd for me a subject of the most intense attraction & admiration; indeed, I am convinc'd that those customs, perspectives, & imaginative reactions which do most to lend the illusions of direction, interest, significance, & purpose to the formless chaos of human existence, are those which spring most directly from man's primitive relationship to the earth, its bounties, its cultivation, & its vary'd phaenomena. When agriculture is totally left behind, there grows up about life a sense of instability, artificiality, & ultimate meaninglessness (born of a separation from the visibly aeternal & cyclick processes of Nature) which cannot but be destructive of the best qualities of civilisation. I agree largely with the eminent Spengler when he affirms, that an agrarian aristocracy is the best form of social organisation possible to mankind. Whilst I have not a personal aptitude for the operations of pastoral & agrestick life, I delight in the antient tradition of country squirearchy, & in my close ancestral connexion with it. You may be assur'd, that my colonial study mantel has swinging from it the undying Farmer's Almanack of Robert B. Thomas[5] (now in its 141st year) which has swung beside the kindred mantels of all my New-England forbears for near a century & a half: that almanack without which my grandfather wou'd never permit himself to be, & of which a family file extending unbrokenly back to 1836 & scatteringly to 1805 still reposes in the lower drawer of my library table . . . . which was likewise my grandfather's library table. A real civilisation, Sir, can never depart far from the state of a people's rootedness in the soil, & their adherence to the landskip & phaenomena & methods which from a primitive antiquity shap'd them to their particular set of manners & institutions & perspectives. God Save the King!

I am glad your domestick affairs maintain a certain quiescence, if not ideal adjustment; & trust that time may do its own salutary & imperceptible modelling toward a stabler & sounder equilibrium. You have no need, I am sure, to lament the absence of grandiose projects in musick; since this is clearly a period of incubation & acquisition in no way to be confounded with idleness. It is pleasant that your friend Wessel can visit you, since I presume you have not many chances to converse with persons whose interests & experiences are so closely parallel to your own.

You are, I think, correct in believing that the thirties will form a rich period for you, owing to the union of a lingering youthfulness with a ripening maturity. Indeed, I believe that the true secret of most creative genius lies in that prolongation of psychological youth which permits of such an union. Nearly all young folk have the sensitive emotions of artists, though without the experience & fund of ideas needed to transform meer feeling into art. Likewise, most persons have by middle life acquired a potentially rich supply of experience & ideas; which, however, remains artistically ineffective because of the loss of the fire & sensitive vision which cou'd advantageously employ it. It is when, in relatively rare cases, the fire & sensitiveness survive to join with the fruits of maturity, that creative work of depth & authenticity is produc'd. If I were you I wou'd indulge to the full any reviving penchant for literature & literary expression. It certainly will not detract from your musical capacity; but on the other hand, will probably prove a stimulus & auxiliary to that side of your personality. Your taste for ideas & their expression in youth was too great not to indicate a powerful & permanent element in your nature, which can never permanently disappear, no matter how many times it may suffer an Alpheus-like submersion. The new delight in physical phaenomena, which you say dates from your Majorcan sojourn, is probably a still further asset to your aesthetick capital. It cannot but add to the products of sensitiveness & experience a poignant touch of reality scarce to be duplicated by those who live with less gusto. This is something I am forc'd to imagine more or less objectively, tho' I suppose I have approximations to it in the pleasure I experience when extreme heat combines with glamourous sun[lit] scenery, bird-songs, floral perfumes, & objects whose tradit[ions] & associations are agreeable to my imagination. I th[en fe]el a kind of buoyancy & elation as much of the body as of [the sp]irit—tho' it fades as soon as the temperature drops [much] below 85 degrees. Obviously, I cou'd never know a life [of] physical gusto in any but a tropical environment. M[ost of] my nearly 43 years in New-England I have spent in [semi]-numbness & shivering from the rarely-interrupt[ed c]old . . . . . . as you can well appreciate from remembering [how] the poor old man shiver'd in Cleveland back in '22 when the 5 o'clock lake breeze began to rattle the library windows![6]

Ah me, good old 1922 . . . . . & what hath time done to the various oddly-assorted figures that knocked about 1537 E. 99th St., 9231 Birchdale, Wade Park, Clark's Lunch, Taylor's Arcade, Eglin's, & all the other half-fabulous landmarks! Despair & the black caves of the sea-bottom for one, for others mediocrity & merging with the crowd, for some progress & growth, for still others a sort of changeless crystallisation, & for a few a stagnation temper'd only by the loss of certain major crudities & inexperienced errors of judgment. How vary'd are the effects of time upon differing types & temperaments! Good old Samuelus is the premier Endymion of them all; he having chang'd less both in mind & aspect than any other of the period I can recall. On the whole, I don't think any one has better prospects for maturity than yourself. With a powerful, quick, & acquisitive intellect at all stages of development, & added to the sum a new physical gusto. What combination cou'd augur better? In truth, you ever had a tendency to join the advantages of different ages. I think it was upon your 17th birthday—in the tense, remote hours before the signing of the armistice in 1918—that I addrest to you some congratulatory lines containing such observations as:

> Is't true, indeed, that thou so short a Time
> Hast known the Air of our terrestrial Clime?
> Art thou not rather some experienc'd Sage,
> Who hast, like *Æson*, lost thy hoary Age?

> . . . . In this fair Train, that rise on ev'ry Hand,
> Foremost of all can gifted GALPIN stand:
> Young as the youngest, brilliant as the best,
> Thy lightening Brain was made to lead the rest.
> 'Tis thine to combat ev'ry ling'ring Wrong;

To help the feeble, and subdue the strong:
Stand forth, bold Youth, within whose Bosom bright
The Past's grave lore, and Future's Force, unite![7]

---

As for local events—aside from the [Great] Migration & the still more recent disaster, they are not many. D[uring] the hot spells I have been active & have taken long & pleasant [ram]bles in the countryside, whilst during the cool spells I have sh[iver'd.] On Sunday, June 11, my aunt & I attended a Musick Festival ([see pro]gramme &c. enclos'd) whose excellence you would doubtless ha[ve appre]ciated far more than I. Amusingly, my back is visible in the group [photogr]aph taken for the press—a copy of which I enclose, together with [some . . . . . .] timely humorous commentary on the whole art of getting into [group pho]tographs.

Fra Samuelus is rejoicing in the acquisition of a *real Grecian sculptur'd head*, which he pickt up with remarkable cheapness at an antique shop in 6th Ave. It is the first thing of its kind he has possesst, & he lately sent me photographs of it, which indicate an object of extream beauty & unmistakable Hellenism.

Klarkash-Ton the Atlantean, High-Priest of Tsathoggua, continues his triumphant course as a master of fiction. Enclos'd is a circular of his recent brochure[8]—containing six phantasies of the highest merit, rejected by commercial magazines because of their lack of rabble-appeal. If you still retain any of those qualities of fancy which produc'd "Marsh-Mad" in the good old days, I recommend this modest collection to you as a rare bargain you will not regret. I have a new tale coming out—with woeful misprints—in the next *Weird Tales*—the one on the stands July 1st.[9] Also—my "Shunned House" booklet may appear at last—finally issued by Walter J. Coates of Driftwind.[10] ¶ Well—may the Muses continue to bless thee!

Yr obt h[blc] Serv[t]—

Grandpa

*Notes*

1. The Samuel Mumford House (1825) at 66 College (later moved to 65 Prospect).

2. HPL designed his bookplate to have a fanlighted doorway. The artwork was made by Wilfred B. Talman.

3. HPL's description here (as in other letters) was later adapted in "The Haunter of the Dark" (1935) to indicate the vista from Robert Blake's apartment in Providence.

4. Non-extant. But see another in *Marginalia* (Sauk City, WI: Arkham House, 1944), facing p. 215.

5. *The (Old) Farmer's Almanack* (1793f.).

6. The ms. is mutilated at this point. The text in brackets here and on subsequent pages is conjectural.

7. From "To Alfred Galpin, Esq." (*Tryout*, December 1920), ll. 21–24, 43–50. The poem was written for Galpin's nineteenth birthday.

8. Clark Ashton Smith, *The Double Shadow and Other Fantasies* ([Auburn, CA]: The Auburn Journal, 1933; *LL* 810).

9. "The Dreams in the Witch House." The misprints are indicated in HPL's letter to Farnsworth Wright of 18 June 1933 (*SL* 4.213).

10. *The Shunned House* was typeset and printed in 1928 by W. Paul Cook's Recluse Press, but the sheets were not bound. In 1933, Walter J. Coates's Driftwind Press was going to bind the sheets but never did so. R. H. Barlow acquired 115 copies in 1934 and 150 more in 1935 but bound only a few copies. Arkham House eventually were bound and distributed the sheets Barlow obtained in 1959–61.

[25] [ALS]

66 College St.,
Providence, R.I.,
Oct[r.] 5, 1933

Son:—

Well, Sir, your Grandpa's glad to hear the news—even though such an annoying item as a salary reduction forms part of the current record. I was certainly interested in the compliment paid you by your noble Austrian friend—& can imagine how pleased you must have been to have your cherished continentalism recognised by a real sprig of the original continental-cosmopolitan culture! It reminds me of the state of ecstasy to which I have twice been raised by having strangers of obvious intelligence & cultivation (both times in Canada, as chance would have it) ask me if I am not of British birth & education. Your Freiherr Karl Tintz zu Schloss Schallaberg &c. would seem to be quite a boy, all told, & I am surely glad you happened to run across him. As for the *Roman* angle—I rather fear the baron had in mind not so much *my* Romans of the hardy age of P. Cornelius Scipio, T. Quinctius Flamininus, Q. Fabius Maximus, C. Laelius, L. Valerius Flaccus, M. Acilius Glabrio, L. Aemilius Paullus, & all the rest, as the *modern* Roman nobility whose origins are in the city-streets of the Middle Ages & of Little Belknap's once-beloved (before he acquired "social vision" & became a young bolshevik) Renaissance . . . . . no mean bunch, at that, though! Probably *you* would like such a comparison much better than one linking you to the Claudii, Julii, Pompeii, Licinii, & Caecilii. Not A. Galpinius Secundus, but Conte Alfredo delgi Galpini! Incidentally, did I ever tell you that you ate dinner with a real Italian nobleman as early as 1922? If not, I may mention that about a year ago I saw an item in the paper stating that our old Cleveland confrere Raoul S. Bonnanno,—the guy who taught me how to eat spaghetti at Luccione's—had fallen heir to 18 titles, several sulphur mines in Sicily, & sundry estates, through a decision of the Italian courts. He is still a member of the N.A.P.A. (there's the democracy of true rank for you!), though I haven't heard from him since the old Birchdale days. Whenever, nowadays, anyone criticises my way of gulping spaghetti, I am prepared to come back with the withering retort that *I* was instructed by a real dago of *title*—no mere peasant or tavern-keeper!

It is gratifying to learn—even tho' it implies no great change in your basick philosophy—that you have extinguish'd the altars of Astarte in favour of those of Urania & Hymenaeus. In your easy recovery from the aberration you might well read a confirmation of what I previously told you regarding the wholly capricious, cosmically un-grounded, & therefore essentially trivial nature of such seizures. They are simply temporary biological-psychological surface twists—& when one thoroughly realises the trivial mechanical character of such emotional phaenomena, he ought to be able to analyse them out of existence whenever they interfere with the well-harmonised & appropriate course of his life, or with the practice of that fairness, honesty, & open, aboveboard conduct which distinguishes artistic living from sloppy, messy living. In the course of time—when the shock of emancipation from religious delusion & ill-based celestial morality has had a chance to subside & reveal the essential squalor & ugliness of disorderly, uncoördinated existence—I fancy that rational aesthetick standards of conduct will be reared anew; replacing the present "lost generation" of anchorless epigoni with a generation once more having loyalties . . . . albeit perhaps loyalties to new & unfamiliar norms. As it is, an element of poignant & definite beauty has been lost from human character.

I trust that your plans for escorting the disorganised young millionaire—whose unfortunate emotional misdirection ought surely to have expert psychiatric attention—will mature successfully, & that the joint European session will not only benefit the patient but prove rewardingly interesting to his guides. You are certainly amply fitted to initiate any neophyte into the arcana of intellectual & artistick Paris! It would surely be providential if circumstances protracted your stay long enough to admit of a Sorbonne degree. Who knows, you might find a permanent berth in La Ville Lumière, become a French citizen, & end up as a Minister of Education or Fine Arts or something of the sort, with a town-house near the Parc Monceau & a villa on the Riviera! But at any rate I trust you'll begin your fuller Gallicisation at Quebec—which is extremely appropriate, since French Canada represents the traditional, pre-revolutionary France of the church & the Capets, logically preceding the liberalised & decadent France which has come into existence on the original ground.

My own Quebec trip of last month[1] was a glorious success—four days of hot & sunny weather in the ancient fortress of the north, beneath the Union Jack of my forefathers. God Save the King! I lingered in all the accustomed spots, absorbing the time-mellow'd sights so dear to my spirit—the frowning citadel, grim city walls & gates, beetling cliff & bristling ramparts, shining silver spires, tangles of centuried lanes, old grey convents, 18ᵗʰ century facades, red roofs, & chimney-pots, dizzying vistas of varied levels, glimpses of broad, blue river, verdant countryside, & far-off purple mountains at the ends of glamourous streets . . . . . & all the rest. I walked to Sillery—3 miles up the river, with its curious headland church—& took a trolley ride to the upper level of Montmorency Falls, where I saw the fine (but now defaced—made into an hotel) Georgian house built by Genl. Sir Frederick Holdimand & later occupy'd (in the 1790's) by H.R.H. the Duke of Kent, afterward father of her late Majesty Victoria. I also look'd up the exact place of Genl. Wolfe's ascent of the cliff—not an easy task, since the spot is not mark'd, nor do the local Frenchmen care to point out the route of their immortal conqueror.

One thing that impress'd me at Quebec was the singular & picturesque aspect of the *sky*—involving odd formations of cloud & mist never seen in more southerly latitudes. This begins, however, as far south as northern New-Hampshire & Vermont—the whole region about Lake Memphramagog having the most fantastick sort of vapours hanging over the peaks & vales each dawn. I do not wonder, in view of this mystical veil of mutation, illusion, & uncertainty hanging perpetually aloft, that the northern races of mankind excel those of the hard-outlined, sunbaked Mediterranean in richness & fertility of fantastick imagination. On this occasion I beheld several atmospherick spectacles of the highest interest, especially one at sunset on Labour-Day. This involv'd a predominantly clear sky & a strangely burning flood of ruddy vespertine light upon roofs, spires, ramparts, & the trans-fluvial cliffs of Levis—coupled with a dense funnel of churning nimbus cloud extending from the zenith to the southeastern horizon. From this interloping mass jagged streaks of lightning darted frequently down to the distant country side beyond Levis, whilst low rumbles of thunder follow'd tardily after. Then, to crown all, a pallid arc of rainbow sprang into view above the verdant Isle d'Orleans, its upper end lost in the forbidding black cloud. The total effect was indescribably stirring to the imagination, & was remark'd by not a few of the several spectators on the lofty citadel whence I witness'd it. My train-ride home was of unusual pleasantness; not only because of the absence of the swinish beer-guzzlers who used to frequent Canadian trains in the days of intensive prohibition, but because of the fine effects of sunset & full moonlight upon the rural landskip of Quebec province. Some of the isolated villages, each clustering in the lee of a quaint, silver-steepled church, are of the greatest imaginable charm; & it was with much pain that I learn'd a fortnight ago of the destruction by fire of one of the churches I saw—that at Valleyfield. Dawn arrived amidst a beautiful lake region in New Hampshire—the train not long afterward taking me within a few feet of the house (now an orphanage) where Daniel Webster grew up . . . at Franklin, formerly Salisbury Lower Village.

On both outbound & inbound trips I paused in Boston to see our good old friend Culinarius. In the outbound trip I also look'd up an extreamly antient house in the suburbs of Boston—the Deane Winthrop edifice, built in 1637 & having a secret room in the vast brick chimney-base. Inbound, I made a side-trip to my beloved old Salem & Marblehead—renewing my acquaintance with familiar antiquities & assimilating a few fresh points. Among the novelties at Salem was a perfect reconstruction of the original pioneer settlement of 1626–30, with the crude shelters, wigwams, huts, & cottages which preceded the building of actual houses of European size, pattern, & solidity. Of course no originals of these rude domiciles survive, but accurate scholarship has been able to fashion pretty definite fac-similes from detailed contemporary accounts. The restored village is situate in a park at the harbour's edge, amidst a landskip made to look as much as possible like the primal topography of Salem. Not only are the early huts represented, but typical industries like blacksmith-shops, salt works, fish-drying outfits, saw-pits, & the like are faithfully shewn. The whole forms the clearest & most vivid presentation I have ever seen of the very first stage of New-England life, & ought to help anyone to reëstablish the true ancestral orientation which these disorder'd times so gravely disturb.

My aunt is now much better, being all around the house on a cane, & each day getting out into the garden for a while. The nurse went nearly a month ago, & in order to emancipate me from door-tending we have install'd an electrical device (one of the few palliating boons of the machine age) which allows my aunt to open the front door from the upper hall. On several occasions I have taken her to walk in the adjacent college grounds, whilst last Saturday she had her first real outing in the form of a motor ride to antient Wickford (one of those quaint villages down the bay's west shoar, which my guest Price[2] & I visited last July) thro' the sunlit autumnal countryside. From now on I shall not be greatly tied up, hence it is possible that I may pay Sonny Belknap a visit in New-York before the month is out, or accompany friend Samuelus to Boston for a museum session if he decides to visit New-England after his return from Cleveland. But all such things are problematical. The approach of cold weather limits my outdoor activities, though I still work in a rural walk now & then, & shall seek to view the turning leaves amidst the mystical silences of the Quinsnicket woods.

Regarding writing affairs—just as I expected, the Knopf bubble duly burst in course of time . . . . differing from the Putnam fiasco only in that the readers praised the stories literarily whilst pronouncing them commercially unfeasible.[3] Since then a man in the state of Washington has broached the subject of issuing my "Colour Out of Space" as a separate brochure[4]—which I shall surely let him do if he wants to, though the project is scarcely likely to mature. I writ a new tale in August, but am very ill-satisfy'd with it.[5] Indeed, I am becoming so ill-satisfy'd with all my attempts, that I have begun a sort of analytical re-reading of the various weird classicks to see if I can discover means of improvement.[6]

Good luck with the painting of Old 536![7] I'll wager it never had such an artistick application of mural colour before! Trust the agriculture will prosper as well. How is Skipper these days? One of my present delights is the club of solemn old Toms which assembles on the roof of a shed across the garden, in plain sight of my study windows. There are sometimes as many as 6 or 7 members present, & I have dubb'd it (in view of the prevalence of fraternity houses in this neighbourhood) the Kappa Alpha Tau. (ΚΩΜΠΣΟΝ ΑΙΛΥ-ΡΟΝ ΤΑΞΙΣ) The huge, sleek, black & white President is grown a great friend of mine, & rolls over & kicks & purrs like a kitten when I approach him. I see him now out the window! Asleep at full length. ¶ Well—be as good a boy as possible, & receive an old man's blessings

    Yr ob[t] h[ble] Serv[t]
      Grandpa

*Notes*

1. The third of HPL's trips to Quebec, the others being in 1930 and 1932.
2. E[dgar] Hoffmann Price (1898–1989), prolific pulp writer, visited HPL on 30 June–3 July 1933.
3. HPL submitted a total of 25 stories to Allan G. Ullman of Knopf on 3 and 16 August 1933, but the stories were rejected. G. P. Putnam's Sons had rejected a collection of HPL's tales in 1931.
4. F. Lee Baldwin of Asotin, WA, had hoped to publish "The Colour out of Space" as a booklet, but it never appeared.
5. "The Thing on the Doorstep," written 21–24 August 1933.
6. This reading resulted in "Weird Story Plots" (unpublished), "A List of Certain Basic Underlying Horrors Effectively Used in Weird Fiction," "List of Primary Ideas Motivating Possible Weird Tales," and "Suggestions for Writing Story" (later "Notes on Writing Weird Fiction").
7. I.e., 536 College Street, Appleton, Wis.—Galpin's former residence.

[26] [ALS]

               Octr. 25[, 1933]

Son:—

  Am I still delighted in my colonial dwelling? Excellent example of needless enquiry! Not only does the charm not fade, but it actually *increases*. This is due in part to the greater degree of orderly settledness attained since the relative recovery of my aunt—who is now all around on a cane, taking strolls in the nearby college grounds & getting even farther afield with my assistance. The rooms are now in better order, the great oil painting is hung over the fatal staircase, & a console slab of veined, yellowish Siena marble (relique of departed glory) is about to go up in the front hall under the wall hatrack & mirror as soon as we can find the ornamental brackets amid our stored household goods. Here is a snap of the place which I took not long ago from the courtyard of the neighbouring college library. I'll ask the return of this. Later I'll send you a fuller, closer view of the house which you can keep if you have any permanent album of such material. I may also send a booklet lately issued by the school department, whose frontispiece exhibits this whole hill neighbourhood & plainly reveals #66 in its retired court.

Glad you had a good Chicago trip, but sorry you picked up a cold. Since I have one myself at the present moment, I can extend a peculiarly vivid message of sympathy, snuffle for snuffle! As for the philosophy & aestheticks of domestick organisation—I still don't agree with your essentially cloudy & ill-defined system of standards. The common emotions connected with primary instincts, & not extensively linked with imaginative associations & a sense of pattern, are undeniably largely mechanical matters which, while *powerful* in the sense that a rap on the head or a siege of typhoid is mechanically powerful in its effect on the system, are certainly not *important* in the artistic experience of complex conscious living. Assuredly, they are not important enough to justify their easy interference with the fulfilment of other emotions whose richness & coördination give them a really pivotal place in an harmonious life of widely-realised possibilities. I feel confident that the current fashionable endorsement of messy living will vastly diminish whenever a reacquired cultural stability gives our most active minds a renew'd chance for mature & leisurely reflection.

Wright seems to be re-using that list of author's friends for which he asked last June. Glad the new W.T. had points of interest for you.[1] My "Festival", written exactly a decade ago, seems somewhat crude & overcoloured upon re-reading. Quinn is a brilliant attorney turned author who could write splendid stuff if he would, but who prefers to cater to the popular market. Sonny Belknap's piece is fair, but not the best the child can do—the horror being somewhat diffuse & strung out. The Klarkash-Ton specimen is excellent, though not illustrating the creator's most imaginative side. If you want to know the contemporary CAS at his best, send to him for that brochure of 6 tales of which I gave you a descriptive circular. Robert E. Howard is an interesting Texas character; only 27 years old, yet as full of the reminiscent lore of the old Southwest as any grizzled cattleman of the 1870's. You ought to see the gigantic set of snake-rattles (12) he has just sent me! He has an odd, primitive philosophy—hating all civilisation (like Lord Monboddo[2] & other devotees of the "noble savage" in my own 18th century) & regarding the barbarism of the pre-Roman Gauls as the ideal form of life. He writes fiction purely for money, hence his more or less stereotyped caterings to popular trends. Once in a while, though, he unconsciously achieves a very genuine power in his depictions of ruins, catacombs, & cities redolent of unholy antiquity & blasphemous elder secrets. "The House of the Worm" is by a new writer wholly unknown to me, but I think it shows a real promise beneath obvious crudities. It has real atmosphere—& that is the big thing in spectral fiction. Yes—I thought I saw touches of my own style here & there.[3] It would amuse me if some writer were to build upon my work & achieve a fabric infinitely surpassing the original! Glad the magazine seems to be selling—for its survival is very precious to those who count on its cheques. Others appear & vanish. Just now *Astounding Stories* is revived—its editor, Desmond Hall, being in touch with Petit-Belnape & others of the gang in N.Y. I doubt if my work would fit this, however. Klarkash-Ton & I are just now unloading a great number of our early & rejected MSS. upon two new magazines (*The Fantasy Fan* & *Unusual Stories*[4]) which don't pay anything. Wright would be glad to see you if you ever called on him. He is probably a good deal more cultivated than his magazine indicates, & shares your devotion to music—being indeed a former critick of that art. He is a sufferer from that odd form of paralysis known as Parkinson's Disease—no longer able to write with a pen, & with a face purged of all flexibility or expression through the failure of the nerves to function.

I've heard of "Wolf Solent", though I haven't read it. Sooner or later I must absorb its contents. I don't think, though, that John Cowper Powys or any of his equally-famous brothers were born in America, though some of them now dwell here.[5] The literary editor of the Providence Journal became especially enthusiastic about Wolf Solent when it first appeared.

Hope your European trip develops successfully . . . I envy you all the time spent in England! Next month I may pay Kid Belknap a visit—though his mamma is now ill from food-poisoning. I've made the most of an unusually mild & sunny October—taking long walks through remote & primitive stretches of countryside. I generally proceed by coach out some main highway, then striking across country afoot till I reach another coach-bearing highway along which I can return. In this way I have explored many regions which I never saw before—some delectably-unspoiled, with narrow rutted roads winding betwixt briar-twined stone walls, ancient gambrel-roofed farmhouses with their barns, byres, & gnarled orchards, primitive well-sweeps & moss-grown water mills, belts of shadowy woodland, distant village spires & glimpses of curving river-valley—all those traditional marks of long, continuous habitation which New England took over bodily from Old England & marked with rich, distinctive touches of her own. Last week I came on a very ancient house built by a lineal ancestor of my own—Thomas Clement—in 1654. It has a great pilastered stone chimney & is still in excellent shape despite its age. Other recent glimpses of the countryside have come through participation in rides given the family convalescent by motor-owning friends. But now the chill of winter is nigh, & desolation looms in the offing!

　　Yr most obᵗ hᵇˡᵉ Servᵗ—

　　　　Grandpa

P.S. Saw a demonstration of *television* last Saturday. Vague & flickering, like the cinema of about 1898. ¶ I enclose the Holland Society's paper with an antiquarian outburst of mine.[6] Our former fellow-amateur Talman edits this sheet. You might send it back if you have no permanent use for it.

*Notes*

1. HPL refers to the following stories from *Weird Tales* (October 1933): "The Festival" (orig. January 1925); Seabury Quinn, "The Mansion of Unholy Magic"; Frank Belknap Long, "The Black, Dead Thing" (later titled "Second Night Out"); Clark Ashton Smith, "The Seed of the Sepulcher"; Robert E. Howard, "The Pool of the Black One"; Mearle Prout, "The House of the Worm."
2. James Burnett, Lord Monboddo (1714–99) gained notoriety and ridicule when, in the first volume of his *On the Origin and Progress of Language* (1773–92), he reported the story of a Swedish sailor named Koeping that there were men with tails living in the Nicobar Islands.
3. Prout's story clearly plagiarizes portions of Lovecraft's "The Call of Cthulhu." See Will Murray, "Mearle Prout and 'The House of the Worm,'" *Crypt of Cthulhu* No. 18 (Yuletide 1983): 29–30, 39.
4. Edited by Charles D. Hornig and William L. Crawford, respectively.
5. John Cowper Powys, *Wolf Solent* (1929), a complex social novel set in Dorset. Powys's brothers Llewllyn and T. F. Powys also were noted authors.
6. "Some Dutch Footprints in New England," *De Halve Maen* 9, No. 1 (18 October 1933): 2, 4.

[27] [ALS]

Nov. 4, 1933

Son:—

Congratulations on the restoration of your creative activity! The words sound tremendously graceful, & accentuate the shivers of the season; & I feel somehow certain that the music is of equal beauty & aptness. There is a genuine originality in that image of the slate-blue sky crawling on the sun & freezing the wind. I wish to hades I had facilities for hearing music well-rendered—if I did, I'd demand a wide variety of your compositions as a loan in order to get an idea of how your genius works in its chosen main line. I shall, indeed, if I ever happen to strike an opportunity for interpretations. I can sympathise with your impatience regarding halts in your course of creation. Just now I am singularly unable to embody any ideas in tales at all satisfactory to me, so that I have devoted much time of late to experiments in new methods & perspectives. Thanks, by the way, for that news item—which surely may prove useful as a story nucleus. Another ocular idea which has long fascinated me pertains to the luminous shapes—geometrical & otherwise—seen against a background of blackness when the eyes are closed.[1] It would be rather good, in a story, to attribute these to scenes in other dimensions or spheres of entity, glimpsed obscurely & fragmentarily when the tri-dimensional world is shut out. One could delineate a person who has cultivated the art of seeing & understanding these alien vistas with especial clearness, & who ultimately learned terrible cosmic secrets from them. In the end the observer might learn of a way to cross bodily to an exotic cosmos, & thus vanish from the sight of man. One stage in this crossing to another plane ought to be just such an inxplicable blindness as that overtaking the Roumanian boy in the item.

Glad the snap of Grandpa's hillside abode proved of interest. Here are some others, which I'll also ask to have returned in the course of time. One shews the whole house at fairly close range. The window above the door is of my bedroom, those at its left being the south windows of my study. (The study also has 2 west windows, at one of which I am now sitting, gazing across the roofs of the ancient hill to a strip of far horizon & a distant steeple[2] on Federal Hill 2 miles away.) Another view is of the colonial doorway in detail (note the fan carving), with my aunt standing in it.[3] A third snap shews my aunt against ancient University Hall (1770) in the neighbouring college grounds. A fourth—of comic rather than serious intent—is of the old gent seated in a corner of the college gateway.[4] The please-help-the-blind effect is caused by the sun in Grandpa's eyes—which were closed when the camera was prematurely snapped. The blurring is due either to the perturbation of the ancient Brownie at its repulsive subject, or to a lack of steadiness in the grip of the photographer. These cheap Brownies have such slow shutter action that they have to be held very still even for allegedly instantaneous exposures. You'll note that Old Theobald isn't such a hippopotamus as he was in Birchdale days—a 50-lb reducing in 1925 having achieved mercifully permanent results. But the old geezer certainly has aged!

By the way—I fear your colleague's Providentian geography is all wet. *Cushing St.* is a full quarter-mile north of here; & instead of going up the great hill, slopes gradually downward from near its summit over the eastward plateau on top. (Like Barnes St.—which is not far away) It is around this street that Pembroke College, the female department of Brown University, clusters[5]—whereas College st. (commonly called "College Hill") tops the main & exclusively masculine part of the institution. In colonial times College St. was known successively as Presbyterian Lane (from the meeting-house at Benefit St., where the great Court House now stands[6]), Rosemary Lane, & Hanover St.—but never as Cushing St. Your friend somehow has the main college mixed up with the women's college in his recollections. College St. has been the accepted name of this thoroughfare since 1771, when the university's classes were transferred here.

Glad prospects still look good for a well-balanced European sojourn. For the past year I have had such a knowledge of Paris that I've felt tempted to advertise my services as a guide without ever having seen the damn place—this erudition coming from a ghost-writing job[7] for a goof who wanted to be publicly eloquent about a trip from which he was apparently unable to extract any concrete first-hand impressions. I based my study on maps,[8] guide-books, travel folders, descriptive volumes, & (above all) pictures—the cards secured from you forming the cream of the latter. Fixing the layout of the city in my mind, & calculating what vistas ought to be visible from certain points (pictures seen under a magnifying-glass furnish a splendid substitute for first-hand vistas), I cooked up a travelogue which several Paris-wise readers have almost refused to believe was written by one never within 3000 miles of the place. If I ever get to your beloved burg I shall be able to start in sightseeing without any preliminary orientation-tour or rubberneck-wagon ride. In my article I took a vicious fling at the ugly Eiffel Tower, & ventured the suggestion that the Victorian Trocadero is an eyesore at close range, but glamourous when seen in the distance against a flaming sunset. Other parts of the text touched on Chartres, Rheims, Versailles, Barbizon, Fontainebleau, & other tourist high spots. I revelled in the *London* section (I studied Old London intensively years ago, & could ramble guideless around it from Hampstead Heath to the Elephant & Castle!), but was not able to do it justice because of the nominal author's hasty passage through it. Nothing but the Tower, the Abbey, & the Cheshire Cheese seemed to give him a first-class kick.

No further word from The Child—I hope his mamma isn't worse. Damn cold today—though Hallowmass, All-Saints', & All-Souls' were admirably sunny. On each of those days I took rural walks—& discovered still another region previously unknown to me. At a hilltop bend of a stone-walled road on the town's northwestern rim I encountered a sunset vista of surpassing loveliness—meadows & orchards sloping down to a pond & river, wooded hills on the western horizon, a steepled village in a northward vale, & a great round moon climbing above the rocky eastward ridge. ¶ Well—try to behave yourself!

Yr obt

Grandpa

*Notes*

1. Cf. HPL's commonplace book, entry 157: "Vague lights, geometrical figures, &c., seen on retina when eyes are closed. Caus'd by rays from *other dimensions* acting on optick nerve? From *other planets?* Connected with a life or phase of being in which person could live if he only knew how to get there? *Man afraid to shut eyes*—he has been somewhere on a terrible pilgrimage & this fearsome seeing faculty remains."

2. St. John's Roman Catholic Church (1871), 352 Atwells Avenue, the edifice that became the Free-Will Church of the Starry Wisdom sect in "The Haunter of the Dark." The steeple fell in 1935, and the church was razed in 1992.

3. See *Marginalia*, photo facing p. 54.

4. See *SL 3*, photo facing p. 134 erroneously captioned "H. P. Lovecraft in Brooklyn."

5. The campus of Pembroke College occupies buildings at 182–222 Meeting Street. The land for the campus was assembled piecemeal early in the 20th century from

lots in the area bounded by Meeting, Brown, Bowen, and Thayer streets. A block of Cushing Street between Brown and Thayer streets eventually was eliminated.

6. The Providence County Court House (1924–33), 250 Benefit Street.

7. Apparently a reference to "European Glimpses" (19 December 1932), a revision job for HPL's ex-wife Sonia H. Greene. It is possible that HPL did not wish to admit to Galpin that he was continuing to do work for Sonia. All the sites in Paris and London mentioned in this paragraph are in fact discussed in "European Glimpses."

8. HPL owned a map of Paris (*LL* 323).

[28] [ALS]

Charleston, S.C.,
April 28, 1934

Son:—

Well, of all coincidences! Look at what I had in my hand just ready to post as I stopped for my mail at the desk of the Charleston Y! Glad to hear from you! Sorry your winter was as bad as Providence's—as it seems to have been. Ours didn't begin so early—I took outdoor jaunts all through October—but when it did set in it sure laid the torture on thick! All the northeast had it just as bad. I almost refused Kid Belnape's holiday invitation—but finally accepted it . . . . . . . using the subway to keep under cover. Feby. 9 was the coldest day ever recorded by any weather bureau in southern New England . . . . it being *17 below* in Providence. That is 5° below any previous known Prov. minimum, & over 10° below any minimum usually reached. What saved the situation for me was the magnificent *heat* at 66 College St.— steam being on in abundance 24 hours a day. But of course I was a virtual prisoner indoors, & as a result felt like a limp rag. I started on my present trip April 14–15, stopping a week at Sonny Belknap's & seeing everybody. One new figure of great interest is Howard Wandrei, brother of the Donald who has been compared to you in physique & iconoclastic genius. This youth is a pictorial artist of macabre & fantastic genius—miles ahead of any of the rest of the gang in his accomplishments, & certain to be heard from seriously in the future. His style is so original that it's difficult to say what its sources & analogues are. One thinks of Beardsley, Sime, Harry Clarke, Goya, & what not. Later on, if you're interested, I'll send you some photographs of his drawings, taken by his brother. Among other new people I met was the fairly famous fantastic magazine writer A. Merritt, whose "Moon Pool" I have admired ever since its appearance in 1918.[1]

Glad to hear you have embarked on an artistic renaissance, & hope it will prove fruitful & permanent. Your whole attitude toward the subject of aesthetic expression is such that I feel certain you have major material in you— & I feel equally confident that you will sooner or later find adequate channels for communicating that material. That's a lot more than I can say concerning many others whom I thought freighted with genius in the old days. All too often later years find these young Shelleys & Baudelaires with no particular message to give, & no sense of uneasiness at being unable to communicate the moods & impressions within them. I myself am still irked & oppressed by my inability to give form & expression to the reactions produced in me by certain phenomena of the external world—& certain combinations of ideas & images—but at my age I know that I shall never be able to utter what I wish to utter. The net result is a barrenness as great as that of the cooled-down young Keatses. I have something to say but can't say it; they could say something if they had it to say, but they haven't it! What a world! But you have more solid gifts, & need only time in order to utilise them. I'll wager this new quintette is an important thing—& surely hope the Chicago orchestra will present your older symphony next season, as hinted by its conductor. The emotional & external sources of your quintette are surely highly interesting to consider—especially the idea from our old friend of 1919 & 1920, the impassioned author of "Zarathustra".[2]

I haven't had much published under my own name recently, since W.T. has acquired a sort of prejudice against my work. In the June issue (I think) will appear a collaboration by E. Hoffmann Price & myself[3] which is virtually all my own. My stuff dissatisfies me so badly that I am repudiating a great many of my old tales, & experimenting with possible ways of eliminating certain characteristic flaws & weaknesses. Just now I have a new tale planned—but it seems puerile to me already—even before the start of the actual writing![4]

Today was cold & overcast—cold, that is, for Charleston at this season; though it would pass for a mild spring day in Providence. I've concentrated on interiors—giving the excellent Charleston museum a rather thorough inspection, & visiting the ancient 44-gun frigate *Constitution*, now very appropriately in the ancient harbour of Charleston. A good old tub—I visited its sister ship the *Constellation* (permanently stationed at Newport, R.I.) when it was in Philadelphia at the Sesquicentennial. The *Constitution*'s home port is Boston .... but I have a habit of visiting New England sites abroad! When at home I take them as a matter of course & neglect them!

Well—in four days I'll be down in Florida. Cold days like this will reconcile me to leaving Charleston, so long as that leaving can be southward!

Regards & benedictions—

Grandpa

*Notes*

1. A[braham] Merritt (1884–1943), "The Moon Pool," *All-Story Weekly*, 22 June 1918; *LL* 17. HPL disdained the later revised version.

2. I.e., Friedrich Nietzsche. Galpin had published "Nietzsche as a Practical Prophet" in Sonia H. Greene's *Rainbow* (October 1921). The same issue contained HPL's "Nietzscheism and Realism," culled from HPL's letters to Greene.

3. "Through the Gates of the Silver Key." It actually appeared in the issue of July 1934.

4. Possibly a reference to the never-written tale described in a letter to F. Lee Baldwin (27 March 1934; ms., JHL): "I'm not working on the actual text of any story just now, but am planning a novelette of the Arkham cycle—about what happened when somebody inherited a queer old house on the top of Frenchman's Hill & obeyed an irresistible urge to dig in a certain queer, abandoned graveyard on Hangman's Hill at the other edge of the town. This story will probably not involve the actual supernatural—being more of the 'Colour Out of Space' type . . . . . greatly-stretched 'scientifiction'."


[29] [ALS]

c/o Barlow, Box 88,
De Land, Fla.,
June 6, 1934.

Son:—

What you say of the possibility of adequate artistic expression on Grandpa's part is surely encouraging, & I wish indeed that I could look forward to such a prospect. Time will tell—though I have less fatuous optimism these days than I had in youth. It's been hard to tell whether or not my subsequent attempts will predominantly reek of New England soil—at any rate, they will be far removed from the pseudo-Dunsaniana of the early 1920's!

I rejoice to hear of your musical prospects in various directions, & hope that your symphony may eventually be played by the Chicago Orchestra.[1] A concert wholly composed of your own work would surely be a notable & helpful event, & I trust that the contemplated Evanston event may materialise. Let us hope, too, that the present stirrings toward new compositions may bear rich fruit.

Your welcome epistle probably crossed the postcard which told of my continued sojourn in subtropical De Land. This is a great place, & the genial climate peps the old man up tremendously. My hosts[2] are so super-hospitable that all suggestions of moving along are violently ruled out—yet before long I simply must get started. Hopes of Havana about gone—but I'll have a week in antient St. Augustine if it breaks me! Shall return north as slowly as possible—haven't yet decided about visiting honest Jawn Milton Samples in Macon. I want to see Charleston again if I possibly can. Expect to stop a week with Sonny Belknap on my way home, & I'll surely give the household your regards.

Glad that the household matters are recrystallising favourably, & hope the dual Appleton-Chicago arrangement may ensure you an ideal summer.

You surely have enough prospects, projects, & activities to keep you pleasantly busy! Assuming that college is closed, I'll address this missive to your natal mansion, the erstwhile 536 . . . . meanwhile keeping your Chicago address in mind. If you're at the latter, you will doubtless receive the document through forwarding.

Enclosed is an item design'd to remind you of old amateur & Mocratick days—a paper containing an article by our good old Sage. I never thought Mocrates could be dragged into amateurdom again, but the persuasion of a bright boy editor turned the trick. By the way—Mocrates' elder son Robert, now graduated from the U. of Wis., has just gone to Erie, Pa. to fill an important position with the Genl. Electric Co. He seems destined to become a technician of some note, & to reflect new lustre upon the already-honour'd name of Moe.

Speaking of old days—my brilliant young host (present story laureate of the N.A.P.A.)[3] is curious to collect certain papers of the past, especially your short-lived *Philosopher.*[4] Have you any residual copies of the latter tucked away in the attic? If so, pray send one to Barlow & make him your lifelong debtor! He surely is quite a kid—a veritable neo-Galpinius in many ways. If he had decent eyesight he'd be even more visibly brilliant than he is.

I guess I described my present temporary habitat on the postcard. De Land is a pleasant little village of modern origin, shaded by great live-oaks & possessing a college—Stetson University. The Barlow place, 14 miles to the west, is in a delightfully lone region of small lakelets, with no other human habitation in sight. I've been taken on various trips to neighbouring regions—including such antiquities as are to be found. No doubt I spoke of the old Spanish mission built in 1696 & demolished by an expedition from South Carolina in 1706. Many of the stone arches & walls are still in existence—thickly clad in vines, & forming by all odds the most picturesque ruin I have ever beheld. Near this mission—at New Smyrna—can also be found vestiges of Dr. Andrew Turnbull's famous indigo plantation of 1768–1783—where he had the Minorcans who later settled in St. Augustine. Turnbull himself ended up as an apothecary in Charleston—founding a shop still in existence, at which I've bought more than one dish of vanilla ice cream.

And so it goes. Let's hear any news that develops, & I'll keep you posted on my moves.

With customary blessings—
    Yr obt hble Servt—
        Grandpa

*Notes*

1. Galpin's *Berg-Symphonie* was performed by the Chicago Civic Orchestra.
2. The young R. H. Barlow and his family.

3. Barlow won the NAPA story laureateship for "Eyes of the God" (*Sea Gull*, May 1933).

4. There was only one issue (December 1920).

[30] [ALS]

Home again—
July 17, 1934

Son:—

Permit me to congratulate a scion of wealth & leisure! I found your note of the 3d upon my arrival home the 10th; but was so ingulph'd by matters demanding instant attention, that no reply was possible till now. This unexpected œconomick boon is surely one of the pleasantest things I have heard of in many a year. True, plenty of young men encounter good fortune; but seldom does that blessing befall one so well-fitted to enjoy & properly utilise it. To the average tradesman-minded youth of America, an income of this sort wou'd mean meerly a nucleus for frantick efforts at senseless multiplication; whereas to you it will serve as a key to the rational savouring & employment of life itself. Again, my congratulations! For once a good thing hath come into the right hands!

You last heard from me, I conceive, in antient St. Augustine; where I spent a delighted week amidst the monuments of a past exceeding even New-England's. It is impossible to describe the fascination of streets & houses which were fifty years old when the first Pilgrim landed on Plymouth Rock—houses older than any *private* dwelling in London itself! And the crumbling city gates— & the massive stone fortress overlooking the tropical harbour—& the great sweep of deserted beach on neighbouring Anastasia Island! It cost me a great pang to quit so venerable a scene, but my reluctance was temper'd by the 2-day stop I was able to make in Charleston. Compar'd with the tropick scenes of Florida, in which I had been so long immers'd, Charleston seem'd relatively northern & barren of vegetation; yet it held a charm of authentick English mellowness & unbroken antique survival which nothing in Florida cou'd equal. It is, without doubt, the most fascinating spot in these colonies. My next stop was Richmond, where I spent a day amidst the boyhood scenes of Poe. Here I was doubly sensible of the northernness of the scenery, tho' I soon became reconcil'd to the traditional landskip which Europe & most of the colonies share in common. After all, this landskip doubtless hath more of artistick fineness in it, than hath the more opulent landskip of the tropicks & subtropicks. The graceful disposition of its parts, & the delicacy of the details, amply overbalance any lack of richness & profusion which it may have. An afternoon in antient Fredericksburg, following upon Richmond, confirm'd me in this opinion; & help'd to reaccustom me to the ordinary scenery of my youth.

I was two days in Washington, during which time I did several things I had never done before—namely, visited Rock Creek Park, explor'd the interior of the Capitol, ascended the Washington Monument (from whose top can be had the finest prospect I have ever beheld—outspread hills & meads & reaches of blue river), & examin'd the furnish'd interior of Arlington, the Custis-Lee mansion on the heights across the Potowomack. This last hath lately been fitted up as it was during the tenancy of the Lees a century ago; & forms the best possible example of a Virginia manor-house.

It was with vast regret that I continu'd north to Philadelphia—but the weather was kind, & kept me surrounded with temperatures of 96° & 97°. In the old colonial metropolis I visited my favourite antiquities (tho' many have vanish'd in recent years) & indulg'd in trips to antient Germantown & the splendid gorge of the Wissahickon. I likewise inspected the home of Poe (1842–44) at N. 7th & Spring Garden Sts., lately open'd as a publick museum. This small brick cottage is precisely as it was in Poe's day, & hath been appropriately furnish'd. In a building adjacent is an ample collection of reliques, including copies of most of the magazines containing the first appearance of the various tales & poems. The effect of the place is extreamly lifelike, & it was not difficult to imagine the bard as present in person to welcome & guide the pilgrim.

Upon reaching New-York, I found Sonny Belknap & his parents about to depart for a 2-day sojourn in Asbury Park & Ocean-Grove, in New-Jersey; & upon their cordial invitation I went along with them. I had not cash enough to linger in Manhattan for any considerable time, hence did not look up any other acquaintances save Brother Samuelus. I came home on the midnight coach July 9–10th, & beheld the spires & domes of antient PROVIDENCE outspread in golden morning light. It was good to behold once more the rolling hills, stone walls, giant elms, & white village steeples of the venerable region of my birth.

Since then I have been struggling with the accumulation of letters, periodicals, & miscellaneous tasks which I found awaiting me. The cold nights are sometimes disconcerting; but the days are reasonable warm, & I take my work out to the countryside each sunny afternoon. I am now on the antient Seekonk river-bank which hath not chang'd a jot since my infancy. But there is a new attraction at home—a tiny coal-black kitten at the boarding-house across the back garden, born last month, & just beginning to be active & playful. He looks like a bear-cub of paperweight size, & promises to become a worthy congener of Felix Baudelaire & Skipper—to which latter gentleman he sends his sincerest compliments.

And so I will conclude, again extending those congratulations which are appropriate to the occasion.

Yr obt Servt—

Grandpa

P.S. An occasion for universal regret amongst the amateurs is the death of the venerable Mrs. Miniter on June 6.[1] ¶ Mocrates attended the amateur convention in Chicago, & appears to have enjoy'd the occasion with extream gusto.

*Notes*

1. Edith Miniter. See HPL's "Mrs. Miniter—Estimates and Recollections" (*Californian* Spring 1938). In his poem "Edith Miniter" (*Tryout*, August 1934) he gives her date of death as 8 June.

[31] [ALS]

Home—July 25[, 1934]

Son:—

Indoors today—too damn cold & dismal for my favourite rural spots. Yet it hasn't rained yet. In fact, except for a couple of very transient showers in Richmond July 1st. I haven't seen a trace of rain since the end of the deluge in De Land June 15th.

Yes—I fancy it's just as well not to advertise your recent good fortune over town. The use so far made of it seems eminently sensible—I recall your having mentioned years ago what a nuisance the Delta Gamma was. It seems to me certainly wise to stick to home soil, where you are already rooted. A modest competence will go farther there than anywhere else; & there is a sense of quiet harmony in an adjustment to native & hereditary lands, which nothing else in the world can supply. My keenest envy is of the man who can die in the house he was born in.

Your "yarb"[1] garden is surely full of interesting potentialities, & I shall delight in seeing samples of its produce. When you have exhausted the gastronomic possibilities of your crops, you can turn to the Æsculapian side & experiment with the many herb remedies which generations of rural New England folklore have extolled. You might even devise a popular patent medicine—Dr. Galpin's Carminative Bitters, or something of the sort. The lore of "yarbs" is a definite element in the colour of early America, & one of the salient features of the reproduced pioneer village in Salem is a garden where all the traditional species are cultivated, so that the visitor may see them both growing, & hung up on walls & rafters to dry.

I trust that the music-copying may not prove unduly arduous. If it affects you as prose-copying does me, you have my sympathy! To me, nothing is more utterly enervating, exhausting, & soporific than the mechanical process of writing (especially on a machine) when unaccompanied by the zest of original creation. In music it may be even worse, since so many complex details have to be kept in mind. At any rate, I feel sure you will have amply earned your vacation when the session of pure recreation comes around—&

trust that season may prove restful & diverting enough to reconcile you to the coming grind in Main Hall 23 at the Methodist Seminary.

Concerning political matters—I trust you won't allow them to engulf your whole personality, as they have with poor little Belnape. That child can scarcely think or talk of anything but his beloved bolshevism these days . . . . . where we used to hear about Baudelaire, Rimbaud, & the virtues of the "sensitive artist", we now hear only of the "infamous American ideology", the "monstrous, sadistic horrors of capitalism", & the need for a sanguinary overturn of all existing values in favour of the Golden Age as now flourishing in Muscovy.

For my part, I believe I am both a fascist & what I would have contemptuously called a "damn socialist" in my younger & middle-aged days. It has become clear to me that, with intensive mechanisation, there will never—even in the most "prosperous" times—be sufficient work to go around amongst the population under a traditional regime of laissez-faire economics. Economy in production will make it possible to supply all human needs with a minimum of labour, so that more & more persons will be *permanently* unemployed. The myth that new needs always arise to take care of the increasing body of the unemployed is now thoroughly exploded. As it is, we know that the effect of "rugged individualism" is to deprive growing numbers of people of any chance whatever to earn food, shelter, & clothing; to reduce still greater numbers to a degrading form of peonage; to increase the prodigious bulk of resources privately owned & withheld from any useful function; & to confirm the vicious enthronement of rapacious acquisitive ability (as distinguished from cultural capacity) as a criterion of human worth. Such a system has nothing whatever to recommend it, & its continuance is now definitely impossible unless it doles out immense sums to provide bread & circuses for the unemployed throngs it creates. Heretofore, general unemployment has been merely temporary. It cannot exist as a permanent condition because an actually starved population will revolt. No state can survive where millions are dying of cold & hunger; for when these millions feel they have nothing to lose, they are certain to strike out desperately in the forlorn hope of keeping alive somehow. The number of desperate unemployed, plus that of those whose insecurity & enslavement make them sympathetic toward any desperate step, is certainly enough to unseat any government or economic order if sufficiently aroused. The question is not an ethical one, as the old-time socialists insisted, but a very practical & material affair. It might be quite all right to 'let the bastards starve' in the approved Hoover way if one could be sure they *would* starve instead of revolting. But one can't be sure. In fact, one can be pretty damn sure of the opposite! And the resistance of the old order is vastly weakened by the fact that nobody under 50 years old really believes in it any more. The concentration of useless resources in the hands of a pushing, parvenu handful of grasping boors while millions starve & the cultivated classes experience varying degrees of hardship is so grotesque a state of things that it cannot be taken seriously. In the past, when resources were scarce, they had to be withheld from the many in order that anyone might have enough to found a tasteful way of life on. Now that machinery has created a plethora of resources, this condition no longer exists. There are enough resources for everyone, & their present useless concentration while millions starve becomes ridiculous through lack of motivation. Thus the capitalists will have to do one of three things: lull the unemployed into quiescence with a dole, accept the destruction & chaos which a revolution will bring, or submit to a governmental supervision which will cut down their profits by distributing work artificially (short hours—more employed) & providing for old-age pensions & unemployment insurance. Of these three courses, it hardly needs to be said that the third is the only sensible one; & we may hope that (in spite of contemporary howlings) capitalists will have the brains to realise it before it is too late. Laissez-faire economics is dead—killed by the machine. No workable distribution of the resources of a group can ever be achieved in future except through a purely artificial allocation—performed by governmental agencies. It is of no use now to drag up archaic & meaningless whines against "the interference of government in business". The welfare of private business is a secondary concern as compared with the primary need of maintaining an orderly society, feeding the population, & creating & distributing the articles necessary to civilisation. Private business, if it cannot fulfil these functions, is no longer worthy of toleration. If it can't justify itself it will have to give place to something which will really work. But of course all change should be gradual. The thing to do now is not to start a general upheaval, but merely to see whether the existing system can be modified enough to work. Give capitalism a chance to see whether it can stand the reduced profits effected by the spread work, pensions, & insurance which governmental supervision will make compulsory. If it can, well & good . . . at least, for a while. If it can't, then the government will have to take over the larger industries & operate them for service & production alone—on a non-profit basis. Actually, there is no reason why anyone should receive resources except in exchange for services performed—it being understood that everyone will be guaranteed a chance to perform services. *Profits* as distinguished from *salary* are fundamentally an absurdity amidst the new conditions of the machine age. However—all this is a far longer way from Petit-Belnape's communism than it is from old-time capitalism. If capitalism is absurd, then so—in tenfold measure—is the Marxian jumble of nonsense about the superiority of manual labour, the ethical need of absolute equalisation, the economic basis of culture, & the need of overthrowing all the aesthetic & intellectual habits of the past. If capitalism is a suicidal ride toward chaos, bolshevism is virtually that chaos toward which capitalism is riding—a wanton & hideous destruction of three-quarters of the imponderable values which create the illusion that life is worth enduring. There is no endurable life for high-grade people save one which has its roots in the past—which has fixed aesthetic points of reference to give the illusion of placement, direction, significance, & interest to the meaningless round of phenomena which bombards our consciousness. And these roots & reference-points bolshevism tends in very great measure to destroy. Therefore I am unalterably against it, let Sonny shriek what he will. Rational adaptation of our economic life to existing conditions need involve no such wholesale holocaust as this. The general cultural values of the past are still valid, & all that we must have is a new way of applying them to the new conditions. Suppose the government *does* own all large industry? It can, as always, reward those who operate the processes according to the quality of the services they perform—with high pay to the brain-workers whose contributions are great & whose scale of life is highly evolved, & with correspondingly lower pay to the labourers whose contributions & needs are less. Pensions & insurance, of course, to be similarly graded. What is eliminated is merely the waste of *profit*—resources foolishly & criminally diverted to those who do not *work*, but who merely "own" . . . . a word describing an artificial condition without basic meaning. And of course all this public ownership would apply only to amounts of resources so large as to form serious economic factors. There is no reason in the world why it should prevent individuals from "owning" homes & all the other accessories of reasonably comfortable living. To those who complain that governmental supervision or ownership of industries would "destroy the hardy initiative of the American character", I have only a thumb upon my nose. In the first place, no quality is worth preserving if it must be preserved at the cost of wholesale starvation & misery. Secondly, it is childish & asinine to measure the qualities of a people by the one standard of material acquisitive ability.

Now as to governmental *methods* as distinguished from *aims*, as I told you, I am an unreserved fascist. A democracy of universal suffrage is today mainly a joke—or a tragedy. More than that, it is a paradox—for it does not & cannot exist. All we can have is something or other masquerading as a democracy. It ought to be plain to all, that in nations of the size & complexity of ours, every problem & issue of national policy is infinitely beyond the comprehension of any but trained specialists. To imagine that the masses are capable of grasping or deciding any measure, or of judging which of many courses is best adapted to the achievement of a given end, is simply infantile in view of the complex technicality of all measures & courses. A vote in the hands of a layman is ridiculous, & a legislature of laymen prescribing acts which they do not even begin to understand is both ridiculous & dangerous. Even when a few people in a democracy understand what is best, the cumbrous processes of legislation generally postpone or defeat the needed measures. Of course, it has to be the bulk of a people who decree roughly what ultimate ends to pursue. If a minority try to depart too far from the collective will, they are unseated by revolution. But, ultimate ends being agreed upon, it will certainly be necessary in future to devise a more intelligent way of effecting these ends. There must be a way to seat governments which not only know how to do what needs doing, but are able to put that knowledge, without hindrance, into effect. And what is that way? Well, so far as I can see, the thing is to simplify government, eliminate needless debate, & place things in the hands of experts in the various subjects involved—all being accountable to some central authority (either one man or a very few men) with power to appoint, depose, & decide without appeal. As to the way to set up such a central authority—I fancy that a very restricted system of voting would be best. Let the qualifications for popular voting be very high—involving examinations in economics & civics, as well as in general cultural subjects. Of course the voters, even so trained, will not be able to grasp all the measures that will be enacted; but they will at least—through general mental discipline—be able to judge of the general worthiness of proposed objectives, & of the general sincerity & competence of the executives to whom they will grant—& from whom they will sometimes take—such absolute & far-reaching quotas of power. This high scholarship requirement for voting will immeasurably raise the intelligence-level of the electorate—thus making its native judgment as well as its fund of knowledge vastly superior to what is now available. Naturally, it will be the duty of the government to see that every citizen has a chance to receive the education necessary for suffrage; but this will not make for rabble rule, since only the superior can master the necessary material & quality for the ballot. If it be complained that no provision is made for a potentially creative leisure class, two replies can be given. First, that any mature government must necessarily regard major aesthetic & intellectual work as a legitimate occupation, & see that first-rate artists & thinkers are duly rewarded for their creative or scholastic efforts. Second, that under a regime of properly spread work virtually everyone will have leisure in sufficient quantities to admit of a rich mental & artistic life, whether or not this life be definitely creative enough to win a governmental subsidy.

As for existing fascist regimes—I fancy Italy's is immeasurably the best so far. Of course, it has many drawbacks, & it does not go far enough in the direction of rational resource-allocation; but it has shown a stability as yet unrivalled. Its worst trouble is the extent to which it meddles in cultural affairs. While a government may well *encourage* trends which it deems sound & *discourage* those it deems unsound, it ought never to carry its preferences to such a length as to imperil perfect aesthetic & intellectual freedom. If the present American regime were evolved enough to be termed true fascism, I'd be inclined to place that above all others; for its efforts to control economic life are wholly free from any corresponding effort to control personal & cultural life. Indeed, I think it is the best possible thing for America at the present time. Intelligent experimentation is all that can be expected at this juncture; & in view of the deadly backward pull of howling, senile reactionaries we need not wonder that unemployment has been only imperfectly palliated. Allowing for all the inevitable mistakes of a pioneering policy, I believe that the much-maligned "Brain Trust"[2] is headed in precisely the right direction . . . . although, ironically enough, I believe that the length to which that direction must be followed is far greater than any which even the boldest Brain-Truster would be willing to endorse at this stage of the game. As for Herr Hitler—I think he undoubtedly means well, & that the Nazi regime is about all that could have saved Germany from collapse last year. At the same time I regret the extent to which the Nazis have interfered with cultural matters—suppressing honest literature & substituting certain arbitrary & often erroneous scientific concepts for actual truth. That is what, in another direction, the bolsheviki have done. Regarding Der Schön Adolf's much-advertised anti-Semitism—the whole question is so damn'd complex that I can only say I'm both for & against him! There is no question but that the Nazis are perfectly right in *two* of their views on the subject: (a) that no minority culture-group ought to be allowed to modify—much less to direct or represent—the main stream of a nation's culture; & (b) that Jewish culture is basically antipathetic to ours—permanently hostile, & incapable of admixture or compromise. It is, therefore, extremely advisable to emulate Nazism in any nation to the extent of restricting influential or "key" positions in cultural life (high executives, judges, large-scale publishers & theatrical producers, educators, attorneys, book reviewers &c) to persons thoroughly belonging to the racial culture-stream of the bulk of the population . . . . . in our case, to Nordic Aryans. It might even be advisable, in the case of an evolved fascistic commonwealth with a small, educationally selected electorate, to make racial-cultural homogeneity an additional voting-qualification. Where the Nazis indubitably go too far is (a) in the extension of alien disqualification to economic matters affecting merely a daily livelihood, & (b) in the adoption of a ridiculously rigid & biologically unsound definition of membership in the dominant Aryan fabric. Point (a) is easiest to excuse, since *at present* private economic resources can prove such a dangerously powerful force in national life that their possession by aliens is potentially dangerous. However, under a fascistic regime of governmental supervision or ownership of resources, no private fortune could attain influential proportions; so that aliens might safely be allowed to share equally with others in the economic as distinguished from the cultural field. Conceivably, though, it might be well to give preference to members of the dominant group when any distribution of opportunities is involved. Regarding point (b)—since the major differences between the Aryan & Semite groups, so-called (actually, each is infinitely varied & lacking in biological homogeneity), is *cultural* rather than *biological,* it is absurd & unwise to carry discrimination to the point of disqualifying thousands of cultural Aryans who may happen to possess a stray drop of Semitic blood. Biology & ethnology reveal the so-called Jewish "race" of modern times as a collection of various mixtures; some totally unrelated to any of the others, & containing every sort of blood from Mongoloid to Mediterranean, Alpine to Nordic, Sumerian to Punic. Its sole claim to homogeneity is a certain persistent *culture*—just as the sole claim to homogeneity of the swart mongrel Sicilian, the erratic, satyr-nosed Slav, the lean, Oriental Spaniard, the mixed, volatile Frenchman, the grave or beefy Englishman, & the stolid, flaxen Icelander is a certain *culture* called Aryan. Now of the various blood-stocks embraced within the Jewish culture-radius, just as of the various blood-stocks embraced within our Aryan culture-radius, some are undeniably lousy & decadent. Of that, a visit to Manhattan's East Side will amply convince one. But on the other hand, the Jewish radius contains many elements biologically equal—& perhaps superior—to anything we can boast. Spinoza—Einstein—Disraeli—Mendelssohn—Maimonides, & so on. Now any biologist knows that innate racial identity plays a damn small part in the moulding of cultural details. The culture a man has is not what is blood has determined, but what the massed impressions & traditions he has received have given him. Jewish culture is not a product of blood, but of historic accident. So is ours. Bring a Jew up in Aryan culture, & he will in the main be a real Aryan unless Jewish ancestral influences get at him . . . & a good or bad Aryan according to his intrinsic biological status. Conversely, any of us could be a Jew if brought up among Jews & severed wholly from our own inheritance. It is, therefore, not at all important to maintain rigid barriers against every trace of Jewish *blood* when our real & legitimate object is merely to exclude Jewish *cultural* influences (which *are* hostile & unassimilable) from our national life. So long as a man has been brought up in our tradition & no other, & retains no vestiges of alien perspective & thought-habits, it does not make a particle of difference whether or not his ancestry contains a trace of blood from any of the other *superior* races—be it Jewish, Chinese, Polynesian, Japanese, Hindu, or American Indian. [The negro & australoid, of course, are another story.] That is, provided his blood-alienage does not involve any marked physiognomical aberrancy of such a sort as to set him apart & drive him back upon his lost alien heritage. It is easy to establish a practical, common-sense classification of persons as to culture-affiliation, even when their blood is not precisely homogeneous. Einstein *is* Jewish—in heritage & loyalties—but what sensible standard would also class as "Jewish" (as outside the Aryan pole) such well-assimilated persons as, for instance, Walter Damrosch, or the publicist Walter Lippmann? These latter men undeniably *think* as Aryans—& therefore any sensible committee on classification (to which, under a rational regime of Aryan fascism, all debatable cases would of course be carried) would group them as Aryans. It is amusing to think of the thoroughly Aryan people who would be placed outside as aliens if the strict Nazi test were made worldwide. Palgrave, compiler of the Golden Treasury[3] (whose sire was born Cohen), the present Lord Rosebery (whose mother was a Rothschild), the aristocratic Belmont family of America (whose forbear changed his name from Schönberg), the Hamiltons of Philadelphia (Andrew Hamilton, the lawyer famous in the Zenger freedom-of-the-press case of 1735 & the designer of Independence Hall, married a Jewess named Franks) & so on! Indeed—since the Nazi ban is not merely on Jews but on all *non-Aryans,* it would come down heavily upon all who bear a trace of *Indian* blood—such as the descendants of Pocahontas, famous throughout Virginia & including men as eminent as John Randolph of Roanoke! Plainly, then, the present attitude of the Nazis on this point is an extreme & unscientific one . . . . . although, as I have said, I certainly believe that actual members of the Jewish culture-group ought to be kept from securing a grip on the legal, educational, artistic, & intellectual life of any Aryan nation. They had gone too far in Germany, & they have gone too far in America—where so much literary & critical material is either of Semitic origin or (through Jew-owned publishing houses) Semitic selection. It is certainly time that the Aryan people everywhere made sure that they are not being led by fundamentally antipathetic aliens, & that they are not permitting such aliens to serve as their mouthpieces of opinion.

Regarding communists & their possible danger in America, it is hard to know what to think. Certainly, the flood of bolshevistic pap that pours out of the ghettoes & Greenwich-Villages of the large mongrel cities is enough to make one see the guillotine's shadow on the next month's calendar page— but after all, the bulk of the natives throughout the country are tremendously against such things. Foreigners, low-grade itinerant workers, & self-conscious parlour intellectuals like Sonny Belknap are the backbone of bolshevism in America. They sound formidable in view of the glib organs of opinion they control—but how much do they amount to when scaled against the solid people, from farmers to merchants & from mechanics to professional men, who still preponderate except in the mongrelised industrial centres? The South is especially firm against radical extremes, & many sections (like the northwest) favouring flexible economic experimentation would come out valiantly against a jump into the ideological excesses of Leninism. I did fear a spread of bolshevism fifteen years ago, but today I really don't think the American people want it. Certainly, they are not satisfied with the present moribund reign of thieving individualism, & might conceivably stage a revolution if Republican obstructionists succeed in slowing up or wrecking the New Deal. But their revolution would never have bolshevism as its object. It would be toward a far milder form of control & collectivism—& if it got out of hand & went bolshevik it would be because of the disproportionate influence of foreigners trained in the technique of revolt. That, of course, is the ever-present peril inherent in all well-meant revolutions . . . . the peril of their going far beyond their original objects. And because of that peril I am devoutly hopeful that a revolution may be avoided through the success & speeding up of the New Deal, with its unmistakable promise of an evolution toward a more rational economic order when conditions are ripe for it. Depend upon it—Grandpa & Little Belknap-Trotsky have many a stirring fight nowadays on the social-political-economic question! You ought to get the little bolshevik going yourself & hear him squeak & sputter!

And so it goes. I'm expecting Morton here next week—August 2–3–4— hence am all primed for three days of continuous oral debate on an interesting variety of themes. Amateur journalism is perking up—& good old Mocrates is beginning to make his comeback even more thorough than I had hoped. He is rejoining both National & [pseudo] United, & has promised to interest his classes at school. First thing we know, there'll be a revival of the *Pippin* . . . . & perhaps the discovery of another Galpinius, if they breed 'em in this puny & decadent generation!

The black kitten isn't visible today, but my older friends of the Kappa Alpha Tau are sedately perched on the shed roof across the garden. As seen from my window, they are marvellous company!

Yrs for the blackshirt march on Washington—

—Grandpa

*Notes*

1. Dialectical variant of herb.
2. Originally a reference to three professors at Columbia University—Raymond Moley, Rexford G. Tugwell, and Adolph A. Berle, Jr.—who advised President Franklin D. Roosevelt on public policy issues before and after his election, and later used to denote the large group of intellectuals who joined his administration.
3. Francis T. Palgrave (1814–1897) ed., *The Golden Treasury: Selected from the Best Songs and Lyrical Poems in the English Language* (1861); LL 671. The senior Palgrave, William Gifford (1836–1888), was a famous traveller.

[32] [ALS]

66 College St.,
Providence, R.I.,
Sept$^r$ 24, 1934.

Son:—

Well—Grandpa certainly had a great time on Nantucket,[1] & a new set of colonial images hath duly taken up its abode in the Old Gentleman's imaginative background! Of the length of my stay & the type of scenes I encounter'd, I believe my card from the antient town itself sufficiently inform'd you. Toward the end of my sojourn I cover'd suburban points on a hired *bicycle*—the first time in 20 years I had been on a wheel! Riding was just as easy & familiar as if I had last dismounted the day before—& it brought back my youth so vividly that I almost felt as if I ought to hasten back home for the opening of Hope St. High School! I think I told you of the earlier coast trip around the island, during which I saw the antient fishing village of Siasconset (locally pronounced *S'conset*).

Nantucket is an island about 15 miles long & 7 wide, situate 30 miles out at sea. The town (call'd Sherburne prior to 1795) lies on a capacious landlock'd harbour on the northern side. It was first seen by Bartholomew Gosnold in 1603, but was not settled till 1659, when some Massachusetts men purchas'd it as a residence to better their condition & escape the savage & illogical Puritan laws of the Bay Colony. At first outside the bounds of any formal colony, it was in 1664 made part of the Province of New-York, then being form'd from the conquer'd New-Netherland colony. In 1692, upon the reorganisation of the colonies after the accession of William & Mary, it was transferr'd to the Province of the Massachusetts-Bay, within which it hath ever since remain'd. The great industry of Nantucket was whaling; first practic'd in 1672, & originally conducted in small boats near the shoar. When, after 1700, whales grew scarce in New-England waters, the practice of equipping large whaling-vessels for distant cruises arose. By 1730 Nantucket whalers cover'd the whole Atlantick, & after 1791 they rounded Cape Horn & made the Pacifick their own. Tho' much set back by the wars of 1775–83 & 1812–14, the industry reach'd its climax around 1842, after which it declin'd. The lessen'd demand for whale oil was primarily responsible for this falling-off; tho' scarcity of spermaceti whales (which yielded the choicest product) accelerated the process. Nantucket whaling ceas'd in 1870, tho' New-Bedford kept the industry alive half a century more—devoting itself to the pursuit of the inferior tho' more common "right whale". After the cessation of whaling, Nantucket came to depend on its summer visitors for a livelihood. The permanent population—some 3800—all descend from the original settlers— Macys, Coffins, Starbucks, Folgers*, Rays, Gardners, Pinkhams, Wyers, Husseys, Colemans, &c.—& when not in the summer real-estate business conduct a rather slim & precarious shell-fishing industry. No other place—except perhaps parts of the South—is so free from foreigners. There are some niggers, but no Jews. At one time Quakerism was dominant on the island, but it is now extinct there. The islanders have a sturdy & distinctive character of their own, & use several idioms peculiar to their domain. The surface of the island consists of treeless, undulating moorlands. Rocks are very rare, & the only groves are of small pines planted around 1845. The town, however, has rich vegetation & fine old trees. Fresh water ponds abound, & their supply is so copious that physiographers are vastly puzzled about the matter. The exact contour of the sandy coast is constantly changed by the sea, which washes soil away in one place & deposits it in another. There was once a sizeable Indian population; which was well-treated by the whites, but which disappear'd altogether not long after 1800.

---

*Dr. Franklin's mother was a Nantucket Folger.

The first village was about a mile west of the present town; the site shifting in 1722, when the earlier harbour was clos'd by a sand bar. Many houses were moved bodily to the new location. Nantucket architecture resembles that of Salem more than that of Marblehead, & possesses many features peculiar to itself. A typical attribute is the rail'd platform on the roof—call'd the "walk", & used for marine observation.

Well—I am glad to hear all the news, & hope you will not find the transition to class work too sudden & arduous. How are the "yarbs" coming along? I enclose something about a similar enterprise. These old cloisters are very familiar to me—indeed, Belnape, Mortonius, & I visited them for the first time not long after our memorable Cleveland sessions of '22.[2] Too bad that discord developed in Mme. Hasting's work, but trust that her retirement to domesticity will not be any grave financial blow. Hope the desiderate touring may materialise when summer comes. As for sites for permanent settlement—I suppose Maine has its attractions . . . . indeed, my aunt has just been spending a fortnight there . . . . . but I wou'd consider it far too cold for hyemal habitation. Florida is the place for year-round residence if I am any judge. But not many would care to leave all trace of home soil behind, so that Madison no doubt has strong claims. For that matter, what's wrong with Appleton? To my mind, the ideal life is that of the man who can live & die in the house he was born in. Your recent enquiring into ancestral pursuits is interesting—& I hope you will eventually get hold of that first bank-note of your father's. Surely you of all persons ought to have it! My grandfather's cousin Gilbert Phillips also followed the banking profession, being president of the Prov. Inst. for Savings at the time of his death.

I don't worry much about politicks, for I think things may naturally drift in the safest possible way. The trend toward the New Deal . . . . toward the policies so long represented by your own La Follette[3] (the "Bearfox" of your allegory of years agone!) . . . . will form a safety valve against any bolshevistic eruption. Sonny Belknap has sold quite a few stories of late, & is getting so interested in money-making that he doesn't remember to cry down the infamous, barbarous, obscene, sadistic capitalistic system quite as continuously as formerly—tho' he is still explicit in outlining his burning, undying hatred of it.

I wish you would look up good old Mocrates in Zythopolis.[4] His address is 1034 N. 23rd St. He still feels rather sore about that tart epistle from 9231 Birchdale 12 years ago, but a cordial word or two ought to annul anything like that in a second. He's a fine, solid old boy, & certainly does know his profession. And that unpublished poetry manual of his actually is a wonder!

Nearly swamped with tasks since my return from Nantucket, especially since a cursed indigestion attack took a clear week out of my programme. I enjoyed the Boston visits with amateurs which preceded the Nantucket trip. Possibly I mentioned that Cook & I went to Haverhill & called on Tryout

Smith, who hasn't changed a bit in the 13 years I've seen him—though he'll be 82 next month.

All good wishes, & hopes for a not too strenuous winter.

Yr most ob^t h^ble Serv^t—

Grandpa

*Notes*

1. HPL visited Nantucket on 31 August–6 September 1934. See "The Unknown City in the Ocean," *Perspective Review* (Winter 1934).
2. HPL refers to the George Gray Barnard Cloisters (now a branch of the Metropolitan Museum of Art) in upper Manhattan. It has an extensive herb garden.
3. Robert M. La Follette (1855–1925), governor (1900–05) and U.S. Senator (1905–25) of Wisconsin. He ran for President as a third-party candiate in 1924.
4. Cf. "An Epistle to the Rt. Hon^ble Maurice Winter Moe, Esq. of Zythopolis, in the Northwest Territory of HIS MAJESTY'S American Dominion" (1929). Zythopolis is HPL's coined name for Milwaukee; i.e., "Beer-town" (from the Greek ζῦθος).

[33] [ALS]

66 College St.,
Providence, R.I.,
Octr. 19, 1934.

Son:—

Glad to receive your bulletin of the 9^th, & trust that by this time the ennui amidst which it was written is fully banished. Too bad someone else got the appointment for which your wife was aiming—but I fancy some sort of substitute activity will develop in time. And your improved status at the quondam Methodist seminary ought to form a strong compensating factor. Glad the faculty replacements have brought you some congenial colleagues. Some of the old-timers must have been rather hard cases. I recall your descriptions of one Farley—who I believe presided over the philosophical department.

I surely hope you will get in touch with old Mocrates during the autumn or winter. In case you've lost my earlier epistle with his address, I'll repeat the latter: *1034 N. 23^d St., Milwaukee, Wis.* After a bit of ice-breaking you both ought to get a real kick out of archaic reminiscence. Every now & then he speaks of his pleasure at running up against some old Appletonian.

No—I haven't had any new stories for over a year. *Weird Tales* rejected some of my best, & I have become dissatisfied with virtually all of my past performances. I am having a sort of intermission, as I did between 1908 & 1917—meanwhile reading the best things I can find in my own line, & pondering on ways to obviate some of the recognised defects in my former methods. Possibly

I'll start up writing a whole series of things before long—& possibly not. I certainly can't until I get some of the circumambient revision out of the way. I'm now debating whether or not to tackle a [. . . . . . .] by old Adolphe de Castro (the friend of [Ambrose] Bierce) which will bring no advance pay,[1] [. . . . . . . . . .] because of the influential sponsoring—[. . . . . . . .] successfully.[2]

Autumn is now here with all its chill, & my outdoor excursions are getting fewer & briefer. I have, however, managed to take enough rural jaunts to see the best of the turning foliage. Fortunately an ideal steam-heating system makes my seat of hibernation safe until April.

All good wishes—

Your ob$^t$ h$^{ble}$ Serv$^t$

—Grandpa

*Notes*

1. See HPL to F. Lee Baldwin (23 December 1934): "The MS. [by De Castro] is a full-length book of miscellaneous social, political, & historical essays rather vaguely entitled 'The New Way', & has very little internal coherence. It appears to endorse the philosophy of Lenin & the bolsheviks, & in certain parts tries to give new & sensational interpretations of accepted history" (ms., JHL).
2. The ms. is mutilated here.

[34] [ALS]

Jan$^y$. 17, 1936

Son:—

Your welcome bulletin of 28$^{th}$ ult. was duly forwarded to Castle Belknap, where the old gentleman was paying another grandchild a New Year's visit. Sonny was as glad as I to hear the news, & you may be having a word from the Child ere long—though since his highly remunerative absorption in the cheap fiction business he has been nearly as bad a correspondent as most of the younger generation!

Needless to say, I perused the current Appletonian chronicle with customary interest, & absorbed with delight the account of Messrs. Skipper & Brokaw. I had been wondering how our inky friend was faring down the years—& I now learn with satisfaction of his continued prosperity & his acquisition of a suitably mettlesome sparring partner. Mr. Brokaw is obviously a personage of distinction, & I heartily congratulate the household upon his affiliation. I can picture him vividly through your admirably graphic description, & can well imagine what a beautiful & fascinating object he must be. His linguistic powers, & his dauntless combative mettle, elicit admiration & respect. Not often is a blooded & pampered patrician of the hearth so definitely a "regular guy"! I can understand his devotion to warmth, & fancy he would appreciate the abundant 24-hour steam piped into this venerable domicile. But for all of Mr. Brokaw I shan't go back on good old Skipper. In some ways the ordinary short-haired feline cannot be surpassed—& surely none of the choice, new-fangled breeds is even half so closely associated with traditional domesticity. Regards to them both—& may they eventually compose their differences & become united in true bonds of fraternal esteem.

While I do not own a cat, I am very frequently a host to the young black gentleman, Mr. John Perkins (b. Feby. 14, 1935), who dwells at the boarding-house across the back garden. He is an elfin creature, with the long legs, large ears, & pointed nose typical of antique Ægyptus' sacred felines. His spirit is exceptionally valiant, & his courtesy to enemies sometimes limited. He has the curiously canine habit of keeping his tail in restless motion—when pleased more than when angered. Indeed, it is a truly eloquent appendage. Mr. Perkins's eyes are large & yellow, & his conversation holds much variety. For minor requests he retains the hesitant, apologetic little "..eew" of his infancy—a characteristic almost amusing in so large a beast. For John has waxed mighty in size, & bids fair to form the leader of the local Kappa Alpha Tau fraternity. The K.A.T., by the way, has fared badly of late. First (last spring) its dauntless fighting champion & Vice-President—the tiger Count Magnus Osterberg—was slain in battle with a vile crawling canine. R.I.P . . . . he never feared any living thing, & is now doubtless dismembering dragons in Valhalla . . . yet he never attacked any adversary first. I weep as I think of his passing. And now—just this month—a further but less tragic loss has occurred—through the removal of the black & white President Peter Randall, Esq., & his tiger brother Stephen (Count Magnus's successor in the Vice-Presidency), from the neighbourhood in conjunction with their human family. Verily, I feel desolated—& the adjacent shed roof seems bleak & barren without the familiar furry forms sprawling in the sun! I must find out where the Messrs. Randall live, & pay them a call.

Some of my friends & correspondents have marvellous felines. Out in California Clark Ashton Smith's coal-black Simaetha has attained an Astonishing age & matriarchal dignity—so that her wizard-master can scarcely recall a day when she did not exist. Not far away the weird writer E. Hoffmann Price has 2 cats, including old pure-white Nimrod, the most intrepid battler & fabulous eater who ever slew & devoured a million gophers in a single night. Down in Florida young Barlow has a teeming feline menagerie whose high spots are two Yellow Persians, Cyrus & Darius; whilst in the Boston zone the amateur E. H. Cole boasts a truly royal tiger-angora companion—Peter Ivanovitch Romanoff—whose purr surpasses in volume any other recorded in history or zoölogy.

Descending to merely human matters—I trust that financial asperities will soon be smoothed out, & that domestic life in general will be clarified by a resigned realisation of the irreconcilability of romantic glamour with middle age. Meanwhile I hope the Ph.D. deal will go through without a hitch . . . for *Dr.* Consul Hasting is a very appropriate designation for a philosopher. Congratulations on your new musical production—& upon the increasingly civilised & contemporary nature of the faculty at the ol' Methodist Seminary. After all, there are several endurable elements in the dragged-out process of human existence!

As for your Grandpa's recent annals—I fancy a postcard hath appris'd you of my second long Florida visit. After pauses in Fredericksburg & CHARLESTON, I reached De Land on June 9th, & remained a guest of my young friend Barlow till August 18. During a part of the time his brother—a fine young fellow, 1st. Lt. of Infantry at Ft. Sam Houston, Texas—was home on a furlough. I had several side-trips to picturesque tropical scenes, & helped my host build a cabin across the lake from his home. In that cabin a printing-press was set up; & there we prepared—as a complete surprise for Petit-Belnape—a 32-page collection of the Child's later poetry . . . all, in fact, since the issuance of "A Man from Genoa" a decade ago. The title of the new volume is "The Goblin Tower"[1]—after one of the constituent poems. Barlow couldn't assemble his binding apparatus till after my departure, but by October he began binding copies one by one. Sonny was prodigiously surprised & pleased—& even forgave us for straightening out the consciously irregular metre in one or two of his sonnets. The typography is nothing to brag about—being a first job for all hands—but there are at least no gross misprints. If you'd like a copy of this collection—which includes, I can assure you, some damned good stuff—just send a dollar to the publisher—R. H. BARLOW, BOX 88, DE LAND, FLORIDA—& he'll bind one up & send it as soon as possible.

On my way back I paused in ancient St. Augustine, magical CHARLES-TON, Poe-remembering Richmond, pleasant Washington, & brooding Philadelphia—finally tarrying a fortnight in N.Y. among the gang . . . staying with Donald Wandrei & having meals up at Belnape's. As usual, I saw everybody—Mortonius, Kleiner, &c. &c.

After my return to 66 I read up 3 months of old papers & magazines—taking a vacation long enough to visit E. H. Cole in the Boston zone & make some pilgrimages in his car . . . to Marblehead, to Cape Cod, & to the wild hills of Wilbraham, where the old-time amateur Mrs. Miniter first saw the light of day in 1867 & breathed her last in 1934. This latter pilgrimage was a sort of funereal mission—its purpose being to scatter on the ancestral soil of Wilbraham (in accordance with the deceased's wishes) the ashes of Mrs. Miniter's mother, Mrs. Dowe,[2] who died in Boston in 1919. Mrs. M. had neglected to carry out this maternal request, & now, after her own death, the duty seemed to devolve upon New England amateurdom in general. It was melancholy to revisit, after the death of those who had been my hosts, the remote & picturesque scenes where I was the guest of Mrs. M. & her cousin

Miss Beebe in 1928.[3] A spectral aura seemed to hang over the immemorial hills—though there were no outward evidences of change since I was there before. Cole & I placed half the ashes in the ancient burying-ground, & half in the deserted garden which Mrs. D. had loved in youth.

On Octr. 8 my aunt & I had a trip to ancient *New-Haven* in a friend's coach—which gave me 7½ hrs. for exploration (I had never before been off a moving vehicle in the town) whilst my aunt did some visiting. The day was ideally sunny (tho' I could have wish'd it warmer), & the ride thro' autumnal Connecticut scenery (100 m = 2½ hrs) delightful. New-Haven is not as rich in colonial antiquities as Providence, but has a peculiar charm of its own. Streets are broad & well-kept, & in the residential sections (some of which involve hills & fine views) there are endless stately mansions a century old, with generous grounds & gardens, & an almost continuous overarching canopy of great elms.

I visited ancient Connecticut-Hall (1752—oldest Yale College building, where the rebel Nathan Hale of the class of 1773 room'd), old Centre Church on the enormous green (1812—with an interesting crypt containing the grave of Benedict Arnold's first wife), the Pierpont house (1767—now Yale Faculty Club), the historical, art, & natural history museums, the Farnam & Marsh botanick gardens, & various other points of interest—crowding as much as possible into the limited time available.

Most impressive of all the sights, perhaps, were the great *new* quadrangles of Yale University—each an absolutely faithful reproduction of old-time architecture & atmosphere, & forming a self-contained little world in itself. The Gothick courtyards transport one in fancy to mediaeval Oxford or Cambridge—spires, oriels, pointed arches, mullion'd windows, arcades with groin'd roofs, climbing ivy, sundials, lawns, gardens, vine-clad walls & flagstoned walks—everything to give the young occupants that mass'd impression of their accumulated cultural heritage which they might obtain in OLD ENGLAND itself. To stroll thro' these cloister'd quadrangles, in the golden light of late afternoon; at dusk, when the candles behind the diamond-paned casements flicker up one by one; or in the beams of a mellow Hunter's Moon; is to walk bodily into an enchanted region of dream. It is the past & the antient Mother Land brought magically to the present time & place. God Save the King! The choicest of the Gothick quadrangles is Calhoun-College—name'd for the great Carolinian[4] (whose grave in St. Philip's churchyard, Charleston, I had visited scarce two months ago), who was a graduate of Yale.

Nor are the Georgian quadrangles less glamourous—each being a magical summoning-up of the world of two centuries ago. Many distinct types of Georgian architecture are represented, & the buildings & landscaping alike reflect the finest taste which European civilisation has yet developed or is ever likely to develop. Lucky (tho' no doubt unappreciative at the time) is the youth whose formative years are spent amid such scenes! I wander'd for hours thro' this limitless labyrinth of unexpected elder microcosms, & mourn'd the lack of further time. Certainly, I must visit New-Haven again, since many of its treasures wou'd require weeks for proper inspection & appreciation.

Oct. 16–18 I had a pleasing visit from our friend Saml. Loveman, Esq.—spent partly in Boston, where we visited the Mus. of Fine Arts & brows'd among the bookstalls. Samuelus hath now left Dauber & Pine, & is the proprietor of an independent establishment call'd the Bodley Book Shop, which holds forth at 104 Fifth Ave., on the 17th floor of an office-building. Also (vide enclosed circular), he is at last the author of a regularly publish'd book.[5] This volume makes a very neat appearance, & is (I hope, since I read the proofs thrice) reasonably accurate as to text.

The autumn was a mild one hereabouts, & I continued to haunt the agrestick meads & groves throughout October. After that something more like hibernation set in, tho' I attended many local lectures of interest. At Christmas we again had a tree, & the air of traditional festivity was considerable.

Dec. 30 I arriv'd at Sonny Belknap's for a week of sociability with the old gang, & succeeded in exchanging greetings with most of the veterans—Morton, Kleiner, Kirk, Loveman, Talman, Leeds, Wandrei, &c. &c. &c. I attended several gatherings, including a dinner of the Am. Fiction Guild, & saw a good many of the cheap magazine hacks whose names are familiar to the reading proletariat. Petit-Belnape & Wandrei are getting deep into hack fiction-writing—to the great financial advantage, tho' to their aesthetick detriment. Sonny sent you his most cordial regards—&, as I have said, express'd a design to write you. By the way—on Oct. 20 Belknap's aunt Mrs. Symmes, the one who financed "A Man from Genoa", was instantly killed in a motor accident near Miami. A bit of tragick irony—even at that moment Barlow was binding a complimentary copy of "The Goblin Tower" for her.

On two occasions—once with Sonny & once with Sonny & Wandrei—I visited the new Hayden Planetarium of the Am. Museum, & found it a highly impressive device. It consists of a round domed building of 2 storeys. On the lower floor is a circular hall whose ceiling is a gigantick orrery—shewing the planets revolving around the sun at their proper relative speeds. Above it is another circular hall whose roof is the great dome, & whose edge is made to represent the horizon of N.Y. as seen from Central Park. In the centre of this upper hall is a curious projector which casts on the concave dome a perfect image of the sky—capable of duplicating the natural apparent motions of the celestial vault, & of depicting the heavens as seen at any hour, in any season, from any latitude, & at any period of history. Other parts of the projector can cast suitably moveable images of the sun, moon, & planets, & diagrammatick arrows & circles for explanatory purposes. The effect is infinitely lifelike—as if one were outdoors beneath the sky. Lectures—different each month (I heard both Dec. & Jan. ones)—are given in connexion with this apparatus. In the corridors on each floor are niches containing typical astronomical instruments of all ages—telescopes, transits, celestial globes, armillary spheres, &c.—& cases to display books, meteorites, & other miscellany. Astronomical pictures line the walls, & at the desk may be obtained useful pamphlets, books, planispheres, &c. The institution holds classes in elementary astronomy, & sponsors clubs of amateur observers. Altogether, it is the most complete & active popular astronomical centre imaginable. It seems to be crowded at all hours—attracting a publick interest in astronomy which did not exist when I was young.

I visited Morton in Paterson on Jan. 6, & that midnight took the coach for home—being delay'd an hour in the sightly colonial village of Hampton, Conn., to await the sanding of a slippery hill. Since my arrival, I have been ingulph'd by an almost unprecedented vortex of tasks—so hopeless that I have had to give over the design of writing a N.A.P.A. critical report. Amateurdom is having a kind of renew'd life—including the usual political warfare.

Clark Ashton Smith's mother died on Sept. 9—an event imposing a severe strain on his nerves. He has now taken up a new artistick pursuit, at which he is succeeding to a remarkable degree—viz. *sculpture or carving* in the soft minerals of his native region. Within the past month or two an unexpected *professional* demand for the products of his chisel has arisen—so that for the moment his writing is quite eclipsed. Most of his statues are miniature grotesque heads or figurines (he has given me two—each representing a monster in some tale of mine), tho' he hath prepar'd several statuettes & bas-reliefs of a more common sort to order.

I surely hope that I can see the cinema "Mad Love"—which several have recommended to me. I was never able to witness "Dr. Caligari", about which I heard so much 13 or 14 years ago. I attend the cinema but seldom—the best production I have lately seen being a highly impressive Irish tragedy intitul'd "The Informer." I also saw "Ah, Wilderness",[6] which made me homesick for the vanish'd world of 1906!

With usual benedictions, & compliments to Skipper, Mr. Brokaw, & everybody, I remain

      Yr ob^t h^ble Serv^t

        Grandpa

P.S. You can find a 3-part story of mine—"At the Mountains of Madness"—in *Astounding Stories*, beginning with the February issue. The W.T. now on the stands reprints my old "Dagon."[7] ¶ You can find stories of Belnape's in many of the current science-fiction & detective magazines.

*Notes*

1. *A Man from Genoa* (Athol, MA: Recluse Press, 1926) and *The Goblin Tower* (Cassia, FL: Dragon-Fly Press, 1935); reprinted in part in *In Mayan Splendor* (1977).

2. Jennie E. T. Dowe. See HPL's "In Memoriam: J. E. T. D.," *Tryout* 5, No. 3 (March 1919): [6] (as by "Ward Phillips").

3. HPL's visit influenced "The Dunwich Horror."

4. John C. Calhoun (1782–1850).

5. *The Hermaphrodite and Other Poems* (Caldwell, ID: The Caxton Printers, 1936; *LL* 550). See also letter 13, n. 15.

6. *Mad Love* (MGM, 1935), directed by Karl Freund, produced by John W. Considine, Jr.; starring Peter Lorre and Colin Clive; *The Cabinet of Dr. Caligari* (Decla-Bioscop/Goldwyn, 1919), directed by Robert Weine, produced by Erich Pommer; starring Werner Kraus and Conrad Veidt; *The Informer* (RKO, 1935), directed by John Ford, produced by Cliff Reid; starring Victor McLaglan and Wallace Ford; *Ah, Wilderness* (MGM, 1935), directed by Clarence Brown, produced by Hunt Stromberg; starring Wallace Beery, Lionel Barrymore, and Mickey Rooney.

7. *Weird Tales,* January 1936.


[35] [ALS]

66 College St.,
Providence, R.I.,
June 20, 1936.

Son:—

Your recent bulletin proved very welcome indeed, & helped to mitigate the woes of a season of considerable asperity. For 1936 has proved a very bad year for the old man—forming, virtually ever since my return from the New Year visit to young Belnape, a continuous chronicle of disaster. First a congestion of thankless & unprofitable tasks which threw my whole schedule awry. Then an attack of grippe which had me flat for a week & multiplied the prevailing chaos a thousandfold. And *then*—before I was well over the grippe—the *real* trouble began! My aunt came down with a grippe attack infinitely worse than mine,[1] so that I was at once reduced to the composite status of nurse, butler, secretary, market-man, & errand-boy. All my own affairs went to hell—revision jobs returned, letters unanswered, borrowed books piled up unread . . . .

> "With ruin upon ruin, rout on rout,
> Confusion worse confounded."[2]

Complications setting in, my aunt had to go to the hospital in mid-March—which altered without materially diminishing my added responsibilities. And the financial aspect can be imagined! Very luckily, my aunt soon began to improve—being promoted to a convalescent home on April 7, & returning to #66 on the 21st. She is now fully ¾ back to normal, having resumed a great part of her usual activities & spending most of her time outdoors in the garden. But my programme remained all shot to hell, & at present I feel just about on the edge of a nervous breakdown. My energy & power of concentration are sunk to a minimum, & my eyesight is not what it was when I was young. The lingering cold of a late spring has helped to keep me down—& I have found it impossible to embark on any trips, notwithstanding a cordial & tempting invitation from Barlow to repeat my Florida visits of '34 & '35. However, the tardy approach of vernal mildness has been of some benefit, & I have been able to keep out of doors to some extent. Would that 98° weather might set in!

Well—congratulations on the new—& first—detective novel, which I know must be good, & which I surely hope to peruse sooner or later! Here's hoping it wins the prize—or, failing that, that it lands advantageously with some publisher in the regular way. Regarding the best markets—I am scarcely an expert in detective-novel placement, but recall that the most prolific author of such material whom I know—your brilliant young fellow-Wisconsinian August W. Derleth of Sauk City—began most successfully with the relatively new firm of Loring & Mussey (now, I believe, called Barrows Mussey, Inc.), 66 Fifth Ave., New York, N.Y. (in the same building with Dauber & Pine, where Samuelus once held forth.) Whether he'd advise that same firm today, I can't tell—but I am asking him about the matter. As the author of half a dozen successful detective novels (the "Judge Peck" mysteries) "The Man on All Fours" (1934); "Sign of Fear" (1935); and "Three Who Died" (1935)[3] & of one serious book ("Place of Hawks"—1935—a group of regional tales with convincing Wis. background),[4] he ought to know a lot more about the game than I do. I have requested him either to write you directly, or to give me all the necessary information for purposes of relaying. I rather hope he'll write you, for you'd find him an interesting cuss. Here is a cutting about him & his work—which I'll ask you to return some time. Regarding the way to fasten a thick MS.—if (as 225 pages probably are) it's too thick to go neatly in a large envelope, I fancy a common elastic band is all that could be demanded. *Permanent* fasteners—i.e., things like the long brass specimens which punch through the top or side of all the sheets to make a sort of quasi-book—are usually not desired by publishers, since they like to be able to separate the MS. into parts if necessary. *Clips* for thin MSS., elastic bands or nothing at all (i.e., just the large envelope in which the MS. is mailed flat) for medium MSS., & elastic bands for very thick MSS. would seem to be the ordinary custom. However, I've asked Derleth if there's any new-fangled professional custom which ought to be followed. As to the date of first financial returns in case of acceptance—I'm inclined to doubt the wisdom of expecting anything this summer. Arrangements differ, of course, & E. P. Dutton Co. used to make good old Everett McNeil small advances upon accepting his various juvenile volumes; but whether this system would hold good in the case of a first novel I can't be sure. Here again I'll seek the latest & most authoritative data from young Derleth. The bulk of remuneration usually comes through "royalties"—a certain percentage of the receipts from sales forwarded at stated intervals when there's anything to forward.

Well—you'll hear again before long, either from Derleth or from me. The outline which you give suggests something of marked power & interest, & the realistic, first-hand nature of the setting ought to remove it considerably from the usual rut. The generous allotment of tragic & violent events is in the best detective tradition (in one of his novels Derleth kills damn near everybody off!), while the dialogue medium surely reflects the prevailing taste. Your chosen title & pseudonym also appear to me to be definite assets. So here's to a bright future for "Marsh-Mad's" first successor! "Strive blindly toward the light that kills, for the eternal hills & valleys will preserve!"*

Any recent story of mine in W T must have been a reprint. My last two published efforts (the first-named of which was frightfully mangled) are "At the Mountains of Madness" (antarctic serial) & "The Shadow Out of Time" (novelette), in *Astounding Stories* for Feb.–Mar–April & June, respectively. Both of these received cover designs,[5] which rather tickled my aged ego.

The few reviews of the Herm which I have seen have been rather discouragingly lukewarm. It is evident that a new generation of modernistic youngsters has seized the critical thrones in most of the papers, & has begun to spread its analytical & subjective doctrines. The tendency is to regard Lovemaniana as something derived from obsolete sources—as a musical echo of images & sentiments no longer fraught with meaning, but merely repeating the emotions of the elder bards. That I thoroughly disagree with such dicta goes without saying—but there's no stopping a pack of young upstarts once they get going! It is this same tendency which has worked to the advantage of poor Crane & made him such a symbol of the poetic present. I can agree with Mr. Untermeyer regarding Crane's unintelligibility,[6] & am myself convinced of the unsoundness of any symbolism whose key rests with the author alone. You may have seen an article—largely based on Crane, & including an image-by-image interpretation (furnished by the poet on request) of one of his shorter verses—on this subject some few years ago in *Harpers* . . . "Poets talking to Themselves", by Max Eastman.[7] He conceded that Crane's obscure allusions are not capricious or irresponsible, but expressed strong doubts of the value of associative processes so purely dependent on the contents & workings of one person's mind.

Amateurdom has had a slight revival this year—owing largely to the return of the old-timer Ernest A. Edkins (now in the Evanston Hospital, alas, with a kidney operation) to the fold. I've sent you a copy of his paper—which contains among other things a not too sympathetic review of Sonny Belknap's new volume of verse.[8] Belnape, by the way, has been having rather a hard time—pushed to the wall with hack-writing, & with both parents recently down with grippe. Samuelus' bookshop seems to keep him amply busy—

---

*From "Mystery", an essay by Consul Hasting, Esq. in *United Amateur* for January 1918.

which is equally true of Kirk's. Good ol' Mocrates expects to get east again this summer—attending the celebrated Bread Loaf Writers' Conference in Vermont. I hope to see him here—for the first time since 1923. In the intervening 13 yrs Grandpa has changed a lot more than he has! His elder son is still doing brilliantly in Bridgeport, whilst the younger is still at college in Seattle.

I hope to see those snapshots of you before long, but trust you'll get rid of the lip-fuzz as soon as the novel is complete! Congratulations on your pleasant spring—bright contrast to the chill & lagging season hereabouts! The landscaping sounds highly interesting, & I trust I may see some photographic evidence thereof. I certainly envy you your ability to dwell down the years in your birthplace! How are the felidae getting along? Sooner or later I want to see your novel—& meanwhile I wish it luck in the contest. I'll shoot along additional market hints at the earliest possible date.

Ever y$^r$ most ob$^t$ h$^{ble}$ Serv$^t$—

Grandpa

P.S. Last moment. I've just recd. the 2nd issue of *Causerie*, & will try to get a copy for you. The criticism of S L is in the main acute & fair, tho' Edkins blames the bard unduly for what he calls his "defeatist" attitude toward life.[9] Actually, a poet's attitude toward life doesn't matter one god damn—so long as he crystallises & transmutes with suitable grace & power, whatever mood or attitude he *does* happen to have.

*Notes*

1. Actually, Annie Gamwell underwent surgery for breast cancer.

2. John Milton, *Paradise Lost* 2.995–96.

3. There were ten Judge Peck novels. HPL owned and read *The Man on All Fours: A Judge Peck Mystery Story* (New York: Loring & Mussey, [1934]; *LL* 234); *Sign of Fear: A Judge Peck Mystery* (New York: Loring & Mussey, 1935; *LL* 236); and *Three Who Died: A Judge Peck Mystery* (New York: Loring & Mussey, 1935; *LL* 237).

4. *Place of Hawks*, illustrated with wood engravings by George Barford (New York: Loring & Mussey, [1935]; *LL* 235).

5. "The Shadow out of Time" and *At the Mountains of Madness*, both illustrated by Howard V. Brown (1878–1945).

6. Louis Untermeyer, *Modern American Poetry: A Critical Anthology*, 5th rev. ed. (New York: Harcourt, Brace, 1936), p. 588: "There will be those who will find Crane's poetry not merely tangential but cryptic. The difficulty is caused by his combination of allusiveness and allegory, especially since the allusions are often remote and the allegorical symbols personal to the point of privacy."

7. Max Eastman, "Poets Talking to Themselves," *Harper's Magazine* 163, No. 5 (October 1931): 563–74.

8. [Ernest A. Edkins], "*The Goblin Tower*," *Causerie* (February 1936): 2–4.

9. Edkins reviewed Loveman's *Hermaphrodite and Other Poems* in *Causerie* (June 1936): 2–4.

[36] [ALS]

66 College St.,
Providence, R.I.,
July 31, 1936.

Son:—

Glad indeed that my recommendation of young Auguste-Guillaume, Comte d'Erlette, proved a good one. I thought he had the skill & experience needed to make his fictional advice of value, & it seems I was not wrong. He is really a great chap—with a driving energy that perpetually astonishes the rest of the gang. Slowly & steadily he is climbing out of the cheap fiction class into the domain of serious writing, & within a decade I believe he will be recognised as a substantial regional novelist. His productivity is almost fabulous—including everything from pulp junk up to Scribner stories & published books. It is impossible to pick up one of the better-grade "little magazines" without coming across his name. Among readers of detective fiction his "Judge Peck" novels are classics of a sort. His enthusiasm in helping & advising fellow-craftsmen is prodigious—& is perhaps one result of his superabundance of energy. I hope you'll have a chance to meet him before long, & believe he'll prove as congenial in conversation as in correspondence. His acute musical appreciation will surely form a link in common.

As to his personality—while I've never met him face to face (though my friends the Wandrei brothers have), & have never formed an intimate picture of his daily life & amusements, I fancy you would find in him a kind of blend of the convivial & aesthetic. He probably changes somewhat as he develops. A few years ago he was an almost amusing egotist who deliberately cultivated egocentricity in order to irritate the complacent bourgeoisie of his somewhat smug & provincial village. He wore a monocle & a flaring-tailed overcoat that almost touched the ground, went outdoors (& once to a social gathering) in a dressing-gown, & had himself snapshotted in all sorts of asinine poses. Now he is maturing & getting over the kid stuff—his ego cropping out in nothing more bizarre than his de luxe letter-heads with different woodcuts for every season. He likes to be thought important, but has a saving sense of humour. I think he enjoys the modest pleasures of society—in fact, he is an avowed enemy to the puritanic attitude—though on the other hand he despises the decadent hedonism of urban & sophisticated circles. He spent a year in Minneapolis as assistant editor of a cheap magazine,[1] & left it in disgust at the affectation, bohemianism, triviality, & laboured "smartness" of the local literary & aesthetic groups. After all, he is essentially a villager with his roots deep in Wisconsin soil. He understands the importance of fixity & of profound geographic traditions, & never writes without a sharp consciousness of the long stream of events, folkways, & personalities behind the "Sac Prairie" of today. To him, basic & permanent human emotions seem to be embodied far more truly & visibly in rural or semi-rural life, than in the rootless, restless, pointless & kaleidoscopic life of a mongrel metropolis. He has never been east or in Europe, nor would he care to live & work anywhere save in his native town. Sauk City appears to be rather an unusual place—a prairie town peopled about 1830 by a small group of Germans of the haute-bourgeoisie & lesser nobility, & sharply differentiated both from such Yankee towns as good ol' Appleton, & from the *peasant*-German areas. Small & self-contained, it has cherished a sometimes enjoyable & sometimes exasperating clannishness. Its old families furnish the curious brooding characters so frequent in Derleth's serious fiction—proud, grim old gentlewomen harbouring various secrets; decadent scions with relentless hereditary taints; patriarchal or matriarchal tyrants dominating individual children or entire households; haughty, destitute aristocrats recalling past glories amidst present squalor, &c. &c. &c. In former years I fancy Derleth was locally disliked for his incessant inquisitiveness regarding the lives & pasts of his fellow-villagers; but he persisted in his "nosey" pestiferousness in order to gain the knowledge of human affairs, emotions, relationships, thought-patterns, & inheritances which he needed for his realistic fiction. Now the natives seem inclined to forgive & respect him—for (having pumped them dry of family secrets) he probably pesters them less with questions, while his growing literary reputation presumably impresses them. In time he will doubtless grow into something like a local oracle—& the outside world may know Sauk City chiefly because of his birth & residence there. No—Derleth isn't a farm boy in any sense of the word. He lives in the village\*, & has a really cosmopolitan outlook. His financial circumstances seem to be moderate; so that he has plenty of time in which to develop his professional writing skill, while he has not been forced to pander to the cheapest editors in order to keep afloat. He is now, moreover, making quite a bit with his stories—so that he paid an income tax for the first time this year. But he is no rich man's son, either—indeed, he used to piece out his spending-money in summer by taking a part-time job in the local canning factory. His tastes would be rather fastidious & sybaritic if he had the means to indulge them, but he is too devoted to literature to attempt commercial enterprises. On the other hand he is a very shrewd business man in the domain of literary marketing, & will probably be financially secure within the next few years. Altogether, Little Augie is quite a boy—amply sustaining the reputation of Old Wisconsin as a nursery of precocious genius. You'll like him.

Sorry the novel needs so much reconstruction—though I suppose the process really forms an invaluable lesson in fictional technique. You can be counted on to use any sound hint to the best possible advantage in the shortest possible order! In the end I hope success will result—favourable professional placement, if not the winning of the coveted Dodd-Mead prize.

---

\* pop. 2000 or 3000

As for the Old Gent—my touristic programme is so far (& is likely to remain) an approximate zero—for reasons which are now (in view of my aunt's recovery) wholly financial. Yuggoth, if I could only get down to Charleston for some life-giving *continuous* heat amidst this chilly summer! I've felt like hell most of the time, though two hot spells helped to brace me up. In mid-July—when a week of 90° weather put me on my feet—I took a boat trip to Newport—rambling as usual around the ancient town & doing considerable writing atop the high, hilly sea-cliffs.

July 18–19 I had an enjoyable visit from our good old colleague Mocrates the Sage, now on a visit to various eastern points after a sojourn at the Grand Rapids N.A.P.A. Convention. It was my first sight of the old boy in 13 years, & I fancy he found Grandpa a damn sight more changed than I found him. He came with his son Robert (now of Bridgeport, Conn.—he visited me twice last year) in the latter's car, & we covered quite a bit of scenic & historic ground in the all-too-brief span of 2 days. Weather favoured us greatly, for we had warmth & sun throughout—whereas the very next day was cold & rainy, with the Old Gent heavily blanketed & shivering over an oil heater. Good ol' Mocrates! We recalled the Kleicomolo & Gallomo days of 20 years ago, dug up issues of *The Pippin* from my amateur files, & in general acted the part of grey, reminiscent elders to the life. I fear young Bob was quite bored to death by the senile gabbling of Pater et Avus!

Had an interesting view of Peltier's Comet on July 22 at the Ladd Observatory[2]—through the 12″ refractor. The object shewed a small disc with a hazy, fan-like tail. I could have seen it through my own small glass but for the obstructed nature of the northern sky in the neighbourhood of 66.

Just at present I have the pleasure of being a sort of long-term semi-host—as Loveman was to us in the good old 9231 Birchdale days of '22—since my young friend Robert Hayward Barlow (my host in De Land, Fla. in '34 & '35) has come to Providence for a sojourn of indefinite length. Some property adjustments about the De Land place are occurring, & Barlow thought this would be a good time to pay the Old Gent a visit & make his temporary headquarters in ancient New-England for a while. I surely am glad to see him—& I forgive him the fierce-looking moustache & side-whiskers he has grown. He has taken a room at the boarding-house across the garden from 66, & will certainly be a most congenial neighbour while he stays. He is full of literary plans—including a realistic novel & the establishment of a high-grade mimeographed magazine of distinctive material.[3] My aunt fears he will go broke because of his ferocious raids upon the local bookstalls!

Well—here's hoping you have a pleasant visit with M. le Comte d'Erlette ere long—& that his critical suggestions may help you to put "Death in D-Minor" across big. Best wishes for the plantation at 726!

Yr obt Servt—

Grandpa

P.S. Loan exhibit of Clark Ashton Smith's grotesque miniature sculpture has reached me at last. Great stuff! Some of the items shew a genius of the most distinctive kind.

*Notes*

1. *Mystic Magazine,* a magazine devoted to the occult.
2. 451 Hope Street in Providence
3. Barlow published two large issues of the mimeographed magazine *Leaves* (1937, 1938).

[37] [ALS]

66 College St.,
Providence, R.I.,
August 9, 1936.

Son:—

Glad to hear of progress on the reconceived "Murder in Montparnasse". You surely have made a radical change in approach & method, & I fancy the present course is much more likely to produce a definitely marketable result. It pleases me to learn that Derleth has been such a help, & I hope you two can meet before long. He refers to you in the most admiring terms in a recent letter, & I have no doubt but that the get-together will be a congenial one when it comes to pass. By the way—if you'd like to see some of Comte d'Erlette's work, I'd be glad to lend you his book "Place of Hawks", or some of his detective novels. Let me know if you wish them. Glad some of your verse is going into M. le Comte's anthology, & hope to see "November" before long.[1] Little Augie is also asking Pater Mocrates for some metrical material—which I imagine the good old boy will be able to furnish, since he's getting rather poetical in his declining years.

Glad you've been somewhat active in music, & hope you'll turn out some memorable compositions before long. Glad also that you've received both *The Dragon-Fly*[2] & *Causerie.* Edkins certainly hit off Samuelus' work finely—so justly that S L is genuinely pleased with the review & has asked for copies.

Sorry to hear of the Appleton drought. Lawns are rather scorched here, but the dessication is on the whole less uninterrupted. I envy you your over-100° temperatures, though a few 90° days have helped to keep me in trim.

Barlow is still here, & last Wednesday the party was further swelled by the arrival of old Adolphe de Castro (erstwhile Gustave Adolf Danziger), one-time friend of Ambrose Bierce & co-translator of the fairly well-known "Monk & the Hangman's Daughter".[3] He was, as you may recall, a revision client of mine in 1928–9[4]—& Belknap wrote the preface for his life of Bierce

published in '29.[5] Old 'Dolph is 77 now, & quite down & out—on public re-
lief in N.Y. His wife died last year, & he is now en route back from Boston,
where he carried out her ante-mortem request that her ashes be scattered
over the ocean off the coast. As usual, the old boy is trying to saddle me with
half a dozen speculative (& undoubtedly unprofitable) revision jobs, but so
far I've succeeded in refusing without offending him. Meanwhile I'm shewing
him the sights of the town, & listening to his tales about all the bygone celebrities (Swinburne, Anatole France, Bierce, Theodore Roosevelt, &c. &c. &c.)
he used to know . . . . how he helped Warren G. Harding become President,
& how his advice also won the presidency for Taft . . . . . . Friday we were all
in the hidden hillside churchyard somewhat north of #66—where Poe used
to wander during his courtship of Sarah Helen Whitman—& each of us (at
Barlow's suggestion) composed a rhymed acrostic on the letters of Poe's
name.[6] Here is mine—the mechanical & inspirationless product of a single
half-hour, writ as I sate upon an ancient tomb:

### IN A SEQUESTER'D CHURCHYARD WHERE ONCE POE WALK'D[7]

Eternal brood the Shadows on this Ground,
Dreaming of Centuries that have gone before;
Great Elms rise solemnly by Slab and Mound,
Arching above the hidden World of Yore.
Round all the Scene a Light of Mem'ry plays,
And dead leaves whisper of departed Days,
Longing for Sights and Sounds that are no more.
Lonely and sad, a Spectre glides along
Aisles where long past his living Footsteps fell;
No common Glance discerns him, tho' his Song
Peals down thro' Time with a mysterious Spell:
Only the Few who Sorcery's Secret know
Espy amidst these Tombs the Shade of POE.

Old 'Dolph's & Barlow's efforts are (pardon the egotism) even worse! Most
emphatically, poetry cannot be written to order.

Today I shall meet Barlow & de Castro at noon, & we shall do the art
museum[8] (only a block down the hill from 66)—which R H B has seen only
in part, & which will be wholly new to Old 'Dolph. There's some pretty good
stuff in it, even if it isn't a rival of the Metropolitan in N.Y. Attached to the
museum proper is a perfect reproduction of a colonial mansion, containing
the finest collection of American colonial furniture in the world.

Well—good luck with the novel, & with all your other ventures. Hope you'll meet the scintillant Comte d'Erlette ere long, & that he will not prove disappointing.

Sir, yr most h^ble & ob^t Serv^t—

—Grandpa

*Notes*

1. August Derleth and Raymond E. F. Larsson, eds., *Poetry out of Wisconsin* (New York: Henry Harrison, 1937). Contains Galpin's "November," pp. 100–101.

2. Edited by Robert H. Barlow.

3. Ambrose Bierce (1842–1914?) and Adolphe Danziger (1859–1959), *The Monk and the Hangman's Daughter* (serialized 1891; book publication 1892; translated from the German of Richard Voss). HPL owned a later edition, *The Monk and the Hangman's Daughter; Fantastic Fables; [etc.]* (New York: A. & C. Boni, 1925; *LL* 90).

4. HPL revised "The Last Test," "The Electric Executioner," and possibly one other story for de Castro from his book *In the Confessional and the Following* (New York: Western Authors Publishing Association, 1893).

5. *Portrait of Ambrose Bierce* (New York: Century Co., 1929). The preface is signed "Belknap Long."

6. The three acrostic poems and others by M. W. Moe and Henry Kuttner were published in David E. Schultz, "In a Sequester'd Churchyard," *Crypt of Cthulhu* No. 57 (St. John's Eve 1988): 26–29.

7. *Science-Fantasy Correspondent* 1, No. 3 (March–April 1937): 16–17 (as "In a Sequestered Churchyard Where Once Poe Walked").

8. Museum of Art, Rhode Island School of Design, 224 Benefit Street.

*Alfred Galpin and his second wife, Isabella,*
*taken at their home in Montecatini Terme in Italy, c. 1975.*

# Works of Alfred Galpin

## *Mystery*

O Man! For what, through infinite aeons, hast thou been striving? For what toilest thou in the monastery, for what delveth thy Science? For what but hounding thy Supreme Lord and Maker, Mystery? What, in thy scale, is the lowest of Humanity? Is it not he, if indeed he exists, in whom there is no longing to *Know*—for whom MYSTERY has no charm? And who the highest, but he whose labors have been most nearly and effectively concentrated toward dispelling that rainbow cloud, Mystery? Truly the aim of thy overlapping days is following to their hidden and unthinkable lairs the greatest possible number of alluring, spectral mysteries.

And yet, what would be thy fate if thou shouldst attain the climax of thy advancing hopes? For what wouldst thou live, O Improphetic? What would thy brain, strained to its corporeal limits of development by the moiling struggle, aid thee? What would become of thy very soul, grown to its fulness of strength and beauty by the food of Perplexity and devouring starvation without it? O pity the Being, for whom there should be no Mystery, no life of mysteries, if, perchance, he should scratch the surface of one, and finding hidden therein the unsounded and immeasurable depths of the Infinite Mystery of LIFE, should find need to pass on.

Ah, Man! Thou art indeed bespoken for a sightless and lovable fool; toiling for the fascination of the toil, and vitally mortal without it; raising thyself against the revealing earth, only to find new breadths of panorama, only to meet with new and greater evils. And truly, it speaketh well for the Eternal Beneficience of Things, that the inevitable and omnipresent LAW checks thee, striving for Psychocide; that all things operate toward Good and toward Evil; that action equals reaction; that all Things have a use and a corresponding abuse; the Eternal and Omnipotent Balance.

So, toil on, O Man! With thy petty troubles of the hour; with thy delving science; with thy selfish, with thy fools, with thy wise, with thy noble. Toil on! What though Eternity; what though Infinity flow and heed thee not? *Strive blindly toward the light that kills, for the Eternal Hills and Valleys will preserve!*

## Two Loves

(After, and with apologies to, Miss Elsie Alice Gidlow in the June *Vagrant*.)

I have two loves, who haunt me unceasingly.
Which shall I choose?

One is ugly to men's sight, and arouses repulsion in them;
Not so to me; for I know the true heart within.
Yes, he is ugly and repulsive to the many—
His robust mien and his plebeian companions dishonour him.
But they are as he:
For his heart is as pure gold, the gold
Scorned in sham by the would-be poetic, but ever true and useful.

He is constant, and I could love him forever;
Yea, with dishonour stamped on his brow by the mob, I yet do love him.
For his heart is as the heart of a thrifty and comely woman sought by all of thought.

He hath a hard skin, and is difficult of acquaintance;
But to him who searcheth beneath, he is a rich mine of delicious treasure.

In my sensuous dreams I behold him, and long for him;
When all the world is heartless and I am weary of it,
Then do I long for him.

The ether I would shun; for he is traitorously fair and beauteous:
But he draws me to him inevitably, as the raft through many streams to the ocean.

His soul burneth as the hot torrents that prompt love—
Ever youthful and daring in heart, but changing ere ultimately carefree;
Inspiring hesitant fear at a distance, but enticing and ever victorious.

He is not constant,
Except as he forceth me to everlasting constancy;
For he is exacting.
He draws me to him and I drink of his luscious beauty—
But O the aftermath! The satient afterwhile!

He would destroy me;
He has become a part of my soul, and meaneth my ruin;
And yet I should die without him.

His beauty sparkles, and is given fastidious care.
His speech flows swiftly and fluently, and is the language of all who are sub-
ject to his sway.
Yea, him I long for passionately, and the other is only a comfort.

I have two loves who woo me unceasingly:
One is bologna and the other Scotch Whiskey:
Which shall I take?

## Selenaio-Phantasma

Dedicated to the Author of "Nemesis"

In Elysium-fann'd fields of my slumber,
    In the wild-tinted beauties of night,
I have feasted on sights without number,
    Recreated all Heav'n with my sight:
And I wake to the sunrise at dawning, fit close to the dusk's mad delight.

Shadow'd visions of beauties unpainted,
    Shifting sights of a Heaven beyond,
Primal nature in pureness untainted,
    Without Man and his slave-making wand,
Meet my sight in procession uncanny, unorder'd, and link'd without bond.

Mingling phantoms above Man's poor notion,
    Phantasmas obscure and unknown,
Undulations and waves of wild motion
    Into infinite variance grown,
I behold in my slumbers of madness, from far shores of mad Cynthia blown.

I have seen things of cryptical meaning,
    Hinting life far above mortal view;
Superstitions of primitive gleaning
    Blend with fancy to forms strange and new;
And my fetterless brain leaps the mountain of Science and dreams 'tis not true.

All the hopes of a life are entwined
    With the greed of a fancy unchain'd.
While my thoughts, by the sleep undermined,
    Wander wordless, uncheck'd, uncontain'd
O'er unearthly expanses of Spiritland, haunting where once they had reign'd.

When, in midst of this immundane dreaming
    Come effulgent the first rays of light,
Bringing back my rapt soul with their beaming,
    Lending splendour to all within sight;
And I wake to the sunrise at dawning, fit close to the dusk's mad delight.

# Remarks to My Handwriting

First form'd by Ibis in Egyptian mud,
Beside the hungry Nile's receding flood,
Thou next becam'st a sacred hieroglyph,
Awkward and cramp'd—gracelessly made and stiff.
Skipping the centuries and the Central Sea,
Latium and France, thou now inhabit'st me.

Yesterday's hen-tracks! Egypt, thou art curst!
Thy offspring's best is but a *pig*-pen's worst!
Could I but change the scrawl to fit my thoughts . . . . . . .
But no—thou mak'st the same old row of blots.
My words are English, but the products strange
When stubborn Ibis waddles without change.
One blessing only lighteneth my load:
Thou art my language and my cipher code!

# Marsh-Mad

A Nightmare

So stifling and oppressive had grown the dank, murkily thickening air of the swamp, that an overwhelming dread of the foul sentience of the vegetation and very atmosphere about me clutched clammily at my senses. The moon-streaked clouds to the north grew more spectrally dark and billowed on toward me. About me clung an all-pervading and indefinite stench that seemed a portent of some grim evil, hypnotic and dreadful. The sudden and unnatural darkness rendered every object in the gloomy swamp vague and ominous. There could be no doubt in my fear-harassed mind that these surroundings, so recently intended for the mere scene of a sportsman's lark, had assumed an aspect of mysterious, thaumaturgic terror.

The omnipresent silence of the place had long irked me strangely. In vain did I attempt to forget my surroundings. I struggled to concentrate my thoughts on the home I had left behind me, but no effort of mind could bring it any nearer than it actually, tantalisingly was; nor could it drive out the sight of this dismal marsh which threatened me at every hand. I tried to think over the many events of my active past, but I obtained only a dim recollection which seemed that of another man, who had lived and died long æons past. All pretense was now fast failing me, and I was forced to confront my situation, unpalatable as it might be, and to renew my long-abandoned efforts to find the path.

The rank vegetation, discolored and overgrown with masses of stagnant, creeping slime, yielded an odor indescribably reminiscent of all the horror of dead things; while the weird, glimmering light turned to a weirder shade under a forbidding canopy of exotic, distorted trees. I was indeed isolated from all that meant a normal state of life, in which Man reigned unhampered by the inexplicable; and the invisible terror of the fen crushed prostratingly upon me . . . . . . And now, as heavy clouds crawled overhead ill-bodingly, a new sense of dumb dread seized me. I felt that the dynamic silence and seeming-solitude of the swamp were soon to be rent asunder in the cataclysmic revelation of the unthinkably HORRIBLE.

How bitterly did I now regret the rashness which had sent me into the unexplored paludal recesses, notoriously teeming with goblindom—which had sent me unescorted and all but unprotected, with the warnings of those who should know dinning against my resolute deafness! . . . . . . I could barely ascertain, with the aid of my pocket compass, the northerly direction in which might lie the commonplace security for which I now so intensely yearned; but ere I might strike out thither a bursting clap as of the explosion of the gaseous atmosphere in that region, precluded the possibility of seeking refuge there. There was the rush of a devastating typhoon to the north, and I fled, panic-stricken, from that which I knew was now inevitable.

As I fled, new terrors made my frenzied path one of such utter fright, that I thought only of fleeing on and on, till flight was no longer possible; but at least till I should succumb in action, and not to the awful influences of the morass. Had I been calmer, I should have admitted the uselessness of this precipitation, and clung to some strong support until the storm had vented itself; but to hesitate, to seek shelter amongst all this—better by far a death of resistance, however mad and inutile! I fled on. The rush of stinking rain seemed a vast excretion which partook of the most noxious characteristics of the swamp. My legs dragged through rotten pools swelling to their angriest filth from the descending torrents. Vile animalculæ swarmed upon me, and my body was racked and torn in concert with my distracted mind.

A newly-impelled sheet of vivid rain swept over the marsh, and lashed its waters into torrents of seething destruction. I was picked up like a rotten log and hurried irresistibly onward.

Grasping all that might impede my course, as unwelcome as my voluntary flight had been relieving, I at first found nothing save yielding slime. At length, as my desperation reached its utmost, my outstretched hands encountered a low-bending limb of a gigantic tree, standing in sinister safety amid the wreck of all about it. A blast of wind seemed to make its branches twirl horribly upward, and I was tossed higher and higher, refused refuge until reaching a high limb I lost consciousness in its foliage. And such a sleep! . . . . . . . . . . . . . . . .

The huge trunk which sheltered me aroused in me an unutterable repulsion, a limitless loathing. Its vilely verdant bark impressed me as most closely resembling the scaly skin of an enormous lizard, and its tremendous limbs seemed to coil about me like savage serpents . . . . Assuredly I was mad! This monstrous organism must indeed be alive! Its great limbs I shed wildly—but against the path of the storm. I peered again. There could be no doubt of it. I heard delirious shrieks as its lesser limbs were torn from it. Its loathsome luxuriance nauseated me. I raved and shrieked in gibbering mania as the incredible Thing writhed and whirled in a world apart from that comforting, sanely furious storm.

I felt the slimy, murderous juices of the Thing eat into my soul. I fell into a lethal state of such pacific horror as no man can feel and remain sane. I felt within me the growing enslavement of the victim of the python, but mine—if it were possible, I shuddered—was of both mind and body. I visualized the unthinkable—saw ridiculous but blanching, revolting visions of the bull slowly succumbing to the gastric juices of the boa . . . . . . and always was that inward sense of grisly decay, a rapid leprosy which embraced my entire being. I screamed aloud in horror. My scream re-echoed and I screamed again. The universe had nothing in it but screams, echoes, screams and unending putrefaction. . . . . . . . . . .

I awoke to find the maggoty corpse of a huge buzzard upon my breast, cast there by the powerful wind of the previous night. Below me lay the swamp, ineffably wet but still navigable; but how prosaic a sight in the cheerful morning sun! I threw back my head and breathed in the pure air of dawn. All about me was the beautiful foliage of Nature; and beyond, not a quarter of a mile to the southeast, lay the fields that spelled home.

## *The Critic*

Clarice is large and blonde, and somewhat dead;
    But still not quite so dull as first she seems.
She's too self-conscious to be quite well bred;
    Her face, though handsome, fails to haunt my dreams.

Peggy's a radiant thing, *petite* and gay,
    As pink and plump and small as one might find;
Her nose is past conception retrousee,
    Then, too, I fear she's shallow as her kind.

Marie's a puzzle: Prettiest of all
    Or too anæmic? Innocent or wise?
She's cute and clever, slight but not too small,
    But still, with her I'm never well at ease.

Then there are others—hosts of them, in fact,
    Who take my eye—unknown more oft than not;
But I have no philandering, smooth tact,
    And so the most of them are soon forgot.

So after all, in writing distant Syb
>That *cher enfant* of high society—
With her amusing genius for the fib,
>There's fun as much as flirting with the three!

## Stars

The glow of youth was in his eyes as he rapped at the first door. A fair maiden appeared in the threshold. The sun glowed white with passion, low in the east.

"Observe the stars," spoke the maiden.

"Ah, there are none while the sun shines; none but your eyes," he replied. She smiled.

"Come in!" and he entered. The room was pink, and sweet with the odor of roses.

"Here will I abide forever with you," whispered the youth.

And when he had feasted upon her eyes, he said, "There are more stars. I must find them."

So he knocked at the second door. There was no answer; then the youth battered it down. The room within was set in golden colors, and filled with strange devices and hidden places. The sun without shone upon the room, and there were reflected the beams of innumerable stars. But the maiden was sorrowful at leaving the first room.

"Observe the stars," she warned, minding sad thoughts.

"Indeed, do they not shine brilliantly here!" exclaimed the man. So they labored with strange devices and searched the hidden nooks for many stars, until they were both gray and aweary with labor. When the dusk impended, they rested and sighed.

"The stars are of tinsel!" cried the man. "See, the dusk is near and they shine but leadenly. But look: is there not a marvelous light playing about next door! There indeed are real stars."

Gathering fair robes about them, he strode in dignity to the third door. It was broad open, and shut behind them. The room was dark with evening, and there were no stars within. When they looked forth, they saw that the glow came from the rooms behind them. They sat and regarded; but they were not comforted.

"There, assuredly, may be the stars; but we cannot reach them," he lamented. And as he sorrowed night came above, but it was not blackness. For far overhead stretched the ribbon of the Milky Way; and countless others, too, gave light.

"Behold! Observe the stars!" cried the woman; and "Behold!" echoed the man. So they drank in the sombre beauty of the infinite stars.

And as they looked, they saw in each other's eyes the gleaming of the brightest of stars.

# Some Tendencies of Modern Poetry

Poetry, like everything else, is undergoing an upheaval. Democracy, a mere shadow in politics, is felt everywhere in the realm of art, corrupting whatever it touches. No longer is literature sacred; but rather it is a means of amusement to the reader, or profit to the writer. So vast is the sea of mediocrity, that each author strives for originality; not within himself, where only genius can look—but to strange forms, forbidden subjects, even to the unspeakably commonplace. To be an artist is unheard of—is it not better to revel amidst shattered idols than to do the things that others have done better before us? So they cry; and with their probings they have perverted the whole trend of English poetry.

Not but that such an upheaval may bring about some things of benefit. Of course the critical-minded iconoclast contributes his share to the progress of art; but he does not contribute art itself. Hence I propose to examine fairly, not the poetry it has produced, but the tendencies themselves that mark modern poetry. Loosely speaking, there are three general notions held by the various revolutionaries. They must ineluctably overlap, and sometimes they become as one; but the theoretical lines of demarcation nevertheless exist. They are, then: first, the cult of impressionism, or a revolution in poetic inspiration; second, the cult of realism, of the commonplaces and routine affairs of life—or a revolution in poetic subject matter; third, the cult of *vers libre*, or a revolution in poetic form. Each of these creeds, as expounded by its most vigorous enthusiasts, is extreme; yet each will no doubt contribute something fundamental to the thought and conceptions of succeeding generations.

Of these three creeds, the first is probably the least reasonable. The poet sits down to composition: Does he rack his brain for thoughts, or work himself into a "fine frenzy" of inspiration? No. The poet, with an effort which becomes easy with constant practice, goes to sleep, arrests himself in the process, and hastily jots down the discordant and disconnected thoughts of the moment. His impressions have but one virtue as poetry: they are indisputably sensuous. But are they simple? impassioned? musical? artistic? do they interpret life? Most emphatically do they fail. The reason obviously is that the "poet" negates intellect. He merely detaches his thinking faculties from his perceptive faculties, and allows the latter to run amuck over the printed page, adorned with rows of dots, dashes, and pretty irregular ripples of text division. So is Amy Lowell, descanting at painful length on her impressions of taking a bath. There is nothing of interpretation here. Even could the impressionist make his work musical and lend it some breath of poetic life, (as some quite frequently do,) there is that fundamental requisite of interpretation lacking. Less violently, impressionism consists in devotion to nothing but the superficial, ignoring basic facts, and the fault is therefore always the same. Like the realist, the impressionist takes out his notebook and copies down a fact or two, leaving the really vital part of the process to the reader. Literature is nothing if not an *interpretation of life;* and mental effort, artistic selection, artistic presentation, all enter primarily into interpretation. These the mere impressionist lacks.

What benefit, if any, may come then from this ephemeral fad? I doubt if anything substantial will result; but at least the great principle of the vividness, the necessity, of concrete detail, has been recognized. Seen through the transcending, imaginative eye of the future, there is wonderful raw material for poetry here. Then, too, imagism has called attention to that fascinating trick of dreaming into semi-consciousness, which may yet serve to the benefit of the poet. So far, it has been productive of much clever phrasing and occasional patches of quaint or even of beautiful imagery.

It is difficult to speak of the tendencies of realism without departing from poetry, which alone is our topic. The desire for lively detail, too, is at the core of all "strictly modern" letters. The extension of this principle into poetry, I believe, is a problem which will perplex critic and poetry alike for decades; but it seems inevitable that Realism must, as representative of the whole age, conquer for that age at least. The whole problem must rest in the æsthetic tastes of the future. If there be anything beautiful, anything worthy of perpetuation in poesy, in Chicago or the life of the average American, Carl Sandburg and Edgar Lee Masters have certainly spied it; but their very means of communicating it introduces the vital question as to the possibility of adapting the exalted forms of poetry to such subjects. If one uses the forms of the past, shall they not be inappropriate? And if one invents new forms, shall they be poetry? It will be seen that this problem includes all that is really vital in the study of poetry today. If America is to contribute anything as individual to English poetry as the short-story to English prose, it will unquestionably be along such lines. But it is doubtful if even the most democratic public mind will long tolerate any great innovation in this respect; for the sublime notes of past centuries upon centuries of accumulating achievement cannot be forgotten—unless indeed our marked degradation in spoken language tells of a change that calls for a new Chaucer of the common people. Even then the foundations of art will not give way. Art must, after all is said and done, be based upon its effect; and the most profound arguments of those who argue principles rather than means, have been brought to naught by the operation of that one neglected principle.

To particularize, then: Realism can only endure as a vital force in poetry as far as it does not nullify the underlying precepts of poetic art. It is to be hoped that the more commonplace types of realism will be confined to prose; that life-as-it-is will not invade poetry of its own virtue, but only selectly, when it contains the loftiness, the beauty, the interest or the passion that is demanded by its vehicle. If hopes will not prevent mistakes at least the reasoning back of hope will force only the worthy to endure; and what endures is alone really worthy of consideration.

The final and most relevant topic of speculation today is in the matter of poetic form. Here there can be no absolutely set dogmas, and the only bounds to experiment can be those of our language and of good taste. Many projectors of inquiry into this field are mere untalented anarchists, making up in audacity what they lack in technique; but there are others who have based their productions upon thorough investigation and good authority. They cite Greek and Latin poetry, early alliterative verse, Japanese, Chinese and other Oriental odes, and could if they cared make much of English blank verse, which is most effective when least distinctively iambic pentameter. Propounding claims little dissimilar from those of Milton, they extend them with intention to revolutionize all poetic form. Their radicals are the inessentiality of rhyme and the independence of rhythm from mathematical, formal rules. This would appear to be a new field for the pioneer; but is it not merely starting anew from the ancient truth which, after centuries of development, have produced our present-day prosody? They forget that the Greeks, the Latins, the Orientals, were not lacking in definite rules; and that these rules were perfectly adapted to the language with which they dealt. So, too, have rules been built up for this language of ours—English, which is still American also. And what are the rules they would propose instead? (assuming that they offer rules, which the more reasonable would do). Fundamentally, they are merely these of simple rhythm, the simple rhythm of prose. The modernist would cast aside the "diagrams" of prosody, in the belief that the freer measures of prose are better suited to his art. [A quotation from *Poetry: A Magazine of Verse* of October, 1918, is typical:

"When . . . Mr. Masters touches on the iambic tetrameter of the *Spoon River* poems, it is hard to see how the term can be of more than faint interest to him. For one thing, it belongs to a lame science, one failing . . . to take note of the large delicate measures possible to prose. . . . Prosody at best provides the poet with but a set of diagrams more or less diverting, of which certainly a work of art, intact, complete, like the *Spoon River Anthology*, bears no trace."]

The selection goes on in painful obscurity, so I have quoted only the more intelligent portions. It would seem here that the modernist is sick of mathematical rules. Wishing to start out on his own resources, he scorns the products of finer tastes than his own. Viewing him thus, we can only tell him that if he prefers prose, let him use it. There is no subtlety in defending the intricate harmonies of prose; rather such a defense is sorely needed in this cacophonic age. And it is with prose, I believe, that this movement will ultimately deal the most; it is prose that will be enriched. If, however, we are to undergo a long period of experimentation with new forms, it is to be doubted whether the research will come to much. The pioneer will be followed by the perfecters; and perfection only comes with definiteness, which we certainly have already. Still, even if innovators are not the best of artists, it is possible that they may perform great services. The realm of blank verse—not of polyphonic prose—is comparatively unexplored beyond the classic heroic line; and if experimentation will serve only to illuminate the distinctions between prose and poetry, it will more than justify itself. Especially will this be so if it finds better means of adapting rhythm to the thought—the real aim of the entire movement.

However this may be, but one fact is evident: That the present age is one of speculation rather than of performance. I have endeavored to point out to what this speculation may eventually come. It will indubitably enrich prose; it should gradually open the way for new fields of expression in the domain of human events; it should clarify man's ideas on poetic form and poetic expression; it should act as a purgative of false notions and ignorant iconoclasm. When this shall have been done, the way will be open to an age that should immortalize American literature.

## The Spoken Tongue

Have you ever stopped to consider what really terrible concessions you must make to spoken language? The man of any human contact must keep a dialect and a special grammar up his sleeve for every class he meets—and he who denies the existence of classes affirms that the section hand talks like a college professor. Such instability of course indicates constant changing of the language; and though my youth may be responsible for the impression, it seems to me that this change is progressing more rapidly every year. The tendency is in the age—together with the split infinitive, "Literary Digest" spelling (even though abandoned) and other amiable freaks.

The ridiculousness of the idea that English has any grammar was brought to me in the few weeks prior to my attendance at a fraternity "formal." My Professors, seniors, juniors, and even lower forms of college addressed me, others, and each other regarding their expected presence at this or some other one of the constituents of "formal" time. They all, with few exceptions, used the form "Who are you gonna take—?" The remainder, as I recollect, said "going" or even allowed themselves the luxuring of a "planning." But not one of this host used "whom." This is the more remarkable in an age in which reading plays so incomparably prominent a part; and the worst newspaper English seldom falls into such errors as the best of us use each day in conversation.

The French, of course, like being told what to say, and their language is the better for it. But all modern language shows a tendency toward monosyllabic expression and dependence upon word order or voice inflection rather than upon grammatical forms. If English is allowed to progress for another century at its present pace, we shall have an interesting product. Two-thirds of the verbs will be compounded with prepositions—even as the Ancient Romans, perhaps—but the prepositions will come after the verb. Witness the innumerable compounds of everyday speech—look out for, look after, look into, look down upon—I have chosen a bad verb for illustration but you may make your own mixtures. Where will our parts of speech be? Especially when the use of the same word in noun, verb and adjective form is becoming so prevalent. Then, too, if spoken language conquers we may have something like Chinese, where voice inflection tells the difference between profanity and a word of thanks. The necessity for some greater master of modern idiom, who shall yet be a scholar and a literary genius, is evident. Oh for another Shakespeare! Without him and his even more influential fellow, Chaucer, should we be speaking French, German, or low Latin today?

## *The World Situation*

The League of Nations is dead; and its greatest supporter has linked his name with the greatest political tragedy of world history. Europe is in chaos. The pitiful council of powerless prestidigitators which still chooses to call itself a League of Nations, is doing nothing to check the plague of wars and uprisings that is sweeping over the recent battlegrounds. Russia, potentially the world's greatest power, is overrun with simple-minded children busy burning their fingers; while what effect she does have on the outside world is disastrous. Germany, sinned and now sinned against, is emulating Russia; and the only survivors seem to be many insignificant neutrals and the nations which seemed destined for the greatest things of the future—Japan, China, England and America.

This is a pessimistic picture; but the most contrarily opinionated person can deny but little of it. Still, I do not wish to be an apostle of desolate despair. Things are indeed in a pretty pass, but before the heyday of our little geoid, Satan demonstrated that wagons which are hitched to a star fall with exceeding force. Instead of placidly tending severally to their own affairs, nations chose in various ways to mix in the world. Some tried to conquer—too many. Others were defenders; others, though also partaking of the preceding classes, had world welfare in mind. From the sorry discord which has resulted, the only cure would seem to be that each large nation resume its own business, interfering only with occasional aid to the downtrodden. It is a disheartening enough end to such a grand affair as our recent World War; but though many refuse to see it, it would appear inevitable.

Here in America, there is less of suffering than of sheer folly. Political ties were forgotten—now they are back again, as bad as ever. Extravagance and other national peccadilloes are in turn asserting themselves; and the only survival of the wartime period seems to be profound hatred for those who don't believe the way we do. But withal we are not starving; the humble workingman, whose slum-born misery has so long been our leading recreation, seems to be enjoying himself; and our quadrennial festival, the Presidential Campaign, seems to be bringing out in all intensity the best and worst in our community existence. There is little to do but strive for sanity and decry the malignant abnormalities of the day. Never, however, ought we to lose sight of the fact that—however we may be interested in promoting our own affairs first—our "splendid isolation" is no more, and that inter-relation has not in the past meant inevitable friendship and amity. Sick as we are of war, it is no phantom which can be "boo-ed" away with disbelief, or considerate germ to be frightened away by the contagious sign of the day before. Adequate preparation to insure international standing in the great international business of war, is the one real lesson which comes to us out of the conflict.

## *The United's Policy 1920–1921*

The ideal of pure literature paramount and unalloyed.

The conduct of the official organ as an exponent of the best in amateur writing, conservative but representative, and impartial in all controversies.

Assimilation of existing recruits rather than intensive recruiting. Promotion of local clubs according to the principles of earlier administrations, especially the Hoffman administration. Closer binding of clubs to the general association, and greater notice for the detached member.

Encouragement of open discussion of all mattes concerning the amateur public, save that political contentions be avoided as far as possible. An impartial and receptive attitude toward all literary questions and disputes.

Encouragement of publishing both individual and co-operative, and recognition of mimeographed and circulated magazines on a basis of equality with printed magazines.

Recognition of the vital distinction between public and private criticism. Greater notice and enlarged personnel for the private bureau. Gradual development of the public bureau into a general topical review of important representative, current amateur literature. (Acknowledgment of current literary tastes as significant if only ephemeral. A. G. Jr.) (Preservation of sound literary ideals in defiance of contemporary decadence. H. P. L.)

Removal of verse and study laureateship classes, and removal of all restrictions regarding the number of entries necessary to ensure awards. Retention of the Literatus title and restrictions connected therewith.

Consolidation of Secretaryship and Treasurership into one appointive office, and consolidation of the two manuscript bureaux into one.

Elevation of entrance fee to one dollar, and dues to two dollars annually.

Maintenance of a special endowment fund for the official organ.

Attitude of amity toward other associations, neither proselyting nor permitting others to proselyte amongst us.

(Signed)
ALFRED GALPIN, Jr., Pres.
H. P. LOVECRAFT, Official Editor

# *Form in Modern Poetry*

## FOREWORD

In putting this essay before the amateur public more than a year after its composition, I feel it essential to declare that it does not represent my attitude at the present moment. I should re-write it, but I am unfortunately less dogmatic in my opinions now, and I should not be able to say so much about it. Briefly, I now regard poetry as rather the essence of all art, independent entirely of form. I should retain the distinction between the two kinds of form, but call poetic form rather VERSE. I am not sure that my conclusions would be essentially at variance with those below, but I am certain that I am now less dominated by professorial card-indices than I appear to be in the essay. The thing is interesting, to me at least, because it represents quite a definite landing-stage in the progress of my thought.

A. G., JR.

The study of form in poetry is to me the most fascinating of pursuits. Poetic distinctions lie at the root of character; and just as everyone feels them, so no one defines them. Every language has its own individual forms, specifically fitted to the national tongue and the national genius. The rude Hebrew sense-rhythm was perfectly adapted to the circumstances of scriptural inspiration; and the prosody of Greece, France or any other race has been a growth depending entirely upon the idiom of that race. In every case, there have been specific rules for imaginative composition, and in every case, these have been differentiated from the rules of plain or prose composition.

In English, twelve centuries of literary evolution have given us some of the most beautiful patterns of versification in any language. These forms have been infinite in possibilities of harmony; flexible, and supremely artistic. The rules lying back of them have not been compulsory. They have been evolved by our finest poetic tastes, and poor taste or bad may use them or leave them as it choose. No poet in the past has achieved immortality—at least as a poet—without employing these models either as he found them or as he was able to modify them. And now there is a widespread revolt against these "diagrams," with much iconoclastic experiment in new and strange fields.

This revolutionary tendency finds expression in a school popularly known as free verse, or *vers libre*. Representative of the modern spirit, there are many other novel fads in the air, and many have allied themselves with this, to its great detriment; but I shall treat only with that part of the movement which has in view an honest literary innovation. Here the claim is that the poet is unjustly restricted by mathematical canons of metre; that rhyme is inessential; and the problem is analysed down to a search for closer harmony between sense and rhythm. A profound task, this: To find for every nuance of thought or emotion, its rhythmical counterpoint!

Yet this seems to me to be the essence of the whole tendency, though it is often clouded over with contributory discussion. However well the aim may sound, I believe there is a serious fallacy back of it.

In the first place, contemporary writers seem to have forgotten the necessity for prose form. In this complex language of ours, both prose and poetry must ultimately recognise the laws of cadence. It is in losing sight of this fact that many have become converted to *vers libre*. Plato, Cicero, Milton, and in recent times Stevenson, Ruskin, De Quincey, Carlyle and all great French prose writers—all these represent a language which is definitely prose, but which is striking for its harmonious cadences. Reading any of these, one is quite likely to think of them as poetry, and in the more impassioned passages to read them as such. Just where the line can be drawn, no man can say save for himself. As a matter of fact, though, there are prose content and poetic content—prose form and poetic form. Just where anomalies like "Ossian" and the better moderns should be placed has always been perplexing, and refuge has frequently been taken in the convenient twilight zone of "prose-poetry." Accepting my rather categorical division, we may say that this generally includes poetic matter in prose form. Poetry should have both characteristics to be genuine. What the *vers libriste* seems to be guilty of, is ignoring the underlying truths of prose modulation.

"Granted," says he, "that innumerable artistic arrangements are possible outside present regulations, have we not therefore the nuclens of a new poetic vehicle, giving greater liberty to poetic inspiration, and yet adjusting sound to sense?" No, my dear sir. I must disagree. You forget that in the expression of any thought there must be a literary structure. Merely to express emotion or love of beauty in nondescript—however congruous—phrasing, is to deny that poetic form is distinct; and though I cannot for the life of me tell you just how it is distinct, I can only point out to you that my ancestors and yours have given us worthy examples for some generations.

Such a response, however, is based upon the assumption that there is no poetic quality in free verse forms. Whether or not this is so, is our real problem. I believe there are some more or less definite points of division in the highly specialised state which our language has attained. The indispensable requisite would seem to be *regularity*—not monotony, nor yet kaleidoscopic variety, but regularity such as constitutes rhythmical *unity*. The basic truth of this principle may be seen in every respectable piece of "irregular" verse in our literature. However mutable be the line-length or the rhyme, the fundamental rhythm never varies. In many long poems, notably the irregular ode of sustained length, there is a procession of patterns, which make together a more or less harmonious whole; but even then the original metric foot almost never changes. The *vers libriste* would abuse this prerogative of adjustment, of variety, until the original purpose of putting his work into verse is utterly forgotten, and the essential unity unrecognisable.

If the radical plead for "larger rhythms," I should have to suggest that any artistic effect of regularity is impossible beyond certain boundaries of the fundamental unit; the limits or nature of the unit depending on the language, and in our case being quite clear. Try as you will to read otherwise, you will find as a speaker of the English tongue that you cannot skip, at the most, more than three short syllables or two normal ones without indicating a beat or accent. Upon this fact is built our prosody. Here, then, is a further distinction. The unit in prose is the phrase, which leaves considerable freedom in interpretation; while the poetical unit must from the fundamental nature of the language depend upon a single vocal utterance, or stress. There is little danger of monotony or maladjustment here to the artist. He employs all the ornaments of melodious wording, well-placed pause and phrase, and the other beautiful subtleties that are first nature to him. Prose, on the other hand, has infinite possibilities of cadence or cacophony—every possibility but that of metrical regularity, which is verse.

Your "larger rhythms," then, are excellent prose; and thus you may flow to thought. In his rougher, freer medium, that is the task of the prose artist. The poet, however he may wish to rebel, must deal with certain pretty patterns. He may distort or re-arrange them at will, but by them he is eventually confined. These give the larger, the more sublime unity of poetry: such unity as is in the slow measures of Tennyson or in the torrential measures of Swinburne. What would these beautiful designs be, had their authors extracted that unity in an effort to fit every meaning to an appropriate but independent rhythm? Independent—that defines it. Poetry is supremely interdependent. The *vers libriste* pleads for larger units of independent rhythm—what is needed is larger groups of interdependent rhythm.

As to rhyme, there is less furore about that. It is a pretty ornament for the lyrist; but our most exalted works have been composed without it. Milton omitted rhyme for the same reason that the Greeks derogated undue embellishments: because his speech was rich enough without it. If the research attendant on the new movement accomplishes anything, it ought ultimately to increase other poetic beauties so that rhyme may be less essential. Blank verse, aside from the classic pentameter, is a realm comparatively unexplored, but fragrant with promise.

And the movement ought really to accomplish much. I have space merely to be theoretical, and in theory the case against free verse seems a bad one. But after all, viewed as an experiment, *vers libre* is a means of great revival of interest in the deeper truths of literature. By it, prose should indubitably be elevated—with the stabilisation, for instance, of "polyphonic prose." And its influence on poetic form should be notable. If any great upheaval is to be effected, it will perhaps go hand in hand with the growth of an independent American idiom. Otherwise, perfection comes only with definiteness, and that we assuredly have today. Many minor developments, perhaps a permanent reaction from some of the more binding restrictions culminating in the Victorian age; but greatest of all—enlightenment.

## *Picture of a Modern Mood*

Outside, a subtle breeze deluded the spirit into warmth and comfort, while it wafted from the flesh all hot humours, all the sere flavour of the sun, all distress. Trees which had yesterday been unmoving skeletons, revealed today the clumsy new colouring of spring, and moved their fragrant twigs in strange rhythms. Nature was green, and red, and unknown browns. Leicester was sure that there had never been another spring like it, even within the domain of his faded infancy.

Inside, Leicester was even now putting together a few scant provisions for a stroll. Few indeed had he chosen thus far. Of the superior merit of Philip Morris cigarettes, he had no doubt, but he hesitated for a long time between "Dorian Gray" and "Le Crime de Sylvestre Bonnard." His indecision revived a doubt which had too long been dormant.

"Certainly I must take pen, paper and writing-board," he decided. "For months I have lounged unassertive about this college, a glutton for the new things it might afford me, for the cruel punishment of social striving—for mere impression. I have longed to write, until that longing has set up a permanent rainbow-future for me; now I must at least for a time seek to set down the strange thoughts I have felt, and cultivate expression."

As he set out, his long-legged gait was almost natural. His head no longer strutted over his right shoulder, but was suspended slightly forward and darted always from one side to the other, searching out some glimpse of undefiled mother earth, so alien in these streets of formless houses. Frequently he met those whom his waking self knew; then he gazed on them blankly or with a slight frown, and mumbled a guttural "H'lo" which would have been polite if it had sounded like English. Clutching the worn black boards of his dilapidated note-book, he strode evenly and swiftly forward, slowing down only occasionally as he deliberated at a crossroads.

It was almost purely an accident that he found a fit object to stay him; and I doubt if he recognised until long afterward how mad he had been ever to leave at all the immense choking wonder of that dam. Within him he was almost unconscious of self, save that he knew he must go somewhere far down the banks of the river and write of the things he saw while going there. This dim urge was almost irresistible, but as he saw the waters tumble insanely through the sluice-gates and converge into a rocky steeplechase, he reluctantly leaped the rampart and walked along the canal-bank until he stood above the sluice.

Never afterward could he tell just how long he stayed there, gazing at the endless permutations of millions of tiny water-drops. In the between states of his consciousness he formed sentences describing it, but afterward he remembered them only as a vague objective mist cast over the splendour of the waters. . . . . . Nearest the bank the swollen river poured through three or four gates, Leicester never noticed just how many. They rolled over the turn, sullen and green, then, like a fountain-head in some wild pagan god-land, burst into a gorgeous eruption of iridescent whites and silvers and pale blue-tinted creams. The foam from this volcano hurled itself backward, then rolled with the undercurrent and came out in a thin stream two yards wide, still more furious than the body of the river, but lower and swifter than the lashed-up crest whence it came. There were bubbles, supernally bright, on this current, and the colours of it were not to be described, for Leicester was not a painter. Other currents, similar, but each with its own beauty, flowed sinuously toward the common vortex; then they grew lower, steadier, more rapid. They whipped through the irregular rock-bed like the weird dance of a far from ugly dragon, twisted around a final submarine promontory, and faded into the shadowed green beneath the bridge. Some of it burst into foam again as it came to the piers of the bridge, but from Leicester's position this was a weak and uncourteous imitation, contributing only to prevent monotony.

Beyond, and sloping a trifle backward from the sluice-gates, was a long stretch of undivided dam. The sun was diagonally over Leicester's head, high enough not to displease his eyes and to imbue the whole vista with light. The brilliant, yet not blinding reflection of the sun was almost all that Leicester distinctly remembered of the broader background. But he never forgot the margin between sluice and dam, where the waters seemed like white-hot molten silver, gurgling in queer bubbles and splashes, and absorbing in some supernatural manner the whole essence, but none of the dazzle of the sun. This margin later united with the quiet places, imparting to them its turbulence without its colour or its gleaming froth. Even this wide roadstead, Leicester saw, was not free from a love of bubble-blowing, and there were winding undercurrents which kept it never the same.

All this Leicester saw, and looked upon it for a long time. But words and the restlessness of words still rang in his head, and he did not stay. Instead he rose with the steadiness of a Philistine and continued plodding in the search for seclusion. Even then he might have remained and tried to write there; but he noted that there were many people of eminent practical curiosity about him, who were gaping at the sight of a huge, black, ugly coal barge, caught by the swirling currents and carried to the edge of the dam. So he went on. His images of the flood were still too stupendous to occupy his mind, and he commenced once more to look about him. He was now wandering in the aisle of a forest of hewn and piled-up lumber, clumsy but immense and admirable. The path was of black cinders, pleasant to walk upon, and Leicester smelt many faint odours of spruce, and pine, and woods he knew not by name. He was still reeling in mind and unconscious of self, for when he made a certain turn he was thrilled by a view of the opposite hillside, fresh with awkward reddish saplings, shrubbery and unsullied greensward—all this seen in a curiously appropriate frame of thick logs, whose brown blended finely, and whose edges cut off just the proper piece of landscape.

But this was almost his last breath of what he remembered thereafter as his "Greek intoxication." He stumbled for nearly a mile along a river shore whose most charming sight, near at hand, was an occasional undwelt-on stretch of green. So in Leicester's mind came once more the daemon Will, with his mirroring attendants Effort and Self-Consciousness. Plain as was the path he walked upon, across the river there were catching panoramas, and the river itself was broad, and clear, and interesting. But he no longer used his eyes, for he had begun to think, and he was already beginning to destroy the beauty he had just experienced. He was moulding it into sentences, enlarging on some chance philosophy that had interjected, re-living the immediate past with the ulterior end of writing it on paper. . . . . . At length he reached a grotto where there was shade, and colour, and the loneliness of Pan.

Hitherto he had maintained the magic of his dying mood by the mechanical exercise of walking; it seemed to instil a rugged re-birth of emotional energy. The grotto was in the hollow of a hillside, overspread with stunted glorious trees, carpeted with moss and dry leaves and peeping wildflowers. Nothing was visible outside of it except an oval portrait of the opposite shore, outlined and gilded through the foliage about him. Leicester chose an inviting spot and sat down; but peace was not in his resting, for there remained the driving motive of pen and paper.

The sentences, pompous and metaphysical, which he had formed so brief a time ago, were confused and vague, and their music seemed mingled with the solemn crashing of the waterfall. The pen said, "Capitalise this scenery; it is very pretty." The trees muttered, "You are a fool, and should be sleeping now." His soul echoed, "You are a fool." Will, the voice of rhythm, interrupted to say, "You must choke back this bitter pessimism in the interests of Art." The old, old mockery of composition re-enacted itself: Leicester scribbled a few sentences, his enthusiasm waned, he knew the phrases were timid and discordant. His *empressment* became a cheaper and cheaper thing in the eyes of the growing monster Discontent. Beauty flew off on the wings of Mood, leaving the grotto sombre and menacing. . . . . .

All this went on in Leicester's head until he had the grace to laugh.

"Poor striver after self-apotheosis," he told himself, "you are an artist reft of the power of expression. Hie you away, Hamlet; and pull your cap over your eyes, for the sun is low and stares you in the face."

The sun, in truth, was reddening; and as Leicester wandered on the return path, he found the discordant elements of his dead mood arranging themselves into a philosophy of decadence, strangely comforting. "It is *fin de siècle*," he mused. "I was a Greek and loved beauty, now I am a modernist and I 'understand' it. This poor rivulet is now nothing other than the Styx. If it be lethal and perhaps lacking in proper illumination, it is at least beyond the ambitious pretence of the world; and it certainly endures longer than Homer himself."

Thus he consoled himself, reconciling the past with the future, which latter was to consist of insipid *bonhomie* and a healthy supper. The road was not long, and he was surprised when he found himself once more on the arched bridge below the dam. He leaned on the stone railing with a melodramatic air of compassion—whether for the insignificance of that bright but public panorama, or for the turmoil it had stirred in his soul, I can not say.

To satisfy a certain pose that grew within him, he took the scratched-up paper which represented his artistic production of the afternoon; crumpled it tightly, and threw it into the teeth of the current. It fell into the maw of a rising breaker, sank, and was seen no more.

"I suppose I shall be obliged to derive several very salutary morals from this experience," sighed Leicester. "Such valuable aids as 'One must have perspective' and 'Art should be spontaneous.' I can see plainly the comfort the English find in platitudes. On the whole, though, I cannot count the afternoon wasted."

A friend, who had been watching for hours the vain efforts of a large squad of coalheavers to extricate the barge from its predicament, slapped Leicester on the shoulder.

"They're going to have a hell of a time getting that thing out of there, aren't they?" said Leicester after a smile of greeting. The two set out for home: but Leicester did not talk much, for smile as he would, he could not shake from his ears the sullen and rapturous rearing of tons of faery-green waters, springing from the mid-stream geysers of Olympus.

## Nietzsche as a Practical Prophet

The problem that Friedrich Nietzsche set himself was a double one. First, he intended to confound and overwhelm the forces of contemporary Christian morality; and then to propose a radical scheme of social organization and of individual aspiration which had as its supreme aim the creation of the superman.

To this problem he brought the genius of his own personality and its hitherto intensely conflicting elements. That is to say, he brought the hard sincerity which was derived from his personal struggle against centuries of tradition crystallized into the modern church. He had himself been a Christian, and a pious one, until his manhood; and yet there was in him that high seriousness of effort, that conscientious endeavor to solve in his own brain the problem of human ends, which refined itself gradually into a religion based on his own worldly and sensitive aristocracy.

Of the many influences which entered into his philosophy either as elements to be combated, or as elements to be absorbed, there were four which might loosely be chosen as the principal ones. H. L. Mencken[1] points out the two most obvious: Greek classicism and the new biology heralded by Darwin. I should choose two others, also, which were nearer to his home, if not to his heart: The scholasticism and ponderous romanticism of his German confreres, and the rather opposite influence of his master, Schopenhauer. The first involved him as a scholar and philologist, but the second opened up the vista of his thought and made possible Nietzsche's defiant emancipation from all the traditions about him.

His philosophy, then, was a revolt against all modern German traditions; it was a purely Nietzschean sublimation of the Schopenhauerian doctrine, a rather confused acceptance of Darwinism, and a straightforward defense of the classical spirit.[2]

To the solution of his problem Nietzsche directed his entire mental energy during the last fifteen years of his sanity. Reasonably enough, he started out with an attack on Christianity, the first bold step without which the remainder would be impossible. He showed that Christianity was a slave-religion, perpetuating the sick and botched while dragging down the strong, the healthy, and the courageous. He traced the origin of its morality and painted it, not as a divine and unquestioned edict, but as a mere perpetuation of customs, stupid customs and decadent at that. He mercilessly attacked the Oriental conception of a supernatural god, and proclaimed "on all walls—I have letters that even the blind shall see"—that since it asserts the supremacy of another world, the whole fabric of Christianity was a contradiction to life, a blasphemy to the soul of man, a stench in the nostrils of the seeing ones, a triumph of unreality, nihilistic pity, and a sickly and putrefied democracy. In the aphoristic books this was carried off with aplomb and a rather ironic analysis; by the time of "The Antichrist" this Oriental faith of Jesus and Paul became to Nietzsche the "one immortal blemish of mankind."

From this new point of view, which was much more penetrating and effective than the old rationalism of Voltaire and his school, Nietzsche practically rewrote the history of man. It seems to me that his most valuable contributions to modern thought are to be found in his piercing analyses of moral and historical problems of the past. Socrates and Christ as the great decadents, Luther and the Reformation as the worst catastrophe of modern times—men, philosophers and states were picked to scraps by his iconoclasm.

This was the achievement of his early aphoristic writings. Before this task should monopolize him or find complete expression, Nietzsche gave the world his constructive doctrines in the poetic testament "Thus Spake Zoroaster." The entire book is infused with the exalted spirit of a new aristocracy—an aristocracy of confident, honorable, ecstatic egoism. "This new

---

1. "The Philosophy of Friedrich Nietzsche," by H. L. Mencken.
2. Many of my facts are derived from the standard biography by Frederic Halevy.

table of values, O my brethren, I set over your heads: Become hard. . . . . Man is something that is to be surpassed." With these famous lines Zoroaster seeks disciples who will labor with him for the ultimate end and flowering of mankind in the superman. Zoroaster is very careful to warn off those who have not the inborn sense of honor necessary for this discipline. He is specific in preserving slave-morality for the slaves—that is, in preserving old moral values as the best protection for, and from, those who are incapable of welcoming his innovations. His is the most limited of aristocracies.

His ethical teachings may thus be summarized. His philosophy, therefore, can be arbitrarily divided into three essentials: (1) The will to power—his debt to Schopenhauer, whose will to live he turned from an abstract motive force of life to a conflict of individual wills, and made it not resigned, but vaunting and glorified. It is probably his most emphasized non-ethical idea. (2) The double morality—herren-moral and sclaven-moral. This presupposed a dual conception of society and was Nietzsche's most terrible weapon against modern democracy. (3) The superman, the quintessence of his prophecy, his most original and daring conception. Of his other novelties, only the eternal return is important, and that chiefly as an evidence of the uncontrolled passion which some call madness.

This, in brief, is the philosophy which, commencing about 1885 and gradually enlarging its scope, has been the horror of the conservative, the Bible of the revolte, the delight of the prose artist and poet. Perhaps no man has ever been more misinterpreted. He has been blamed, more or less justly, for German militarism, the sensual licenses of "modern moral degeneration," modern atheism, and, in general, for the failings of those cheaper souls whom he so well foresaw, playing the part of his disciple, proud of this high sanction for their sins.

But his influence was a greater and more positive thing than misconception and misrepresentation. He is one of the great prophets of this liberal age, and acquaintance with his writings has touched profoundly the lives of nearly all those leaders of men who have followed him. Today he is beginning to be understood.

In relation to his time, Nietzsche was obviously the enemy of everything most truly contemporaneous. He opposed democracy, scholasticism, romanticism, Christianity, and Christian ethics of all types. He attacked nearly every man who approached his eminence or who came into direct contact with his philosophy. He invented modern German prose and defied every rule of literary tact and coherence. From his mountainous isolation of thought he viewed the entire path of human history in a light that contradicted every current attitude. He arraigned every past philosopher, and when he borrowed an idea he infused into it the vigor and elevation of his own personality.

Back of this anachronism there is no mere perversity, still less reaction. There is rather the spirit of power, dynamic energy, of the glory in life and the striving for individual and social betterment. His time was "out of joint;" it worshipped abstractions, and Nietzsche held up vital energy as the a priori fact and the highest value. In this trait he was a true prophet and he anticipated with his quick and lively intuition much that is salt to modern minds. He saw directly into the workings of the human spirit, and made psychological advances informally which the technical and objective psychological schools were slower in reaching. For instance, in "Prejudices of Philosophers" he briefly analyzes the psychology of the philosopher, and then proposes that only psychological facts, not Greek abstractions, should be the basis of philosophy. Here and elsewhere he spoke vaguely of the "new psychology" as he did of "philosophers of the future." And he was partly justified in the appearance of Bergson and James, both of whom embody a great deal of the Nietzschean love of life. For example, Nietzsche anticipated James' pragmatism, his voluntarism in psychology and his temperamentalism in philosophy. Bergson's catchword "Creative Evolution" might be the very method for the superman, and Bergson also bowed to creative, vital energy. It is therefore quite likely that when Victorianism and its contemporaneous German culture have been forgotten, Nietzsche instead will be remembered as the very incarnate spirit of his time—not of the time in which he lived, but of the time with which he was pregnant. In the accidental timbre, the spectroscope test of his genius, he was in every sense a true prophet. So much for his greatness of soul: what of the logical fabric he created?

The most apparent thing about it is that Nietzsche had no metaphysical insight or logical subtlety—he could not leave the realm of life. I have been able nowhere in his works to find any clear statement of his metaphysics. He evidently accepted the biological data of Darwin, yet he attacked Darwin personally and tried to overthrow his theories. He did the same with Schopenhauer's will to live—altered it arbitrarily to fit into the pattern of his temperament. He spoke of will to power as a profound philosophical doctrine when it was merely the psychological fact of personal assertion, and when his own application of it rendered it futile as an explanation of the universe. Nothing is more evident than that he accepted evolution because it suited his love of the world, and the will to live because it suited his love of both will-power and life.

Even his ethical edifice will not stand the test of logic. The superman starts out by overlooking the conclusions of modern anthropo-biology, that man is incapable of development beyond his present biologic power[3] and that his future evolution must be selective and, more especially, social. One indication of this which everyone will recognize is illustrated by the fact of insanity, which is, in many cases, the result of mutations in the evolutionary scale.

---

3. "The Direction of Human Evolution," by Conklin, is a rather dull treatment of this point.

The "sport" is abnormal, and is combated by the fundamental instincts of the race. More technically the conclusion is upheld by the fact of man's high degree of specialization, which brings about a decrease of adaptability. But even granting the possibility of a noble and select aristocracy, immune from the ordinary weaknesses of man, glowing with strength a race of creators of rulers—even this race is obviously not a surpassing of mankind, but an artificial culture separated from mankind in the mass by a long and arduous chain of sacrifice and peril, the product of which is its own negation. Nietzsche himself was the first to admit the immense labor necessary for the superman, but he had a passion for aristocratic perfection which overleapt all humanity. Going farther, Nietzsche knew too that the modern democratic freedman hated the aristocrat and would never sacrifice his own material interests for the fostering of genius. He would view the superman as a mere rhetorical tour de force, which in actual life could mean one of two things: Nobility, which he hates, and genius, which he leaves to chance.

I need go no farther on this via dolorosa to show what was already clear; yet I must admit the fascination of the idea, and the apparently powerful influence it is having on modern philosophies of evolution. The fault lay in the radical temper of its creator, not in the conception itself. This radicality of thought makes impossible a literal application of his dual morality, yet this also is valuable in theoretical ethics and may be applied, following Nietzsche's own example, to every factor of human progress.

Nietzsche was, therefore, as a thinker, a great prophet of revolt, a great iconoclast, a great innovator. If I may broaden the use of the ambiguous term "practical prophet" to include his influence in general on modern times, there remains a consideration of his personality, his artistic genius—its influence on his philosophy and on present-day thinkers and artists.

Probably the most emphasized trait of his personality was that unfortunate neuroticism which later led to his total insanity. I say unfortunate when I do not really mean it, because it is better to undergo savage derogation than to have written nothing worthy of such notice. And it is certainly obvious that we owe the superb literary finish, the whole bravura and fire of his philosophy, to that internal and agonizing emotional stimulus. He was like the nightingale and the thorn, like Shakespeare and his tragic passion for Mary Fitton.[4] He was in torture, but in exquisite torture. And it is a final and subtle shibboleth of one's taste, whether or not one is repelled by that beautiful instability which would wreck the efforts of the mediocre but which intensifies the purely instinctive thinking-in-words of genius.

It is to this insanity, such as it is, that we, therefore, owe his genius; but it will prevent his literal acceptance and make him rather a source than an

---

4. I have this on the word of Mr. Frank Harris in his great book, "The Man Shakespeare."

authority. For him to win any significant literal disciples in practical affairs would mean that he must create aristocrats; and an aristocrat needs no Nietzsche. He was a philosopher, not a sociologist, and held always to the necessity of radicalism in thought.

And the final touch to his temperament was that hardness of soul, that revulsion which Chesterton calls a philosophy of "weak nerves." To me this shutting off of all but the emotions of personal glorification is the most vulnerable point in Nietzsche. I think Chesterton is almost justified when he says that truly great men are ordinary men. At least the really great man in my estimation is the man who accepts his own greatness without social prejudice, who has that overflowing soul which has no time for egoistic ecstasy, and who if he loves himself has love and pity to spare for those less fortunate beings whom he can by no honest interpretation avoid recognizing as his fellow men.

But this also is a fault in Nietzsche, and not in his glorious prophecy. No one with the artist soul to which he makes his strongest appeal can overlook the terrible soddenness, the weakness of will, the intrusive stupidity and filth of the modern mob autonomy. We must love mankind, but there must be discrimination. It is easier to love men from the cave of a hermit than from the window of a city apartment where the odor of democracy and the contemptible viciousness of the newspaper crying its wares offend the senses. Nietzsche teaches men the message that the soul of a strong man is precious and may not be poisoned with the conglomerate Freudian complexes of a herd. He was a poet, and will never lack hearers; his life was a tragedy, he will never lack sympathy. He possessed the essence of that noblest of all souls, the artist who can bear the brunt of truth and its pity; but he sacrificed everything in him that he thought was "soft" for the one purpose of perfecting his philosophy.

He pointed out the errors of our present democracy and opposed thereto an opposite equally fallacious. But life moves forward by opposites, and if he can gain hearers the future ought to tell how much of his proud and brave insight humanity can bear.

Voila tout.

## To Sam Loveman

Ah, there are many ways to Arcady!
    Some purple-tinted in the evening haze,
    Some strewn with fresh-expired regrets, and some
That wind forever, with no destiny.

I, who have strewn too many of these with wan
    Dismemory'd ghosts and harsh-uprooted flowers,
    Knew that the search was vain, until there came
The fluted minstrelsy of fallen Pan

And cry of old Apollo in the night
 Of Beauty and the tyranny of fools.
 And I, too, raise my voice to hymn the pain
An ecstasy that *you* bring to the rite

Of your ancestral bacchanals—my friend,
 I'd never dare to call you that, but know
 Somewhere within that pagan heart of yours
The homely Nazarene is denizen'd.

*Oct. 19, 1921*

## The Vivisector

An invitation to criticise the last two issues of *The Wolverine* gives one an excellent opportunity for evil-doing. One might in some cases take advantage of such openness, but this time one can't, because *The Wolverine* isn't that kind of magazine.

It is easily the best contemporary publication of the new typewritten sort, and is likely to remain so unless *Corona* or *Pine Cones* be resurrected. Indeed, if the last two numbers are an indication of those to follow, even these excellent veterans might have to yield first place. So much for praise, now for a little criticism.

"Facts Concerning the Late Arthur Jermyn and His Family", by Mr. Lovecraft, shows another phase of that writer's gloomy but powerful genius. It is perfect in execution, restrained in manner, complete, and marked by Mr. Lovecraft's uniquely effective handling of introductory and concluding portions. The legend is not so powerful as many of Mr. Lovecraft's dreamings have been, but it is unquestionably original and does not derive from Poe, Dunsany, or any other of Mr. Lovecraft's favorites and predecessors. Its affiliations are rather closer with Ambrose Bierce, and I personally should place it beside much of Bierce's best work without fearing for the fame of the United's representative. Mr. Lovecraft is unquestionably a man of distinguished genius in the short story, but he is unfortunate in coming rather late in the line of macabre writers, and in lacking many of those elements of sophistication which are so imperative in our times. For example, his critical faculty is poor and his stories are almost entirely at the mercy of his mood. Moreover, he is singularly lacking in psychological perception, a thing which is essential to immortalize any tale except that of the sheerest and most Shelleyan fiber. As a consequence of this latter lack the plot of the Jermyn tale is a trifle obvious, and its principal character is wooden. But with all these drawbacks Mr. Lovecraft is deserving of a fame much broader than he chooses to seek. For the power and persuasion of his style, and for the gripping, unearthly cast of his imagination, he is as great as any living author in his field and in the range of my acquaintance. He certainly excels Lord Dunsany in directness of narration and the whole realm of the horrible in imagination. If the reader be astonished at this praise, let him read "Polaris" and "The White Ship" for beauty of style, "The Doom that Came to Sarnath" or any of his temple or city fables for luxurious detail, or "Dagon", "The Statement of Randolph Carter", and "Nyarlathotep" for sheer wonder of imaginative power, and then he will merely have scratched the man's personality.

Next in importance to the serial tale are the editorials by Mr. Lawson. They are well-written, honest, and straightforward, thoroughly likeable without exception. I should, however, like to disagree with our editor on public criticism; for he suffers from the widespread and apparently ineradicable delusion that private criticism should be run in public columns. I say again, and would shout it from the housetops if I could, that when a writer wants personal, constructive criticism the place for him to seek it is the private critical bureau. Public criticism, I am weary of saying, should be of some decent literary caliber and should deal with works of public importance, not with infinitesimal details. Once admit private criticism into the public bureau and you have not only a repetitious series of admonitions, all about the same, but a troublesome obligation to include everything, entirely everything, or hurt someone's feelings.

For this occasion I continue in the old private-critic rut so well ploughed in *The United Amateur* by Mr. Lovecraft, and take up *The Wolverine* in detail. "At the Nadir" shows good writing ability on the part of a hard-working and earnest beginner, but the plot is very, very trite and the conclusion anticlimactic. Mr. Lehmkuhl knows better and will do good work later. My "Zoilian" colleague shows fine common-sense in the March number, but reveals prejudice in June: he seems on the one hand sadly bitten by Galpinitis, while on the other hand he is ridiculously unjust to Mr. Lovecraft's "Polaris", which is one of the best stories in amateur journalism.

The verse matter interests me a trifle less, but is of relatively high merit. "When Clover Blooms" is sincere, "Time" is excellently sentimental. "Appreciation" has a touch of exuberance about it, offset by the sly and pert correctness of Mr. Lovecraft's careless effusion in his favorite "Theobaldian" heroics, the instrument of his dull moments.

Another than Lovecraft had recourse to a pseudonym to cloak recent work. Like him a laureate in her department, Mrs. McMullen cannot help being graceful; but there is little substance in "Why" and the piece is impaired by mixture of archaic and modern verb-forms. "Afterwards" is of the same type—feminine and pleasing, but unimportant. Miss Pierce's poem may be put in the same category: it shows a certain plaintive sincerity but needs technical improvement.

So much for the two issues. Certainly, *The Wolverine* has amply proved its right to the laureateship bestowed by the National; and one can but hope that it will maintain an equally high standard in future numbers.

# Four Translations from Les Fleurs du mal by Charles Pierre Baudelaire

## Au Lecteur

Folly and error, lust and avarice,
Enwrap our souls, and vex our flesh amiss;
  As beggars their own vermin, so feed we
With sweet remorse our worn-out wickedness—

Pliant remorse, that yields to stubborn sin;
Time eases high resolves, and we begin
  Once more the gay and muddy pilgrimage,
Relying on vile tears to wash us clean.

On sorrow's pillow, Satan Trismegist
Enchants and slowly rocks our spirit to rest;
  And the rich metal of our will is molten
And vapouris'd by this wise alchemist.

It is the devil pulls our puppet-strings . . .
We are attracted by repugnant things;
  One step the nearer every day to Hell—
The horror wanes, but the hot odour clings.

Like a poor rake that in his wild unrest
Gnaws at some ancient harlot's martyr'd breast,
  We lie in wait and snatch clandestine pleasures,
And squeeze them dry, as oranges are prest.

Serried and swarming, like the Helminthes,
Ghouls in our brains wriggle in drunken sprees;
  And when we breathe, the unseen stream of death
Flows in our lungs, and leaves each hour his lees.

If club or dagger, poisoning or flame
Have not yet scroll'd the tokens of their fame
  On the bare canvas of our destinies,
'Tis merely that our spirits are too tame . . .

But with the panthers, jackals—with the lice,
The apes and serpents, scorpions, rats, and mice,
  The vultures, and the monsters of all shapes
In the menagerie that breeds all vice,

There's one the ugliest, wickedest of all;
He stirs not much; he makes but little brawl,

Yet is on leash to devastate the earth,
And with a yawn can make a god his thrall.

'Tis Boredom! Lost in some wild dream or other,
He weeps, and smokes his pipe—but why this pother?
For well you know this dainty monster, Thou
Hypocrite reader—fellow man—my brother!

## L'Ennemi

My youth was but a vagrant thunderstorm,
    Travell'd in some scarce moments by the sun:
Lightning and rain have made such ravage there
That all my garden's crimson fruits are gone.

Now I have reach'd the autumn of my thought,
    And soon—so soon!—must ply with spade and rake
To smooth again those riven furrows, where
The flood has left a graveyard in its wake.

And who knows? The new flowers that I dream
    May find this newly-laven soil, to teem
With unseen tonic for another start . . .

—O sorrow, sorrow! Time eats up our lives,
    And the obscure Enemy that gnaws each heart,
On our most precious life-blood feeds, and thrives!

## Remords Posthume

At last, when you and your dark beauty sleep
    Beneath a black and marble monument;
    When you shall have for couch and tenement
A hollow grave, and vault with sides that weep;

When, with the stones that sift down through the heap,
    Your breast is batter'd, and your lithe flanks bent,
    And all the power of your heart is spent,
And these your wayward feet not even creep:

Then, in the waste of that great lonely night,
    Often the tomb will wail around your bed
With its deep homeless voice, mocking your plight.

And say, "What is it to you now, frail corse,
    That once you did not know the cry of the dead?" . . .
And the worm will still devour you, like remorse.

## L'Ange Gardien

What are your thoughts tonight, poor solitary soul?
What do you say, my heart, that has been so wither'd,
To the most beautiful, the most good, the most dear,
At whose divine glance you have so suddenly blossom'd?

—We forsake all pride to sing his praises,
Nothing of ours can give you the sweetness of his direction;
His god-like flesh bears the perfume of the Angels,
And his eye clothes us in garbs of light.

Whether in the night and the solitude,
Or on the street, among the populace,
His ghost dances like a flame in the air.

Sometimes he speaks, and says: "I am beautiful, and I command
That for love of me you love only the Beautiful;
I am the guardian Angel, the Muse, and the Madonna!"

## *Scattered Remarks upon the Green Cheese Theory*

The moon, says a notorious cynic of the sixteenth century, is in the last analysis a large chunk of fibre, which has chipped off all sorts of ligneous splinters and carelessly left them to their own generation. Their decay into flesh-seeming substance, during which period the Old Block lost track of them, was followed by a pathetic assumption of directly solar origin on the part of the Matches, which a half-witted child of the demi-god Tyrrilongko had whittled, on a sunny day, from a fleshified spruce log. My authority explains the matter thus: Squeechum, a great bullying sort of spirit, who delighted in frightening children, came along as the poor child was seeking diversion in this already old-fashioned manner; and knowing the timid nature of his victim, he scared him half to death by imparting combustible Heads, or Skulls, to the newly shaven loglets. The child dropped his jaw in astonishment, and shivered like the wind-god on a cold autumn day. Squeechum was not half satisfied with this bit of diabolism, and went so far as to give the Skulls some special properties of his own contrivance. The chief of these was the necessity for friction, by which the creature's capital pieces might slowly be fretted into flame, to their great enjoyment and eventual dissociation. Thereupon the whole heap had in no time at all fallen to scraping one another; they were in danger of disappearing the next moment, but Squeechurn—with that rare presence of mind which has preserved demons as a separate species even unto our day—endowed this union with a function, and behold! they rubbed off splinters even as did their distant ancestor, the Old

Block. They then spent their burning-out years in rearing the splinters to maturity. It is from this epoch of Tinderkind that the great fear of inflammatory thoughts and contacts for the young, is first known to have swayed society.

When they were nicely spread out on the little boy's playground, Squeechum sneeringly left the latter to his own devices with them. The divine progeny, however, was as weary of the business as his crony, and was no longer even afraid of them. He found that their flame was harmless to his empyrean integument, and disgustedly sauntered off for a thrill at the hive of the Hybla Bees.

This carelessness properly redounded upon him, for the Tinderkind soon overspread his peninsula, and thence migrated to the remotest lunar caverns. The manufacture of Splinters was still a prime diversion, and had resulted in a dual differentiation of the species, but this manner of inciting combustion was soon found monotonous. They next turned to the Sun, and by their complete acceptance of his Ascendance received many sparks, which produced several fine bonfires and a great deal of eloquence. Like all civilised excrescences, they developed a language, but my authority hints slyly that Squeechum had an elbow in the affair. Be that as it may, it served to amuse the fire-seeking Splinters, and after some generations was employed to proclaim their direct filial importance to the Sun.

The gods and demons in this neighbourhood of space were a criminally negligent lot, and had not endowed their shavings with anything so clever as Squeechum's Skull; so pretty soon they waxed envious and quarreled among themselves about the right to set them on fire. While they were thus hotly engaged, Squeechum gathered up a plenteous handful and made Safety Matches of them. This he accomplished by squeezing their tops tightly and surrounding them with another layer of secret compound. This compound would inflame only through those portions of the natural environment which were sacred to Squeechum. He was making rapid headway with this cony-catching trick on his confreres when they discovered his absence and spied on him. By introducing variations of their own, they soon had the race divided into innumerable compartments, or Match Boxes.

"Within the last few centuries," says my cynical informer, "the Superhuman Powers have busied themselves in more cerulean employments, and the Tinderkind, following the empty-headed example of their first hewer, wander the globe in bewilderment. They have worn out their Patent Scratchers to the number of thousands; most of them, having lost the old spontaneity of the Lucifer Match, are content to frizzle out their existence on the first snitch of sand-paper they run across, endowing it with all the graces of language which have descended to them from a nobler epoch. Intermarriage between boxes has produced even more bewilderment, and the old standards of division by Scratching Shrines have disappeared almost even in name. Instead can be seen any number of single Matches, sick of poring over their genealogical tablets, who have found new uses for their top-pieces. They devote themselves to the collection of grains of sand, fretted from the old sand-paper of the race, or to speculation on the reaches beyond their globe. Their descent from the Sun is a favourite topic of argument, and has succeeded in inflaming a number of them; Squeechum and the unknown descendant of Tyrrilongko still figure in their folk mythology. But to me (continues the original narrator) the point of interest still lies in their uppermost Protuberance, for which they have discovered such various and novel uses. I was led into a deep maze of cogitation upon this unhappy race by hearing a vagrant member, whose red head showed signs of Luciferian atavism, complain as follows:

"'Great Spirit of the air, where are your lightnings? The sand-paper of our forefathers is uneven; it is rough, or it is smooth, and the dregs of the race have recourse to it. Great Spirit! You are not divine, you shall have no sawdust from me, if you can no longer circle this head with flame. Great Spirit! Our own altars inflamed us; but since you are quiet, even they no longer burn. The noble Match Box of my forbears is fallen and vanished, and I no longer know my own brethren. Give us, Great Spirit, a ball of fire from your hidden coffers, that our points may bow thereto and we may chant, united about it, something to our ashes of the song that inspired Tyrrilongko when first he made Match! Great Spirit!—'

"But I dissolved in tears, and heard no more.—"

My informer has carefully explained his cynicism on every page of his book; it was a rare attitude in those dark days. But poor old duffer! To weep at the aberrations of the merest of smoker's accessories shows indeed some deep well-spring of corruption in his soul; and I am forced to consider his cosmology a fabrication.

## Department of Public Criticism

The third issue of Samuel Loveman's amateur magazine The *Saturnian*, which is known to several members of the U. A. P. A., contains more of magnificent poetry than any other publication which has ever been connected with the society. More in quantity; in quality it yields only to its own first issue, with Mr. Loveman's odes to Apollo and Dionysos, and the poem "Oscar Wilde."

The substance in the issue consists in the translations from the two French poets, Charles Baudelaire and Paul Verlaine. Such translations seldom appear. Judged simply as English poetry, they have a quality of beauty all their own; as renditions from a foreign tongue, they are almost beyond criticism.

The Baudelaire poems are the more numerous, and include some of the best translations ever made in the language. More than Verlaine, Baudelaire was susceptible of translation. He insisted upon music as a prime factor in his poetry, but the music is obtained with the old devices of smooth rhythms and richness of phrase which were not unknown before him in both English and

French—indeed, his Alexandrines have much of the quality of English blank verse. This quality Mr. Loveman has rendered perfectly. In turning this highly polished and classical poetry into his own peculiar idiom, Mr. Loveman has lost some of its studious art; there are some overwrought phrases, touches of hectic colouring, and less regard than other translators have paid to the logical unfoldment of the thought. He has made it English rather than French, but all this is easily forgivable; for the faults are Baudelairian in their error. The poems are virile, alive, sensuously beautiful; and in not a single line or phrase is there the commonplaceness which Baudelaire so detested.

The versions are no more literal than was Baudelaire's translation of Poe. I can vouch, however, for Mr. Loveman's sureness of touch. He has altered much, but every alteration brings with it either idiomatic or imaginative force. More than once Mr. Loveman has actually improved upon the classical original. For example, the first four lines of "Exotic Perfume":

> When, with eyes closed, a sultry autumn night.
> I breathe the odour of thy vehement breast,
> I see myself upon strange beaches rest,
> Dazzled and charmed in the unsetting light.

I venture to say that there is a higher quality of imagination in this than in the original:

> Quand, les deux yeux fermes, en un soir chaud d'automne,
> Je respire l'odeur de ton sein chaleureux,
> Je vois se derouler des rivages heureux
> Qu'eblouissent les feux d'un soleil monotone.

Here the essential details of the image are strengthened in a shorter compass. The passage in question is one of the most musical in "Les Fleurs du Mal," but surely the translation has come as nearly as possible to equalling that factor.

Two other translations which equal or surpass the original are "Causerie" and "La Musique." The rich intensity and virile compression of the former make it a masterpiece purely as an English poem, yet the translator has taken fewer than his customary liberties. "Music," one of the most spiritual of "Les Fleurs," loses nothing in the translation.

I have carefully looked up the Modern Library Edition and the one or two other books where translations of Baudelaire are to be found. They are occasionally more faithfully literal, but without an exception mediocre in atmosphere and with scarcely a conception of phrase-making. I say with considerable assurance that every one of the *Saturnian* translations, down to the poorest, is superior to all that have preceded it.

The Verlaine poems are no less remarkable, but are rather an exhibition of virtuosity. Verlaine's music is purely French, and much of it derives more than half of its effect from intangible Gallic rhythms and assonances. The poems chosen for translation are among Verlaine's prettiest, and the renditions are amazingly skilful, but the results have much less poetic value than the more vital "Fleurs du Mal." Yet they contain many exquisite things; and in a completer volume of translations would be memorable. They recall the similar grace and sympathy of the Heine translations, in the second *Saturnian,* which suffered likewise from their fragmentary condition. One poem stands out particularly; a fragrant flower of a poem, commencing "La lune blance Luit dans les bois, "of which I recall seeing three other versions by more or less well-known poets, among them Arthur Symons. I refer the inquisitive to Mr. Symons' version in the appendix to his "The Symbolist Movement in Literature." The exquisiteness and grace of Verlaine live only in Mr. Loveman's version, which is short enough to quote entire:

> The moon of snow
> Shines in the wood;
> From every bough
> Thin voices brood
> That the green sprays cover. . . . .
>
> O my dear lover.
>
> The pool at our feet
> Profoundly traces
> The silhouette.
> Of the willow that faces
> The bleak wind's power. . . . .
>
> Muse on: it is the hour.
>
> A vast and far
> Content is given.
> And where we are
> Descends from heaven
> Air irised star, a flower. . . . .
>
> It is the exquisite hour.

To set off the exoticism of these poems, Mr. Loveman prints several simpler pieces of his own. They are less ambitious than some of his work, but are not entirely the losers for that reason. The poems are all quite brief, but are instinct with beauty and humanity, and show that Mr. Loveman, unlike any other who has ever been connected with Amateur Journalism, has something of infinity in him.

# Intuition in the Philosophy of Bergson

The idea of intuition, while not the most novel of M. Henri Bergson's singular contributions to contemporary philosophy, appears to be fundamental to his entire system; and is indeed the key to understanding the methods by which this strange personality arrives at his notions. We find scattered throughout his writings several attempts to analyze it, more frequent references to its value as a new philosophical *method,* and a continual practice, quite consistent with his preaching, from which he derives many essentials of his philosophy.

This insistence upon mystical method is perhaps Bergson's most vital connection with contemporary thought, and therefore one of the chief causes of his now fading popularity. This is palpably an age in which mysticism, if not dominant, is at least an element to be reckoned with. Moreover, it makes acceptance of Bergson's system easier to the normal person, because it seems to lend an extra-intellectual plausibility to many of his vagaries.

While reference to it is so frequent in his works, particularly in his *magnum opus,* I have been unable to find a reasonable analysis of the method anywhere. In chapter two of "Creative Evolution," after stating that instinctive and intelligent life are two complementary directions of the central life stream, he says, "There are things that intelligence alone is able to seek but which, by itself, it will never find. These things instinct alone could find; but it will never seek them." There seems to be a difficulty here, which Bergson recognises even more explicitly a trifle later: "But a glance at the evolution of living beings shows us that intuition could not go very far. On the side of intuition, consciousness found itself so restricted by its envelope that intuition had to shrink into instinct."

The difficulty here is heightened by the difficulty of finding any experiential background for this analysis—it is another offspring of Bergson's "intuition." I have shown that his analysis of the functions of instinct and intellect, overlooking its other faults, seems unable to give us any clearer comprehension of intuition; but some of his other statements are superficially more satisfactory. In one place he says that intuition is "instinct that has become disinterested, self-conscious, capable of reflecting upon its object and of enlarging it indefinitely." The word "reflection" would seem to posit a certain co-operation of intellect in the process, and elsewhere Bergson recognises this. His view seems to be perfectly honest, and fairly consistent. He is in possession of a certain rather undefinable method of thinking, closely connected with the traditional sense of the word "intuition." He makes laudable efforts to explain this process, and manages to convey to us, in an indirect way, much of its essence.

Assuming, therefore, that Bergson is unable to give a scientific justification of his method, still is it not superior to that of the intellect? Bergson apparently thinks so. His whole analysis of the function of the intellect is a marvellously clever demonstration of his claim that intellect can not handle life, but is only at home in restricted spaces, with inert matter. But does his own method negate intellect? He is unable to define it, however nebulously, without including its expressed enemy. He admits outright more than once, that his "instinct" is by itself as helpless as intellect—indeed more so, for how can instinctive knowledge become conscious knowledge except through intellect? He does not say; therefore we may assume that instinct plays the initiatory role, but that it can only become knowledge when it reaches the higher thought centres.

There is, however, a vital contradiction to intellectualism, in that the intellect is not accepted as the ultimate source of knowledge, or judge between contradictory sources, and is discredited as far as possible from any participation in the knowing process. This is Bergson's mysticism; what does it mean?

The basic assumption in his plea for a new method, is that this "letting oneself go," this mystical *introspection,* can produce uniform results if philosophers apply themselves to it with proper zeal. There is something ludicrous about the vision that comes to my mind when Bergson pleads for a "new method" in philosophy. What a waste of perfectly good mathematical ability! Why not import spirit mediums into the profession, and be assured of fuller, if perhaps less accurate data? But that is beside the point, which is to find out what Bergson's intuition is and whether it will do all he thinks it will.

In the case of Bergson himself, there is apparently a large element of imagination, particularly of a *visual* sort, in his mentality. His figures of speech are distinctly pictorial; he has a habit of mistaking a particularly clear figure for a logical explanation. His picture of the vital impetus, of the evolution of life, is especially strong in imaginative quality. One is led to suspect, then, that his own "intuition," from which he apparently derives the general notion of the process in others, has a great deal of the poetic imagination in it.

Now, the difficulty about imagination, however well it be grounded in reliable "instinctive knowledge," is that it differs so markedly in the individual. It is an attribute of genius, perhaps the most inseparable of them all, but geniuses are notorious for following their own bent, and for being different from all who have come before. In Plato it gave the supra-sensible world, in Spinoza the "all," in Leibnitz the monad. And worst of all, it is impossible to argue with the authoritative visions of genius. The whole panorama is a vast postulate, no part of which will its parent allow to be argued from the rest. While intellect is a common meeting ground, in which all ideas must subscribe to the laws of logic and common experience; on the other hand, intuition is so indefinite that no two individuals can possibly have the same understanding of it, and it authorises the individual experience in sharp distinction from the common.

Reality, reached in this clandestine and subjective manner, becomes determined by the emotional association of the individual. And at this point Bergson seems to stop. He is effective from some points of view, in attacking the intellect; but his own vision is not of the sort which spreads, like that of Swedenborg or Bruno, or Plotinus. Intuition, as far as I can see it, becomes contradictory to real philosophy when it is emphasised in preference to reason. It necessarily gives the individual his data for speculation, and is a necessary attribute of great philosophy. But to seek the intuition rather than the why and wherefore, is an emotional process, which modern psychology is gradually showing to be merely one form of self-delusion. In persons of strongly imaginative temperament it means much; in art, literature, and the more refined contacts of life, this vague fellow-feeling is much more necessary than conscious syllogism. But it is not philosophy, and to ask philosophers to adopt it as a method is ridiculous.

The real effect of Bergson's plea is to make disciples of a certain cosmic temperament akin to his own, and to give them the groundwork of an inner mystical life. But it does not stimulate research into reality. If you care to agree with Bergson you will probably have little independent contribution to make. If you don't, more than likely you will reach a reality entirely distinct from the reality of Creative Evolution; or your introspection may lack the credibility of Bergson's, and you may be forced to abandon the method entirely.

The whole appeal, then, as I see it, is for people to sympathise with the opinions of this queer, this unique thinker. His philosophy is almost entirely without social connections, in essence or in presentation. Other philosophers feel themselves one of many, or at least recognise themselves as philosophers. Bergson seems to think of himself as an eye apart. He speaks disapprovingly of "metaphysics," "philosophers," "scientists," "the intellect," and even of his old occupation, mathematics. His intuition is personal, it places originality higher than consistency, and it seeks personal participation. For this reason it always seems to me that Bergson is persuading rather than convincing. He wants to wheedle one to his side, and he will use the most plausible argument at hand.

On the other hand, adopting a broader and sympathetic attitude, one may see much of value in the emphasis, at least, in Bergson's method. Like James, Nietzsche, and other typical modernists, he wants to inject *life* into philosophy. But Nietzsche puts life above truth; James makes life the criterion of truth, while Bergson has fundamentally nothing more to contribute than the mystics of the past. He wants, it might be put, to make philosophy interesting—he is in a certain sense a romanticist, even an impressionist. But I rather fear he is working in the wrong material. Philosophy is an ancient and sedate institution; break through it, like one of Bergson's rockets, and when the sparks have died down the eternal Logical Mind must analyse the light and bring it into focus with proved or accepted facts of past philosophers. His own most important additions to the stream of thought have been those in which he was most consistent, either within himself, or with experience. Apart from these isolated arguments; his temporalism, his conceptions of life and intellect, and so on, he is important only because of his spirit—his intuition. He had a gorgeous cosmic vision and he used every resource of argument, language, and feeling to make that vision common to mankind.

# Ennui

When the earth blossomed and was green again, I denied the god of desolation and went among the trees. I breathed incense, and I knew that the gods of the forest were breathing their offerings to the implacable blue sky. I breathed of it as would the sky, had it any soul, and knowing that the sky had none, I was a god. For a moment joy was in me.

But the spirit of desolation was angry, and smote me. I did not see him; the grass, the flowers, sun and wind still moulded their evanescent palaces of warm perfume; but the will of my god is mighty, and he supplants these things. Then desire glistened in my brain, like a grey moon when the stars are out; I desired joy and lo! it had slipped away, and left not even sorrow in its place. And my desire grew strong, and I felt the strength of it through all my spirit; and I envisioned my dead sister Pain and would have sung to her in a high and melancholy voice. I would have sung to her of the cruel and moist lips of love, and of the agony that creates hope, of immeasurable fair gardens that mock the frenzy of fine words, of the ruin that comes to dreams in the morning; I would have chanted to the lonely bones of the desert the purity and exaltation that was once Pain. But the words were harsh, and the savour of their sickly passion suddenly cast me into despair. "Ai; Ai! Thou that dreamed of mountains and would be a God! Thou that spurned men and re-built fallen castles, and sang at night, in the desert, the anthem of your immemorial pride! Thy voice is pallid, it is not the voice of man, it is not the hymn of thy sister Pain; and as you speak you dishonour the crystalline vapours that are words, for your soul is empty, and its voice is hollow." And I beat my breast, and quaffed unspeakable red wines, and called to my garden the dancers of Eudemia, who danced before me with no garment, and were not ashamed, for they loved me. And I cried at them to go away, and pored over the beautiful mad parchments of old poets, and knew the thing that drove them mad. But in all this the voice of despair laughed always as men do not ever laugh, while it sucked the blood of my heart and sent it poisoned through strange channels in my breast.

Then I regained my voice, and it rose to the grey mansion of my God, saying, "Behold, you have taken away joy and beauty, give me now suffering, that I may feel one of men, and let me weep with the beggar at the crossroads!" But my God spoke only in his old accents of despair. . . . . .

Then I grew angry, and denied again my God. And the mocking sharp voice of despair rose higher and became pale song. And this is what it sang, to the tepid sands of my little desert, as the sky was silent.

# A Critic of Poetry

An article by one Michael White has been called to my attention, in which Mr. White, apparently one of Amateurdom's uncrowned Sainte-Beuves, makes some remarkable revelations about the poetry of my friend, Samuel Loveman. Mr. White marshalls a number of immortal names to crush his palpitating adversary—Barry Cornwall, Edgar Allan Poe, John Keats, and that distinguished critic Lord Macaulay. Mr. White is morally certain that these personages, in our modern age, would have joined the National Amateur Press Association, if only to deplore, with Mr. White, the decline of poesy. The companionship of Lord Macaulay has rendered him clairvoyant, and his rich comprehension of Keats has kindled in him a boundless store of friendly and paternal admonitions. He has theories of his own, like his predecessor in American scholarship, Mr. Poe.

"When he ceases to preach from Olympian heights and descends among men and women of the world, and interprets their heart songs, and adds his protests against the evils of the age," says Mr. White with prophetical benignancy, "then indeed shall he come into his own, a prophet and a teacher whose lips have been touched by the divine fire." He goes deeper than this. He reveals the secret springs of action which have brought upon us this masterpiece, his article; he is displeased that my friend, Howard P. Lovecraft, should have been enthusiastic about "A Triumph in Eternity"—such unscholarly methods lead astray the young men, now members of the National Amateur Press Association, whom Mr. White is going to make the prophets and teachers of the not too immediate future. As a critic of the modern—and quite un-Olympian—psychological school, Mr. White should be acquainted with the amiable and not too strictly discriminating enthusiasm of my good friend Mr. Lovecraft; but such oversights may be pardoned him, for with his great precursor, Matthew Arnold, Mr. White possesses "high seriousness." Poetry, and the criticism of poetry, are serious matters to Mr. White, who is pained at Mr. Loveman's "insincere misanthropic philosophy," and warns him that Poe dwelt among the morbid horrors of the tomb. Serious, Mr. White is not a mere impressionist in his criticism; he is something of a classicist, and a passionate advocate of good grammar and of the clear-cut, chiseled imagery of Alexander Pope and Edgar Guest. He does not allow the rapture of versification to seduce him from his conviction that the dead do not speak, particularly when their mouths are clogged with roots. He objects to one of Mr. Loveman's most simple and poignant pieces, after a medical examination of its tropes, with "there is no sequence—the closing lines leave us just where we were in the beginning." Alas! "This is the doctrine of Poe," who was not interested in politics. Like his contemporary rival, Mencken, Mr. White is interested in the doctrines and beliefs of his subjects. Mr. Loveman's theories are pernicious. He belongs to a school, and that school is dead, and I am ashamed of Mr. White's erudition that he didn't quote Swinburne to prove it—or disprove it. Alpheus and Arethusa, by the simple venom of their presence, will undermine, nowadays, the most exalted prophet, and seduce the reformer of society from his task. When the diapason of Mr. White's learned style has receded from the ear, one rests with the unbending conviction that Mr. Loveman is inferior to Keats and Milton, but that if he will follow Mr. White's directions, there is yet hope for him.

Let me do Mr. White justice—Mr. Lovecraft's criticism was "strictly Swinburnian," and I can agree with him that "A Triumph in Eternity" is rather exasperating. Beyond that point I should like to disagree with Mr. White but for his own rather unlyrical obscurity, which leaves me in considerable doubt as to his intentions. It would seem as if Mr. White did not know what he was talking about. And indeed, one does not criticise poetry by comparing it to Keats, or by resenting its syntax. Above all, one does not criticise poetry—of all things—by a series of negations. If Mr. White had any interest in writing articles, except perhaps to wield the dung-fork which his species are reported to bear in their hands at birth, he would at least have taken pains to find out something of Mr. Loveman's own type of mind and his reasons and methods in writing poetry. This is best done by putting, not Keats, but oneself, in the place of the writer, a suggestion perhaps a little malicious in the case of Mr. White. But it is rarely possible that his seer-like intelligence might then have divined that "A Triumph in Eternity" (although a legitimate subject, on account of Mr. Lovecraft's eulogy) was written very many years ago, and is no more representative of its author's mature creation than "Queen Mab" is prophetic of "The Sensitive Plant." Certain young persons, Mr. White, are often seized with a vicious and unphilosophical enthusiasm for good literature, particularly poetry. They have the atrocious and Nietzschean egoism to wish to emulate these productions; and if they be sufficiently young, and untroubled by vicious thoughts of their epoch, they are frequently known to imitate Milton, Swinburne, and even to poach upon our critic's preserves, and pay the "highest compliment" to Keats. Mr. Loveman, being a man of very profound sensibility to the best productions of the creative mind, has passed through that stage—very well through, I assure you, Mr. White. His personal and strictly original output since then has been small, but it has been sincere, intimate, poignantly felt, and exquisitely realized. And he has maintained his artistic integrity by attending strictly to his own affairs and leaving the evils of capitalism to Upton Sinclair, who has studied economics; and be it said, by leaving the heart songs of the men and women of the world, to Edgar Guest.

# From the French of Pierre de Ronsard ("Amours"—Livre II.)

## Aubade

Awake, my Mary, my fair indolent:
    Now the gay lark thrills, lyrically high,
    And Nightingale in rich-exhaling sigh
Murmurs, against a thorn, his love's complaint;—

Arise! over a pearl-embossed lawn
    Come with me: here's your pretty rosebush, red
    With opening buds; carnations, scarce have shed
The dew last night you fed them: it is dawn.

Last night you vowed, at bedtime, by your eyes,
    To wake before me; but Auruara's want
Still holds them in her veiling sorceries.

There there! a hundred kisses on them, and
    Upon your breasts a hundred, sweetly warning
My love to wake up early in the morning.

*1924*

# Echoes from Beyond Space

*Ebony and Crystal* by Clark Ashton Smith (printed by *The Auburn Journal,* Auburn, Calif.) (1922).
*The Star-Treader, and Other Poems* by Clark Ashton Smith. (A. M. Robertson, San Francisco. (1912).

Here is a book, from an obscure newspaper office, which should be seen by every one who really cares whether good literature is written in America or somewhere else. For more than ten years Mr. Smith has been writing poetry of an amazing force and originality; has published three volumes, of which "Ebony and Crystal" is the latest; and our intensely occupied literati have never heard of him outside of his own state. This book challenges the reading public in more ways than one. Its chief poem "The Hashish-Eaters, [*sic*] or the Apocalypse of Evil" is the longest and most imaginative, to my mind unquestionably the greatest, poem in the literature of the grotesque. It does not stand alone. Line after line, poem after poem, is stamped with the idiom of a unique creative imagination. Obscurity has taught the poet to scorn contemporary notice and he has written with utter defiance of the unimaginative, critical minds that constitute the literary body politic. Why has he remained unknown? He has been closely contemporaneous, for one thing, with the intellectualised trend of ultra-modern writing, and his work makes no pretensions to analytical power or intellectuality. Then, connoisseurs of the grotesque are few; and the average man of culture, finding much of the book below the author's best level, turns away and loses the gold with the sand. But he has the examples of Bierce and Poe for company in his obscurity, both of whom have been powerful influences upon his writing.

I cannot attempt in this brief compass to justify my claims about Mr. Smith's ability, particularly since comparatively few amateurs have seen the works in question. But for a casual sample, here is the closing sestet from his sonnet, "To Life:"

> "Fair as the moon of summer is thy face,
> And mystical with cloudiness of hair. . . . . . .
> Only an eye, subornless by delight,
> Shall find within thy phosphorescent gate
> These caverns of corruption and despair
> Where the worm toileth in the charnel night."

But no single passage can give a notion of his sheer power and the surprising variety which it casts upon so limited a universe—it is a Baudelairian volume to the core, from that point of view.

The poet concentrates all the force of his imagination and of his immense and exotic vocabulary upon single lines, careless of the rules of perfect art, swooping through his unearthly outer world only to report, seldom to discriminate. Like Poe, he is the "haunted sot." But without Poe's superb art or his keen and versatile mentality, Mr. Smith is perhaps more naive; reading his volume gives me the same sort of delight that endears to me the minor Elizabethan drama—one can ramble on infinitely, now and then finding passages which repay an hour of drearier stuff. Naive, Mr. Smith is young. He writes as a schoolboy plays, with big words and big images and big effects which fail as often as they succeed—but succeed stupendously well. "The Hashish-Eaters" is a gigantic fib in which the events are very limited—the hero ascends into a universe of such processional horror and beauty as no one has painted before, and after a considerable fright, is left there with escape or awakening his only recourse. I would not have it well written for anything—the vocabulary is intolerably outlandish, and there is absolutely no conception of varied beat in his blank verse—it is too gloriously uplifting as it is and when there is a particularly good whopper, one can smile. It must be taken in its entirety, and so must the volume as a whole.

Mr. Smith was born in Central California in 1893, and has always lived in Auburn with his mother, writing poetry, making love, doubtless something of a local deity. He has never sought a "higher education." His first volume, "The Star-Treader," contains some of his finest work, written before his nineteenth year! He is certainly America's most prodigious boy-wonder, if one must collect such things. Perhaps his finest poem belongs to this early period, "Nero," which expresses with a horror that is truly and everlastingly sublime, a lust to be among the gods and to play sadistical tricks with the stars. This is Mr. Smith's province, the terrific and infinite void, which only such a whimsical imagination as his own can justly populate. But if you think he is powerless before other topics, read his love poems. He has written many, quite as astoundingly bad and good as the rest, with some which ought to outlast most of the American verse with which I am acquainted. But we cannot discuss his genius until some one has bought his books, and the professional haters of the new and daring in literature are likely to hold the field for some time yet.

## Red . . .

My love's a blood-red-brilliant rose:
    My lady is a rubied wine,
A sparkling Burgundy, that glows
    With sunset-luster, crystalline.

Here on this hand, where I caressed
    That rose, are bitter flecks of red;
And the rich wine that thrills my breast
    Flows bitter, as if surfeited.

*1930*

# En Route
# (An American to Paris, 1931)

## I. New York Harbor

Hail, thou Sea!
Liberator, Ocean, we hail thee!
Salt are thy waters,
Pungent the breath thereof,
Passionate thy striving—
Hail!

Strident ships and sailors,
Laughter, and sun, and wind
Congregate to greet thee—
Hail!

Quiver we before thee
Like beasts, wind-driven,
Seeking the open, the sunlight.
Grant us, O fathomless

Siren, breast unheeding,
Storm unending—sweep us
At last, to freedom!

## II. On Deck

I wonder what the fish are doing
        'Way down there.
What a field for meditation
They must have; no noise or bustle,
        Free from care!

Fish, they say, are splendid brain-food.
        If that be so
The big chaps are in clover.
                  Perhaps not;
Natur's an inconsistent damsel,—
        They may not know.

Lord, if I had their chances, now,
        No more excuses!
No city din—no heartless public—
But scenery, quiet, isolation,
        All that conduces

To first-rate head-work. Of course, there's not
        Much atmosphere,
But then I'm from the Middle West,
I could survive.
            Yet . . . . for the present . . .
        I'll stay up here.

## *November*

Above the plain sighs the evening wind,
        A cold breath,
Withering leaves, and grass, and the soul within me.

The slate-blue sky crawls against the sun,
        And freezes
The very wind that shudders now beneath it.

O wind! O sky! Night is coming after,
        And darkness,
And the clear naked limbs of trees . . .
                and silence.

# A Partial Bibliography of Alfred Galpin

"The Critic." *Philosopher* 1, No. 1 (December 1920): 9. As by "Consul Hasting."

"A Critic of Poetry." *Oracle* 4, No. 2 (August 1923): 8–10.

"Department of Public Criticism." *United Amateur* 21, No. 5 (May 1922): 54–55.

"Echoes from Beyond Space." *United Amateur* 24, No. 1 (July 1925): 3–4.

"Ennui." *Conservative* No. 13 (July 1923): 10–11. As by "Anatol Kleinst."

"En Route." Unpublished.

"Form in Modern Poetry." *United Amateur* 20, No. 3 (January 1921): 34–36.

"Four Translations from 'Les Fleurs du mal' by Charles Pierre Baudelaire." *United Amateur* 21, No. 4 (March 1922): 39–40.

"From the French of Pierre de Ronsard ('Amours' Livre II)." Unpublished.

"Intuition in the Philosophy of Bergson." *Conservative* No. 13 (July 1923): 5–9. As by "A. T. Madison."

"Marsh-Mad: A Nightmare." *Philosopher* 1, No. 1 (December 1920): 7–8. As by "Consul Hasting."

"Memories of a Friendship." In H. P. Lovecraft et al., *The Shuttered Room and Other Pieces* (Sauk City, WI: Arkham House, 1959), pp. 191–201. In *Lovecraft Remembered*, ed. Peter Cannon (Sauk City, WI: Arkham House, 1998), 164–72.

"Mystery." *United Amateur* 17, No. 3 (January 1918): 40. As by "Consul Hasting."

"Nietzsche as a Practical Prophet." *Rainbow* 1, No. 1 (October 1921): 4–7.

"November." In *Poetry Out of Wisconsin*, ed. August Derleth and Raymond E. F. Larsson (New York: Henry Harrison, Poetry Publisher, 1937), p. 100–101.

"Picture of a Modern Mood." *United Amateur* 20, No. 4 (May 1921): 61–64.

"Portrait of a Father." *Wisconsin Magazine of History* 63, No. 4 (Summer 1980): 263–77.

"Red . . ." Unpublished.

"Remarks on My Handwriting." *United Amateur* 19, No. 1 (September 1919): 4.

"Scattered Remarks upon the Green Cheese Theory." *United Amateur* 21, No. 4 (March 1922): 37–39. As by "Anatol Kleinst."

"Selenaio-Phantasma." *Conservative* 4, No. 1 (July 1918): 3.

"Some Tendencies of Modern Poetry." *Philosopher* 1, No. 1 (December 1920): 10–11.

"The Spoken Tongue." *Philosopher* 1, No. 1 (December 1920): 11–12. Unsigned.

"Stars." *Philosopher* 1, No. 1 (December 1920): 9.

"To Sam Loveman." Unpublished.

"Two Loves." *Conservative* 4, No 1 (July 1918): 8. As by "Consul Hasting."

"The United's Policy 1920–1921" (with H. P. Lovecraft). *Zenith* (January 1921): 1.

"The Vivisector." *Wolverine* No. 11 (November 1921): 16–18. As by "Zoilus."

"The World Situation." *Philosopher* 1, No. 1 (December 1920): 12. Unsigned.

De Sanctis, Francesco. *De Sanctis on Dante*. Ed./Trans. Joseph Rossi and Alfred Galpin. (Madison, WI: University of Wisconsin Press, 1957).

Fauriel, C[laude] C[harles] (1772–1844). *Fauriel in Italy; Unpublished Correspondence (1882–1825)*. Ed. Alfred Galpin. Roma: Edizioni di storia e letteratura, 1962.

Galpin, Alfred Maurice, Isabella Panzini, and Marilyn Schneider. *Beginning Readings in Italian*. New York: Macmillan, [1966].

Galpin, Alfred Maurice. *French Prose: An Intermediate Reader*. New York: Macmillan, [1965].

# Index

CPSIA information can be obtained at www.ICGtesting.com
Printed in the USA
LVOW12s1513071213

364283LV00003B/233/P